中国公民出境旅游
服务质量解析

A Focus on Service Quality of
Chinese Citizens' Outbound Tours

徐辉著
By Xu Hui

浙江工商大学出版社
ZHEJIANG GONGSHANG UNIVERSITY PRESS

图书在版编目（CIP）数据

中国公民出境旅游服务质量解析：汉英对照／徐辉
著．—杭州：浙江工商大学出版社，2017.9
ISBN 978-7-5178-2171-7

Ⅰ．①中…　Ⅱ．①徐…　Ⅲ．①国际旅游－服务质量－
研究－中国－汉、英　Ⅳ．①F592.3

中国版本图书馆 CIP 数据核字（2017）第 105781 号

中国公民出境旅游服务质量解析

徐　辉　著

责任编辑	沈　娴
封面设计	许寅华
责任印制	包建辉
出版发行	浙江工商大学出版社
	（杭州市教工路 198 号　邮政编码 310012）
	（E-mail：zjgsupress@163.com）
	（网址：http://www.zjgsupress.com）
	电话：0571-88904980，88831806（传真）
排　　版	杭州朝曦图文设计有限公司
印　　刷	杭州五象印务有限公司
开　　本	710mm×1000mm　1/16
印　　张	33
字　　数	485 千
版 印 次	2017 年 9 月第 1 版　2017 年 9 月第 1 次印刷
书　　号	ISBN 978-7-5178-2171-7
定　　价	68.00 元

版权所有　翻印必究　印装差错　负责调换

浙江工商大学出版社营销部邮购电话　0571-88904970

FOREWORD(1)

As is known to all, the world has entered an era of "Experience Economy". In this epoch of Internet+, service is embedded in our daily lives where our activities are supported by series of interconnected service systems.

Tourism has now become one of China's fastest growing industries. As the forerunner of the service industry, tourism is one which perceives service provision as its basic connotation. Without service, tourism is simply wishy-washy. Therefore, tourism enterprises, constituting the major market of the tourism industry, see services as the core of their business operations. Not only does the quality of service enable tourism enterprises to gain broader market acceptance, but also determines whether customers will participate in a tourism itinerary.

With China's sustained economic growth and rapid increase in the level of its national income, the development of China's tourism industry has undergone unprecedented change. The potential of the Chinese outbound tourism market have also attracted global attention, while the lucrative outbound tourism market of China has concerned both domestic and overseas travel agencies. How do international tour guides (tour guides & tour escorts) provide excellent services when leading outbound tours? Or how do they provide services that satisfy their customers or even exceed their customers' expectations? This new book authored by Royal Xu Hui, Associate Professor of the Tourism College of Zhejiang, Hangzhou, China offers fruitful discussions. Focused on the outbound tourism perspective, the author elaborated the quality of tourism services from a new angle through deliberations of relevant case studies and analyses; while at the same time integrated marketing, public relations, tourism psychology, tourism economics, and other tourism related disciplines into the case studies and analyses with a view to inspiring tourism professionals in better service provision. This novel bilingual volume will surely enlighten each and every reader offering or accepting tourism services.

Mr. Xu Hui has extensive work experience in the hospitality and travel industries. He obtained his Master's degree from the School of Hotel and Tourism Management at the Hong Kong Polytechnic University. Mr. Xu is currently a faculty member of the Tourism College of Zhejiang, Hangzhou, China and is enthusiastic in his pursuit of the tourism career. His exertion and dedication to always learn, reflect, and enhance oneself at work are truly valuable to the hospitality and tourism profession.

Professor Haiyan Song
Associate Dean & Chair Professor
School of Hotel and Tourism Management
The Hong Kong Polytechnic University

序（二）

　　认识徐辉老师很多年了。他在旅游业工作长达 30 余年，既有在杭州香格里拉饭店等高星级酒店工作的经历，又有在浙江省中青国际旅游有限公司担任部门经理的经验，是一位具有丰富实践经验的老师。2004 年我校请他给旅行社管理系导游专业、旅行社经营管理专业学生开设一些讲座，涉及出入境旅游、旅行社运营、旅行社市场营销与计调等，受到师生的好评。他对旅游教育充满激情与热忱，2011 年从企业来到学校工作，正式成为一名旅游教育工作者。来校 5 年有余，他很快完成从职业经理人到人民教师的转型。本书是徐辉老师通过长期从事国际旅游业的积累和观察，对旅游服务形成的一种解读，也是从教 5 年多来工作的思考和总结。

　　2015 年，我国公民出境旅游人数达到 1.2 亿人次，继续保持"世界第一大客源地"的地位，是全球众多目的地国家或地区的重点目标客户。随着中国公民出境旅游越来越大众化，让中国公民了解出境旅游的相关知识，让旅游从业人员了解现代国际旅行社的基本运营模式和操作方式，显得更为重要。

　　本书按照不同的旅游服务类别，通过对中国公民出境旅游经典案例的分析，以新的体例与模式的整合，简述出境旅游服务的内涵。它涵盖了旅行社门市接待、出入境旅游体验、航空交通服务、品牌酒店服务、高品质国际导游（中国领队与境外导游）服务等方方面面，突出主题，彰显对策。同时，通过出境游案例这个切入口，对银发旅游市场、亲子游市场、自由行市场、散客市场进行了深入的剖析；对邮轮旅游、研学旅游、结伴旅游等新型旅游模式也有所涉及与研究。书中大量的案例分析和思考使本书高潮迭起又峰回路转，让你爱不释手。

　　本书是徐辉老师几年来笔耕不辍的成果，饱含他多年来的心血和智慧。通读全书，发现有几点鲜明特色。其一，主题突出，内容完整。全书所有案例都是公民出境旅游时的不同场景，紧紧围绕旅游服务这条主线，从八个方面展开，基本展现了出境旅游服务的全貌，同时又能使读者从各个服务侧面获得对优质旅游服务的整体认知。其二，理实融合，知行统一。本书通过案例展示和评析，把旅游理论与服务实践有机结合，具有一定的思想深度和理论高度，使读者学有所获，学以致用。其三，文风朴素，热情洋溢。本书的所有内容基本都来自作者本人的亲身经历，可谓有感而发，一气呵成。文字朴实无华，但内容十分丰富，体现了作者对旅游服务的用心体验和深入思考。其四，敢于创新，大胆探索。近年来作者一直尝试在国际导游专业进行中英文双语教学，本书主要为双语教学服务，所以对写作要求很高，完成此书实属不易。

　　毋庸讳言，该书紧跟中国旅游产业发展的步伐，密切关注行业现状与大旅游发展动态，突出高职教育课程的专业性和时代感，贴近旅游服务第一线，是一部值得细细品读的作品。

　　感谢徐辉老师的精心耕耘、潜心钻研，感谢徐辉老师在教学改革上的探索。

　　在此预祝本书顺利出版。

浙江旅游职业学院党委书记　教授

王昆欣

2016 年处暑夜于千岛湖校区

前　言

据世界旅行及旅游业理事会（WTTC）预测，中国将在 2023 年成为世界第一大旅游经济体。中国出境旅游市场因其爆发式的增长速度，正在成为全球瞩目的热点。旅游专家认为，今后 5 年中国公民出境旅游总人数有望突破 4 亿人次。2016 年，中国出境游人数已达 1.22 亿人次，同比增长 4.3%。从总量上来看，已经连续 5 年成为世界排名第一的旅游客源国。截至 2017 年 1 月，中国公民组团出境旅游目的地国家和地区已达 151 个，中国公民可组团前往的国家和地区达 117 个。

出境旅游与境内旅游不仅仅是旅游目的地自然条件和旅游距离上的差异，由于跨越不同社会经济制度，存在不同的民族文化，以及使用不同语言文字，在许多方面与境内旅游有所不同。如出入境必须准备中华人民共和国护照或通行证，健康检疫进行疾病预防，各国海关有不同的规定等；还有目的地国家或地区语言文化环境对旅游服务产生的额外要求，由于时差等因素在境外出现问题与境内通信联络的不便以及不同政治、法律、经济制度造成的麻烦等。随着出境旅游越来越呈现出大众化的倾向，中国公民增加出境旅游的相关知识及了解旅行社的基本运营模式显得尤为重要。

本书系浙江省社科联社科普及课题（13ND43）的研究成果，并被列为 2017 年度浙江省社科联社科普及出版全额资助项目和省社科规划课题（17KPCB07YB）。课题的研究是从以下三个方面展开的：

其一,作者通过五年时间的积累与总结,撰写并从中精选了80篇与出境旅游服务质量相关的案例文章及评析,并将文章翻译成了英文。全书共分8个篇章,从旅游者赴旅行社报名参加出境旅游,办理证照、签证等出境手续开始,到自由行旅游者或者出境游领队带领旅游者在境外游览,涵盖了出入境程序、航空服务、全球导游服务、品牌酒店体验、出境游领队服务等方面,最后,以旅游者入境返回的流程为主线,以"案例"为主体,以"评析"作为案例的衍生,从中延伸出与出境旅游相关的各种旅行知识。书中的每一个案例均上升到理论高度并归纳出处理的方法。各篇通过案例有机结合,融为一体。读者通过此书,能够了解旅游者在出境旅游时必须注意的事项,并让旅游者明白旅行社从业人员在出境旅游过程中发生紧急情况时应采取的具体对策及解决问题的最佳方法。

其二,本书的另一个意图,也就是本课题研究的另一个着眼点,是跨文化交际。作者拥有行走60多个国家和地区的经历,以中国出境旅游者的出境流程为线索,将全球各地的多元文化展示在中外读者面前,既能让中国人了解境外的风光与文化,也可以让更多的外国人了解中国人出境旅游的行踪。同时,该书能将复杂而又令人费解的市场营销、优质服务和服务关系学融会贯通到具体的案例细节中。能达到化繁为简、深入浅出的境界是需要对理论研究和实践经验有深入理解和丰富体验的。本书还跳出旅游业看旅游者的方式,把旅游作为交叉学科来进行理性探讨。

值得一提的是,本书所精选的案例多数是作者亲身经历过的,或者是向旅行社出境游领队、销售人员等一线从业人员调研获得的。本书题材广泛,内容丰富且真实。

其三,本书以中英双语的形式撰写,填补了这方面领域的空白。一方面,让读者、旅游从业人员了解全球范围内出境旅游业的最新动态及服务艺术。另一方面,让旅游从业人员、旅游专业的高校学生通过双语阅读,来熟悉出境旅游业的英语,特别是一些专业术语,以消除部分人员对英语学习的恐惧感,增加对英语学习的兴趣。希望此书能对未出校门的旅游专业的学生和旅游工作者的学习和工作起到一定的帮助作用。也希望能为高校旅游专业教师的案例教学提供一份良好的素材。此外,由于该书是以中英双语的形式写作,既可以作为英语爱好者英语学习之用,也可供常住中国的外籍工作人员及在华留学生阅读。书中所有的案例与评析均在 2012—2016 年度的浙报传媒《江南游报》上发表过,受到同业人员及读者的好评。

在本书的研究与撰写过程中,香港理工大学酒店及旅游业管理学院副院长宋海岩教授,全球旅行与旅游业合作组织(GTTP)亚洲/中国区总监邱汉琴教授,浙江旅游职业学院张建融教授、汪亚明教授,杭州市旅行社行业协会会长、浙江省中青国际旅游有限公司总经理张勤先生和杭州市中国旅行社有限公司董事长朱光明先生,在繁忙的工作之余,对本书提出了宝贵的意见。浙江旅游职业学院李晓红教授、严一平副教授,澳大利亚威廉·安格理斯学院(William Angliss Institute)特聘英籍教师 Tamlan Saoudi 先生,浙江省中青国际旅游有限公司国际旅游中心资深翻译朱霄波先生分别对全书的中英文内容进行审稿并提出修改意见。浙江旅游职业学院厉玲玲、陈建新与徐颉成老师,全球旅游案例研究大赛冠军、香港理工大学酒店管理专业张佳蓉学士参与了部分文章的翻译工作。浙报传媒《江南游报》江如文总编辑给予积极支持,在显著的版面上连续刊登作者的案例描述及实证研究评析,使高校、企业与媒体的互动形成良性循环。另外,浙江省中青国际旅游有限公司出境旅游总部朱小军副总经理、领队部陈曦经理、资深出境游领队陈雪峰女士,杭州海外旅游有限公司资深出境游领队童智毅先生,浙江长征职业技术学院吴小川老师,浙江旅游职业学院饶华清副教授、陈积峰老师提供了书中的部分案例素材,为实证研究奠定了坚实的基础。在此一并表示感谢。

由于本书涉及的内容广泛,专业性强,我们的学识水平有限,难免存在不足之处,恳请各界读者匡正赐教,以期通过不断的修订进行完善和提升。

2017 年 3 月于杭州

目录
CONTENTS

[第一篇]
Chapter I
旅行社门市接待篇
Branch Office Reception of Travel Agencies

随"百变自由行"，在巴厘岛度新婚蜜月 /017
Changeable Self-service Travel, Honeymoon in Bali Island

"丰富的目的地服务+专业的旅游资讯+精选的酒店+可选的机票"，
这就是中青旅的"百变自由行"

CYTS' Changeable Self-service Travel offers rich destination service,
professional tourism information, selected hotels and optional air tickets

赴毛里求斯度蜜月 /022
Honeymoon in Mauritius

演员陈小春和应采儿就是在毛里求斯的红顶教堂结的婚

Movie stars Jordan Chen and Cherrie Ying
married at the red roof church in Mauritius

一本特殊的"账本"通行证 /030

An Account-book-style Travel Permit

被小孩涂鸦过的护照内页。 这样的护照是无效的哦!

A passport with a kid's scribbles cannot be used！

境外旅游意外保险 /035

Outbound Tour Accident Insurance

100%纯净新西兰南北岛8日游

100% pure 8-day Travel in the North and South Islands of New Zealand

终于赴日本看上了滨崎步演唱会 /042

Final Success in Attending Ayumi Hamasaki's Concert

日本歌手滨崎步演唱会不能错过

Japanese singer Ayumi Hamasaki's concert should not be missed

"湿" 而复得的护照　/048

How to Do When the Passport Is Wet

杭州出发，无须转机，直飞美国

Direct flight from Hangzhou to the US without transfer

当从网上购买的旅游产品与旅行社包价游产品相撞时　/053

When Travel Agency's Package Product Meets the Product Purchased Online

要选择有资质的网上旅游产品哦!

Please choose qualified tour products online!

怀孕了，还能旅行吗?　/058

Travel During Pregnancy ?

你喜欢这样的旅行社门市洽谈区吗?

Do you like such a reception area of a travel agency?

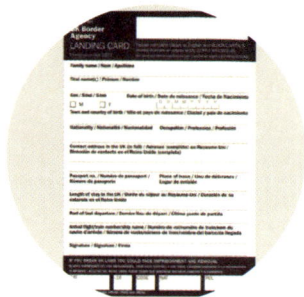

誊抄英国入境卡　*1062*

Fill in the British Landing Card

入境目的地前别忘了填写入境卡

Don't forget to fill in the landing card
before entering a destination

上海飞伦敦还是北京飞伦敦?　*1067*

From Shanghai to London or from Beijing to London ?

作者带团赴伦敦时，客人兴致勃勃地拍摄伦敦塔桥

When the author took a group to London, the guests were taking
photos of London Tower Bridge with great interest

Chapter II

出入境体验篇

Dealing with Exit and Entry Inspection

客人分别从新德里、巴黎、伦敦和哥本哈根转机回上海 /077
Transferring from New Delhi, Paris, London and Copenhagen
to Shanghai Respectively

当你在印度旅行时，大街上的印度女人会让你大饱眼福
When you travel in India, please feast your eyes on those Indian ladies on the street

领队的名下托运了28件行李 /082
28 Pieces of Luggage under the Name of the Tour Leader

越来越多的机场开始有自助值机柜台，这是澳大利亚悉尼机场
自助值机柜台

This is a self-service kiosk at Sydney Airport, Australia, and
there are more and more such kiosks at airports

印尼落地签　　/086

Visa on Arrival in Indonesia

在"落地签国家"尼泊尔奇它旺野生动物园骑大象其乐无穷

Riding elephants in Chitwan Safari in Nepal, a country where
Chinese citizens are granted visas on arrival, offers a great joy

在悉尼转机与退税　　/091

Transit and Tax Refund in Sydney

世界各主要机场的免税店都有会讲中文的售货员，这是新西兰奥
克兰机场的免税店

This is a duty-free shop at Auckland Airport, New Zealand. Now
there are salespeople who can speak Chinese in all the major
airports in the world

您来新西兰的目的是什么？　　/098

Why Do You Come to New Zealand?

新西兰的剪羊毛表演是每个旅游者必看的节目

Shearing show is a must for every tourist in New Zealand

在成田国际机场办理"夏威夷蜂蜜"的托运
Consignment of "Hawaii Honey" in Naria International Airport

除了美丽的夏威夷，美国还有壮观的大峡谷
Besides beautiful Hawaii, there is Grand Canyon in the US

终于离开了素万那普国际机场
Bidding Farewell to Suvarnabhumi International Airport

泰国曼谷素万那普国际机场
Suvarnabhumi International Airport in Bangkok, Thailand

Chapter I

旅行社门市接待篇

Branch Office Reception of Travel Agencies

[本章导读]

随着中国国民旅游走入大众化时代和旅游市场的成熟,旅行社全面铺开的连锁经营门市带给了旅游者诸多便利,社区里、大街上、超市中,旅游者可以方便地咨询、报名、付款和签订旅游合同。旅行社门市部也开始脱离片面的销售功能,更注重接待服务的功能。

本篇通过描写中国公民为出境而赴旅行社门市咨询和报名的过程,提醒旅游者赴旅行社参加出境报名时应注意的事项,以及旅行社门市接待人员与销售人员应如何做好接待工作。

[Chapter Outline]

With the growing and maturing of tourism market in China, the tourism industry has entered an era of mass tourism. Numerous branch offices set by travel agencies have facilitated tourists, who can consult, register, pay, and sign travel contracts conveniently in communities, streets and supermarkets. Instead of partially focusing on their selling function, branch offices of travel agencies start to emphasize improving the quality of reception service.

Chinese citizens who want to participate in an outbound tour usually consult and register in branch offices. By analyzing the process of consulting and registering in the offices, the author in this chapter attempts to tell tourists what to consider before the registration, and at the same time offers some constructive suggestions for the receptionists and sales people about how to do the reception work in a proper and efficient way.

随"百变自由行"，在巴厘岛度新婚蜜月

　　黄小姐计划 9 月份结婚，办完结婚仪式后就赴国外度蜜月，因此她和未婚夫一起前往中青旅咨询适合度蜜月的旅游线路。

　　在门市销售人员的推荐下，结合自己的预算，黄小姐与她的未婚夫决定前往印度尼西亚的旅游胜地——巴厘岛。但是，看了些旅行社门市摆放的旅游线路，黄小姐发现或多或少有些购物安排，而且旅游团入住的酒店比较普通，和黄小姐印象中巴厘岛左手梯田、右手海洋的酒店完全不同。这时门市的销售经理小沈向他们推荐了巴厘岛的自由行产品。黄小姐觉得自由行确实好，但是自由行需要自己做目的地攻略，到时候需要用酒店接送车也是比较麻烦的，而如果天天在酒店待着，不去当地特色的景点又很无聊。见此情形，小沈笑了笑，把中青旅的"百变自由行"特别旅游产品向他们做了介绍。"百变自由行"就是针对希望自由旅行，但又对旅游目的地不太了解的游客的，在传统自由行产品基础上，结合了旅行社机票、酒店等资源方面的采购优势，增强了目的地资讯方面的服务。黄小姐他们可以选择符合自己需求的航班、酒店及目的地的附加服务，如接送机，当地租车，导游服务，景区景点一日游，代购景点门票、船票等，包括为热门自由行目的地设计旅游手册，为自由行目的地提供 24 小时中文电话服务等。在团队机

票的优势上,小沈又向黄小姐推荐了一些如 Ayana Resort 和 Laguna Resort 这样具有巴厘岛文化特色的酒店供他们选择。最后,黄小姐选择了"百变巴厘岛 4 晚 6 天自由行(东航直飞)"的行程,即:2 晚 Melia 酒店＋2 晚 Seminyak 别墅,含早餐及酒店间往返接送,五星酒店与特色别墅经典混搭,体验多种当地风情。黄小姐选择了自己喜欢的酒店,预定了一日游等项目,高高兴兴地离开了中青旅门市柜台。

[评析]

中国旅游研究院、携程旅行网共同成立了"旅游大数据联合实验室",并发布了《2016 中国出境旅游大数据》。2016 年我国出境旅游者花费高达 1098 亿美元(约 7600 亿元人民币)。

报告分析认为,2016 年我国出境旅游人数达 1.22 亿人次,同比增长 4.3%,其中旅行社组织的出境旅游人数预计超过 5000 万人次,出境自由行规模超过 7000 万人次,其中 56% 是女性,44% 是男性,"70 后""80 后"是出境游的中坚力量,占比近 50%,银发族及"90 后""00 后"的出境游人数也逐渐增加,2016 年最年长出境游客达到了 101 岁。自由行人数的比率逐年提高,市场存在着巨大的发展空间。

作为中国现代旅游服务业的领航者,中青旅率先顺应了旅游行业散客化、个性化的发展趋势。2008 年,在依托既有品牌影响力的基础上,集中优势资源,向市场全力推出了中青旅又一崭新的业务品牌——百变自由行,致力于在传统团队业务之上,为旅客提供更加多元化的服务。

中青旅百变自由行＝丰富的目的地服务＋专业的旅游资讯＋精选的酒店＋可选的机票。丰富的目的地服务指的是完善的地接网络,提供一日游、租车、代购门票等多种当地旅游服务。专业的旅游资讯指的是专业资讯团队提供的热线咨询和景区景点、旅行须知、游记攻略等全方位旅游资讯。精选的酒店指的是提供全球精选的高品质酒店,保证旅行的绝对享受。可选的机票指的是提供多种航班搭配和丰富航段时间,客人可自主选择。

实际上很多旅行社都认识到自由行变得越来越具有市场潜力。只要品牌过硬，大多数旅游者还是会找上门来，寻求更专业的服务。以上案例就说明，正是中青旅"百变自由行"的魅力和专业服务留住了客人。

Changeable Self-service Travel, Honeymoon in Bali Island

Miss Wang was going to get married and planned to spend honeymoon abroad after wedding. Therefore, she and her fiancé came to Zhejiang CYTS together to inquire about traveling route for honeymoon.

According to the outlet staff's recommendation and their budget, they decided to go to Bali Island, the famous tourist destination in Indonesia. However, the traveling routes showed that shopping arrangements were inevitable and the hotels tourist group was going to stay in were so ordinary, which was totally different from what Miss Wang expected. At that time the sales manager, Mr. Shen, recommended a self-service traveling product to them. However, Miss Wang thought it was troublesome because she had to make a tourist destination strategy by herself and let the hotel pick up and drop off. And it would be boring if she just stayed in the hotel instead of going to local scenic spots. Knowing her confusion, the sales manager, Mr. Shen smiled and made a detailed introduction to this changeable self-service traveling product. Actually this product is designed for those people who want a self-service traveling but know little about the tourist destination. It takes advantage of travel agency in booking plane tickets and hotels and enhances destination information service for tourists. Miss Wang and her fiancé could choose which flight to take, which hotel they want to stay in and extra information service of destination, such as pick-up service at airports, renting local car, tour guide services, one-day traveling in scenic spots, booking tickets of scenic spots and steamer tickets. It includes designing traveling brochures for popular self-service traveling destinations, providing 24-hour Chinese telephone service and so on. Besides the advantage of group plane tickets, Mr. Shen also provided them some hotels, featuring Bali culture, such as Ayana Resort and Laguna Resort, for them to choose from. At last, Miss Wang chose changeable self-service traveling in Bali Island for 4 nights and 6 days (China Eastern Airlines non-stop flight). It was 2 nights in Melia hotel and 2 nights in Seminyak villa including breakfast and hotel round transfer service. They could enjoy five-star hotel and special villa service, fully experience local culture. At last, Miss Wang chose her favorite hotel, booked a one-day tour and so on before leaving Zhejiang CYTS happily.

Comments

China Tourism Research Institute and Ctrip have co-founded Tourism Big Data Joint Laboratory, releasing 2016 China Outbound Tour Big Data. A total of USD 109. 8 billion (RMB 760 billion) was spent by Chinese outbound tourists in 2016.

According to the report, there were nearly 122 million outbound trips of the Chinese people in 2016, an increase of 4. 3% from last year. Among them, travel agencies organized over 50 million trips, while the number of self-guided tours reached 70 million. Females accounted for 56%, while males 44%. Young people born in the 1970s or the 1980s took up 50% as the mainstay. And the percentage of senior citizens and those born in the 1990s and the 2000s increased as well. The oldest outbound tourist in 2016 was 101 years old. There has been an increase in self-guided tourists, indicating a huge market potential of this group.

As a leader of Chinese modern tourism service, CYTS followed the developing trend of individual and personalized service in tourism. In 2008, based on the existing influence of the brand, CYTS collected advantageous resource and built a new business brand to the market-changeable self-service traveling in order to provide more kinds of service for guests besides traditional group service.

CYTS changeable self-service traveling = various destination services + professional traveling information + selected hotels + optional plane tickets. Various destination services mean a perfect local traveling service network, such as providing one-day traveling, renting car, booking scenic spots tickets and so on. Professional traveling information means there is professional information group providing hotline consultation, information about scenic spots, traveling notice, travel strategy and other information. Selected hotels mean proving global selected hotels with high qualities to insure absolute traveling enjoyment. Optional plane tickets mean there are different flights and fight times that you can choose freely.

Actually many travel agencies realize that the market potential of self-service traveling becomes wider and wider. Only if your brand is good enough, most tourists will come for more professional service. The above case manifests it is the charm and profession of changeable self-service traveling of CYTS that attracted tourists.

赴毛里求斯度蜜月

毛里求斯、马尔代夫、塞舌尔并称为印度洋上的三大明珠。毛里求斯清澈的海水、洁白细腻的沙滩为人们所推崇，一直以来是欧洲人度假的首选目的地。

某国际旅游公司门市的欧阳小姐正在接受一对"85后"夫妻询问关于海岛旅游的事宜。这对刚结婚的年轻夫妇想去国外的海岛度蜜月，结婚前他们去过泰国的普吉岛、菲律宾的长滩岛等岛屿，觉得老是在亚洲范围内旅游，异域风情不够浓郁，此次想去马尔代夫度蜜月。年轻夫妇将自己的想法告诉了门市的欧阳小姐，希望欧阳小姐能够做一个推荐。欧阳小姐立刻向小夫妻推荐了赴毛里求斯度蜜月，并给出了三大理由。

第一，马尔代夫政府花了很大的精力与财力来做旅游推广，所以马尔代夫知名度很高。在中国的出境游市场，只要提到海岛旅游，马尔代夫必为首选。但马尔代夫位于南亚，毛里求斯则位于非洲，从异域风情来讲，毛里求斯更胜一筹，它曾经是英国的殖民地，融合了亚洲、欧洲和非洲的各种文化。

第二，大多数旅游公司所销售的马尔代夫的包价旅游产品，往往是每天只含一顿早餐，午、晚餐需要客人自理，而毛里求斯的包价旅游产品含"一顿早餐＋一顿晚餐"，而且旅游费用要比马尔代夫低。从 2011 年 7 月 4 日毛里求斯航空首航上海以来,从中国到毛里求斯的游客人数增长势头强劲。2012 年来自中国的入境旅游人数增长 38%,毛里求斯旅游当局也看到了中国出境游客的大幅增长,以及中国游客在境外的巨大消费潜力,决定大力向中国市场推广毛里求斯旅游。所以,从 2013 年 1 月起,毛里求斯航空公司开始每周运行两班直飞上海的航班,大大方便了旅游者的出行。

第三,目前,浙江省的散客拼在一起时,将会由专门负责毛里求斯旅游的专线业者来操作。业者将与毛里求斯的旅行社直接对接,而不是通过上海、北京的旅游中间商来完成地接操作。这样,就大大减少了中间环节沟通不畅所造成的麻烦。接着欧阳小姐又补充了一句:"你们是新婚,还可以向当地酒店申请蜜月超值特惠:一顿烛光晚餐、NIRA 温泉水浴一次、花瓣浴一次,如房间允许,升级房型。"年轻的夫妇考虑了一下后跟欧阳小姐说:"我们回去讨论一下,明天给予答复。"

第二天,年轻的夫妇拿着护照等相关证件又来到门市柜台,找到了欧阳小姐,决定参加毛里求斯 8 日游。他们真诚地告诉欧阳小姐:"我们昨晚在网上搜了一遍关于毛里求斯的旅游产品,没有与贵公司旅游线路相同的,我们觉得你们选择的酒店是当地的品牌酒店,整个线路有新意。所以,我们决定参加贵公司的毛里求斯 8 日游。"

[评析]

目前,操作出境游的旅行社对目的地的选择基本上是面面俱到。只要是对中国公民开放的目的地国家和地区,旅行社都想方设法去开拓,进行地接操作,以显示旅行社服务的大而全,这种方式在旅行社人力、精力顾不过来的情况下,不是一个最好的选择。出境游中旅游专卖店(专线旅游)的开设在美国、新加坡、日本等国家和地区早于中国形成。这些旅行社往往对旅游者只卖一个旅游目的地国家(地区)的旅游产品,旅行社从业人员对所卖的线路或者目的地国家(地区)往往非常熟悉。开设专卖店的愿望就是要让每个游客都能在这里找到适合自己的产品,最大限度满足游客的需求。

在杭州的旅游市场上，旅游专卖店（专线旅游）的模式正在形成。美国、日本、印尼、伊朗等出境市场的旅游专卖店（专线旅游）已经形成，杭州某旅游公司在2012年得到毛里求斯航空及毛里求斯当地最大的地接社的支持，有幸成了毛里求斯在浙江市场的专线操作者，专门销售及操作毛里求斯的旅游产品。也就是说，这家公司充任了一个专项批发商的角色。它的一个非常重要的推广功能是将毛里求斯的各种旅游产品设计好，分发给同业（包括代理点及其门市收客点）。

随着互联网技术的日益发达，许多旅游公司都开设了网站，同时游客们也习惯于以网络上的价格作为基准来进行比价，而某些大型的专业旅游网站凭借自身的优势，往往会推出几个价格超低的产品来吸引旅游者的眼球。这给专线旅游的销售造成了很大的困难。面对这一现状，毛里求斯专线旅游针对他们的目标市场采取了差异化的销售策略。在毛里求斯地接社的大力支持下，他们拿到了毛里求斯当地品牌酒店的优惠价格，这些酒店无论在酒店建筑、服务还是价格上相对于国际连锁酒店都有优势，在同业或者直客的销售过程中他们会避开网站上推广的"大路"酒店，做到同一产品，不同内容，不同品质，保证价格的独特性。对游客来讲，比价就失去了实际的意义。而且他们在价格的制订方面把大部分的利润让给同业，这样就大大增加了同业销售的积极性。案例中，年轻的夫妇在网上搜索了毛里求斯的旅游线路，却没有发现相似的线路，使旅游者对该旅游线路的原创性更坚定了信心。

专线旅游产品制作者请专人设计，利用毛里求斯旅游局提供的官方高清图片，设计了大量精美的宣传册和宣传海报及毛里求斯官方推广视频赠予同业。同时，对同业销售及其门市销售人员进行了有关目的地国家——毛里求斯及旅行线路的培训。如果说宣传海报和推广视频这两项是推销毛里求斯旅游产品的基础，那么门市销售的技能培训就是推销能否成功的关键所在，因为客人最后下单与否大多取决于门市的销售水平。案例中，欧阳小姐推荐年轻夫妇赴毛里求斯旅游的三大理由，就是门市销售人员专线旅游培训的成果。没有对产品的研究就不能总结出这些道理。

随着近几年来中国公民出境旅游人数的增多,中国公民对很多目的地国家和地区并不陌生,对于一些经常出境旅游的人而言,东南亚已经不足以引起他们的兴趣。如何将新开放的旅游目的地国家或地区介绍给旅游者,除了推销技巧本身外,以产品多样化、个性化,地接操作专业、性价比高为特色的旅游专卖店(专线旅游)的模式来面对出境旅游市场,是一个非常值得推广的形式。

Honeymoon in Mauritius

Mauritius, the Maldives, and Seychelles are called the three Pearls of the India Ocean. The crystal clear water and white fine sandy beaches in Mauritius are adored by people; it has been a vacation destination for the Europeans.

A young couple who wanted to have their honeymoon in foreign islands were consulting Miss Ouyang for island tourism information in a travel agency. They had been to Phuket in Thailand, Boracay in the Philippines and so on. In order to experience the exotic views, they wanted to go to the Maldives for their honeymoon. They expected some recommendations from Miss Ouyang, who immediately recommended Mauritius to the young couple for honeymoon for three reasons:

Firstly, the Maldivian Government has devoted a great deal of energy and money to do market promotion in China to make the Maldives into a holiday destination, and therefore the Maldives are more famous in China. In China's outbound tourism market, as long as people refer to islands tour, the Maldives will be preferred. The Maldives are located in South Asia, while Mauritius is in Africa, and the latter must outrace the former in terms of exotic views. It used to be the United Kingdom's colony, and is the integration of the various cultures of Asia, Europe and Africa.

Secondly, most Maldives travel packages sold in tour companies only include breakfast. Lunch and dinner are not included. However, Mauritius travel packages include breakfast and dinner (lunch excluded). Moreover, the travel cost is lower than that of the Maldives. On July 4, 2011, Air Mauritius had the inaugural flight from Mauritius to Shanghai and since then it has witnessed the remarkable growth in the number of tourists from China to Mauritius, a 38% increase in the number of inbound tourists from China in 2012. Mauritius tourism authorities have also seen the substantial growth of Chinese outbound tourism and the huge consumption potential of Chinese tourists abroad, so they decided to promote Mauritius tourism to the Chinese market. As a result, from January, 2013, Air Mauritius has been running two direct flights to Shanghai every week, greatly facilitating tourists' travel.

Thirdly, at present, individual guests in Zhejiang Province are combined into a group, and will be accepted by professional travel agencies specializing in handling Mauritius tourism, rather than through the Shanghai or Beijing tour companies to complete the traveling, which greatly reduces the inconveniences in intermediate communication. Then Miss Ouyang added that as they were newly married, they could also apply to local hotels for honeymoon promotions, that is, a candlelight dinner, a NIRA spa bath, a flower bath, and room upgrading if possible. After considering a moment the young couple wished to go back for discussion and would make the decision tomorrow.

The next day, the young couple holding passports and other related documents came to the sales counter of the travel agency and they decided to take part in the 8-day tour of Mauritius. They told Miss Ouyang that they searched on the Internet last night again for Mauritius tourism products, but there were no identical travel routes with that of the company, and they believed that the hotel chosen enjoyed some reputation, and the entire schedule was new. Accordingly, they decided to participate in the 8-day tour of Mauritius travel organized by the company.

Comments

At present, travel agencies operating outbound travel service provide almost all the outbound travel destination choices to customers. As long as the travel destination countries or regions are open to Chinese citizens, travel agencies often try to develop such markets for local operation to show their strengths. However, this may not be a good choice due to limited manpower. The exclusive travel agency for outbound tourism has been more rapidly developing in the United States, Singapore, Japan and other countries than in China. These agencies tend to sell only a few tourist routes or tourism products of only one tourist destination. Staffs in these travel agencies are very familiar with the destinations they are dealing with. The main aim is to enable every visitor here to find suitable products to meet their own demands.

In Hangzhou's tourism market, exclusive travel agencies emerged. Exclusive travel agencies for the United States, Japan, Indonesia, Iran and so on, has been formed. Luckily, a travel corporation in Hangzhou became the travel store for Mauritius in 2012, specializing in sales and operations in Mauritius tourism product with support from Air Mauritius and Mauritius' largest inbound tour operator. In other words, the tourism corporation has played a special role of the wholesaler of

Mauritius tourism products. A very important promotional function is to produce good Mauritius tourism products, distributed to the peers (including agents and their travel stores).

With the development of the Internet technology, lots of travel agencies have their own websites, offering competing prices to attract customers. As we all know, customers like comparing the prices on the Internet, which undoubtedly poses great challenges to these exclusive travel agencies. Facing the competition, the exclusive travel agencies of Mauritius have adopted different sales strategies. They have offered local renowned hotels with competitive prices supported by local travel agency partners. Different from international chain hotels, these local hotels are not only unique in architecture but also reach the international service standard. What is more, they offer attractive prices. Though the tour products are the same, the contents and qualities are different, and hence guarantee the uniqueness of price. For tourists, it is pointless to just compare the prices. Meanwhile, they have given most of the profits to the sales partners, greatly promoting the motivation of the sales. In the above case, the young couple searched the Mauritius routes, but didn't find similar lines, which convinced the tourists of the originality of the tour product.

Based on the Mauritius tourism official HD pictures, they designed a number of brochures, posters and official promotional videos of Mauritius through professional designers. At the same time, sales and retail sales staff are trained about the country of destination, Mauritius, and its tourist routes. If the posters and promotional videos are the base to promote Mauritius tourism products, the retail sales skills training is the key to success of the final sales, because whether guests buy or not depends mostly on retail sales levels. In the case, Miss Ouyang explained to the young couple three reasons to visit Mauritius. The three reasons were the result of the training of retail salespeople. Without studying the products, she could not have concluded all these reasons.

With the increase in the number of Chinese outbound trips in recent years，many destination countries and regions are very familiar to Chinese citizens. For those who've traveled abroad for so many times，outbound tourism in Southeast Asia can no longer attract them. How to introduce newly-opened tourist destination countries or regions to tourists，in addition to selling techniques，exclusive travel agencies with product diversification，personalization，professional local travel agency operating，and cost effectiveness should be considered as a way worth popularized.

一本特殊的"账本"通行证

年近 68 岁的杭州王奶奶,老伴在两年前去世,在家独居。王奶奶有一个独子,在外地工作,由于工作繁忙,也不能经常陪伴在王奶奶身边。但是她的儿子很孝顺,一有空就会回来与母亲团聚,也希望母亲有时间就出去旅游。

2014 年 4 月的某一天,王奶奶独自去了杭州某家国际旅行社,准备办理出境旅游的手续。进入旅行社门市后,接待人员很热情地让她就座,并拿出旅行社新推出的几条出境旅游线路给王奶奶看,也耐心地做了解释。王奶奶看了几条线路,感觉都还不错。但是,事实上她更想去香港看望她的妹妹,于是工作人员小胡就推荐她让旅行社单独买来回机票,并帮她做签注。王奶奶觉得这个主意不错,决定以这种方式赴香港看望妹妹。王奶奶告诉小胡,她的港澳通行证上个月就去公安局办好了,已经带在身边。小胡就让王奶奶把通行证出示一下。小胡拿到通行证后翻了一下,发现在通行证的最后一页空白处全都是王奶奶记的账。原来,王奶奶把通行证当成了记账本,账本的内容全都是买菜花了多少钱,儿子又给了多少钱,这个月还剩下多少钱之类的。

小胡微笑着跟王奶奶讲,她的通行证上由于有乱涂乱画的痕迹已失效,在中国边防出境时出示,边防是不会让她出境的。如果她要赴香港看妹妹,只能重新去公安局办理一本通行证了。

王奶奶带着无奈的表情，向小胡点了点头，并同意去申请一本新通行证。

[评析]

据报道，一位中国男子在微博上发帖求助，称一家人去韩国旅游，但他的护照却被不懂事的儿子涂得乱七八糟，结果无法通过边检，被困在韩国境内。为此，该男子希望网友支招，让自己早日回国。

护照、港澳通行证及大陆居民往来台湾通行证是重要的出境旅行证件。这个案例使我们认识到：在门市接待客人时，对客人的证件检查一定要十分仔细，避免出现不必要的麻烦。同时，门市销售人员也要了解相关证件的使用注意事项。按照国家有关规定，护照、通行证上是不能乱涂乱画的。王奶奶把最后一页当成了账本，这样的通行证是过不了中国边防的。

同样，旅客在出境时必须证件齐全，尤其是护照必须在有效期内。有时会在机场的关口遇到护照或通行证过期的旅客，可能他们在办理签证（签注）时并没有过期，到了出发时却已过期。只要出境时护照、通行证显示有效期不足6个月，边检就不会放行了。

因此，游客们要保管好自己的护照、通行证等，避免其被乱涂乱画。同时，护照、通行证等证件也不得存在破损，否则证件就会失效。护照、通行证的有效性也是门市工作人员在收客时需要重点关注的内容之一。

An Account-book-style Travel Permit

The nearly 68-year-old lady Wang lived in Hangzhou alone, as her husband had passed away two years ago. Her only son was working in another city busily, so he could just spend a little time with his mother. Luckily, the son was so filial that he would come back home to stay with his mother if he was free and he also hoped that his mother would have time for traveling.

One day in April, 2014, Ms. Wang went to an international travel agency alone in order to go through the formalities for outbound travel. When she arrived at the sales counter of the travel service, the receptionist helped her with enthusiasm and showed some new outbound travel routes to her with patient explanation. The old lady was satisfied with these routes. But in fact, she wanted to visit her sister in Hong Kong. Considering this situation, the receptionist Hu suggested that the travel agency buy a round-trip ticket and help her with the endorsement. She thought it was a good idea and decided to follow this suggestion.

Ms. Wang told Hu that she had already gotten the Exit-Entry Permit for Travelling to and from Hong Kong and Macao last month from the public security bureau. Hu asked Ms. Wang to show it to her and surprisingly found that the last page's blank space of this permit filled with Ms. Wang's own accounts. Obviously, Mr. Wang regarded her permit as an account book and the contents were all about how much the food she bought cost, or how much money her son gave to her, how much money left this month and so on.

Hu told Ms. Wang with smile that because she scrawled and kept accounts on the permit, the permit was invalid and the immigration officers would not permit her to pass. Therefore, a new permit had to be applied for.

After hearing that, Ms. Wang felt disappointed but she nodded to Hu and agreed to apply for a new permit.

Comments

It was reported that a Chinese man posted a message for help on micro blog saying that his passport was scrawled on by his naughty son and this made him fail to go through the immigration inspection and was forced to stay in Korea. Therefore, he hoped some netizens could give him some advice so that he could go back to China as soon as possible.

Passport, Exit-Entry Permit for Traveling to and from Hong Kong and Macao and Mainland Residents Traveling to Taiwan Permit are all very important international travel documents. From this case we can realize that travel sales staff should check the certificates very carefully when receiving the guests in order to avoid unnecessary troubles. At the same time, the salespeople of the travel service should know how to use and keep these certificates. According to relevant regulations, passports and permits cannot be scrawled and scribbled on. Ms. Wang used the last page of the permit as the account book and thus this kind of permit cannot be used to go through the Chinese border checkpoint.

Similarly, tourists must take all the certificates needed for departure and especially make sure the passport or the permit must be within the validity period.

Besides, you'd better leave the country 6 months before the expiration of the validity or you will be refused to obtain the visa because of the short valid period. Sometimes we can meet the tourists whose passports or permits are invalid at the border checkpoint of the airport. Maybe their passports or permits were still valid when the visas was issued, but when they depart the passports or the permits have just expired. In a word, if the validity of period is less than 6 months the border checkpoint will not let you go through it.

In conclusion, tourists should take care of their own passports and permits. In addition, all the certificates will be useless if they are spoiled and the staff of travel service should take the validity of passports and permits as one of the most important concerns when receiving the guests.

境外旅游意外保险

新西兰仅 400 万人口,有辽阔的空间容纳不胜枚举的风光胜景。这里有绵延约 550 公里的崇山峻岭、面积相当于一个小国的火山口湖泊、4 座活火山、14 个冰河雕砌的峡湾、约 4 万平方公里的天然森林,以及完美的海滩。伟大的地质构造造就了新西兰得天独厚的地理风貌。

自新西兰航空公司开通了上海—奥克兰的直飞航班后,新西兰旅游局向中国华东地区各省(市)旅游局推广了"100%纯净新西兰之旅"的各种线路,掀起了中国公民赴新西兰南岛、北岛旅游的高潮。浙江几家旅行社在浙江主要的报纸上联合刊登广告,联合收客,保证了每一个预控机位的团体均能组团成行,建立了浙江(杭州)出境游组团社客人单独组团成行的出境旅游操作新模式。

某国际旅行社领队部安排了小许担任"100%纯净新西兰南北岛 8 日游"的领队。出发前,小许来到旅行社与出境旅游中心澳新部计调人员陈小姐交接工作。当陈小姐将带团的资料交给小许时,小许一眼发现"中国公民出国旅游团队名单"中一位客人的年龄是 81 岁。小许立刻问陈小姐客人是否购买了境外旅游意外保险。经陈小姐与收客的门市销售员核实,该客人只购买了一份几十元的意外保险。小许凭他多年的带团经历,又向门市销售人员询问了该客人的身体状况,销售人员告诉小许:"老人的报名是由他的儿女来办理的,共有 6 名亲属一同前往,老人有国际旅行健康证明书。"接着,小许又问:"你与老人见过面吗?"销售人员告诉他:"几次到旅行社来送报名及签证材料的均是他的儿女,所以一直没有见到过老人。"小许心想,虽然老人有国际旅行健康证明书,但销售人员没有见过面,总是觉得不踏实,万一老人在新西兰旅游时发生意外,没有购买高额保险,理赔起来就比较吃亏。于是,小许将自己的想法与陈小姐进行了交流,陈小姐将该事情向澳新部经理做了汇报。考虑到老人是该旅游公司的常客,且年龄超过 80 岁,经商量决定,旅游公司出钱给老人购买价值 300 元的境外旅游意外保险。险种包括:

①境外旅游意外伤害保险,涵盖意外身故、残疾及烧烫伤;

②境外旅行附加医疗费用补偿保险,涵盖意外和急性病医疗补偿;

③境外旅行附加紧急医疗救援,涵盖医疗运送和送返、亲属慰问探访补偿等。

旅行开始的那一天,小许比预定集合时间提前半小时抵达集合点。抵达后首先主动打电话给与老人一同前往旅行的 6 人中的负责人,询问老人是否已经安全抵达集合点。与老人见面后,老人对小许的特别关注感觉非常安慰,因为毕竟是老人,他非常需要有人来关心。

一路上,小许与客人游览了南岛的花园城市基督城,穿过坎特伯雷平原前往库克山区参观了牧羊人教堂、美丽的蒂卡普湖泊,而后抵达蹦极发源地皇后镇,在被美国有线电视新闻网评为最佳景观餐厅之一、拥有 330 个座位的天空缆车餐厅享用晚餐,同时欣赏皇后镇街景、瓦卡蒂普湖和周边的壮观景色。接下来,团体又乘坐游轮、接驳大巴游览了神奇峡湾,观赏冰河时期的奇妙景观。结束了南岛的旅行后,老人与团体又兴奋地飞往北岛的奥克兰与罗托鲁瓦,当参观罗托鲁瓦爱哥顿农场,喂小羊、小牛和鹿,看到其毛有软黄金之称的羊驼,参观奇异果园,品尝奇异果蜂蜜时,老人笑得似乎回到了童年。

旅行的最后一天,从奥克兰飞往上海的飞机起飞前,小许将旅行社特地购买境外旅游意外保险的事情告诉了老人。老人兴奋地告诉小许:"此次新西兰之旅要比欧洲旅行更惬意。下次旅行一定来找你们旅行社,如有可能也希望你能再次陪我们一同前往世界各地。"

[评析]

随着对中国公民开放的目的地国家和地区不断增多,以及中国公民收入水平的不断上升,越来越多的中国公民赴境外旅行。而且,子女带老人旅游的这份孝心已经从境内旅游慢慢渗透到出境旅游。通常来说,各使(领)馆在办理签证时,对70岁以上老人要求出示国际旅行健康证明书,也就是说,使(领)馆对70岁以上老人的健康安全特别关注。而旅行社在接受70岁以上老人报名的时候应要求家人陪同前往旅行,并应该告知老人最好购买相对高额的境外旅游意外保险。该案例中,旅行社门市销售人员没有及时告知客人购买相对高额的境外旅游意外保险,而老人的团费已经支付,合同已经签订,签证也即将获得,一切都准备就绪。在这种情况下,旅游公司考虑到老人是回头客,权衡了该事件的利弊关系,毅然决定由旅行社出钱为老人购买一份保险,以应付突发情况。

领队在与计调人员交接工作时,应该根据客人的年龄结构进行分析,重点关注团队中的那些特殊客人,比如年长者、婴儿、媒体工作者等,尽量争取在出发前将准备工作做到位。

另外,旅行社在经营管理中不能仅看到当前的利益,而应该从全局考虑。案例中,虽然旅行社在客人全然不知的情况下,为他购买了高额境外意外保险,但是确保了客人的全方位安全,赢得了回头客,值得业界学习。

Outbound Tour Accident Insurance

With a small population of four million, New Zealand has numerous tourist attractions within its vast territory. There are mountains stretching over about 550 kilometers, crater lakes with an area equivalent to a small country, 4 active volcanoes, 14 fiords, natural forests covering an area around 40,000 square kilometers and perfect beaches. Great geological forces created a unique landscape in New Zealand.

Since the opening of the direct flight between Shanghai and Auckland by Air New Zealand, New Zealand Tourism Bureau had promoted various lines of "100% Pure New Zealand tour" in provincial tourism bureaus in eastern China, setting off a climax of traveling in South Island and North Island in New Zealand. Outbound tour agencies in Zhejiang placed ads together on major newspapers in Zhejiang and received tourists to ensure the success of every tour group. It marked the establishment of a new mode of travel operation in Zhejiang (Hangzhou).

An international travel agency appointed Mr. Xu as tour manager of the "8-day Tour of 100% Pure North and South Island of New Zealand". Before departure, he handed some work over to the operator Ms. Chen. When Ms.

Chen gave him the group information, he soon found that there was an 81-year-old guest in the group. Thus he immediately asked if the guest had taken out outbound tour accident insurance. After verification with the salesperson by Ms. Chen, they confirmed that this guest only arranged accident insurance worth only a few dozen *yuan*. Based on his many years' work experience, Mr. Xu inquired the salesperson about the physical condition of the guest. The staff told him that the guest's children handled his application and six of the family would travel with the guest. Also the elderly had the international travel health certificate. Mr. Xu then asked if the staff had met the guest in person. The answer was no since all the paperwork including application and visa were handled by his children. Xu was still worried. If the guest should be in an accident during the tour, he would suffer losses in insurance claim. Thus, he shared his ideas with Ms. Chen, who reported the matter to the department manager. After discussion, they decided to take out overseas travel accident insurance worth RMB 300 for the guest because he was the company's regular. The insurance includes the following types:

1. Overseas travel accidental injury insurance, covering accidental death, disability and burns;

2. Additional medical expense compensation insurance, covering accidents and acute disease medical compensation;

3. Additional emergency medical rescue, covering medical evacuation and repatriation, visit compensation, etc.

On the first day of the tour, Xu arrived at the assembly point half an hour earlier than the scheduled time. Upon arrival, he first called the man who was in charge of the six family members and asked if the old man had arrived safely. After meeting Xu, the old man felt comforted due to Xu's consideration, since he really needed some care.

Along the way, Xu led the group to view the Garden City of Christchurch on South Island, and visited the Shepherd Church, beautiful Lake Tekapo across the Canterbury Plains in Cook region. Then they arrived at the birthplace of bungee jumping in Queenstown and enjoyed dinner in the 330-seat Skyline Restaurant, which was rated as one of the restaurants with the best views by CNN. Meanwhile they also appreciated the streetscape and spectacular view of Lake Wakatipu. Their next stop was at the fjords by cruise and shuttle bus to enjoy the wonderful landscape of the Ice Age. After the trip on South Island, the group flew to Auckland and Rotorua on North Island and visited Agrodome Farm in Rotorua, where they fed lambs, calves and deer. They saw alpaca whose hair is called soft gold, visited a kiwi fruit ranch, tasted kiwi honey, which brought the old man back to his childhood.

On the last day of the tour, before taking the flight from Auckland to Shanghai, Xu told the old man about the specially purchased insurance. The old man excitedly told him that the trip in New Zealand was more pleasant than that in Europe. He would choose the same agency next time and hoped that Xu could accompany them to different places around the world.

Comments

With the increase in the number of destination countries and regions for Chinese citizens and in the income of Chinese citizens, more and more Chinese citizens are traveling abroad. Moreover, the number of young tourists taking their parents abroad for showing filial duties is also growing. Generally speaking, consulates usually require people over 70 to show international travel health certificate in the process of visa application, showing its particular concern over senior people. Travel agencies often require escorts for people over 70 and advise them to take out relatively expensive outbound tour accident insurance for precaution. In the above case，the sales staff did not advise the old man to purchase relatively expensive outbound tour accident insurance before he signed the contract and paid for the tour. In this case，the travel agency decided to pay for the insurance of the old people for precaution since he was the regular.

The tour manager should analyze the age structure of the guests when the work is handed over from the operator，focusing on those special guests，such as the elderly，infants，and media workers. Sufficient preparation should be done before departure.

In addition，the travel agency should view its interests in a long run. The case shows that although the travel agency paid the insurance fee for its guest without noticing，it won the guest's recognition and ensured his total security，which proves to be valuable field work experience.

终于赴日本看上了滨崎步演唱会

　　我朋友一家在杭州某旅游公司满心欢喜地报名参加了 6 月 19 日至 28 日的"荷法意瑞 10 日游（杭州出发）"。朋友的女儿甜甜 5 月初在网上订好了 8 月份去日本的来回机票、酒店及滨崎步演唱会的门票。在各旅游公司的网站上找了很久，觉得该旅游公司 6 月 19 日出发的团在时间上非常符合他们的要求，认为从欧洲回来后还有一个月的时间可以办理销签，全家便赴旅游公司报了名。按正常程序，旅游公司在 7—15 个工作日内就可以完成销签工作，所以，我的朋友毫不犹豫地付清了团费。

　　但是几天后甜甜从另一家给她做日本签证的旅游公司得知：7 月 16 日之前若无法拿回护照交予日本领事馆签证，日本签证将无法保证办理。那么甜甜面临的将是损失往返机票、酒店两晚的房费、演唱会门票等各项费用。情急之下甜甜联系了旅游公司操作欧洲游的门市销售陈小姐。陈小姐称已跟旅游公司欧洲部确认了这个情况，提出可以去申请当面销签，届时会帮忙跟领事馆申请。于是，甜甜放心地参加了"荷法意瑞 10 日游"。

　　从欧洲回来后，甜甜联系了办理欧洲游的旅游公司。陈小姐告诉她这个团没有抽到面销，而且要等好几批团面销结束后，领事馆才能将全部的护照交还给旅游公司。简言之,该旅游公司的态度就是没有办法申请面销。

为了安抚客人的情绪,陈小姐当着客人的面联系了欧洲部的计调人员王小姐,王小姐表示她会盯住领事馆进行销签工作,预估在 7 月 18 日前可以将护照拿回来。回家后,甜甜感觉时间上的悬念太大,心里还是没有把握。

第二天,甜甜又一次来到该旅游公司,提出面销通知下来后,她可以自己去上海领取护照,这样可以节约路程时间,还能直接将护照送到日本领事馆做签证。而旅游公司也提出,希望她能自己去盯盯法国领事馆,同时,该旅游公司在上海负责送签的公司会予以配合。可是眼看最后期限慢慢地接近,旅行社却一直没有告知甜甜何时能去上海的领事馆领取护照。

过了一周,无奈之下,甜甜再一次来到该旅游公司找到了出境旅游中心欧洲部经理,说明了她立刻需要护照是因为马上要办理下一个目的地国家的签证,而且,出发之前陈小姐是答应她可以申请当面销签的。于是,欧洲部经理答应甜甜会和上海的送签公司联系,将护照拿出来进行当面销签。

三天后,甜甜接到了旅游公司陈小姐打来的电话,通知她可以赴上海法国领事馆销签。甜甜在上海完成销签后,立刻又将护照送到了日本领事馆做日本签证。

8 月份,甜甜终于如愿以偿地飞往日本,按原计划看了滨崎步的演唱会。

[评析]

护照销签,就是注销签证,主要目的是让相关国家领事馆通过护照和登机牌等确认所有团队游客已按时返回。随着中国旅游的逐步开放,虽然各国的签证都有有效期,但日本、德国、芬兰、意大利等许多国家的领事馆都要求团队游客回来后必须销签。

一些国家的当面销签是有条件的。譬如,抽到的客人需要跑到领事馆证明自己已经从该国回来。各领事馆的销签政策也一直在变化之中。有时旅游公司将护照及材料送进领事馆时,领事馆就会告诉送签的旅游公司哪些人是需要回国后面销的;有时在旅行团出国前的一两天,领事馆的工作人员才会告诉旅游公司哪些人是需要面销的;有时在整团回来后,才会告诉旅游公司面销的人员名单。

据笔者所知,申请面销有一定的难度,需要旅行社跟领事馆多次沟通,讲清楚申请面销的原因,也就是与领事馆的中文秘书沟通。该案例中,门市销售人员已经答应客人替她申请面销,就应该等客人回来后,设法为客人办理申请面销的事宜,而不应该让客人一次又一次地上门,直到找部门经理才解决这一问题。

Final Success in Attending Ayumi Hamasaki's Concert

A family of my friend joined a 10-day tour in Netherlands, France, Switzerland (starts from Hangzhou and lasts from June 19 to June 28). My friend's daughter Tiantian had planned to Japan in August and had booked a round-trip ticket, a hotel and a concert ticket for Ayumi Hamasaki. She prepared all these things in the early May. The family searched on the Internet and thought the date of June 19 would be the best choice for them to go to Europe. According to the general procedure, travel agencies could finish the visa cancellation in 7—15 workdays. After they came back they could have enough time to cancel their European visa. So the family happily decided to join the group and my friend paid all the money to the travel agency without hesitation.

But several days later, Tiantian was informed by the travel agency in charge of her Japan visa application that if she could not hand in the passport to the Japanese consulate before July 16, the Japanese visa would not be done. In this situation, Tiantian would have to cover the loss of money including the round-trip ticket, the two nights' accommodation and the concert ticket. She urgently contacted Ms. Chen, who was the saleswoman operating European travel market. Ms. Chen said she had checked with the European department about this issue that the family could apply to cancel the European visa in their presence. The agency would help them do the application. Finally, Tiantian got assured and had the 10-day tour in Europe.

After they came back from Europe, Tiantian called the agency that operated the Europe tour, but Ms. Chen told her that they could not manage to arrange the presence cancellation for her, and they had to wait to get the passports after several groups in front of them.

In order to soothe the emotion of the customer, Ms. Chen contacted the Europe operator Ms. Wang. Ms. Wang told them they would follow this case and could probably get the passports before July 18. Coming back home, Tiantian still thought the time was too limited and the chance was slim.

On the next day, Tiantian went to the travel agency again proposing that she could go to Shanghai to get the passport by herself. In this way, she could save time on the way and directly hand in the passport to the Japanese consulate in Shanghai for the visa. The agency suggested that she push the French consulate, and meanwhile, the company in Shanghai in charge of delivering visas would help her urge the consulate to be faster. The deadline June 16 was approaching, but Tiantian still didn't get any news about when to get the passport in Shanghai.

One week later, she had no choice but to go to the Europe department again. This time she went to the manager of the department for help. She explained that she needed the passport urgently to apply for the visa for Japan, and before leaving for Europe, Ms. Chen promised her that she could have the presence cancellation. Finally, the manager agreed to contact the visa company in Shanghai to apply for presence cancellation.

Three days later, Tiantian got the call from Ms. Chen and was told she could go to Shanghai with her parents to do the presence cancellation. She succeeded in visa cancellation and took the passport in a hurry to the Japanese consulate for Japanese visa.

In August, she flew to Japan and watched the concert of Ayumi Hamasaki. She finally made her dream come true.

Comments

The purpose of visa cancellation is for the related consulate to check whether all the tourists have come back on time by the passports, the boarding passes, etc. Most countries have a certain period of validity on the visa, but many countries like Japan, Germany, Finland and Italy still require the group tourists to do the visa cancellation after they come back to China.

Some countries have certain conditions for doing presence cancellation. For example, the passenger who gets the chance needs to go to the consulate to prove that he or she has come back from the country. Sometimes, the consulate will tell the travel agencies who need to do the presence cancellation as soon as they hand in the passports and other data; sometimes, the consulate will give the notice one or two days before the group leaves and it's also possible for the consulate to inform the agency after the whole group has come back.

As I know, to do the presence cancellation is difficult. The agency needs to talk to the consulate for many times and explain clearly about the reasons. The

中国公民出境旅游服务质量解析

046

Chinese secretary in the consulate has to be communicated with. In this case, as the sales staff has already promised the customer to apply for the presence cancellation, they should do their best to help the customer rather than solve the problem after the customer has talked to the department manager for several times.

"湿"而复得的护照

美国是许多游客向往的国家,大家平常所熟悉的大多是纽约、华盛顿等非常具有代表性的城市。2014 年 4 月,小伊有幸担任了"美国西海岸 8 日团"的领队。该旅游团的特色是深度游览美国西海岸最负盛名的三大城市——洛杉矶、拉斯维加斯、圣地亚哥,自由选择游览美西大峡谷、胡佛水坝等著名景点,欣赏圣地亚哥老城风光,畅游圣地亚哥"中途岛号"航母。

行程是从杭州飞往广州再转机到洛杉矶,团队将在洛杉矶住 3 个晚上。其中,第二天从洛杉矶到圣地亚哥进行一日游,第四天再从洛杉矶坐车赴美国赌城——拉斯维加斯,这是一座建立在沙漠上的繁华城市,同时,又是美国的会展中心之一,世界级拳击比赛首选地和世界著名的婚礼之都。游客将在拉斯维加斯住 2 晚。在赌城游览期间,大家会坐汽车前往科罗拉多大峡谷参观。行程的第六天游客将从拉斯维加斯坐车回到洛杉矶。最后,从洛杉矶出发,乘坐飞机返回中国广州。

出发的那一天,团队乘坐的航班从广州白云机场起飞,经过 13 小时左右的飞行,于同一天的 18 点抵达美国西海岸最大的城市、"天使之城"——洛杉矶。一落地,迎接大家的就是一场大雨。虽然团员们都带了雨伞,但无奈雨势太大,领队身上的双肩包还是被雨淋湿了。当时领队小伊也没太在意,回到酒店后发现放在双肩包最外层的护照被雨水打湿了,水已经渗开,护照里面部分颜色已经染开,拿在手里已经呈现"水肿"状态。小伊当时第一反应是庆幸客人的护照没有放在他这里,在确认旅游团成员的护照没有像他的一样被淋湿之后,小伊松了一口气,还好只是一本护照有问题。于是,小伊立刻打电话给中国驻洛杉矶领事馆,询问该护照是否可以继续使用。领事馆工作人员告诉他,打湿的护照不可以继续使用。考虑到这几天在美国境内旅游都是坐大巴,暂时用不到护照,于是,第二天下午小伊将护照的复印件留下,原件送到了洛杉矶领事馆,以补办一个旅行证明,方便从美国洛杉矶回中国时办理出境手续。就这样,小伊又继续开始带领客人游览。第六天从拉斯维加斯返回洛杉矶时,小伊从领事馆获取了补办的旅行证明,顺利地离开了美国,结束了美国西部之旅。

[评析]

按照《中华人民共和国护照法》中的有关规定,有下列情形之一的,护照持有人可以按照规定申请换发或者补发护照:

(一)护照有效期即将届满的;

(二)护照签证页即将使用完毕的;

(三)护照损毁不能使用的;

(四)护照遗失或者被盗的;

(五)有正当理由需要换发或者补发护照的其他情形。

案例中,领队由于对护照保管不当,致使护照被雨水淋湿,无法正常使用。为了不影响接下来的行程及顺利回国,领队就需要尽快采取弥补措施。幸好只是领队一个人的护照出了问题,而团队内其他客人的护照完好无损,而且由于团队在美国境内的行程无须坐飞机,不需要使用护照。所以,领队有充足的时间前往我国驻洛杉矶领事馆,补办一个旅行证明。不然,领队也许就不能随团一起活动了。

一名出境游领队,在带团过程中,不仅需要有服务意识、安全意识,还必须具备很强的证件意识。出境旅游没有护照、签证，旅途简直是举步维艰，所以领队在保管好自己证件的同时，也要竭力提醒团内的每一位客人，一定要保管好各类证件。如：专门用一个防水性极好、较轻便且较牢固的袋子来保存护照之类的重要证件，放置在身上或背包里也要时刻检查一下是否安全无失，这样，就会大大减小证件丢失、损毁、被盗的可能性。

How to Do When the Passport Is Wet

The US is a country that many tourists desire to visit. There are many cities with distinguished characters and people are normally familiar with，such as New York，Washington，etc. In April，2014，Ms. Yi fortunately became the tour leader of "8-day Tour along West Coast of the US". The specialty of this tour was to visit the three famous cities along the west American coast：Los Angeles，Las Vegas and San Diego. And the tour was optional for a visit to the famous scenic spots like the West Grand Canyon，the Hoover Dam as well as enjoying the old city view and the Midway Aircraft Carrier in San Diego.

The group was scheduled to fly from Hangzhou to Guangzhou，then to Los Angeles. The group would stay for three nights in Los Angeles. And on the second day，one-day tour in San Diego was scheduled. On the fourth day，the group would go from Los Angeles to Las Vegas by bus，a bustling city built on the desert, one of the exhibition centers in the US, a famous wedding city as well as the world class boxing competition venue. The tourists would stay there for two nights. During the visit in Las Vegas, the tourists would also go to the Great Colorado Canyon. On the sixth day, the tourists were supposed to be taken back to Los Angeles from Las Vegas and then fly to Guangzhou.

On the departure day, it took 13 hours from Baiyun Airport in Guangzhou to the biggest city in west American coast at 18:00—the City of Angel, Los Angeles. Upon arrival, there was a heavy rain. Even with an umbrella, the tour leader still got her bag wet. At that time, Ms. Yi, the tour leader, did not pay attention to it until she found the passport was wet at the outside layer of the backpack when she arrived at the hotel. The passport was wet and swollen by the rain, so the pages inside had got dyed. Ms. Yi felt fortunate that the guests' passports were not in her hands and got wet like hers. Ms. Yi called the Chinese consulate in Los Angeles to ask if the wet passport could be used or not. The staff in the consulate told her that the wet one could not be used. Considering that the following itinerary was in the country by bus and the passport was not needed, Ms. Yi kept a copy of her passport and sent her passport to the Chinese consulate in Los Angeles to get a traveling certificate. This certificate should help her get the customs procedure done when she came back to China. The tour leader went on traveling with her guests. On the sixth day, when the group came back to Los Angeles from Las Vegas, the tour leader got the traveling certificate from the Chinese consulate and left America. This was the end of the story.

Comments

According to the Passport Law of the People's Republic of China, the passport holder may apply for the renewal or renaissance of his or her passport if the following situations happen:

(1) The passport is going to expire;

(2) The pages in the passport are used up;

(3) The passport is destroyed and cannot be used again;

(4) The passport is lost or stolen;

(5) The other situations with proper reasons.

In the above case, the tour leader did not take good care of her passport and made the passport wet by the rain. It might affect the following itinerary and even the tour leader might have problems when she was going back to China. So the tour leader had to take action as soon as possible. Luckily, it was only the tour leader's passport that got wet and the other guests' passports were fine. And when traveling in the America, the group didn't need to take the plane. The passport was not needed. So the tour leader had enough time to go to the Chinese consulate in Los Angeles and apply for a traveling certificate. Otherwise, the tour leader could not have finished the journey with the group.

As an outbound tour leader, he or she must not only have the sense of service and safety, but also keep an eye on certificates. Without the passport and the visa, traveling abroad is impossible. Therefore, the tour leader has to take good care of his or her own certificates as well as remind the group. For example, it is necessary to prepare a waterproof, light and secure bag to keep the passport or other important certificates, and also check them from time to time. With cautions, people may reduce the chances of losing their important certificates or having them destroyed and stolen.

当从网上购买的旅游产品与旅行社包价游产品相撞时

　　泰国普吉岛的游览行程基本都是 4 晚 6 日。徐领队所带的团,前两天进行得很顺利,但在第三天时有一对来度蜜月的夫妇向领队提出:他们想在第五天自由活动时,参加他们在某网站购买的珊瑚岛一日游的活动。

　　领队小徐翻看行程表核对后发现,第五天的确写着早餐后自由活动,晚上在幻多奇主题公园享用自助餐后前往机场。但是,由于这个团是购物团,所以购物项目会穿插在每天的行程中,并且已经在附加协议上注明是什么时间进行。由于导游是有权利在不增减行程景点的情况下改变前后游览顺序的,所以导游将所有购物点全部挪至第五天这段自由活动时间内进行,并且已经征得了客人的同意,其中有两个购物点明确表示会在第五天早上和下午进行,同时第五天全天是含餐的(因为如果是自由活动那就会显示不含餐)。同时,泰国的接待旅行社有一条规定:不走购物点的旅游者需要每人交给导游人民币 800 元,方能离团自由活动。领队将上述情况告知客人之后,建议他们取消网上的行程预订,但是这对夫妇说他们已经付清了所有款项,而且网店的工作人员解释说如果取消,就是全损。

　　这对夫妻表示无法接受这个事实,觉得旅行社没有在合同内明确购物点时间安排与 800 元脱团费的问题,是旅行社的失职,要求旅行社补偿他们在网上购买的旅游项目的全部损失,或者免去他们每人 800 元的脱团费。经过领队与客人一段时间的协调之后,客人还是坚持自己的观点。于是,领队向客人要普吉岛当地负责人的电话号码,帮助进行沟通协调。由于他们在网上购买的旅游项目是一个散客拼成的一日游,店家只给了一个当地的导游名字,所以,客人也没办法给出接待社的联系方式。这样的旅游产品,其安全性也有待考量。

另外,本次行程的普吉岛地接社也明确表示不会同意客人的解决方式,坚称如果客人一意孤行要去参加自行购买的项目,那必须向两位客人加收一共 1600 元的脱团费。在调解无果的情况下,领队与计调讨论之后决定给出下列答复。方案一:①让客人继续和店家谈谈能否退还一定量的费用。②如果一定要参加他们自己购买的项目,那就签下"自愿离团"的协议,一切费用自理,自己注意安全,出任何意外组团社不负任何责任,并且一定要在规定时间到达幻多奇主题公园,放弃午餐并且不退还午餐费用;如若不能在规定时间到达幻多奇主题公园,就视为主动放弃接下来的行程,不退还任何损失;若耽误回程飞机,一切后果自负。③每人 800 元的脱团费组团社将和地接社再进行协商,尽量压低价格,但不能保证协商成功。方案二:放弃网上自行购买的项目,自行承担所有损失,随后按照原定行程参加购物项目。将这两个方案给客人之后,领队再三解释,请他们第二天早上集合的时候给予答复。

最后,小夫妻还是选择了方案二,大家的行程也就继续按照合同进行了下去。

[评析]

旅游行程中,所谓的自由活动也是必须在领队、导游的引领下进行的,而不是完全脱离团队单独进行自由活动。

目前,网上的预订多种多样,我们暂且先不去管它的安全性、可行性与合法性等,我们只想说,旅游者如果已经参加了旅行社的包价旅游产品,就应该在购买其他旅游产品时,问一下报名参加旅游的旅行社,是否有矛盾存在,这样就不会发生案例中的情况。案例中,该团明确是购物团,也就是说,购物是整个行程中不可缺少的一个环节,该客人想参加自己购买的其他旅游活动,显然是与原来的行程相抵触的。

When Travel Agency's Package Product Meets the Product Purchased Online

Normally the trip to Phuket, Thailand, lasts 4 nights and 6 days. Xu, a tour leader, took a tour group to Phuket. The first two days went smoothly. On the third day, a newly married couple came up to Xu and told him that they would like to take part in a tourism product they purchased online when they were in the free accivity time.

Xu checked the itinerary which showed that the guests were going to have a free day after breakfast and then have dinner at Phuket Fantasea theme park and finally to the airport. However, due to the fact that the group was a shopping group, there would be shopping activities on their everyday itinerary, which had already been informed on the additional agreement. As tour guide had the rights to change the time schedule of each activity on the itinerary, Xu had moved all the shopping activities on the fifth day, which was under permission of all the guests. Meanwhile, two of them were clearly informed that the shopping would be done in the morning and afternoon and the meals were included, as meals would be showed on free day itinerary. Furthermore, another policy made by local travel agency was that anyone who refused to take on original route on the itinerary had to pay extra RMB 800 for leaving the group. Xu told the couple the policy and suggested that they cancel the product they bought online. However, the couple mentioned that they had already made the full payment of the product with no refund.

The young couple complained that the agreement of the travel agency product didn't mention anything about shopping schedule as well as another RMB 800 for compensation and the agency were liable for the negligence. They insisted that the travel agency should either be liable for all the loss for the product they purchased online or not charge them the extra RMB 800 per person. The negotiation didn't work out very well between the two parties. The guests still insisted on their own opinion. Therefore, the tour leader tried to get in touch with the local leader who was in charge of the online product. However, the guests didn't have the contact of the leader. Therefore, the safety became another concern.

In addition, the travel agency at the Phuket also disagreed with the suggestion of the guests and they insisted that if the guests really wanted to take part in the program they purchased online, they had to pay for RMB 1,600 in total for leaving the group. Finally, the agency offered two options for the guests to choose from.

Plan A:

1. Get in touch with the online agency to see if the payment could be refunded.

2. If the guests insisted on participating in the program, they had to sign the "agreement of voluntarily leaving group" with no liability of the travel

agency. Meanwhile, they had to arrive at Phuket Fantasea in time with no lunch provided(not refundable). If the guests couldn't arrive at the theme park in time, it would be regarded as quitting the whole program with no responsibility of the travel agency.

3. Local travel agency and China travel agency would negotiate to see if they could charge the guests for leaving the group with a lower price(lower than RMB 800).

Plan B:

Quitting the online product and following the original travel route and guests taking on the responsibility themselves.

Xu explained and passed the two plans to the couple. They were required to give Xu a reply by the next day.

In the end, the couple decided to choose Plan B and everything was followed by the agreement.

Comments

During the trip, any free activities should be led by tour leaders instead of having guests leave the group to have free activities alone.

Currently, there are a great number of tourism products online. Regardless of their safety and legality, if tourists have already signed up for the trips provided by travel agencies, they are required to consult the agencies to see if there is any conflict existing to avoid the situation mentioned in the above case. In this case, the group was a shopping group. Therefore, shopping was supposed to be a must during the trip. If the guests intended to participate in the product they purchased by themselves, the conflict apparently existed between these two tourism products.

怀孕了，还能旅行吗？

　　一对新婚夫妇满心欢喜地参加了某旅行社组织的"纯泰6日游"。在旅行社门市报名时，两位新人选定了行程，旅行社门市销售人员给他们办理了报名手续，祝愿他们新婚快乐，旅途愉快。

　　前四天的行程非常顺利。可是到了第五天，不幸的事发生了：旅游大巴在从芭提雅回曼谷的路上翻车了。小王被送到曼谷国际医院治疗，确定为骨盆骨折，需要手术并大约需要三个月的治疗时间。其间，医生给小王做了一个全面检查，结果发现小王已经怀孕一个月了，但她自己却不知道。由于小王在全面检查之前，已经用了许多不利于胚胎成型的药物来治疗骨盆骨折，显然，将胚胎留在肚子里是不利的，小王想人工流产。但是，根据泰国的法律，泰国医院是不能给小王做人流的。而且，小王在泰国医院所花费的医药费是由境外保险公司支付的，如果小王要回到国内做人流并治疗骨折，那境外保险公司就不会给她支付医药费。况且，骨盆骨折一下子是无法痊愈的。无奈之下，小王只能在泰国医院治疗，两个月以后，在还没有痊愈的情况下，小王飞回了中国，然后再进行流产手术。

　　原本是一场完美的蜜月旅行，却造成了这样遗憾的结局。

[评析]

对于新婚夫妇来说,他们在报名参加旅游时可能并不知道女方是否已经怀孕。但有些旅行者来旅行社报名时,明明知道自己已经怀孕,还要来冒这个险。孕妇如隐瞒怀孕实情报团旅游而发生意外,自身需承担相关责任。同时,旅行社门市接待人员有义务提前告知孕妇行程安排,要善意地提醒她们孕妇旅游时所存在的风险,并提出相关建议。孕妇如果坚持出行,应向旅行社出具正规医院所开的健康证明,证明身体能承受旅途造成的劳累等;另外,出行前旅行社应与之签订需"特殊照顾"的补充合同。案例中,门市销售人员没有对来报名参加旅游的新婚夫妇做出提醒和建议也是一个严重的失误。

医生一般不建议孕妇在怀孕 3 个月内旅游,因为这段日子容易流产;也不赞成孕妇在 7 个月以后旅游,这一时期如果发生意外,易引起早产。其他的时候如无流产、早产迹象,在孕妇身体允许的情况下是可以出游的。但即使可出行,孕妇也应选择较轻松的旅行项目。最好不要出境,毕竟各地水土不同而且旅途比较遥远。

Travel During Pregnancy?

A newly married couple joined a 6-day trip in Thailand organized by a travel agency. They picked up their own travel itinerary while signing up for the tour at the agency. The salesman helped them go through the application procedure and wished them a wonderful trip.

During the trip, the first 4 days went smoothly. However, there was an accident on the fifth day when the tour bus overturned on the way from Pattaya to Bangkok. Wang, the wife, was sent to Bangkok International Hospital and was confirmed having pelvic fracture in need of surgery with 3 months of therapy. Meanwhile, Wang was accidentally found her pregnancy for a month during the medical examination. Due to the fact that Wang was taking meds for pelvic fracture which impacted the health of the fetus, the baby was clearly not in good health condition. Wang wondered whether she could have an induced abortion right away. However, having an abortion was not allowed in Thailand. Meanwhile, all the expenses in Thailand would be paid by the insurance company overseas. If Wang did the abortion and fracture therapy after getting back to China, the insurance company would have no obligation to pay the bill. Other than that, pelvic fracture cannot be healed in a short period of time. Reluctantly, Wang had to receive treatment in Thailand and then fly back to China after two month of therapy for the abortion.

Sadly, the wonderful honeymoon trip ended up in hospital.

Comments

For most newly married ladies, they might not make certain that if they are pregnant or not. However, some of them try to hide the truth on purpose when applying for the tour.

Salesmen have the duty to inform pregnant tourists potential risks as well as to give suggestions for traveling during pregnancy. If they insist on traveling, tourists are liable for offering health certificates provided by hospitals to prove they can endure tiredness that may occur during the trip. Meanwhile, a "special treatment" should be signed between tourists and travel agencies. In the case above，the salesman should take on responsibility for failing to inform the couple of the potential harm caused by pregnancy.

It is not suggested for pregnant ladies to take trips during their first and last 3 months of pregnancy，which may cause miscarriage and premature birth easily. In the other months of pregnancy，pregnant women can choose leisure trips if they are physically able to do so.

誊抄英国入境卡

资深领队钱先生此次将带一个赴英国和爱尔兰两国旅游的旅行团。老钱在接受旅行社计调人员交接的行程表时发现,由于国庆期间直飞伦敦的机位非常紧张,所以,改成了从杭州飞阿姆斯特丹转机,再飞伦敦。老钱发现,在阿姆斯特丹史基浦机场的转机时间有 2 个小时,转机时间倒是充裕,但出现的新问题是,每个团员均需要填写一张英国入境卡。可旅行社由于最近英国团较多,英国入境卡所剩无几。如果让客人在阿姆斯特丹飞伦敦的飞机上自行填写入境卡,客人会有许多困难。阿姆斯特丹飞伦敦的时间是 1 小时 20 分钟,如果 32 张入境卡全部让领队填写,时间比较紧张,也会导致入境英国前的准备不够充分。

于是,钱领队从网上下载了一张英国入境卡,先将诸如出入境的日期、在英国所下榻的饭店等信息填写好,复印了 32 份,开始分别为每一位团员填写。

出境的那一天,钱领队将填写好的入境卡复印件放在随身的文件夹里。在阿姆斯特丹机场转机时,钱领队将团员带到阿姆斯特丹机场飞伦敦的登机处,将填写好的英国入境卡复印件发给每一个客人,让他们先熟悉入境卡的内容。然后,钱领队告诉客人,上了飞机后,请大家按照每人手上拿的入境卡复印件的内容,将其抄写到正式的入境卡上,并对大家的配合表示感谢。大家拿到这张填写好的入境卡复印件后,互相争着谁的英语理解力强,遇到疑问时,还向钱领队求证,气氛非常好。

登机后,钱领队马上用熟练的英文问了空中服务人员,索要了 32 张入境卡,告诉服务人员:"我们是旅行团,领队会统一发入境卡给团员的。"考虑到客人可能会忘了带笔,钱领队还带了一捆笔,发给那些没有带笔的团友。由于"样本"在手,等飞机起飞时,全团的客人基本上都已经填写完毕,并按照领队的吩咐将入境卡夹在了自己的护照里。

飞机落地伦敦时,客人拿着护照(含签证)和填写好的入境卡,有序地通过了移民局的检查。

[评析]

随着中国经济的腾飞,越来越多的旅游目的地国家和地区对中国开放,然而,旅行社不一定储备着所有旅游目的地的入境卡。借助网络下载,给客人预先填写好样本,领队在飞机上领到入境卡后让客人照着样本来填写入境卡上的各项内容,也算是一种服务创新。

传统的做法是,旅行社领队先将入境卡的信息填写好,然后让客人签个名,省了让客人填写的麻烦。但对于年轻的旅游者,应让他们自己填写,他们会觉得这是一种旅游体验。所以让他们自己填写是完全没有问题的。然而,对一些年老的旅游者或者小孩,领队应该帮他们填写。

如今,随着网络时代的发展,旅行社之间的竞争也变得越来越激烈。旅行社只有做好服务工作,抓好细节,才能在客户中赢得好评。

Fill in the British Landing Card

Mr. Qian, a senior tour leader, was going to take a group to visit the UK and Ireland. When the operator transferred the itinerary, he found out that the direct flight to London had been changed due to the tight flight schedule during Chinese National Holidays. They had to fly to London through Amsterdam. But Qian noticed that there was enough time for them to catch the connecting flight with the two-hour layover at Amsterdam's airport Schiphol. At the same time, another problem popped out that the travel agency didn't reserve enough landing cards since there were many groups to the UK recently, but everyone in his group needed a landing card. It's difficult for them to filling in the cards during the flight from Amsterdam to London. If tour leader filled out the forms and asked them to sign their names, there would be short of time for finishing the 32 forms since the flight from Amsterdam to London only lasted one hour and twenty minutes. Besides, they couldn't be well prepared for the entry.

Then, an idea came to Qian that he downloaded a UK landing card from the Internet. He then transcribed the shared information on the card, such as date of entry and exit, hotel to stay in the UK, travel agency to work with. After that he made 32 copies and put the individual information, like name and gender on the cards.

On the departure date, Qian put these cards in his file folder. During the transferring time, he assembled the visitors in front of the boarding gate to London, handed out the copied landing cards to each of them and asked them to get familiar with the details of the card. Then, he told them to transcribe the shared information on the copy to the official landing card and extended his gratitude to everyone.

After the copies were delivered, he checked with the visitors to see if they understood the English meanings of the information on the copies. Tourists competed to comprehend the meanings better and came to explain when having questions. What a wonderful atmosphere!

After boarding, he requested 32 landing cards from the flight attendant with fluent English and explained that he would deliver landing cards to the group. As soon as the visitors got the cards, they began to transcribe. Almost everyone had finished copying before the plane was ready to take off, and then they put the cards in their passports as requested by the tour leader.

When landing at the airport, visitors got through the immigration's inspection in order with their passports (including visas) and landing cards in hand.

Comments

With the rapid development of Chinese economy, more and more destination countries and regions open their gates to Chinese citizens. Under this situation, the travel agencies may not reserve enough entry/arrival/landing cards of destination counties and regions. It would be counted as a service innovation if the tour leader could download the cards from the Internet, write down the information beforehand and ask the visitors to copy the details from the sample card to the official cards.

Conventionally, the tour leader will fill in the cards and let the visitors to sign, which will save their efforts to do it. But as for the young travelers, they will consider it as a tourism experience if they could do it by themselves. Of course, for the aged and children who can't do the job, the tour leader should assist them to transcribe.

In the Internet era, the competition among travel agencies becomes more and more intensive. Only offering excellent services and paying special attention to details will win the customers.

上海飞伦敦还是北京飞伦敦？

　　2013 年 7 月，上海某具有出境资质的旅行社组织了一个去欧洲的出境旅游团，共 43 人。这是一个散客拼团，游客分别来自杭州、宁波、绍兴、温州、上海、南京、苏州等地。该团出发地为北京，由北京飞往伦敦，全程领队兼导游是欧洲地接社派的台湾人黄先生。考虑到团队人数比较多，上海的组团社也派了一名领队小吴，让小吴协助黄先生来共同完成领队及导游工作。

　　由于正巧是夏季，天气变化多端，雷电、台风较多，航班延误时常发生。上海、南京、杭州和宁波等地飞往北京的航班出发前一天临时取消，只有温州飞北京的航班正常起飞，当台湾领队用繁体字发送短信给温州客人中的 4 位老年客人时，他们却看不懂。所以，4 位老人在温州机场办理登机手续时，没有告诉值机人员他们要在北京转机去伦敦，因此，值机人员只给他们办理了温州至北京的登机牌，行李也只托运到北京，没有同时办理北京至伦敦的第二程登机牌和行李从北京到伦敦的托运。4 位温州客人抵达北京首都机场后干等了 4 个小时，他们不知道如何办理去伦敦的登机牌和行李托运。

　　与此同时，小吴却仍在上海，因航班取消，没能按原计划时间抵达北京。4 位老年游客通过温州当地旅行社联系上海出境社，上海出境组团社计调再联系小吴,让他与 4 位老人联系。小吴在电话中,告诉他们如何抵达登机门,结果 4 位老年游客听不懂"G28 登机门"的英文表达方式,小吴只好发短信告知具体位置,让他们把短信给机场工作人员看。在机场工作人员的帮助下,4 位老人终于在航班起飞前 20 分钟赶到登机口。同时,小吴也赶到了 28 号登机口。4 位老年游客见到小吴后非常生气,连续 3 次把行程单丢到地上,以宣泄不满的情绪。

南京游客在飞机起飞前 10 分钟赶到,小吴多次与机长沟通,希望能延迟 15 分钟起飞。但北京飞往伦敦的航班上有近 300 名游客,有些乘客抵达伦敦后还要转机,因此机长不予同意。南京游客因在南京禄口机场不能取得去北京—伦敦的联程登机牌,行李没能直接托运伦敦,只能抵达北京后再办理飞伦敦的登机牌和行李托运。但因飞机即将起飞,工作人员不予办理登机手续,南京游客错过了原定的 14:10 飞伦敦的航班,后改签为 18:30 的航班,又因飞机故障推迟到次日 9:30,导致南京游客去欧洲旅游整整推迟一天。

[评析]

目前,欧洲线旅游(如:荷、法、意、瑞 10 日游)的领队、导游安排的模式往往是客人在机场集中,由欧洲派来的领队兼导游给团体办理登机手续,然后一同飞往欧洲旅游目的地。如果人数比较多,组团社还会派一名中国领队一同前往欧洲,客人出入境的服务工作是该领队的主要工作。到了欧洲境内,领队与导游的工作往往由一人来担当,这个人被称作 through guide。他(她)的工作除了讲解以外还包括接送团,酒店及餐饮的安排,景点门票的支付,游船预订等一系列工作。他们所带团的旅游线路往往要跨越几个国家。这些领队兼导游往往会几种工作语言(如:英语、法语、西班牙语等)及中国方言(如:广东话、闽南话等),方便与景点、餐厅、酒店、车队、机场的相关工作人员交流。通常他们均为受过良好的高等教育或者从小在国外出生、长大的华人,也有部分中国留学生。

旅行社在操作欧洲团体时,无论是机票的成本原因,还是机位的问题,抑或是出于多种原因考虑,总的来说,华东地区的客人到上海集中出发飞伦敦显得比较合理,不应转机北京集中后再到伦敦。在这种情形下,上海组团社应该叮嘱温州的代理社派一名送机人员协助 4 位老年客人办理登机手续,那就不会出现案例中的情形了。4 位温州客人在案例中遇到的问题,如果有专业的送机人员,他肯定会按照"如果需要乘坐转机的航班,行李应当托运到最终的目的地"的原则来办理。如从杭州飞澳大利亚的珀斯,乘坐香港港龙航空公司与香港国泰航空公司联合推出的杭州—香港—珀斯航班,虽需要在中国香港经停转机,但从杭州出发办理行李托运时,应该将行李直接托运到终点站珀斯。

很多时候领队带团的成功与否与计调的前期工作也有直接关系。如果计调在出发前能将工作做得很细的话,团队的运作就会顺畅一些。

作为领队,要有面对航班临时取消,游客滞留或误机的心理准备,要有处理此类突发事件与安抚游客负面情绪的能力。

From Shanghai to London or from Beijing to London?

In July, 2013, a qualified travel agency in Shanghai organized a group of 43 people to travel to Europe. It was a group of travelers from Hangzhou, Ningbo, Shaoxing, Wenzhou, Shanghai, Nanjing, Suzhou, and so on. The group would depart from Beijing to London, and the guide and leader of the whole journey was Mr. Huang from Taiwan. The travel agency in Shanghai also sent a leader Mr. Wu to help Mr. Huang because the number of tourists was large.

It was during summer, and flight delay often happened due to bad weather such as typhoon and storm. Flights from Shanghai, Nanjing, Hangzhou and Ningbo to Beijing were all cancelled the day before their departure from Beijing. There were only flights from Wenzhou to Beijing. Mr. Huang then informed 4 elderly passengers in Wenzhou via short messages in traditional Chinese characters. Unfortunately, the guests couldn't read that. So when these four guests checked in, they didn't tell the staff that they would take a transfer in Beijing to London. So the staff only gave them the boarding passes from Wenzhou to Beijing and the luggage were all shipped to Beijing. They didn't get the boarding passes from Beijing to London, nor their luggage. When they got to Capital Airport, they waited there for 4 hours and didn't know how to check in for their flight to London.

Meanwhile, Mr. Wu didn't get to Beijing as scheduled because the flight was cancelled in Shanghai. Those 4 elderly tourists in Wenzhou asked for help from the local agency and the agency in Shanghai. Finally Mr. Wu made a phone call to them and told them the way to get to the boarding gate G28. Because they were not able to recognize the English letter "G", so Mr. Wu sent a short message to them and they four got to the boarding gate 20 minutes before the plane took off with the help of the airport staff. When they saw Mr. Wu at the boarding gate, they threw their schedules on the floor for three times to express their dissatisfaction.

The tourists from Nanjing arrived at the airport 10 minutes before the plane took off, and Mr. Wu asked the captain several times to postpone taking off for 15 minutes. The captain refused to do so because there were more than 300 passengers on the plane and some of them needed to take a transfer in London. Those tourists from Nanjing could not get the boarding passes from Beijing to London in Nanjing Lukou International Airport and thus they could not ship their luggage directly from Nanjing to London. They had just missed their flight on 14:10 and had to endorse their flight on 18:30. Unfortunately, that flight was postponed to 9:30 the next morning due to mechanical difficulties. They were a whole day late to Europe.

Comments

Recently, the regular procedure of tour group to Europe(such as a 10-day tour to Netherlands, France, Italy and Switzerland) is to ask the tourists to meet at the airport, and the leader and tour guide from Europe will help them with check in and fly to Europe with them together. If it is a large group, the agency will send a tour leader from mainland China to help the group with check-in and going through customs. When arriving in Europe, the job of the leader and the local guide will be handled all by one person, the through guide. He or she needs to do all the arrangement during their travel in Europe, including the transportation, the hotels, meals, tickets, as well as the on-the-spot narration. Usually the through guide can speak several working languages, such as English, French, Spanish, as well as Chinese dialects for effective communication. They are usually well educated. Most of them are born or grew up in foreign countries. Some Chinese overseas students would also do such jobs.

When tour agencies organize those European groups, there are many factors for them to consider, including the cost or seats of the flight. But generally speaking, it is quite reasonable for the tourist from East China to depart from Shanghai to London, not from Beijing. In this case, the agency in Shanghai should have asked the agency in Wenzhou to send a staff to help those 4 elderly tourists with their check-in. They would have their boarding passes from Beijing to London and their luggage would be shipped directly to London. There is a basic principle: If it is a transfer flight, the luggage will be shipped to the final destination. For example，one is to fly from Hangzhou to Perth in Australia，and if he needs to take a transfer in Hong Kong，his luggage would be shipped to his final destination，Perth.

If the group operator of the travel agency could do his work more carefully，the group would run more smoothly.

Facing with the frequent flight cancelling and delay，a tour leader should have the ability to move the stress away from tourists and deal with various situations properly.

第二篇

Chapter II

出 入 境 体 验 篇

Dealing with Exit and Entry Inspection

[**本章导读**]

　　随着中国经济的腾飞和出入境管理政策的放宽，近些年我国公民出境人数急剧上升。从中国出境到他国（地区）的入境阶段，要通过中国和外国的海关检查、卫生检疫检查、边防（移民局）出入境检查、登机安全检查等十几个关口。购买自由行产品的旅游者和旅行社出境游领队要对所要通过的关口、所要办理的各项手续十分熟悉，才能顺利完成从中国出境到他国（地区）入境的所有烦琐的手续。

　　本篇通过记录作者及其同事出入境、抵离他国（地区）时，在边防、海关、卫生检疫、购物退税等环节的经历，让读者了解出入境的各流程及注意事项。

[Chapter Outline]

As the taking-off of Chinese economy and the relaxing of immigration control, the number of Chinese citizens traveling abroad has been sharply increased in recent years. Leaving from China and entering other countries(regions), travelers need to go through Chinese and foreign customs, health & quarantine inspections, immigration offices, boarding and security checks and so on. Individual tourists and tour leaders of groups must be quite familiar with all these complicated formalities of going through all different checkpoints. Only in this case can you successfully leave China and enter into other countries(regions).

In this chapter, by sharing this author's and his colleagues' experiences of dealing with formalities of entry into and exit of China, passing through the customs, immigration offices, health & quarantine, entering other countries (regions) and refunding shopping taxes, the author attempts to show readers exit and entry procedures and points for attention.

客人分别从新德里、巴黎、伦敦和哥本哈根转机回上海

　　领队老徐所带的欧洲 11 日行程的团到第十天的时候,原计划是上午游览城中之国——梵蒂冈和罗马的许愿泉、古罗马废墟外景、古罗马角斗场、古罗马凯旋门等景点后,下午从罗马到法兰克福转机再回上海。

　　当导游和领队协助客人在罗马机场办完客人购物的退税手续,过完安检正准备登机时,他们却被告知:罗马机场发生火灾,罗马飞往法兰克福的航班将延误,延误多少时间暂不知道。全团共计 34 人,在法兰克福转机逗留的时间只有 2 小时,时间一分一秒地过去,最后整个航班延误了 3 小时才起飞,导致大家延误了下一程法兰克福飞往上海的航班。抵达法兰克福机场后,航空公司安排团员们在法兰克福机场附近的酒店入住。

　　次日一早,领队与导游带着客人来到值机柜台,开始办理法兰克福飞上海的机票改签手续。由于同一时段共有 4 个团的 145 名客人赶不上飞上海的航班,隔天法兰克福又没有飞上海的航班,这就意味着大家只有转机才能回到上海。而值机人员获取机票的方式是能从系统中找出几张票就先走几个,所以就算转机,整个团的客人也不可能安排在同一架飞机上。

　　此时客人叽叽喳喳地议论开了,由于大部分游客均不会讲英语,让他们单独

转机会有许多困难,这也给领队及导游造成了人员分配上的难度。

领队、导游经过和客人一段时间的相处,发现团里有一个家庭的父亲是某大学的教授,其儿子是毕业于某外国语学校的准大学生,可以考虑将这户家庭拆开,带领并帮助别的客人一起转机。于是,在征得客人的同意后,这位教授和他的儿子临时充当了领队的角色。

其中,团里有个含外公、妈妈和小孩的 4 人组,从法兰克福飞哥本哈根被分在两个不同的航班。领队就与航空公司商量,请航空公司安排轮椅,将老人送上飞哥本哈根的第一个航班,到了哥本哈根再用轮椅将老人送往下一个航班的登机口,与带着两个小孩的妈妈会合。此外,领队自己带着 19 人从巴黎转机。其间,领队也不时通过电话,对仍滞留法兰克福机场,准备第三天出发的两批客人进行询问、安排及安抚。

就这样,连同领队在内的 34 名客人分两天,分别从新德里、巴黎、伦敦和哥本哈根转机回到上海。

［评析］

在境外旅游,由不可抗力所造成的行程延误是经常会发生的。案例中,意大利罗马火灾造成的航班延误,导致旅游者赶不上后段航程。

领队遇上此类情况时,首先,应该尽量和航空公司说明团队的人员组成,因为大部分中国游客没有国际转机的经验和良好的英语表达能力。其次,应先让妇女、儿童、老人及残疾人先飞回始发地。同时,领队、导游应该利用团里英文好的团友帮助别的团友来完成转机等事宜。案例中,领队主动与航空公司商量,使用轮椅的方式解决了 4 人分两个航班会合的问题。

Transferring from New Delhi, Paris, London and Copenhagen to Shanghai Respectively

Xu, a tour leader, took a 11-day-tour group to Europe. On their tenth day, they were supposed to visit Vatican, Trevi Fontana, Foro Romano, Roman Amphitheatre as well as Roman Arches according to the itinerary. They would then head to Rome airport and transfer from Frankfurt before they flew back to Shanghai.

When the guests were escorted through the security check after finishing the tax refund procedure for shopping, the group was informed that there was a fire at the airport and the flight was going to be delayed and the delay time was unknown at the moment. There were only two hours for the group to get on board at Frankfurt Airport. Finally, the flight was delayed for three hours, which caused the group to miss the flight to Shanghai. After arriving at Frankfurt Airport, the airline staff arranged the accommodation for the group right away.

The next morning, Xu took the group to check in together with the tour leader for rescheduling their flight to Shanghai. Meanwhile, there were another 4 groups who also were unable to get on the flight to Shanghai.

However, there was no straight flight to Shanghai the next day, which meant they all, had to take connecting flights to Shanghai. What's worse, the airline staff could only get a few air tickets from their booking system. Therefore, not all the guests couldn't get on the same flight home. At that moment, the guests started to complain about the situation. As most of the guests in the group couldn't speak English, it was a challenge to distribute the guests.

During the trip, Xu found that there was a guest in the group who was a university professor and his son was studying at a foreign language university. Therefore, they could probably let the father and the son take different flights respectively to help other guests transfer to Shanghai. After having their permission, the father and son served as temporary tour leaders in the group.

There was a family of the grandfather, the mother and kids in the group who were going to fly from Frankfurt to Copenhagen by taking two different flights. After Xu discussed with the airline, the airline agreed to prepare for a wheelchair for the old man on the way to Copenhagen and then escorted him to the next gate meeting up with the kids and their mother. In addition, Xu took a small group of 19 members transferring from Paris. He also kept in touch with the guests who were still waiting at the Frankfurt for their flight the next day.

In the end, a group of 34 guests, together with the tour leader, took two days flying to Shanghai from New Delhi, Paris, London and Copenhagen separately.

Comments

Due to the act of god, tour groups often encounter delays. In the case above, due to the fire in Rome airport, the guests couldn't catch the flight in time.

When tour guides face such a situation, the first thing they have to do is to explain the condition of the group to the airline staff such as guests' lack of travel experience, language barrier, etc. Meanwhile, the tour leaders should let women, kids, the elderly and disabled people get on the flight first. Other than that, tour leaders and tour guides should encourage the guests who can speak English in the group to help other guests who don't speak a foreign language. In the case mentioned above, the problem of the family of 4 got solved by asking the airline staff to use the wheelchair to escort the grandfather.

领队的名下托运了 28 件行李

出境游领队小章带的一个 30 人的 5 天港澳游团队马上就要结束行程回杭州了。行程的最后一天是从澳门坐船到香港海天码头,然后再搭乘飞机从香港国际机场飞回杭州。

香港国际机场非常大,办理了登机手续后,要进行安检,再坐机场小火车至离境大厅。从离境大厅到最远的登机口岸走路需要 10—20 分钟,到有些登机口还要再次乘坐机场小火车或穿梭巴士。小章在海天码头替客人办好登机手续,换取了登机牌,马上将登机牌分发给客人。因为离登机时间近了,领队小章怕时间来不及,轮到团队托运行李时,小章就将所有客人的 28 件行李全部托运在领队的名义下,自己只要点一下行李件数就能完成托运。况且,虽然航空公司规定每位旅客只能托运 20 公斤行李,但办理团体托运时行李可以按照人数叠加重量。之后小章迅速带着客人通过安检,坐小火车到达登机口。

这时离登机口关门只有 10 分钟了,小章在确认客人是否都已登机时发现少了 2 名客人。小章马上原路返回寻找这 2 名客人,结果丢失的 2 名客人登机了,小章自己却错过了最后的登机时间。香港航空规定机舱门关闭后就不能再打开。小章无奈,眼睁睁看着自己的航班离港起飞。同时,由于小章没有登上飞机,航空公司将以小章名义托运的 28 件行李全部从飞机的行李舱上卸下来,取消了托运。

　　事情发生得那么突然,领队小章马上订了下一趟最快回杭的航班,但是当他再办理登机手续时,值机人员告诉他只能托运 20 公斤的行李,剩下的行李全部要按超重来计算。无奈,小章支付给航空公司 2 万元人民币的行李超重费。

[评析]

　　海天客运码头是附属香港国际机场的跨境渡轮码头,位于机场的东北面。来自珠江三角洲其他城市及澳门的旅客,经此码头搭乘香港国际机场的航班,无须办理香港的入境手续,可以立即进入机场的管制区域(视为香港境外);搭乘航班抵达时转搭渡轮离港亦可。

　　此案例告诉我们,领队在带领客人离境、转机时,一定要留有足够的时间。在时间很紧迫的情况下,客人也需要积极配合,特别是赴新加坡、法兰克福、香港等城市的大型机场乘机,更需要留有足够的时间。以上案例告诉我们,换乘飞机需要领队的组织与客人的配合。领队必须睿智且灵活应变。另外,在办理行李托运时,最好不要采取将所有的行李以领队名义托运的方式,而应让客人单独办理行李托运。否则,万一遇到以上的特殊情况,就会造成巨大损失。

28 Pieces of Luggage under the Name of the Tour Leader

The tour leader Mr. Zhang, together with his group of 30 members, was coming back to Hangzhou from a 5-day Hong Kong and Macau trip. The group was supposed to come back to Hong Kong Sky Pier by boat from Macau, and then fly to Hangzhou from Hong Kong International Airport.

Hong Kong International Airport is large. You need to check in, pass through the security and then arrive at the departure lobby by airport train. The longest distance from departure lobby to the boarding gate is a 10—20 minute walk. Some of the boarding gates require passengers to take the train or the shuttle again to get to. Mr. Zhang checked in for the guests at Sky Pier and got the boarding cards. He then distributed those cards to the guests. Because the boarding time was approaching, Mr. Zhang consigned the 28 pieces of luggage totally under his name, for the sake of saving time and convenience. The airline company has the rule that if the guests conduct group consignment, the weight can be added according to the number of the group member. And every guest can check in 20kg luggage free of charge. After the check-in, the tour leader led the guests to pass through the security and arrived at the boarding gate by train.

It was 10 minutes before the boarding gate closure. The tour leader found that two guests were missing. He turned back to look for the two guests and it turned out the two guests boarded on the plane already. But the tour leader himself thus missed the plane. The Hong Kong airline has the rule that once the gate is closed, it cannot be opened again. The tour leader had to see off his flight. Meanwhile, because the tour leader was not able to board on the plane, the 28 pieces of luggage under his name were unloaded by the airline company.

It was really an accident. The tour leader Mr. Zhang booked the next flight back to Hangzhou immediately. But when he checked in again, he was told that he was only able to check in 20kg luggage and the rest was counted to the overweight luggage. Mr. Zhang had no choice but to pay the overweight

中国公民出境旅游服务质量解析

luggage about RMB 20,000 to the airline company.

Comments

Sky Pier is a transboundary pier affixed to Hong Kong International Airport. It is located at the northeast of the airport. Tourists coming from other cities in Pearl River Delta and Macau need no entry procedures when taking the flights in Hong Kong International Airport through Sky Pier. Those tourists may enter into the airport control zone (regarded as outside the Hong Kong territories) directly. They only need to take the ferries to leave Hong Kong when arriving by plane.

The case shows that the tour leader must set aside enough time for the tourists to depart and transfer. When the time is kicking, the tourists also need to cooperate with the tour leader. Enough time must be saved, especially in a large airport, such as that of Hong Kong, Singapore, Frankfurt. The above case tells us, the cooperation between the tour leader and the tourists is essential. Also the tour leader must be flexible and wise. Besides, when checking in the luggage, the tour leader may not be suggested to get the tourists' luggage under his or her name. Let the tourists check in their own luggage. Then it will result in less loss when there's an accident.

印尼落地签

2012 年 12 月,我准备赴印尼雅加达参加一个国际会议。由于决定出发的时间比较晚,申请普通签证估计来不及了,所以,我向某五星旅行社出境中心负责印尼市场的计调人员请教,得到的答复是:只前往雅加达、泗水或巴厘岛等主要城市或旅游度假胜地,可以直接办理落地签证,不需要将护照等材料送到印尼驻上海领事馆。于是,我立即在网上预订了一张上海—雅加达的来回机票。

第三天,我乘坐上午 10:05 从上海出发的航班,于下午 3 点多抵达了雅加达国际机场,飞行时间约 6 个半小时(雅加达时间比北京时间迟一个小时)。其间,在上海浦东机场办理登机手续时,仅需出示护照和打印出来的电子机票。过中国边防检查时,出示护照和登机牌即可。

飞行途中,空中小姐分发了印尼入境卡让每位乘客填写,这是办理落地签证和入关必须要做的。到达目的地后,在前往移民局柜台的通道内很容易看到办理落地签证的窗口。我先到缴费窗口缴纳 25 美元(如果需要对方找钱,一般会找给你印尼盾,汇率比自己去兑换会稍微低一些,所以尽量准备正好是 25 美元的纸币),然后去签证申请窗口,交付护照、入境卡、费用收据和电子机票(最好打印英文版的)。签证官问了我一个简单的问题:"你来印尼的目的是什么?""开会。"我回答。签证官对了一下护照上的照片与我本人,立刻在护照上盖了章。此时,我抬头看到了这样一条标识:Bribers and grafters will be heavily punished(行贿者和受贿者将会受到重罚)。我顿时想到:20世纪90年代我来印尼工作时,雅加达移民局、海关有腐败的现象,最突出的是官员受贿。经过当地政府的整顿,现在风气好多了。因此,只要你材料齐全,不用担心对方会敲诈你。签证办完后,过了移民局,就可以取行李,出海关,然后走出机场大厅,继续印尼之行。

会议开完后,出境时办理登机手续,还需缴纳15万印尼盾的机场税。如果用美元缴纳还要贵一些。

[评析]

所谓落地签证,是指申请人不直接从所在国家取得前往其他国家的签证,而是持护照和该国有关机关发给的入境许可证明等抵达目的国口岸后,再签发签证。落地签证通常是单边的,但往往需要两国间的海关协商,双方同意以后,中国海关才能让团体客人或散客从中国出境。

为方便各省(区、市)旅游局统计通过旅行社口径参加出境游的旅客人数,即使游客是经过具有出境资质的旅行社来办理机票购买、境外酒店预订等事宜,仍需要办理落地签证。旅行社会为这些散客上传经各省(区、市)旅游行政部门(旅游局)盖章的"中国公民出国旅游团队名单表"至省(区、市)旅行社协会,以方便出境游人数的统计。另外,旅行社有了客人的个人档案,万一游客在境外有突发情况,旅行社就可以提供详细的资料给省(区、市)旅游局,以方便联系我国驻目的地国家(地区)的大使(领事)馆。

值得注意的是,无论哪个国家,都要求旅游者持有往返机票或是前往第三国的机票和正确的旅行证件,以及足够支持旅行的资金。

Visa on Arrival in Indonesia

I planned to attend an international conference in Jakarta, Indonesia in December 2012. The time for applying regular visa was insufficient because the decision of leaving was late. Therefore, I consulted the staff in charge of Indonesian market in the outbound operation center of a five-star travel agency and the reply was that visa on arrival could be available if the destinations were some major cities or tourists attractions, including Jakarta, Surabaya, Bali and so on. The passport and relevant materials were not needed to be sent to the consulate in Shanghai. So I booked a round-trip flight ticket on the Internet (between Shanghai and Jakarta).

On the third day, I arrived at Jakarta International Airport at 3:00 p. m. by Garuda Indonesia Airline from Shanghai. The departure time was 10:05 a. m. and the trip lasted six and a half hours (time in Jakarta was one hour later than Beijing time). At Shanghai Pudong International Airport, I only needed to show the passport and electronic ticket. When I passed the Chinese frontier defense for inspection, the passport and boarding card were required.

During the flight, the stewardess distributed entry cards to every passenger. Entry card is the necessity for you to get the visa on arrival and enter the country. When you arrive in your destination, the visa on arrival counter is easily seen at the pass to the immigration office. I paid USD 25 over the counter. (The changes will be rupiah and the exchange rate is not as good as you have in banks. So preparing the exact amount of USD 25 is strongly recommended.) The next step was to approach the visa application counter, to hand in the passport, entry card, receipts and electronic ticket (better in English version). The visa officer asked me one simple question: "Why do you come to Indonesia?" "Conference." I answered. The officer checked my photo in the passport, looked at me, and then stamped my passport. At that time, I noticed a slogan above, "Bribers and grafters will be heavily punished". I suddenly felt that the situation got better and better in Indonesia after the hard working on bribes by the local government. In the 1990s, I went to work in Indonesia. And there was corruption in the immigration and customs offices, especially the grafters. But now, you only have to prepare your materials well and do not have to worry about being taken advantage of. After getting the visa, I passed through the immigration office, got the luggage and went out the Customs. The trip in Indonesia turned out to be very smooth.

After the conference, I paid another 150,000 rupiah when boarding at the airport. It would be more expensive if you paid in US dollars.

Comments

Visa on arrival relates to the situation that candidates who have not got the visas in their own country obtain the visas when they arrive in the country with the passports and entry cards, etc. Such kind of visa is normally single-sided, and needs the agreement by the two Customs of the related countries. After the agreement, the Chinese customs let group guests or FIT pass through the Chinese frontier.

The tourists who process their flight tickets，book hotels through travel agencies still need get the visas on arrival. In order to count the number needed by the provincial tourism bureau，the travel agency will upload the Chinese Citizen Outbound Travel Group Name List stamped by provincial or municipal tourism administrative departments for the guests. Besides，the travel agency may provide detailed information to the bureau so as to contact the destination's Chinese embassy(consulate) if there should be an accident to the guest.

Tourists are required to hold the round-trip ticket or ticket to the third country，proper travel certificate，and enough money for traveling no matter which country they are going to visit.

在悉尼转机与退税

2012 年 8 月，我有机会赴澳洲墨尔本学习，在上海与墨尔本间来回，均从悉尼转机，从中获得了转机的新知识。

在上海浦东机场办理乘机手续时，我拿到了两张登机牌，即从上海飞往悉尼的 QF130，悉尼飞往墨尔本的 QF431，但值机人员告诉我们，抵达悉尼时，就得办理澳大利亚入境手续，然后，转飞澳大利亚国内航班 QF431 赴墨尔本。也就是说，到达悉尼后要将行李拿出来重新托运。

经过 10 个小时的飞行，第二天当地时间 8：30，飞机缓缓地降落在悉尼机场。落地后我们到了查验证照的柜台处，顺利通过了移民局官员的检验，继而照着电子看板上显示的飞机航班与行李转盘所示，很快拿到了托运的行李。接下来的步骤是赴海关，办理检验检疫手续。早就知道澳大利亚的卫生检验检疫非常严格，所以在出发前，我将自己所带的药品、榨菜等食品装在一个口袋里，免去打开整个行李箱检查的麻烦。在海关排队时，工作人员会询问游客需要申报哪类物品，根据物品的不同，将游客安排到不同的海关检验处，即使没有任何物品需要申报，也必须通过所有的申报程序。海关官员依旅客排队顺序，选 6 人一组，与各自所带的手提行李排成一队，然后让一条警犬来闻一闻旅客所带的行李。幸运的是我没有被抽到打开行李检查,很快地通过了海关的检查。之后,我拖着自己的行李来到 Qantas Domestic Transfer(澳航国内转机),转了一个弯,即刻看到了 Qantas Domestic Check-in(澳航国内办理乘机手续)的大厅,在办理乘机手续柜台的最边上,柜台显示屏上打出"bag drop"(行李托运)的字样,大家又将行李交给工作人员重新托运。至此,乘客再过安检,重新登上悉尼至墨尔本的飞机。

一个月后,在墨尔本的学习结束了。我从墨尔本启程,准备在悉尼转机回上海。9月的一个早晨,那是墨尔本的初春,天气晴朗,我抵达墨尔本机场办理登机手续,将行李直接托运到上海,也就是说,到悉尼转机时不需要将行李提出来。可是,我在墨尔本买了一些商品,可以在出关的机场退税。根据澳大利亚海关规定:退税前必须将所购买的物品给海关办公室的官员检查、盖章后方可拿到退税款。经过询问我们才知道,我们这种乘坐同一航空公司的航班且以国内段加国际段的飞行方式出关的,在悉尼方可进行退税,也就是说,我们在悉尼过了移民局以后才可以拿到退税的款项。但这里有一个问题:因为行李是直接托运到上海的,我买的商品又需要给海关办公室的官员检查,难道我们得提着刚购入的所有商品坐上墨尔本至悉尼的飞机,等到了悉尼再进行检查、盖章?地勤人员告诉我:在墨尔本机场就可以检查、盖章,然后,将检查过的行李托运。于是,我在墨尔本就将所有要退税的商品集中放在一个口袋里,办理乘机手续时,先到一楼国际抵达处的海关办公室给海关官员检查。他在我的收据上盖了 TRS 的印章,我们再将这些物品办理行李托运。

一个半小时以后,我们抵达了悉尼,下了飞机后,顺着国际转机的指示牌很快找到了移民局,办完了离境手续后,马上看到了 Tourist Refund Scheme(游客退税中心),我将在墨尔本机场由海关人员盖过 TRS 印章的发票交给了工作人员,其很快将款项退给了我。

［评析］

转机由于比直飞廉价,是许多人出国旅游、留学等的选择。旅游者可以在出发前向航空公司或在办理乘机手续时向工作人员,询问有关转机的要求。

案例中,我乘坐的是同一航空公司的航班,出入境均在悉尼,入境时上海—悉尼为国际航班,悉尼—墨尔本为国内航班,出境时,先飞国内,再飞国际。在该情况下,旅游者最关心的是转机时的行李托运和退税办理。

尽管悉尼和墨尔本的均是国际机场,但国际惯例往往是以抵达目的地国家的第一个机场作为入境口岸,或是以离开一个国家的最后一个城市的机场作为离境口岸。同样的运作也发生在中国的航空公司:中国某航空公司的杭州—广州—迪拜及杭州—广州—墨尔本航线就是以广州作为出入境口岸的。

在澳洲或别的地方旅游,旅游者离境前不要忘记去退税中心办理退税,这是旅客的权益。在悉尼国际机场退税有两种方式,一为"仅限托运的退税物品",像绵羊油、香水及不可带上飞机的各种液态乳状类物品,二为"可带上飞机的退税物品"。

仅限托运的物品退税步骤:

步骤一:抵达悉尼国际机场后,先至入境楼层,寻找号码为 A18 的商店,找到海关办公室,进去后直接至柜台办理退税手续。

步骤二:出示护照及预退税物品收据,海关人员会查看购买物品时的收据,以及行李箱内的免税品。检查后在收据上盖上退税中心印章,然后你再将所买商品打包托运。

步骤三:经过护照检验,根据指示寻找退税中心,拿到刚才盖章后的收据进行退税。

可携带上机的退税物品退税步骤:

只要按照一般离境程序,在过移民局后,寻找退税中心,出示你要退税的物品,以及收据、护照即可。

如何取得退税税款?

退税无法直接支付现金,以下三种方式可取得退回的税款。一是退回旅客所选用的信用卡(Master Card,Visa,American Express 等),二是打入澳大利亚银行账户,三是各种货币的退款支票。

Transit and Tax Refund in Sydney

In August 2012, I had the opportunity to go to study in Melbourne, Australia. I flew between Shanghai and Melbourne with both transits in Sydney, from which I gained new knowledge of transit.

During the check-in at Shanghai Pudong International Airport, I got two boarding passes, namely QF130 from Shanghai to Sydney, and QF431 from Sydney to Melbourne. However, the check-in staff told me that I had to go through immigration procedures when I arrived in Sydney before transferring to the Australian domestic flights QF431 in Melbourne. In other words, after arriving in Sydney my luggage must be checked out.

After a 10-hour flight in the next morning, the aircraft landed slowly at Sydney Airport at local time 8:30. We reached the inspection counter, and successfully passed the test by the immigration officials. According to the electronic billboards that displayed the flights and luggage carousels, we quickly got our our luggage. The next step was to go to the customs for inspection and quarantine procedures. It has long been known that health inspection and quarantine in Australia are very strict. So before departure, I parceled my own medicines, preserved Sichuan pickles and other food in a pocket, eliminating the inconvenience to open the entire luggage for check. Queuing at the customs counter, we were asked by the staff the kind of items we needed to declare. Different items would be assigned to different customs divisions for inspection. Even if there is no need to declare any items, they must pass all of the procedures. Customs officials divided people into groups of six by queuing order with their hand luggage, and then let a dog to smell their luggage, but did not find any contraband. Fortunately, I was not chosen to open my luggage and quickly went through the customs inspection. After that I dragged my luggage to the Qantas Domestic Transfer, turned a corner, and instantly saw the Qantas Domestic Check-in hall. At the counter edge for the boarding procedures, there displayed "bag drop", so I took the luggage to the staff for re-checking in. At this point, the passengers underwent the security check again before re-boarding the aircraft from Sydney to Melbourne.

A month later, at the end of my study in Melbourne, I departed from Melbourne for Shanghai, having the transit in Sydney. It was a September morning in Melbourne's early spring, so the weather was gorgeous. I arrived at the domestic departure of Melbourne airport for check-in (this was a domestic flight), so my checked luggage would be directly shipped to Shanghai. That was to say, we wouldn't need to take our luggage during the Sydney transit. However, I was entitled to tax refund for some products I bought in Melbourne. According to the Australian Customs regulations, tax refund can only be claimed after inspection and sealed by officers of the customs office. We were told that we must claim tax refund in Sydney in our case, which meant we could get back the money only after going through the immigration counter in Sydney. The problem was that we tried to ship the checked luggage directly to Shanghai, so we could not possibly take out the products from the checked luggage for tax refund inspection. The airport staff told me that we could have the inspection and stamp in Melbourne before having the luggage checked. Thus, I put all the products subject to tax refund in the same bag, and took it for tax refund inspection at the customs office during check-in. The inspector stamped TRS seals on the receipts and then we could have our luggage checked.

One and a half hours later, I arrived in Sydney. Having got off the plane, I saw the sigh International Transfer and by following this sign, I quickly found the immigration. After finishing the departure clearance, I immediately saw the Tourist Refund Scheme, and I handed over the TRS invoice with the seal I had got from Melbourne Airport Customs officers. She quickly refunded me.

Comments

A transit flight often happens to outbound travel, studying abroad, etc., as it is cheaper than a direct flight. Tourists, before departure, may inquire the airlines staff about transit flight requirements.

In the above case, I took the same airline, departing and arriving both in Sydney, namely domestic flight for Shanghai / Sydney and international flight for Sydney / Melbourne. In this case, tourists were most concerned with the luggage transfer during transit and tax refund.

Sydney and Melbourne both have international airports, but more often the first city to arrive in the destination country is seen as the port of entry, or the last city to leave the country as the departure port. The same operation also occurs in Chinese Airlines: for China Southern Airlines flight Hangzhou / Guangzhou / Dubai and Hangzhou / Guangzhou / Melbourne, Guangzhou serves as the exit and entry points.

Do not forget to go to the Tourist Refund Scheme for tax refund in Australia or other countries before departure, which is the right of tourists. There are two ways at the Sydney International Airport for tax refund: one is only for checked items, like sheep oil, perfume and other liquid items that cannot be taken on board; the other is for the items that can be taken aboard.

The steps of tax refund for checked luggage only are:

Step one, arrive at Sydney International Airport, get to the floor for entry, find Shop No. A18, that is, the Australian Customs & Quarantine, go directly to the counter for refunds.

Step two, produce passports and pre-tax refund goods receipt. The officers will check the receipts of the duty-free items as well as the luggage compartment. After the officers' checking, the receipts will be stamped with the seal of the Tourist Refund Scheme(TRS), you may arrange shipment of the goods or take the carry-on luggage aboard.

Step three, after the passport inspection, find the Tourist Refund Scheme according to the instructions to get stamped receipts for the tax refund.

Steps of tax refund for carry-on luggage are as below:

Just follow the normal departure procedures. Go across the immigration office, find the Tourist Refund Scheme and show the items you want for tax refund, as well as the receipt and passports.

How to obtain tax refund?

The cash cannot be refunded to you directly. There are usually three ways to get the money: first, travelers' credit cards（Master Card，Visa，American Express，etc.）; second, an Australian bank account; third, a refund check for multi-currencies.

您来新西兰的目的是什么？

出境游领队小陈所带的"纯净新西兰8日游"团队抵达新西兰第一大城市——奥克兰后，在他的带领下，客人手持新西兰入境申报卡，在标有"Other Passport（他国护照）"字样的5号口排队过关。团队中大部分客人顺利地通过了移民局的检查。这时，两位新西兰移民局的官员走到一位正在接受护照查验的客人身边，与当班的移民官交流了一下，就把这位客人带进了移民局办公室。客人回头焦急地寻找着领队。

领队小陈看到此景，向移民官表明自己的身份后也一同进了移民局办公室。领队拿出团体签证给移民官查看，并向客人询问事情的经过。原来，客人是一位不懂英文的中年妇女，她用手势比画着表示听不懂，移民官就拿出一份翻译成中文的新西兰入境卡给该客人参考。在新西兰入境卡上有这么一条"Are you coming to New Zealand for medical treatment or consultation or to give birth? Yes. No.（您来新西兰是为了求医治病，或是进行医疗方面的咨询，或是进行分娩吗？是，否。）"当时可能是太紧张了，中年妇女竟然选了"Yes"，所以就被移民官带到了办公室。领队和中年妇女交流了一下，了解了事情的经过，向移民官解释道：我们是来自中国的旅游团，来新西兰的目的是旅游，这是我们的团体签证。

该客人年纪稍大,也是第一次出国,她听不懂英文,更不会说。她不明白刚才你们所问她的问题,很紧张,所以才会选择"Yes"这一项。听着领队的解释,移民官们又交流了一下,但好像没有要放人的意思。这时领队凭着多年的实战经验,立刻让该客人把刚才在"Yes"上打的钩画去,在"No"上打了个钩,并让客人签上自己的中文名字。做出了这个举动后,移民官才同意放行。

所有客人拿完行李后,领队带着客人去过海关检查,这时候问题又来了,整个团队都被带到了海关办公室。海关官员问领队:"为什么所有的客人都穿着一样的新旅游鞋?"领队灵机一动,告诉海关官员:我们是来自中国同一个乡村的旅游团队,穿新鞋是我们乡村的一种民俗,这样能为远行的人带来好运。没想到这次海关放行很快,他们能接受这样的解释,西方人的思维方式和中国人有时会有差异的。

最后,团队出了海关,导游已在外面等候多时。此时此刻,大家才真真切切进入了新西兰,以最快的速度上了车,开始了新西兰8日游之旅。

[评析]

随着电影《指环王》的热映,这个被誉为"地球上最后一片净土""长白云之乡"的美丽岛国,以她特有的魅力吸引着来自世界各地的人民。新西兰正成为中国游客最喜爱的旅游目的地之一,中国已跃升为新西兰第二大客源国。然而,不少人对于新西兰的认识仅限于在北岛走马观花,而对于独具风采,集天然风景之精华的南岛却无暇顾及,实在有如登黄山而不临天都,是个很大的缺憾。"纯净新西兰8日游"正好是为配合"星空联盟"成员之一——新西兰航空公司开通上海及香港直航往返奥克兰航班而设计的旅游新线路。通过奥克兰中转能连接新西兰国内超过25个目的地及澳大利亚与斐济、大溪地等西南太平洋群岛。

当你抵达奥克兰,下飞机后,随着人流一直往前走,就会来到移民局设在机场的入境审查通道。这里排着两个队,一队是持新西兰和澳大利亚护照的人,另一队是持其他国家护照的人,中国公民就是在此列中。轮到你的时候,向入境官员递上你的护照、在飞机上填好的入境卡以及机票。当然,入境官员可能还会询问你一些问题,如"您之前来过新西兰吗?""这是您第一次到新西兰吗?"等等,非常简单的问题,不必紧张。然后,入境官员会给你的护照加盖一个印(如是移民,盖上的印签是 Residence Permit,如果是留学生,则是 Student Permit,其他还有相应类别的 Permit)。通过入境审查后,你就可以到行李传送带上取登机前托运的行李了。

下一步是通过海关检查。首先要选择走哪条通道,红色的还是绿色的。由于农业和畜牧业是新西兰最重要的两个产业,因此为防止外来植物和病菌入侵,对农牧业产生危害,新西兰海关对动植物、食品及沾有泥土的物品的检查非常严格。如果你在入境卡上填携带有上述物品,便只能走红色通道(Goods to Declare Way Out);如无申报物品,则走绿色通道(Nothing to Declare Way Out)。海关人员可能会要求你打开行李接受检查,让警犬稽查毒品,用 X 光扫描行李(安检)。如无问题,海关检查就此结束。

案例中,领队在带团工作中非常注意细节,如:在过移民关时领队让客人先过关,自己最后过,当出现问题时比较方便应付解决,以保证每一个客人都能顺利通关。对于中国客人出门一起穿新鞋的情况非常巧妙地用"民俗"二字来解释,绝对是恰到好处。另外,领队了解到西方人是非常注重签名的。所以,在处理"您来新西兰是为了求医治病,或是进行医疗方面的咨询,或是进行分娩吗?是,否"这一问题时,领队让客人将"Yes"上的钩画掉,在"No"上打个钩,并签上客人自己的中文名字,最终赢得了移民官的信赖。做出这个举动,完全是靠领队的睿智和对中西文化的了解。

Why Do You Come to New Zealand?

The outbound tour leader Mr. Chen, together with his tour group "8-day Tour in Pure New Zealand" arrived at Auckland, the largest city in New Zealand. Following Mr. Chen, the guests lined up at Gate 5 with the sign "Other Passport". Most guests passed through the inspection of New Zealand Immigration Office. Just at that time, two officers from the immigration office walked near a guest whose passport was being checked. After communicating with the officer on the shift, they brought the guest to the immigration office. The guest was looking for the tour leader anxiously.

Mr. Chen noticed the situation and declared his identity to the officers. Following the officers and the guest, Mr. Chen came into the office too. He took out the group visa and showed it to the officers and asked about what was going on. The guest was a middle-aged lady who did not understand English. She had gestured that she could not follow the officer. So she had got an entry card in Chinese. There was one item on the New Zealand entry card: "Are you coming to New Zealand for medical treatment or consultation or to give birth? Yes. No." At that moment, the lady had been so nervous that she had chosen "Yes" for the question in the card. This was why she was in the office. The tour leader communicated with the lady and explained to the officer, "It was the first time that the middle-aged lady went abroad. She didn't understand English, let alone speaking. And she was so nervous that she made the wrong choice." The officers exchanged their opinions for a while, and still did not seem to release the guest. Based on his experience, the tour leader told the guest to correct the card. She deleted the tick on "Yes", chose "No" and signed her Chinese name. After that, the immigration officers granted the lady's entry into New Zealand.

When all the guests got their luggage, the tour leader brought them to the customs. Another problem popped out. The whole group was brought to the customs office. The officer there asked the tour leader why all the guests wore the same new sports shoes. Such kind of question may seem weird in China, for Chinese like to wear new shoes when they go out. The tour leader made a quick response, saying that the members in this group were coming from the same village. They believed that new shoes would bring good luck for traveling people. The customs officers accepted this explanation.

The group finally got through the customs. The tour guide had been waiting for them for a long time outside. Everybody got on the bus fast and truly began their 8-day tour in New Zealand.

Comments

Influenced by the movie *The Lord of the Rings*, New Zealand, known as the "last pure land on earth" and "the land of the great white clouds", attracts people from different parts of the world with her distinguished charm. And this country also becomes one of the hot destinations for Chinese visitors. China becomes the second tourist source country for New Zealand. However, the Chinese people's knowledge of the island is limited to the north island. We know little about the south island which has wonderful natural sceneries. It's a pity if tourists go to Mount Huang without going to Tiandu. Similarly, tourists will have a great loss if they go to New Zealand without arriving in the south island. Cooperating with New Zealand Airline Corporation, one of the Star Alliance, "Pure New Zealand 8-day Tour" enjoys the advantages that the corporation opens new flights from Shanghai to Auckland and Hong Kong to Auckland. In Auckland, people may make the transferring to 25 destinations in New Zealand, Australia, Fiji, Tahiti and the islands in southwest Pacific Ocean.

When you arrive in Auckland, follow the crowd, you will get the entry check set by the immigration office. There will be two lines—one is for the people holding New Zealand and Australia passports and the other is for people from other countries, including Chinese. When it is your turn, hand in the passport, the entry card that you filled in on the plane and the ticket to the officer. Of course, the officer may ask you some simple questions, such as "Have you ever been to New Zealand before?""Is this your first time to come to New Zealand?" Try not to be nervous. Then the officer will give you a stamp (Residence Permit for immigrant, Student Permit for overseas students, and other permits). After the entry check, you may collect your luggage consigned at the luggage conveyor.

Customs check is the next step. Your first choice is to select which pass you should go through: the red exit or the green exit. Because agriculture and animal husbandry are two major industries in New Zealand, the customs strictly check the plants, animals, and goods with dirt to prevent the potential damage brought by the outside plants and viruses. If you have brought the above items, you need to go through Goods to Declare Way Out (the red exit). If you don't have any declarations, you may go to Nothing to Declare Way Out (the green exit). The customs officers may ask you to open your luggage and check it. They also use dogs to check drugs, X-rays to scan bags. If nothing is wrong, then you pass the customs.

In the above case, the tour leader paid a lot of attention to details. For example, he let the guests go through the customs first and himself the last. When there was a problem, he could solve it instantly and make sure every guest could pass the customs. He delicately explained the situation that village guests like to wear new shoes when going out with "folk customs". Besides, the tour leader knew westerners respect signatures. So he told the guest who made a wrong choice on the entry card to correct her mistake and signed her name, while making the officers believe them again. Thanks to the tour leader's wisdom and knowledge of Chinese and Western cultural differences, the problem finally was solved.

在吉隆坡转机时，少盖了一个"过境章"

某旅游公司员工小钱，担任入境旅游英文导游 6 年后，转做入境旅游销售工作，主要负责亚洲市场。2014 年新年过后，小钱准备赴新加坡做一次促销，将中国的经典旅游线路逐一介绍给新加坡做中国团的旅行社。

考虑到杭州有马来西亚亚洲航空运营的杭州—吉隆坡的廉价航班，小钱出发前订了杭州—吉隆坡—杭州的来回机票，准备从吉隆坡进入新加坡，回程从新加坡返回吉隆坡再回杭州。

在订好来回机票到出发前，有 3 周左右的时间。新加坡旅行社客户推荐小钱从吉隆坡到新加坡最好能搭乘跨国长途巴士，从而多一种体验。但是，从新加坡到吉隆坡还是希望他能乘坐飞机，毕竟乘坐飞机，时间上可以大大缩短。小钱采纳了新加坡旅行社的建议，又购买了一张新加坡飞往吉隆坡的亚航的回程机票。正好，与之前购买的吉隆坡—杭州的机票的路线衔接上。小钱在出发之前了解到，马来西亚对中国公民有 120 小时的过境免签。这样，回程在吉隆坡的转机应该没有任何困难。

小钱顺利地按照计划拜访了客户，结束了销售工作。在新加坡樟宜机场办理乘机手续准备回国时，小钱告诉值机人员，将行李直接托运到杭州。但是，值机人员却告诉小钱,由于没有同一时间购买联程航班,所以飞抵吉隆坡后他只能先出关,提取行李,再重新办理登机。无奈,小钱只能按照值机人员的要求来做。

亚航所在的新航站楼,在海关处有一个专门的通道给过境旅客出去。抵达吉隆坡后,小钱随着人流走过过境通道,工作人员给了小钱一张出入境卡,小钱并没有在意,径直前往行李认领处提取行李。重新办理登机手续后,过移民局出境时小钱遇到了麻烦。工作人员查看小钱的护照后,并没有找到过境盖章的页面,于是,移民官员开始了一系列的问询,在小钱多次解释之下,最后工作人员允许他出关,并且告知下次过境一定要盖过境章。

[评析]

一国公民国际旅行时,除直接到达目的地外,往往要途经若干个国家(地区)才能最终进入目的地境内(多见于使用联程机票,搭乘国际航班转机的情况)。这时不仅需要取得目的地国家(地区)的入境许可,而且还必须取得途经国家(地区)的过境许可,这就称为过境签证。而"过境免签"是指外籍人士依据过境国家或地区的法律或有关规定,从一国经转某国前往第三国时,不必申请过境国签证即可过境,并可在过境国进行短暂停留的政策。

马来西亚对中国公民有 120 小时的过境免签时间,大家在过境时带好护照以及前往下个目的地的机票,在过境时一定要让工作人员盖上过境章,不要因为工作人员的疏忽给自己带来麻烦。案例中,小钱因为是第一次以这样的方式转机,也根本没有留意到盖过境章的柜台,因此,就漏了这个步骤,出关时就遇到了移民官长时间的盘问。

同样,为延长外国游客在中国一些旅游城市的停留时间,经国务院批复同意,我国目前共有北京、上海、广州、成都、重庆、大连、沈阳、西安、桂林、昆明和杭州等 18 个城市对 51 个国家的公民实施 72 小时过境免签。

在实行免签政策的城市,来自英国、美国、澳大利亚、韩国等 51 个国家的公民只要持有第三国签证和机票,不需要我国签证便可入境,并在入境城市范围内停留 3 天。

Lack of One "Transit Stamp" When Transferring in Kuala Lumpur

Mr. Qian, a member of a travel agency, has been working for 6 years as an English-speaking tour guide in inbound tourism and then he was responsible for inbound tourism sales. After the new year of 2014, Mr. Qian planned to go to Singapore promoting classic Chinese traveling itineraries to the travel agency in Singapore who receives Chinese groups.

Considering Malaysia's Air Asia had budget flights from Hangzhou to Kuala Lumpur, Mr. Qian booked a round-trip ticket between Hangzhou and Kuala Lumpur before leaving. He planned to go to Singapore from Kuala Lumpur, then returned to Kuala Lumpur and at last go back to Hangzhou.

After having booked the ticket, before departure, there were three weeks or so. Therefore the travel agency client in Singapore recommended that Mr. Qian take a transnational long-distance bus from Kuala Lumpur to Singapore to get a special experience. In the meantime, he recommended that Mr. Qian go to Kuala Lumpur by air because flying was the quickest and the most convenient and could save a lot of time. Naturally, Mr. Qian took the advice and bought another plane ticket of Air Asia from Singapore to Kuala Lumpur and thus could connect to the flight from Kuala Lumpur to Hangzhou perfectly. Before leaving, he also noticed that Chinese citizens could transit in Malaysia without visa for 120 hours and therefore there would not be any trouble when transferring in Kuala Lumpur.

Mr. Qian visited his client according to the plan successfully and finished the sales work. Then he went to the Singapore airport to go through the boarding formalities and prepared to go back to China. However when Mr. Qian was checking luggage, the staff of the airport told him that because of not having bought the interline tickets at the same time, Mr. Qian must exit first to pick up his luggage and then go through the boarding formalities again. Mr. Qian had to do what the staff asked.

There was a customs passage especially for transit tourists in the new airport terminal of Air Asia. Mr. Qian went through the cross-border passage with the stream of people after he arrived at Kuala Lumpur. Then the staff gave Mr. Qian an arrival card and a departure card which Mr. Qian did not pay enough attention to. He went to the baggage claim area to pick up his luggage. Unfortunately there was some trouble after going through the immigration formalities again. The staff did not find the transit chapter when checking Mr. Qian's passport and then the immigration officer started a series of inquiry. After explaining for several times, Mr. Qian was allowed to exit and was noticed to have to get the transit stamp next time.

Comments

When a country's citizen is traveling among countries, except going to the destination directly, he can also go through several other countries/regions and eventually arrive at the destination(usually seen in interlining and international connecting flight). Under such a situation he needs both the entry permit of the country/region he is going to and the crossing permits of the relevant countries/

regions and they are the so-called crossing visas. Visa-free transit is a policy that foreign visitor does not have to apply transit visa of the transit country and can stay for several hours when he comes to the third country according to the policies and laws of transit country.

There are 120-hour visa-free transit in Malaysia for Chinese citizens. One should carry his own passport as well as the ticket to the next destination and get the crossing stamp from the staff when transiting in order to prevent him from getting troubled due to the carelessness of the staff. In the case mentioned above, because it was the first time to transfer in this way for Mr. Qian, he even had not noticed the counter of sealing crossing stamp. There was one important step missing and it led to a long time inquiry when exiting the customs.

In addition, in order to delay the duration of stay in some Chinese tourist cities for foreign visitors, there are now 72-hour visa-free transit in 18 cities including Beijing, Shanghai, Guangzhou, Chengdu, Chongqing, Dalian, Shenyang, Xi'an, Guilin,Kunming and Hangzhou in China for citizens from 51 countries, which are permitted by the State Council.

In these cities which perform the visa-free transit policy, citizens from the UK, the US, Australia, Korea and other countries included in the 51 countries can enter into China without Chinese visa and stay for three days in these cities as long as they arrive in these cities with plane tickets and visas of the third country.

第二次入境新加坡时发生的故事

　　在中国出境旅游的发展历史上，1990年出境游领队开始率团到东南亚旅游，揭开了中国出境游领队带团到国外旅游的第一页。从开始出境旅游，"新马泰"旅游一直是国人比较追捧的一条线路，20多年过去了，首次赴境外旅游的中国国民，依然对"新马泰10日游"的线路情有独钟。10天时间可以游览3个国家，经济实惠。

　　出境旅游领队小全带的是一个标准的"新马泰"旅游团队。团队从杭州直飞新加坡之前，领队小全告诉团里抽烟的客人们：新加坡是个法律制度严格的国家，新加坡海关规定，首次入境的客人是不能携带香烟的，但是一般客人身上如果有拆开的烟，那么也就视作默认，但是身上所有的烟加起来不能超过19支。

　　当这个团从马来西亚出关，要再次进入新加坡移民局时，领队在旅游车上宣读了新加坡的法律，并再次告诫所有吸烟的客人，因为是第二次进入新加坡，所以一支烟都不能带，和第一次是绝对不同的，如果查到一支最少也要罚200新币，相当于1000元人民币。新加坡政府通过加重烟税，希望大家都不要抽烟。所以，在新加坡买一包烟的价钱是在中国的3到5倍。

　　由于新加坡和马来西亚之间有柔佛海峡相隔，走陆路从马来西亚再到新加坡要通过跨海大桥,即:新加坡岛北侧正对马来西亚柔佛州首府新山的铜锣湾桥,从马来西亚的新山关口到新加坡的关口只有 10 分钟车程。马来西亚的物价低,因此,人们会从马来西亚带烟进入新加坡。

领队在大巴上讲解完了进入新加坡时的注意事项和禁忌之后,就带领大家过新加坡入境移民大厅了,并要求大家过完海关后在旅游大巴上集合。一个半小时过后,大部分团员都回到了车上,只有一对退休的老年夫妇始终没有出现。

领队再次回到出关大厅的门口,焦急地盼望,终于盼到了这对夫妇中的女士。只见老太太也正焦急地找着领队,说她先生在过海关查行李的时候被工作人员带走了。领队有种不好的预感,马上问老太太有没有带违禁品。老太太说:"没有啊,我们什么也没带,你看行李都在我这里。只是烟有没有问题啊?"

领队当时就憋了一肚子火,但还是理智地压住了。领队转身对老太太说:"我刚才在大巴车上讲过,不管你身上有多少烟都要丢掉,一支都不能带!你看现在我们大伙都在车上,就等你们了。我们还要赶赴机场坐飞机,如果因为这个原因误了航班,损失将会非常严重。"老太太焦急地说:"我们普通话不好,车上只顾看风景,没有听明白你说的注意事项。"

领队一边说着一边让老太太先上车,自己去了移民局办公室找老先生。看到那位老先生正和移民局办公室的官员比画着,领队上前第一句就悄悄地问老先生,带了多少烟。老先生说共两包,一包新的,一包已经拆开。领队询问官员这样的事会怎么处理,官员说:"你作为领队知道新加坡的法律,应该告知你的团员,在新加坡一支烟就可能罚到 200 新币,这次你的客人带了 35 支烟,但因为是初犯,所以我们就罚 200 新币。"

领队一边向移民官员说抱歉,一边解释说:"我作为领队对每位团员都已经告知了新加坡的法律,但是这位先生上了年纪,他只会说方言,对于我所说的话他可能是一知半解,才会违反了新加坡的法律,对不起,我们今天是从马来西亚过境新加坡飞泰国。"听了领队的解释,新加坡海关官员最后不仅没有罚款,还将已开封的一包烟还给了那位老先生,但对那包没拆的烟做了当场销毁的处罚。

上了大巴,领队再一次清点了所有的客人,全车人踏上了奔赴新加坡樟宜机场飞往曼谷的旅程。

[评析]

新山(Johor Bahru)又名柔佛巴鲁,是马来西亚柔佛州的首府。它是位于马来半岛最南端,也是欧亚大陆最南端的城市,与邻国新加坡隔着柔佛海峡,有"大马南方门户"之称。它以一道长堤衔接新加坡,是柔佛州的10个属县之一,为马来西亚第二大城市。从新加坡走陆路进入马来西亚就可抵达新山这个城市。

《中华人民共和国旅游法》第四章第四十一条明确规定:导游和领队从事业务活动,应当佩戴导游证,遵守职业道德,尊重旅游者的风俗习惯和宗教信仰,应当向旅游者告知和解释旅游文明行为规范,引导旅游者健康、文明旅游,劝阻旅游者违反社会公德的行为。由于旅游活动通常要跨越一定的区域,旅游者将置身于陌生的环境中,旅行社必须履行告知的义务。上至旅游目的地的法律规定、民情风俗,小到气候变化、餐饮特色,特别是要阐明旅游目的地和旅游者居住地的差异。告知义务应做到事无巨细,详尽周全,其目的就是让旅游者事先知道旅游目的地的相关情况,为顺利开展旅游活动做好准备。

案例中,领队小全确实两次告知客人关于新加坡法律规定入境新加坡带香烟的规定。但是,最后游客还是违规带了香烟。幸亏领队详细并诚恳地跟海关官员做了解释,才减轻了处罚。因此,履行告知义务必须看具体对象。针对旅游者不同的文化背景、身体状况、生活环境,采用不同方式履行相关的告知义务,如旅游者来自农村,领队、导游在履行义务时,要非常详尽地介绍旅游目的地的情况,甚至是要告诉旅游者如何横穿马路、交通红绿灯代表的意思。所以,对案例中的这对夫妇的情况领队最好是观察到后,能单独给他们再做详细的说明。这样,发生违规的概率就会相对小一些。

The Story of Second Entry into Singapore

In the history of China's outbound tourism since 1990, outbound tour leaders firstly began leading a tour group to Southeast Asia, which unveiled the first page of Chinese outbound tour. Since the beginning of Chinese outbound tourism, Singapore-Malaysia-Thailand tour has always been attractive to Chinese citizens. After more than 20 years, for those traveling abroad for the first time, Singapore-Malaysia-Thailand tour still has great attraction, because in 10 days tourists can visit 3 countries. The tour is economical and affordable.

Mr. Quan is the tour leader of a Singapore-Malaysia-Thailand tour group. Before boarding the flight from Hangzhou to Singapore, Mr. Quan told the whole group that as Singapore is a country with a strict legal system, tourists are not allowed to carry more than 19 cigarettes for the first time when entering Singapore according to the Singapore Customs regulations.

When reentering the Singapore Immigration Office from Malaysia, the tour leader reconfirmed the Singapore's laws about taking cigarettes into the country to the smoking guests. As it was the second time to enter Singapore, tourists were not allowed to take even one cigarette. Tourists taking one cigarette would be fined at least 200 Singaporean dollars, which is equivalent to

RMB 1,000. The Singapore Government hopes that everyone smokes less through the provision of increased duties on tobacco. Therefore, in Singapore the price of a pack of cigarettes is three to five times of that in China.

Since Singapore and Malaysia are separated by the Straits of Johor, passengers traveling on land from Malaysia to Singapore would take the sea-crossing bridge, Causeway Bay Bridge. It is only a 10-minute drive away from Malaysia's Bahru immigration and Singapore immigration. Because goods in Malaysia are much cheaper than in Singapore, people from Malaysia would bring cigarettes into Singapore.

After explaining the matters needing attention, the tour leader led the group through the Singapore immigration hall and asked everyone to wait on the tour bus after passing through the customs. One and a half hours later, most of the members returned to the bus, and only a retired old couple did not come back.

The tour leader anxiously went back to the immigration lobby to look for the old couple only to find that an old lady was anxiously looking for him. She said her husband was taken away by the customs staff. The tour leader immediately asked if they had brought any contraband in their luggage. The old lady said, "Would it be the cigarettes we are taking?"

Hearing this, the tour leader said, "I just told that you are absolutely not allowed to take any cigarettes with you! You see, other tourists are waiting for you. We need to get to the airport. If you miss the flight for this reason, the losses would be very grave." The old lady anxiously said, "Our mandarin is not good, so we just focused on seeing the landscape, and did not understand what you said."

The tour leader first let the old woman get on the bus, and went to the immigration office to find the old man. The old man was actively communicating with the customs officials by gestures. The tour leader quietly approached the old man, and asked how many cigarettes he took. The old man said two packs—a pack was new, and the other was opened. The tour leader asked the officials about what they would do with the old man. The officials said, "As the tour leader you must know about Singapore laws, you should inform your members that in Singapore having a cigarette could be fined up to 200 Singapore dollars. Your guest has brought 35 cigarettes. As it is a first offense, so we just fine him 200 Singapore dollars."

The tour leader apologized to the immigrant officials, and explained, "As a tour leader, I've told my tourists about Singapore laws before. But the old couple can only speak Chinese dialect, and can't understand me fully. Today we are flying to Thailand by transiting via Singapore." Having heard the explanation, the Singapore customs officials canceled the penalty, returned the opened pack of cigarettes to the old gentleman. But the new pack was destroyed at once.

Comments

Johor Bahru is Johor's capital in Malaysia. Located in the southern tip of the Malay Peninsula, as well as the southernmost city of the Eurasian continent, it is the main entrance city in south of Malaysia. With a causeway linking Singapore, it is one of the 10 districts of Johor. It's Malaysia's second largest city. Johor Bahru is a must for those traveling from Singapore to Malaysia.

According to the Tourism Law of People's Republic of China, when in work, tour guides and tour leader must wear tour guide badges and tour leader badges, comply with professional ethics, respect the customs and religious beliefs and inform the tourists about civilized codes of conduct. They should also introduce healthy and civilized activities to them and discourage anti-social behaviors of tourists. In traveling, tourists usually find themselves in a new environment, so travel agencies must fulfill the obligation of informing. Information of legal provisions, customs, climate change, special meals should be given. The differences between tourist destinations and the tourist residence should be especially clarified. Informing should be done in detail, whose purpose is to let tourists get familiar with tourist destinations in advance.

In the above case, the tour leader had told the guests about the Singapore laws twice. However, tourists still brought illegal cigarettes. Thanks to the leader's detailed and honest explanation, the punishment was reduced. Therefore, fulfilling the informing obligation must be done concretely. Tourists have different cultural backgrounds, so tour guides must do very detailed introductions of the tourist destination like how to cross the road, the meaning of traffic lights. If the tour leader had introduced the Singapore laws to the old couple alone and in detail, the chance of violation would have been relatively slim.

戴高乐机场转机时的"危机"

墨西哥有充足的阳光和美丽的海滩。墨西哥的旅游官员说,在 2008 年,他们发现 3‰ 以上的到访游客旅游开支增加了 4‰ 以上,甚至在发生全球经济危机的情况下,仍然有大量的游客涌向墨西哥的海滩和用鹅卵石铺设的街道。据美国《今日美国报》报道,墨西哥正借着比索对美元疲软的机会,吸引在经济衰退中消费谨慎的各国游客,以振兴其作为外汇收入主要来源的旅游业。

资深领队小刘带领 5 位客人从上海出发赴墨西哥游览,在 8 天的旅程中客人无不为这个"壁画之都""宫殿之城"所深深吸引,同时也为领队小刘全程的优质服务所折服。然而在离开墨西哥返回中国时,机场所发生的那一幕却给了小刘一个巨大的考验……

原计划最后一天是从墨西哥城出发,途经美国与墨西哥交界的城市——提华纳返回上海。可墨西哥国际航空公司在团队离开墨城的前一天,突然取消了此航班,而将墨西哥城—提华纳—上海的航线分两段卖给了两家航空公司。即:从墨西哥城至巴黎,由法国航空公司承运;从巴黎途经北京至上海,由中国国际航空公司承运。

无奈之下,小刘与 5 位客人只得选择墨西哥城—巴黎—北京—上海这一航当客人抵达巴黎戴高乐机场转机时,国航的值机小姐却告知小刘并没有他们 6 人的预订,且机位已满,并补充说墨航曾提及他们 6 人的预订,但未最终确认。领队问了小姐,接下来有没有航班飞往北京或上海,回答是:没有,但明天有一个同样的航班飞往上海。这一突如其来的消息让团员傻了眼,不知所措。但此时小刘并没有慌张,因为他心里明白自己是团体的核心所在,自己都慌了,客人必定都会急得像热锅上的蚂蚁,乱成一团。小刘镇定自如地向客人做了解释并安抚好了他们,然后立刻联系墨西哥航空公司驻巴黎办事处,可电话却无人接听。同时,由于时差的关系,国内此时是深夜,组团社已经下班。

突然间,他灵机一动,想到墨西哥国际航空公司与法国航空公司是"天合联盟"的成员,墨西哥国际航空公司没有做好确认工作以至于客人不能顺利回国,如今客人从墨西哥城飞来巴黎,可客人并没有进入欧盟的签证,法国航空公司的承运显然是非法的,那么法航必须把他们立刻送回原出发地——墨西哥城或者安排下一程的飞行,让客人回国。

于是,小刘便立即联系法国航空公司驻巴黎机场办公室,用娴熟的英语与法航办公室交涉,法航终于认识到由于疏忽所造成差错的严重性,赶紧给客人安排了巴黎—香港—上海这一联程航班。同时,法航为表示歉意,将 6 位客人巴黎—香港的舱位提升为头等舱。客人抵达香港后,只在香港等候 2 小时,便搭乘港龙的飞机,飞回了上海。舒适而温馨的头等舱的礼遇,使客人把在巴黎戴高乐机场的那一幕遭遇抛诸九霄云外。同时,客人们都禁不住啧啧称赞起资深领队小刘的沉着、机智与危机处理能力。

[评析]

本案例的起因是领队遇到航空公司取消航班,将航线分别卖给了两家航空公司,如果两程机票都是确认好的,且能顺利抵达目的地,那也罢了。但恰巧,中间环节出了问题。领队不是以被动地等待一天来处理此问题,而是想到了"旅客只有机票而没有签证,航空公司是不能承运的"这一理由,并将此作为支点,展开了与法航的交涉。最后,法航不但重新开出联程机票,而且将巴黎—香港的舱位提升为头等舱。此事的处理相当完美,这与领队小刘良好的英语语言表达与技巧、沉着的应变能力是分不开的。

案例中小刘的机智为客人的墨西哥8日游画上了一个圆满的句号。这份机智源于他平时知识的积累,这积累使得他在巴黎机场这个舞台上尽情地展现了自己。沉着冷静,灵活应变,有智有谋,不禁让我们为他喝彩,更值得旅游业同行学习。

另外,旅行社计调在安排出境旅行团来回机票时,遇到需要转机的情况,应尽量使用同一航空联盟下的航空公司,例如:星空联盟(Star Alliance)、寰宇一家(One World)。这样,若遇到问题,各联盟航空公司处理起来就相当方便。以上案例中,法国航空与墨西哥国际航空同属"天合联盟",它们两家航空公司可以互为结算。法航为客人开了巴黎—香港—上海联程机票,可以向墨航结算。

A Crisis When Transferring at CDG Airport

Mexico has plenty of sunshine and beautiful beaches, said one Mexico's tourism official. In 2008, they found that more than 3% of the visitors' travel spends increased by more than 4%. Even in the economic crisis, there were still a lot of visitors going to Mexico's beaches and the streets made of cobbles. According to *USA Today*, Mexico has been reported to take advantage of the exchange rate between the peso and the weak USD to attract cautious tourists during the economic recession to revitalize tourism, the major source of foreign exchange income.

Senior leader Liu led 5 guests from Shanghai to Mexico. In the 8-day tour, all the visitors were deeply attracted by the city's murals and palaces. At the same time, they were satisfied with the leader Liu's high-quality service. However, when they left Mexico to China, something happened in the airport that proved to be a highly frustrating experience for Liu.

The original plan was to start from Mexico City on the last day, through a city called Tijuana at the border between America and Mexico, and then back to Shanghai. But Aeromexico Airline suddenly canceled the flight before they left Mexico City, and divided the air of Mexico City/ Tijuana /Shanghai into two parts, that is, from Mexico City to Paris by Air France, Paris to Shanghai via Beijing by Air China.

Mr. Liu and the 5 guests had to settle for the flight of Mexico City/Paris/Beijing/Shanghai. However, when the guests arrived at Paris Charles de Gaulle Airport, Air China's operator told them that there was no reservation for them and the flight was full. She also said, "Aeromexico Airline had mentioned the 6 people, but not confirmed at last." Mr. Liu asked the operator weather there were other flights to Beijing or Shanghai, but the answer was no. There would be the same flight to Shanghai tomorrow. The bad news left the tour group dumbfounded. But Liu was not panic because he knew that he was the center of the group. If he showed panic, other guests would feel more anxious. So he calmed down and explained to the guests. Then he tried to contact the Aeromexico Airline office in Paris at once, but the phone calls were not answered. At the same time, due to the time difference, when he contacted the agency in China, everybody was off work.

Suddenly, he thought that Aeromexico Airline and Air France were

SkyTeam Alliance members, and Aeromexico Airline did not do a good job of confirmation for their guests, so some guests could not return home smoothly. Now the guests had taken a flight from Mexico to Paris, but they didn't have the visa of entering the European Union. Obviously, Air France's conduct was illegal, which meant that Air France must arrange them back to the original starting point, Mexico City or arrange for the next flight, letting the guests return home.

Therefore, Liu contacted the Air France office at once, negotiated to the staff with fluent English; Air France finally realized its serious negligence. So they arranged the guests to take the Paris/Hong Kong/Shanghai's connecting flight. At the same time, the staff upgraded guests to the first class in the Paris/Hong Kong's flight. After the guests arrived in Hong Kong, they only waited for two hours in Hong Kong before taking a Dragonair flight back to Shanghai. Comfortable and warmhearted treatment made guests forget the thrilling things that happened at Charles de Gaulle Airport. Meanwhile, they praised Liu's composure and tactful capacity of crisis management.

Comments

The cause of this case was the cancellation of flight, and the airline transferred the business to two other airlines. It seemed logical that if the two flights were confirmed, the group would return home smoothly. However, there was something wrong in the middle link. The tour leader dealt with the problem in a proactive way. Instead he found a special reason that if guests had air ticket instead of visa, the airline shouldn't carry. He negotiated with Air France staff. Finally, Air France not only offered them connecting flights again, but also moved them to the first class in Paris/Hong Kong's flight. The problem was handled perfectly due to Liu's good English and strain capacity.

In this case, Liu's tact put a final seal on the happy 8-day trip. This tact was achieved by his usual accumulation of knowledge. His calmness, agility and tact are worth drawing upon attention.

In addition, when travel agency staff arrange outbound tour groups' round-trip tickets, and find a transfer to another flight is necessary, they should employ the same airline alliance of airlines, such as Star Alliance, One World. Thus, when we need to transfer to another flight, it will be simpler to deal with. In the above case, Air France and Aeromexico Airline belong to SkyTeam, They can make mutual settlement. When Air France plans a connecting flight Paris/Hong Kong/Shanghai for guests, it also can be settled by Aeromexico Airline.

在成田国际机场办理"夏威夷蜂蜜"的托运

"美加之旅"的最后一站是夏威夷。它因盛产檀香木,亦称檀香山。在夏威夷旅行,街上燃烧着天然气作为路灯,横穿马路时行驶的汽车会主动停下来做个手势让行人先通过,奇异的街景,礼貌的行为,无不给人留下深刻的印象。

行程的最后一天,我领着团体来到火奴鲁鲁国际机场,准备乘机经东京成田机场转机返回上海。在机场,我脑海里还萦绕着典型的夏威夷文化:呼啦舞、四弦琴、花环、阿罗哈(Aloha)。对夏威夷的感受真的是人各有异。对初访者,它是充满新奇的发现;对恋人们,它是充满浪漫的天堂;对其他人,它是闹市中的桃源。夏威夷是每个游客一生不能忘怀的记忆。伴着回忆,我见到一位团友在机场的商店里买了一小瓶产自夏威夷大岛的蜂蜜,准备带回国送给母亲。

从夏威夷出发,飞行了 9 小时后,大家抵达了日本东京成田国际机场。按惯例,在转机口还要进行安全检查,对随身携带的行李做检查。按日本国土交通省的规定,乘客不能携带超过 100 毫升的液态物品。而一瓶蜂蜜有 300 多毫升,这可怎么办呢?我告诉了客人这一规定,但客人还是抱着侥幸的心理,把蜂蜜放在手提旅行包里。当然,这没有逃过 X 射线透视仪器的检查。当那位客人的手提旅行包放到输送带上过安检时,检查员通过监视荧光屏观察到了包里的蜂蜜。

机场安检工作人员告诉那位客人，蜂蜜不能带上飞机，但客人不想把蜂蜜丢进垃圾箱，于是向安检人员表达了想要把蜂蜜带回中国的意愿。安检人员在请示上级后，拿了一张指示图，让客人前往日本航空的柜台办理托运。

日航办理登机手续的柜台在日本移民局之外，按常理需要有日本签证方可出关。于是，我对安检人员说："My guest doesn't have a Japanese visa.（我的客人未持日本签证。）"安检人员查看了我和客人下一段的登机牌是前往上海，就告诉我：你们去日航的登机柜台办理吧，你们有 3 个小时的转机时间，足够办好托运。

我和客人怀着忐忑不安的心情，拿着护照、登机牌和蜂蜜来到移民局。我替客人把事情的原委向移民官陈述了一遍，没想到移民官很快给我们俩的护照粘了一个"口岸通行"（SHORE PASS）的纸条，黏纸上注明，通行时间有 3 天，出日本的活动范围限在东京和千叶地区。

我们很意外也很兴奋，手里拿着盖有"口岸通行"章的护照、东京—上海的机票及登机牌找到了日本航空办理登机手续的柜台，顺利地给这瓶已经乘坐了 9 小时飞机的蜂蜜办了托运手续。

[评析]

实际上，只要有第三国签证并且有下一段的飞机机票及登机牌，均可在日本停留 3 天时间（往往由所购买机票的航空公司来做担保）。然而，现场申请短暂停留和持入境日本签证的旅客均需要填写入境卡和海关申报单，现场申请者可能会被拒签。移民局往往会根据申请者的出国记录来决定是否许可其出入关。

出境领队在带领客人转机赴第三国时，会发生意想不到的情况。大部分转机的旅客是无法出入关的，但也有一些航空公司会允许转机时间较长的旅客（通常是超过 6 小时）办理转机城市的出入境手续，安排免费市内观光游。

领队在处理此事的时候，套用了内地居民通过香港赴第三国政策，即：自内地途经香港，如持有中国护照、联程机票外，还持有前往国的签证，或合法居留证（如美国"绿卡"），可在香港过境停留 7 天，无须办理进入许可。但并不是在任何境外城市转机都可以套用在香港转机的方法。

领队大胆灵活处理问题的能力，也是职业领队应该具备的一种素质。

Consignment of "Hawaii Honey" in Narita International Airport

The last stop of the tour to America and Canada is Hawaii. It is also called Honolulu, as it abounds in sandalwoods. Many tourists are much impressed by the gas streetlamps and the good manner of local drivers, who let pedestrians go first by stopping car and making a gesture.

In the last day of the route, I took the tour group to Honolulu International Airport for a transfer flight from Narita International Airport to Shanghai. Even at the airport, the typical culture of Hawaii, such as hula dance, ukulele, floral hoop and Aloha kept running through our minds. Each had a different feeling towards Hawaii. It is a fancy discovery for new visitors, a romantic paradise for lovers and a fairyland for all. Hawaii tour was an unforgettable memory for visitors throughout their life. At the airport, I saw one guest of our group buy a small bottle of honey which, as a souvenir, was made from Big Island of Hawaii.

After 9 hours flying from Hawaii, we all arrived at Narita International Airport, and were waiting for security check. According to the airport rules, it was forbidden to carry more than 100 mL of liquids. The bottle of honey had a capacity of more than 300 mL. I informed the guest of this rule. However, the guest put the honey bottle into the luggage in the hope that he could escape the examination. When he put the luggage on the conveyer belt for check, the airport officials saw the honey bottle hidden in the luggage through the monitor screen, and told him the honey bottle was forbidden to be taken on board. The guest didn't want to just throw it into the trash, insisting to take it back to China. Finally, the airport officials gave him an index map, asking him go to the JAL counter for consignment.

As the JAL counter was outside Japanese Immigration Office, a Japanese visa was a must for passing through the customs. So I informed the airport officials that this guest had no Japanese visa. When the airport officials saw the destination of boarding card was Shanghai, he told us that it was OK for checking in at JAL counter, and there were totally 3 hours for consignment.

With a bit sense of unease, we went to the immigration office with passports, boarding cards and the honey bottle. Beyond our expectation, the immigration officer soon stuck the label of "SHORE PASS" on our boarding cards after I told him the whole story. The period of validity of this label of SHORE PASS was 3 days within Tokyo and Chiba area. With effective SHORE PASS label in the passports, we gladly went to the JAL counter for consignment successfully.

Comments

Actually, there is a 3-day transit in Japan if the tourists have the third country visa and the boarding pass(guaranteed by the airline company). Besides, tourists who want to apply for a short stay with a Japanese visa need to fill in the landing card and the Customs Declaration Form, and the applicants may be rejected for the visa by the immigration officers according to abroad records.

Unexpected situations may happen when tour leaders take tourist groups to the airport for a connecting flight. Mostly the tourists cannot get through the customs, but for those who need to take a long time (generally over 6 hours) for transferring, the airline company would allow them to go through the customs for a sightseeing tour.

In this case, the leader of the tour group adopted the policy of Chinese citizens going abroad via Hong Kong. That is, "With the passport, joint-way air tickets, visa, legal residence permit like US green card, Chinese citizens those who go abroad via Hong Kong can stay in Hong Kong for 7 days without departure and arrival procedures". But this policy for a connecting flight is not available in all countries.

The ability of solving problems with flexibility and boldness is the key quality for being a professional tour leader.

终于离开了素万那普国际机场

马年的 11 月 23 日,出境游领队詹姆斯带领由某集团工会组织的 32 名员工赴泰国旅游。

旅行团乘坐中国春秋航空公司的航班,于晚间 8:35 准点由杭州直飞泰国的首都曼谷。抵达曼谷素万那普国际机场,办理好入关手续后,泰国美女为团员们献迎宾花环,坐上旅游大巴已经是凌晨 1 点多。詹姆斯和亲切的泰国导游接洽后,由导游带领团友前往酒店入住。

第二天,团友们参观了汇集泰国建筑、绘画、雕刻和装潢艺术精粹的大皇宫以及与大皇宫相邻的玉佛寺,寺里供奉着一尊价值连城的国宝——玉佛,该玉佛是由整块翡翠雕成的,团员们看后惊叹不已。随后大家乘坐长尾船畅游湄南河水上市场,参观水上人家的生活及水上市场的交易情景。紧接着,团员们参观了泰国的白宫——阿南达沙玛空皇家御会馆,该会馆是泰皇与皇后在登基 60 周年纪念日,接受来自 25 个国家的国王及王室成员祝福的地方,会馆中珍藏了很多精工细琢、独具匠心、闪闪发亮的镶嵌宝石的手工艺珍品和供品。

第三天,午餐后,团员们乘车前往有"东方夏威夷"之称的度假胜地——芭提雅。一路上,团员们参观了独具特色的热带龙虎园,在园内欣赏到了鳄鱼、老虎及小猪等的表演。傍晚前后，一行人前往芭提雅2013年7月最新开张的米默莎迷你人妖城与欧式建筑拍照取景地游玩，并享用了泰式酒楼柠檬石斑鱼晚餐。

行程的第四天早上，在游览了芭提雅的一些景观后，团员们乘车返回曼谷。一路上团员们在土产店和 King Power 国际免税店购买了一些喜爱的商品，觉得心满意足。整个旅行给大家留下了难忘的回忆。

行程的第五天，大家带着在泰国购买的大包小包的商品到达机场办理回程手续。就在办理行李托运的时候，意想不到的事情发生了。

按照中国春秋航空公司的规定，每位经济舱的旅客包含随身携带物品在内只能带15千克的免费行李。而团体客人从中国飞来泰国时行李的重量就已经接近这个标准了，更何况客人在泰国旅游期间买了很多泰国特产。毫无疑问，每个人的行李都是超重的，而春秋航空规定，超重的部分按每千克400泰铢付费，相当于人民币80元。说实话，买的东西可能都不用这么贵。这时，所有乘坐该航班的团体客人都开始埋怨了，有些客人和机场地勤人员发生争执，有些客人开始向领队及泰国导游抱怨，也有一些客人为了不付超重费，开始扔多余的东西。总之，当时的场景一片混乱。最后，詹姆斯所带团的客人们将行李拆东补西，总算大部分过了行李托运这一关，只有两名客人无论怎样都要支付行李超重费。这两名客人和值机人员吵了起来，这时离登机时间已经很接近了。詹姆斯为了不让这两名客人误机，主动替客人付了行李超重费，办好了行李托运。领队与这两名客人赶到登机口，检票人员在登机牌上扫过条形码后，工作人员就关闭了检票口。

詹姆斯登上了飞机，发现自己出了一身冷汗。飞机起飞后，他总算放心了，心里嘀咕着，终于离开了素万那普国际机场。

[评析]

廉价航空发端于20世纪70年代的美国，以美国西南航空公司的创立为代表。所谓廉价航空，最显著的特点就是低成本、低票价。这一模式在经历几十年发展后，现已在全球航空市场占据了一席之地，成了全球民用航空公司发展最快的一个领域。在此期间,涌现了大批较成功的航空公司,如欧洲的瑞安航空公司、澳大利亚的维珍航空公司、马来西亚的亚洲航空公司和新加坡的虎航。中国的春秋航空公司也在这波廉价航空大潮中得以发展。

根据春秋航空的行李规则,如果旅客购买的是春秋国内航班的"轻松特价行"特价组合产品,无免费托运行李额度,只可免费携带 7 千克以下且尺寸不超过20×30×40厘米的非托运行李(手提行李)进入客舱。非"轻松特价行"旅客可携带的免费行李,包括托运行李和非托运行李,总计为 15 千克(手提行李限 7 千克以内)。事实上,出境游领队在出发前都已经告诉客人乘坐春秋航空时的这个规定。当时,客人都表示知晓该规定,但当真正要额外支付行李超重费时,客人又会按照原来脑海里固有的理解方式来要求对方。

见多才能识广,案例中的出境游领队有着足够的国际旅行经历和国际交际能力,他从大局出发,在整个出境游的最后一步毅然决定替个别客人支付行李超重费,以避免事态进一步扩大,是一个非常明智的做法。

Bidding Farewell to Suvarnabhumi International Airport

On November 23rd, 2014, James, a tour leader took a group of 32 employees from the same company to Thailand.

The group took a China Spring Airline flight to the destination. At 8:35 p.m. the flight took off in time from Hangzhou to the capital of Thailand,

Bangkok. Out of Suvarnabhumi International Airport the group was warmly welcomed by Thai beauties with flowers. It was after 1:00 a.m. that the guests got on the tour bus. Afterwards, James met the local tour guide, and then the tour guide took the group to the hotel.

The next day, the group visited the splendid royal palace with Thai architectures, paintings, carvings and decoration arts, and the Jade Buddha Temple which was close to the palace. Inside the temple there was a priceless national treasure called the Jade Buddha. The Buddha was carved with jade, which impressed the customers. Later on the group took a long-tail boat heading to Menam floating market, visited people who lived on the water and witnessed the trades conducted in the floating market. After that, the group visited the white house in Thailand, Ananta Samakhom Throne Hall, where the king and the queen received blessings from 25 countries around the world during the ceremony of their 60th Accession Day. In the hall, there were various handicrafts with gem as well as tributes.

On the third day after lunch, the group took the bus heading to Pattaya, which was a perfect vacation paradise. The place was also called oriental Hawaii. The whole group got really excited about it. Along the way, they also visited the unique tropical zoo with performances given by crocodiles, tigers and piggies, etc. At dusk, they went to see a newly-opened M's Sally mini town for ladyboys and European style architectures for pictures. In the evening, they had lemon garrupa for dinner at a local Thai restaurant.

On the forth day, after visiting some other attractions in Pattaya, the group took the bus heading back to Bangkok. On the way, the customers went shopping at the local store and King Power international duty free shops, which made them feel very satisfied. The whole trip left the customers a very good impression.

On the fifth day, everybody went to the airport with lots of packages and were about to take the flight back home. However, something unexpected happened.

According to the regulation of China Spring Airline, every customer in the economy class can only carry 15 kg of luggage free of charge. However, on their way to Thailand the group's belongings had already reached the maximum weight. Besides, they had also bought a lot of extra stuff during the trip. Certainly, all the suitcases were overweight. China Spring Airline has made it clear that extra weight costs extra fees, THB 400 per kilo, equal to RMB 80. But actually the things tourists bought weren't supposed to be that expensive. So some of the guests started to complain, some had a quarrel with the staff working at the airport, some started to throw away things they bought earlier. In a word, it was really a mess. Finally, most guests managed to have the luggage checked. There were still two who had to pay for their overweight luggage. They quarrelled with personnel at the airport. It was really close to the boarding time at that moment. In order to catch the flight in time, James paid for extra fees for his customers by himself and helped them have the luggage checked. They got to the boarding gate and had the barcodes on their boarding cards scanned. The staff out there closed the entrance right after they got on board.

At this moment, James found himself completely wet with cold sweat. He murmured to himself, "Finally we're home-going."

Comments

Budget airline originated from the US in the 1970s, which was represented by the establishment of Southwest Airlines. The most striking feature of budget airline is low cost and low fare. After years of development, it has already played an important role in the global airline market. Meanwhile, it has also become a field with fast development. During the period, a lot of successful airlines emerged, such as Rayanair from the EU, Virgin Atlantic from Australia, Airasia from Malaysia and Tigerair in Singapore. Spring Airlines is also one of them.

According to the regulations made by Spring Airlines, if the guest purchases the tickets with special prices, he or she can only carry 7kg suitable with volume less than 20 × 30 × 40cm to board the plane. Other guests are allowed to have luggage weighing 15kg including carry-on (lighter than 7kg) as well as checked suitcases. This was already informed by the tour leader before departure. At that time the customers seemed all aware of that. However, when they actually faced the situation, the guests were not willing to follow the regulation.

The tour leader mentioned in the case above was very experienced and sociable, and he placed the general interest above the individual's interest. At the last minute, he decided to pay for the extra weight by himself in order to catch the flight in time, which was very wise.

第三篇

Chapter Ⅲ

航空服务延伸篇

In-flight Services

[本章导读]

　　出境旅游者外出旅行的主要交通工具是汽车、飞机、火车和轮船。飞机是出境旅游活动中最主要的交通工具，它具有快速省时、安全舒适的优点。旅行社推出的中长途旅游产品中，基本上都采用飞机作为旅游出发地和目的地之间及目的地国家（地区）各个城市之间的主要交通工具。

　　乘坐国际航班是出境旅游必不可少的一个环节。本篇通过记录作者及其同事乘坐国际航班、游轮等的经历，让读者了解乘坐国际交通工具的注意事项及基本常识，如转机、航班经停、航空服务等。

[Chapter Outline]

For outbound travelers, their main transportation means are coach, airplane, train and ship. Because airplanes are fast, time-saving, safe and comfortable, air transportation becomes the major transport in outbound tourism activities. The mid-long distance travels designed by the travel agencies usually employs aircrafts as main transport between origin and destination countries/regions and between the cities in the destination countries/regions.

For most outbound travelers, taking an international flight is a step that can't be skipped. By sharing his own and his colleagues' experiences of taking international flights and cruises, the author intends to introduce some do's and don'ts for outbound travelers and some basic knowledge about taking international transport, such as transfer, stopover, cabin services and so on.

在澳洲航空的飞机上品尝牛肉馅饼

我曾赴澳大利亚的东海岸城市墨尔本、凯恩斯（大堡礁）、布里斯班（黄金海岸）、悉尼旅游，全程乘坐了 7 次飞机，均是澳大利亚航空公司（Qantas Airways）的航班，从中感受到了澳洲航空服务的与众不同。

我们一行从悉尼金斯福德·史密斯机场飞往墨尔本图拉曼里机场时，乘坐的航班 13:00 起飞，14:45 到达，这个时间段让我们无法用正式的午餐，只能在机场随便买点面包等食品充饥。

飞机于 13:00 准时起飞，前往墨尔本。没过多久，空中服务人员开始派发软饮料（如可乐、柠檬水、矿泉水、橙汁等）。我向一位资深女空乘（看上去 50 岁左右）要了一瓶柠檬水，顺便问她是否有花生米供应。女空乘告诉我，花生米没有，但有 Pretzels（椒盐卷饼）可做替代。我回应"好的"，她迅速地从机舱后面的餐柜里拿了一包给我。

接下来，空乘人员开始分派食品——牛肉馅饼配番茄汁。这种食品形状类似葡式蛋挞，里面的馅是剁得很碎的牛肉，热乎乎的，味道鲜美无比。我问邻座的同行者这个食品的名称，他也不知道。于是，我又问女空乘："刚才我们享用的食品非常好吃，请问它的名字叫什么？"她说："Meat Pie and Sauce（肉馅饼与汁）

是澳航集团的全资子公司——澳航餐饮集团有限公司悉尼饮食中心制作的。集团主要经营两大类别的饮食业务：Q Catering 和 Snap Fresh。Q Catering 目前在悉尼、墨尔本、布里斯班、凯恩斯、阿得莱德与珀斯 6 个澳大利亚机场分别设立了饮食中心。Snap Fresh 是建于昆士兰省的一家先进的食品中央生产商，专门为各大航空公司供应飞机餐膳，同时，其产品也直接向非航空市场进行销售。"接着我又好奇地问："哪里可以买到？"她微笑地回答："诸如 Seven-Eleven 等超市都会有，但味道不一定一样。您想再要一个吗？"我不好意思地回答："我不需要了，我们随行的一位儿童需要一个。"（正好坐在我后面的一起来的小孩也在听我们的对话。）她说："那好。"没过多久，这位空姐递给我两个肉馅饼，并告诉我："比较烫，小心点。"此时，我心里觉得一阵温暖，在澳洲旅游七八天了，仍不适应这里的饮食，但这顿简单的机上午餐，却缩短了南半球和北半球的距离，也让我对澳航这些年龄较大的空中服务人员的善解人意由衷地敬佩。

想着想着，只听机上广播说飞机就要降落了。于是，我将这两个肉馅饼转交给了小孩的妈妈，让她拿回酒店后再品尝。

[评析]

澳洲航空公司（简称澳航）于 1920 年在澳大利亚昆士兰省创立，全名为昆士兰省与北领地航空服务有限公司。卓著的声誉使澳航成了航空业可靠、安全、先进技术及优质客户服务的象征。

如今，澳航已成为世界领先的长途航空公司及澳大利亚最强势的品牌之一。

中国人的观念中，空中服务人员（空姐或空少）应是比较年轻的，然而，由于国外劳动力比较紧缺，特别是欧美、大洋洲等的一些国家，出现在顾客面前的机上服务人员往往会比较年长，有些甚至是爷爷奶奶辈的。比较年长的从业人员，通常会更加善解人意，对顾客的心理把握比较好。

案例中，这位空姐非常了解中国人的心理，含蓄、内敛是中国人的一大特点。心想再吃一个，但不直说，而是通过孩子的需求将意思委婉地表达出来。空姐凭她多年对客服务的经验，把握准了顾客的心理，让顾客的满意由衷而发，实现了让顾客"满意＋惊喜"的效果。

Tasting a Beef Pie on a Qantas' Aircraft

Having gone to Australia on the east coast city of Melbourne，Cairns （Great Barrier Reef），Brisbane （Gold Coast），Sydney，I took 7 flights of Qantas Airways and enjoyed the distinctive Qantas services.

We started from Sydney Kingsford Smith International Airport to Tula Man in Melbourne Tullamarine Airport. The flight was about to take off at 1： 00 p. m. and landing at 2：45 p. m. We could not use a formal lunch，so we bought bread and other food as meal at the airport.

The plane was scheduled to fly for Melbourne at 1：00 p. m. Before long， the air services began distributing soft drinks （such as cola，lemonade，mineral water，orange juice，etc. ）. I asked for a bottle of lemonade to a senior female flight attendant （who looks about 50 years old），and also asked her whether there were peanuts available. The female flight attendant told me there were no peanuts，but they had Pretzels as an alternative. I said OK，so she quickly took a packet to me from the back of the cabin sideboard.

Then the flight attendants began to distribute food，beef pie with tomato juice. The food was similar to the Portuguese egg tarts，and inside the meat was finely chopped beef that tasted warm and delicious. I asked the passenger sitting next to me the name of the food, but he had no idea. So I asked the female flight attendant, "The food we have just enjoyed is very tasty. What is its name?" She said, "Meat Pie and Sauce. It is made by a wholly owned subsidiary of the Qantas Group, the Sydney Diet Centre of Qantas Catering Group Limited. The group principally operates in 2 broad categories: Q Catering and Snap Fresh. Q Catering has division centers in 6 Australian airports of Sydney, Melbourne, Brisbane, Cairns, Adelaide and Perth. Snap Fresh is built in central Queensland as a state-of-the-art food manufacturer, to supply aircraft meals to major airlines as well as to non-aviation market." Then I curiously asked, "Where can I buy it?" She answered with a smile, "Such as Seven-Eleven convenient shops, but the taste is not necessarily the same. Do you want to have one more?" I was embarrassed to answer, "I do not need it, but a child traveling with us needs one (just sitting behind me)." She said, "Well." Not long after, the flight attendants brought me two meat pies and told me, "It is hot, so be careful." At this point, I felt warm. We spent 7—8 days in Australia, and this simple lunch shortened the distance between the northern and southern hemispheres. We were convinced that in Qantas the old air service personnel always serve with sincerity and consideration.

While I was pondering on this, the broadcast informed us that the plane was about to land. Thus, these two meat pies were handed over to the child's mother for food when they went back to the hotel.

Comments

Qantas Airways (abbreviation: Qantas) was founded in 1920 in Queensland, Australia. The full name is the Queensland and Northern Territory Air Services Limited. It is reliable, safe, advanced and a symbol of quality customer service.

Today，Qantas has become the world's leading long-haul airline and one of the most powerful brands in Australia.

In Chinese people's minds，air service personnel should be a group of young people. However，due to a lack of labor force，the flight attendants are often elder people in countries of Europe and America，Oceania，etc. Old employees would show more understanding with a better mental grasp of the customers.

In this case，the elder flight attendant knew much about Chinese passengers' thoughts. Chinese people always display a subtle and restrained attitude toward many things. He might want one more，but felt embarrassed to express his idea. And the flight attendant，with her rich experience，had a precise understanding of the passenger's thoughts and thus met his demand.

如果空姐换一种口吻说话……

2014 年 11 月下旬,我赴韩国首尔参加第十五届国际暨世界文化旅游大会。空中旅行的经历让我感触颇深。

8:20,我们一行 5 人登上了杭州飞往首尔的航班。登机牌上显示我的座位是 24J,这是一个靠过道的位置,我在办理登机手续时特地向值机人员要求的。登上飞机后,我走到 24J 号座位旁,发现位子上坐着一位中国客人。我怕自己搞错了,就将登机牌交给站在一旁引领乘客就座的空乘人员,让她再确认一下我寻找的座位是否正确。空姐一看登机牌,我的座位确实是靠走道的那个座位,便示意座位上的男子让座。这时,坐在我座位上的那位男子很委屈地告诉我,他自己的座位被一位韩国人占了。于是,我们要求空姐帮我们问个明白。经过询问,空姐对我说:"他们都是韩国人,那你只能坐在后面一排他们空出来的位子上了。"听到这样的解释,我非常不满意,于是,我对空姐说:"对不起,我不同意调换座位,我喜欢坐在靠走道的座位。"

空姐立刻将我的话翻译了过去,并对大家说:"请大家都按登机牌上的座位号就座吧!"无奈之下,韩国客人很不情愿地把座位让出来。24 及 25 排这两排座位上的乘客一下子都站起来进行换位,飞机上顿时一阵混乱。我身边的那位中国人回到了他的座位上就座，我也坐上了 24J 这个靠过道的位子。

[评析]

空中旅行时，乘客互换座位是经常会发生的事情。处理这类事情时，空中服务人员的态度非常重要。一项社会心理学研究认为：相互理解＝语调（38％）＋表情（55％）＋语言（7％）。空乘人员的语言艺术、语音语调以及对客人说话时的表情都是换座位是否成功的关键因素。案例中，如果空中小姐能将对被调换座位的乘客说的话改成"对不起先生，他们都是韩国客人，想坐在一起，跟您换个位置，行吗？"，我想，自己一定会同意的。

互换座位，表面上看起来是乘客之间的事情，但实际上跟空中服务人员在中间的协调是有很大关系的。特别是国际航班上，乘客来自世界各地，各个国家的文化背景不一样，有时语言沟通也有障碍，更需要空中服务人员以殷勤好客的态度、谦和的语言来解决这类看似简单，但处理起来又需要讲究一点艺术的事情。

If the Airline Stewardess Changed Her Tone ...

During the last 10 days of November, 2014, I got a chance to take part in the fifteenth international world conference on cultural tourism in Seoul, Korea. My experience of air trip was very impressive.

Five of us boarded the flight from Hangzhou to Seoul at 8：20 in the morning. The boarding card showed that my seat number was 24J, which was an aisle seat, because I asked the check-in staff for that when I was checking in. After boarding I walked to the seat and found that there was a Chinese sitting on that seat. I thought maybe I made a mistake, so I gave my boarding card to the stewardess who was settling passengers down on seats, and asked her to confirm whether the seat I was looking for was right or wrong. After seeing this, the stewardess told me the seat I found was mine and asked the man on that seat to return the seat to me. At that time, the man told me with grievance that his seat had been taken by a Korean. Then we both asked the stewardess to help us talk to the Korean. Later the stewardess told us that they were all Koreans and I had to sit on the vacant seats in the row behind them. When I heard this explanation I was very unsatisfied and then I told the stewardess I was sorry and I would not agree to change the seat because I preferred the aisle seat.

Immediately, the stewardess translated what I said to those people and said: "Please take your seats according to the boarding cards." Reluctantly, the passengers of 24th and 25th row had to stand up and change seats, which caused a chaos. The Chinese returned to his own seat. So did I.

Comments

Changing seats among passengers during the air tip is very common and it is very important for flight attendants to deal with it. A research of social psychology shows: understanding with each other = tone (38%) + facial expression (55%) + speaking (7%). Language art, intonation, pronunciation and facial expression are the key factors to success of changing seats. In this case, if the stewardess can change her words like "I am sorry, sir. They all come from Korea and they want to sit together. Could you please change the seat with them?", I think I will agree with that.

On the surface，changing seats in the plane is something among passengers. But actually it has a lot to do with flight attendants' efforts. Especially on international flights，passengers come from all over the world，so sometimes it is difficult for them to communicate with each other. Thus it calls for polite attitude and gracious words to solve problems，which seems simple but requires something artistic.

坐火车在"翡冷翠"游览

佛罗伦萨是一座具有悠久历史的文化名城,它既是意大利文艺复兴运动的发源地,也是欧洲文化的发源地。大诗人徐志摩把它译作"翡冷翠",这个译名比另一个译名"佛罗伦萨"来得更富诗意,更具色彩,也更符合古城的气质。

"法意瑞"的行程中,第九天的安排是这样的:早上从博洛尼亚出发,驱车赴佛罗伦萨,游览完后再驱车前往罗马。

领队小于所带团队的司机来自克罗地亚,才第二次跑"法意瑞"这条线路,全程靠 GPS 来导航。有的时候 GPS 所指的路不一定正确,往往要绕路才能抵达目的地。从佛罗伦萨到罗马有 300 公里的车程,在欧洲,大巴一天用车时间不能超过 12 小时,导游石小姐担心司机由于不熟悉路线而超时,便决定改乘火车进佛罗伦萨城游览,乘火车期间既可以让大巴和司机休息,又可以让客人有在意大利乘坐火车的别样体验。

取得客人的同意后,石小姐对行程进行了调整,大家从佛罗伦萨郊区 Sesto Florentino 的火车站上车,前往新圣母玛利亚中心火车站。一路上客人边欣赏着沿途的风光,边闲聊着,充分感受到了乘坐意大利火车的新鲜感。下了火车,导游在前领路,领队在后压阵,一行人顺利地进入了领主广场。团员们首先欣赏了

《大卫》的复制品。然后，大家跟着佛罗伦萨的导游来到世界上最美的教堂——圣母百花大教堂。大教堂有一个橘红色的巨大圆顶，所以很明显，远远就能看见。教堂的右侧，还有世界上最漂亮的钟楼之一——高达 82 米的乔托钟楼。与其他教堂不同的是，圣母百花大教堂是世界上第一座带有大圆顶的教堂，圆顶由 10 块浮雕组成，顶内有螺旋形阶梯直通穹顶，可鸟瞰佛罗伦萨市风光，这也成了佛罗伦萨的重要地标。团员们无不为这个欧洲文艺复兴的代表城市——佛罗伦萨惊叹。

　　游览完了佛罗伦萨已是午餐后，导游、领队带领团队从新圣母玛利亚中心火车站坐上回 Sesto Florentino 的火车。下了火车后导游和领队让客人按组进行报数集合（导游已将团队分成了若干组），每组都反馈人已到齐，列车员就让火车开走了。等团队走出月台，有一个带着女儿的女子突然说："我的丈夫还没有下车。"听到这个消息，大家都傻眼了，不知如何是好。事态紧迫，导游、领队定了定神，立刻打了电话，对方说：他已坐上返程的列车。15 分钟后，心急如焚的领队终于又接到了这位客人。

　　于是，大巴又一次启动，朝新的目的地城市——罗马奔去。

[评析]

　　旅游者在进行旅游活动时，他们的思维有时可能会"短路"。也就是说，有时他们会做出异常行为。案例中，由于座位不够，有一户家庭的丈夫、妻子和女儿只能分坐在不同的车厢。下了火车，妻子想当然地认为丈夫已经下了火车，在没有完全确认的前提下，就说丈夫已经到了。哪知道丈夫在火车上由于旅途劳累而有些昏昏沉沉，结果坐过了站。因此，领队和导游一定要反复强调下车的站点，在下车之前要快速清点人数，看客人是否到齐，若没有到齐应提醒一起的同伴，以防遗漏客人。而旅游者本身也应该多留意这些关键点。

　　另外，旅途中万一碰到此类情况，其处理方法是：第一，如果客人懂目的地国家（地区）的语言或英语，可询问站台工作人员，乘原火车返回（因为类似意大利这种城际火车，几乎 5—6 分钟就是一个站，10 分钟左右就会有一班火车经过）；

第二,若能在语言上沟通顺畅,可直接出火车站坐出租车返回始发地(可以将电话拨通,让出租汽车司机与导游交流,导游会告诉司机抵达地点);第三,就站在下车的地点,通过电话告诉导游下车站点的名称,让导游或领队坐火车来接。但是以上方法的前提是旅游者的手机开通了国际长途。

A Train Tour in Firenze

Florence is a famous cultural city with a long history. It is where Renaissance and European culture originated.

During the tour in France,Italy and Switzerland,the 9th day's itinerary was as follows:the tour group started from Bologna in the morning,then arrived in Florence and finally went to Rome.

The Croatian driver of the group led by the leader Mr. Yu relied on GPS all the way,because it was his second time driving along the route. Sometimes the group had to make detours,as the route set by GPS was not always correct. Rome is 300 kilometers' away from Florence. In Europe,the coach bus is not allowed to be on the road for more than 12 hours. Considering the time restriction,Ms. Shi,the tour guide,led the group to Florence by railway. Taking trains in Italy gave tourists a special experience and also a break to the coach driver.

Ms. Shi made some little adjustments to the itinerary with consent from all the tourists. The group started from the railway station in Sesto Florentino in Florence suburbs to Stazione di Firenze Santa Maria Novella. The tourists had a fresh feeling taking trains in Italy while chatting and viewing the beautiful scenery along the way. The group soon arrived in Piazza della Signoria with the guide and leader in the front and rear of the line respectively. The tourists first appreciated the replica of David, the statue. Then they arrived at Basilica di Santa Maria del Fiore, renowned as the most beautiful church in the world. It is quite eye-catching with the gigantic orange dome. On the right lies the 82 meter-high Giotto's Campanile, one of the most beautiful bell towers in the world. Santa Maria del Fiore is the first church with a great dome composed of 10 reliefs. Tourists may have a bird-eye view of Florence through the spiral stairs to the dome. The cathedral is surely the landmark of Florence. All the tourists were fascinated by Firenze, the representative of the European Renaissance.

When the tour in Florence was finished, it was after lunch time. The group was ready to go back to Sesto Florentino. The train departed after each group reported their members were all present. (The guide had divided the tourists into several groups.) However, upon arrival on the platform, a lady with her daughter said, her husband was still in the train. Everyone was at a loss. Fortunately, the guide and leader calmed down and made a phone call. The railway station said the man was on the way back. 15 minutes later, the man joined the group again.

The coach set off for the new destination, Rome.

Comments

Tourists may experience "brain short circuit" during the tour. Sometimes they may conduct abnormal behaviors. In the case, the husband, wife and their daughter had to sit in different coaches on the train. Upon arrival, the wife figured that her husband must have got off the train. However, he didn't. He was sleepy due to the tiredness. Under this circumstance, the guide and leader should always make sure every member is present, getting them ready for getting off the train. Tourists should also pay attention to it when traveling overseas.

Under such circumstances, the solutions are as follows. First, if the tourist understands English or the local language, he can inquire for the return trip. The inter-city train in Italy comes approximately every 10 minutes. And it takes 5—6 minutes to drive to a station. Second, the tourist may go back to the station of departure by taking a taxi if he can communicate with local people. If not, the tourist may hand the phone to the taxi driver to contact the tour guide to make sure he gets the destination right. Third, the tourist may just wait in the station and inform the guide to go and pick him up. All the above-mentioned ways could be adopted provided international direct dial service is available for the tourist.

徜徉在夜巴黎中

在"法意瑞"的游览线路中,法国往往会被安排在第一站。抵达巴黎的第二天,客人们兴致勃勃地游览了罗浮宫、凯旋门、香榭丽舍大道和协和广场,大家完全沉浸在初抵巴黎的兴奋之中。下午,导游向客人推荐了夜巴黎游览的自选活动。出乎意料的是,团队中除了一名 71 岁的老人晚上要早点休息,其余的客人均报名参加了这个活动。

晚间 8 点,大巴在用餐的餐厅接我们上车。夜游导游是个北京人,侃侃而谈。第一站,我们去了西堤岛上的巴黎圣母院。巴黎圣母院矗立在塞纳河畔,位于整个巴黎城的中心,它的地位、历史价值无与伦比,是历史上最为辉煌的建筑之一,也是古老巴黎的象征。哥特式风格的基督教教堂以其建筑风格,祭坛、回廊、门窗等处的雕刻和绘画艺术,以及堂内所藏的 13—17 世纪的大量艺术珍品而闻名于世。

参观完巴黎圣母院出来,走过一条街就到了巴黎拉丁区。拉丁区位于巴黎五区和六区之间,是巴黎著名的学府区。拉丁区这个名字来源于中世纪,这里以拉丁语作为教学语言,拉丁区是巴黎的大学集中的地方,这里有好几所大学,包括著名的索邦大学。因此,拉丁区自然就成了知识分子云集的地方。这里横街窄巷多,空气中弥漫着咖啡、烤面包、烤肉的香味;这里旧书店、旧电影院、画廊多,夹杂着一些文艺复兴前后的古老教堂,建筑也大都可以上溯到文艺复兴前后时期,浸润着一种历史感。由于纬度高,巴黎在夏季晚上 9:30 以后,天空才开始慢慢地暗下来。夜色渐浓,大家不知不觉地走进了一家土耳其店铺,店里卖一种小吃,是烤肉和洋葱夹着串在铁棍上烧烤,土耳其人叫这种吃法为"沙威玛"。买的时候厨子用利刀一片片切下来,裹在薄饼中吃,每个卖 5 欧元。大家都尝了尝,真的很香。此时此刻大家真正感受了巴黎人的夜生活。接下来大家在大王宫前拍照留念。

第四站,我们抵达了荣军院。荣军院在国王路易十四统治时期是安置伤残军人的医院,拿破仑一世的棺椁如今依旧陈放在此。荣军院的金色穹顶在夜色中显得格外醒目,是这座建筑的标志。

22:40 左右,我们的旅游大巴慢慢地驶向此次夜游的最后一个景点——亮灯的埃菲尔铁塔。埃菲尔铁塔被称作"钢铁夫人",由工程师古斯塔夫·埃菲尔为 1889 年的世界博览会设计。这是一座名副其实的技术里程碑,324 米高,重达 1 万吨。当时钟敲响 23 下,埃菲尔铁塔上所有的灯都亮起的那一刻,所有提前等候在那里的游客纷纷拍照留念,点灯和闪灯的时间持续了 5 分钟。

在回程的路上,导游告诉我们:考虑到点灯成本过高,巴黎市政府可能会取消每晚点灯和闪灯的节目。到时,要是再来巴黎,就欣赏不到这个景观了。大家听了越发觉得这个自选项目值得参加。

[评析]

自选活动或自费项目是常规游览项目的延伸或补充。一个普通的旅游者可能一辈子只会去一次某个旅游目的地国家或地区,所以,安排合理的、有新意的、有亮点的自选活动,很多旅游者还是愿意参加的。案例中的夜巴黎游览就可以说是自选活动的经典。第一,所有的景点与白天的游览项目不重复。第二,能让旅游者或多或少了解一些目的地居民的普通生活。如徒步拉丁区。第三,整个夜游有新意和高潮,埃菲尔铁塔的点灯和闪灯就是其中之一。

但是某些东南亚国家的自选活动往往活动内容无特别之处，收费过高，有导游硬性要求客人参加的嫌疑，这往往导致客人非常反感，不愿意参加。旅行社或导游推荐的自选项目是让旅游者能真正欣赏到常规行程以外的，能体现本地特色的项目，还是完全以盈利为目的，明白人一看就清楚了。因此，客人是否参加自选活动，不是看客人，而是看旅行社设计的旅游产品如何。

Evening Wandering in Paris

　　In the itinerary for a tour of France, Italy and Switzerland, France is usually the first destination. Upon arriving in Paris, tourists visited Louvre, Arc de Triomphe, Avenue des Champs-Elysees and Place de la Concorde. Every tourist was quite excited about the Paris tour. In the afternoon, the guide recommended an optional activity in the evening to the group. All the tourists agreed to attend it except a 71-year-old guest who needed a rest early.

　　We got on the coach at 8:00 p.m. The guide for the evening tour was a nice and talkative man from Beijing. The first stop was the Notre Dame de Paris on Cite. Notre Dame de Paris is located at the center of Paris city, along the Seine. It is the symbol of ancient Paris and one of the most magnificent buildings in the history with incomparable value and status. This Christian church is well-renowned for its Gothic style, sculptures and paintings in temples, corridors, windows and artworks in the 13rd—17th centuries.

After visiting the Notre Dame de Paris, the group crossed a street and arrived in Latin Quarter, Paris, located between Le 5e and 6e arrondissements de Paris. It is famous for its universities and colleges. The area is called Latin Quarter because universities and colleges like the famous Université Paris-Sorbonne conduct teaching and research in Latin. Latin Quarter with narrow alleys was where intellectuals got together. Buildings here like ancient bookstores, cinemas, galleries and churches can be traced back to the time of the Renaissance. People can smell coffee, baked bread and barbecue in the air. Actually, they can sense the long history here. There comes the darkness after 9:30 p.m. in summer in Paris due to the high latitude. The tourists went to a Turkish stand selling barbecue and onions strung together on a cord. Turkish people call it Shawarma. The chef sliced pieces down and got them wrapped in thin pancakes. The tourists bought some at 5 euros for each. It was tasty. They really had a wonderful time in the evening Paris.

The tourists then took some photos in front of Grand Palais. The 4th stop was L'Hotel des Invalides. L'Hotel des Invalides was the hospital where disabled soldiers were received under Louis XIV's reign. Napoleon I's coffin is still there. The golden dome of L'Hotel des Invalides is quite eye-catching.

Finally, the group went to the last scenic spot, the Eiffel Tower, to enjoy light show at 10:40 p. m. The Eiffel Tower is renowned as Iron Lady. It was designed by French engineer Gustave Eiffel for World Expo 1889. With a height of 324 meters and weight of 10,000 tons, it is definitely a technical milestone among buildings. When the bell rang for the 23rd time, all the lights on the tower were turned on. The show lasted 5 minutes.

On the way back, the tour guide said that the Paris authority was considering cancellation of the light show due to high cost. People might not be able to see it next time. The tourists felt it was really worthwhile attending the optional activity.

Comments

Optional activities or chargeable ones are an extension or a complement of regular tour activities. A common tourist may have only one opportunity to visit a certain place in a lifetime. Therefore, new and interesting optional activities with reasonable prices would be accepted by many tourists. Evening tour in Paris in the above case is a classical example. First, all the scenic spots are new. Second, it may help tourists know something about local people's life like the wandering in Latin Quarter. Third, the evening tour usually needed a climax like the Eiffel Tower light show.

However, optional activities in some Southeast Asian countries' tours don't have fun and special contents. Some even overcharge tourists. Tourists can easily tell whether these activities are valuable or just for profit. Therefore, the quality of tourist products determines the number of tourists attending this kind of activities.

航班延误的赔偿：200 元＋一项自费活动＋一顿晚餐

芽庄气候宜人，是越南的海滨旅游胜地。随着杭州直飞芽庄包机的开通，越来越多的人选择出境赴越南中部港市、庆和省省会——芽庄度假。

出境游领队小符此次所带的越南团是从杭州萧山国际机场直飞越南芽庄的"一地团"。此次包机出游是由杭州三大出境社合办的亲子游产品，客人多为三口之家。出境游领队小符早早地恭候在杭州萧山机场，客人们也都准时在规定的集合时间到达机场并向领队报到。办理好登机牌，过了海关、中国边防，抵达登机口。正当小符在心里暗暗祈祷一切顺利的时候，却被告知原本预定晚上 7:30 起飞的航班由于航空管制不能按时起飞。

小符预感到航班的延误可能会耽搁后面的行程，便立刻向机场的相关负责人反映，并表示团队里有很多小孩，请求尽可能早点起飞。

同时，小符第一时间向机场要来了毛毯、饼干和饮料，在一定程度上缓解了客人的情绪。但直到凌晨，从越南过来的飞机还是没有落地，更别说起飞了。团队的客人开始围着登机口向工作人员讨说法，有个别家长的情绪非常激动，大人、小孩乱成一团。面对如此局面，几个团队的领队立刻介入其中，与航空公司交涉。直到凌晨 1:30，旅游团才开始登机。

按照中国民航总局的规定，延误4—8小时的航班，航空公司有义务赔付每一位乘客200元人民币的现金，但是客人表示旅行社也要做出相应的赔偿。小符积极向计调反映这件事情，经商议，最终三家出境旅行社决定增加一项自费项目和一顿晚餐，作为对客人的额外补偿，另由越捷航空做出每人200元人民币的现金赔偿。条件谈妥后飞机才得以起飞，此时已是凌晨2:30。

[评析]

关于飞机误点，一直有不同的说法和定义。据了解，美国航班统计延误率以15分钟为限，中国航空业内默认的标准则宽松到30分钟。有民航专家认为，航班起飞时间比计划起飞时间（航班时刻表上的时间）延迟30分钟以上或航班取消的情况称为延误，延迟30分钟以内算合理。还有一种说法是：航班降落时间比计划降落时间（航班时刻表上的时间）延迟30分钟以上或航班取消的情况也属于延误。

飞机延误4—8小时（含8小时），航空公司还需向旅客提供价值300元的购票折扣、里程或其他方式的等值补偿，或是人民币200元。延误8小时以上则要向旅客提供价值450元的购票折扣、里程或其他方式的等值补偿，或是人民币300元。

出现案例中这样的延误情况，实际上旅行社本身是没有责任的。客人提出补偿要求，看起来比较无礼，但也是宣泄情绪的一种途径。从表面来看，旅行社似乎有损失，但从另一个角度来讲，也是给旅行社树立良好口碑的一个机会。相信那额外的一个自费项目和一顿晚餐，也会给客人留下难以忘怀的记忆。

Compensation for Flight Delay: RMB 200, a Self-funded Activity and a Dinner

Nha Trang is regarded as a seaside resort of Vietnam for its perfect weather. As the direct flight from Hangzhou to Nha Trang is available in Hangzhou Xiaoshan International Airport, a great number of tourists fly to Nha Trang for vacation.

Fu, a tour leader, took a tour group flying from Hangzhou to Nha Trang, Vietnam. The group consists of families with kids organized by three top travel agencies in Hangzhou and most of the tourists in the group are families of three. On the departure day, Fu arrived at the airport early to welcome his guests. Fu felt incredibly blessed that all the members of the group arrived on time, carried the boarding cards, passed the customs and the security check and reached the boarding gate smoothly. However, he was informed that their flight scheduled to take off at 7:30 p.m. was going to be delayed for air traffic control.

Fu had a feeling that their trip schedule was going to be postponed because of that. He consulted the airport staff whether the flight could take off as soon as possible as there were a lot of kids in his group. Meanwhile, he also got blankets, cookies and some drinks from the airport for the guests to ease their nerves. Unfortunately, the flight didn't arrive even after midnight. The customers started to complain and some of the parents in a rage argued with the airline staff. Some tour leaders held a discussion with the airline about the issue. Finally, the passengers started to get on board at 1:30 a.m.

According to regulation of CAAC, airlines are liable for flight delay from 4 to 8 hours with compensation of RMB 200. However, customers also asked for compensation from the travel agencies. Fu reported the case to the tour operator and the travel agencies agreed on making a compromise by adding a self-funded activity as well as an extra dinner for the customers. The flight finally took off after settling down everything at 2:30 a.m.

Comments

Regarding flight delay, there have always been different perspectives and definitions. American airlines see taking off 15 minutes behind schedules as delay. In China, the standard has been extended to 30 minutes. Some professionals believe that flights taking off within 30 minutes should be considered reasonable and acceptable. Another theory is that if the landing time of a flight extends by 30 minutes or longer, it is a flight delay.

Airlines are liable for flight delay of 4—8 hours (including 8 hours) by providing RMB 300 flight discount or RMB 200 direct compensation; 450 RMB discount or RMB 300 direct compensation for more than 8 hours.

In the case above, the travel agencies had no responsibility for the incident as it was caused by the third party. However, they still provided compensation for keeping reputation and maintaining customer relationships. The self-funded and extra dinner could certainly leave a deep impression on customers. Therefore, solving problems by losing profit can also be considered as a favorable method for airlines.

入关时，入出境许可证遗失了

宝岛台湾在 2008 年 7 月对大陆居民开通旅游后，游客纷纷报名，台湾迎来了旅游的高峰。

资深领队小刘正是赶上了台湾旅游的高峰时段带团去台湾，此时他还不知道有一个极难解决的问题正等着他。当时赴台湾旅游一票难求，所以很难乘上直航的飞机，而这个团队也是因为这个原因，去台湾是从香港转机的。首先乘坐的是到香港的中国东方航空的飞机，然后到了香港再转华航的班机，问题正是在下了华航的飞机后发生的。

下了华航的飞机后，领队让客人上完洗手间后集合，然后向所有客人发放入台证，并按照相关部门的要求，让所有客人把入台证夹入大陆居民往来台湾通行证内。向客人解释过注意事项后，领队带领所有客人向入境大厅走去。走着走着，一位客人突然叫了一声，回头一看，原来这位客人的入台证居然滑入了扶手电梯的缝隙里，就这样没有了。客人不知所措，小刘却临危不乱，马上想到了两点：第一，马上到相关部门报备；第二，找到华航的工作人员，请他们帮忙和相关部门交涉。左思右想，小刘采取了第二种方法，因为他想到，如果自行去找相关部门，要 24 小时才能做新的入台证，另外，相关部门肯定不相信会有这种事件发生,他们会让华航遣送客人返回出发地,而客人是夫妻同来,那就意味着两人都要回去,那事情就会变得更加复杂。而且华航有责任帮助搭乘其航班的乘客去解决这一类事。

于是领队小刘马上找到了华航工作人员。华航先帮助他找到了电梯修理工程师,准备让电梯暂停,拆开电梯来取入台证,但是工程师马上否决了这个方法。因为电梯拆卸需要很长时间,况且就算找到了,也肯定压坏了,不能再用了。所以,华航立刻帮助领队写了一份情况说明并且和相关部门描述了所发生的情况。基于华航和相关部门长期合作的友好信任关系,相关部门立刻在短短的一个小时内,给这位客人做了一张临时入台证,而且告诉领队,回来的时候,可以再找到华航柜台,拿着客人的照片重新办理一张入台证。于是,这位客人拿着补办的入台证顺利开始了台湾之行。

[评析]

世界之大,无奇不有。这是一个非常罕见的案例,领队却处理得非常漂亮。一般碰到此类事情,领队都会采取第一种方法,而该领队非常机智,马上想到第一种方法的弊端,如果采用第一种方法,无疑增加了解决问题的难度。

领队想到华航,知道自己的力量没有华航的力量大,华航呈交给相关部门的情况报告远远比领队所写的情况报告更容易让其相信;再加上华航是一个服务性质的企业,如果客人坐它的飞机来台湾而没有进关的话,它也有推卸不掉的责任。所以,华航一定会认真地处理这件事。如果是相关部门就不同了,它必须要按规定办事。因此领队找华航处理该事件的选择是完全正确的。

入台证是大陆去台湾观光的游客所持的一次性通行证,客人在飞机落地3小时后未办理手续的话,入台证就会自动作废。而领队考虑到这点,在3小时内将问题处理完毕,事半功倍。这是一个经验与智慧完美结合的案例,值得旅游业的同行学习。

The Entry and Exit Permit Is Missing When Entering the Customs

Taiwan witnessed its tourism peak since the July of 2008 when it allowed mainland inhabitants to travel to Taiwan.

The senior team leader Mr. Liu guided a group to Taiwan during this peak period. At that time he didn't expect that a tough problem was waiting for him. Those days, the tickets to Taiwan were in short supply and it was very difficult to take a direct flight. Therefore, this group flew to Taiwan via Hong Kong. They first took a China Eastern Airlines flight to Hong Kong and then took a China Airlines flight to Taiwan.

After getting off the plane of China Airlines, the team leader asked the group to gather after they went back from the washroom. Then he handed out the entry cards of Taiwan, and let the group members put them inside Mainland Residents Traveling to Taiwan Permits according to the requirements of the relevant department. He declared some notices and guided the tourists to the hall. Suddenly he heard a scream. He turned back and found that a tourist's entry card fell into the gap of the elevator.

The visitor didn't know what to do, but Mr. Liu acted very calmly. He came up with two solutions, that is, report to the relevant department or find the stuff of China Airlines and ask for their help. After careful consideration, Mr. Liu took the second solution because he thought that if he went to the relevant department by himself, it would take 24 hours to make a new entry card. Besides, if the relevant department did not believe in this kind of case, it would let the China Airlines send the tourist back to his departure place. As the group member came in couple, and that meant both had to go back, which would make things more complicated. What's more, China Airlines had the responsibility to help its passengers solve such problems.

So Mr. Liu found the staff of China Airlines immediately, who found a repairman to stop the elevator and open it for the card. But the repairman turned down this suggestion because it would take a long time to open the elevator. Even if the card could be found, it must be crushed. Therefore, the China Airlines worker wrote a report for the team leader and declared the case to the relevant department. Due to the long-term friendly relationship between China Airlines and the relevant department, the latter made a new temporary card for the visitor within 1 hour. The relevant department also told the team leader that when he came back, he could carry a photo of the group member and made a new entry card on the China Airlines desk (to be used when leaving Taiwan). Finally, the group member, with the temporary entry card, began his visit in Taiwan.

Comments

Everything could happen. This was a very rare case, but the team leader dealt with it very properly. Generally the leader in this case would take the first solution, but this leader was very clever and he thought about the disadvantages immediately. If he took the first solution, it would be more difficult to solve the problem.

The team leader thought about China Airlines because he knew that it was more powerful, the report made by it would be much more dependable and believable. Besides, China Airlines is a service company, so it has an unshirkable duty if its passengers couldn't enter Taiwan. Thus it would probably deal with this case more seriously. But the relevant department is different. It should obey rules. In conclusion, the team leader's decision of turning to China Airlines was quite right.

The entry certificate is a disposable permit for the visitors who came from the mainland to Taiwan. It would become invalid automatically if visitors don't go through the entry formalities within 3 hours after the plane landed. Thinking about this point, the team leader solved the problem within 3 hours efficiently. It is a case which combines rich experience and wisdom, and tourism practitioners should learn from it!

终于飞到了世界上最北的国家——冰岛

　　小宣是"0517欧洲全景游21天团"的领队。5月17日早上,领队小宣带领客人从上海浦东机场出发,于18日凌晨抵达德国巴伐利亚洲的首府——慕尼黑。此行程中,游览的目的地国家包括德国、冰岛、卢森堡、比利时、捷克、斯洛伐克、奥地利。客人来自同一家公司,共计30人。

　　下午2点团队抵达慕尼黑机场,准备搭乘冰岛航空公司的航班前往冰岛首都雷克雅未克。团队顺利地办理了登机手续,拿到了登机牌,托运了行李,和导游告别后进入候机大厅。客人在等候了一小时后被告知飞机将延误两小时,客人虽有抱怨但仍继续等待。时间又过去两个小时,显示屏上显示的"延误"字样突然变成"取消"。于是客人纷纷要求航空公司给个说法。小宣赶忙先稳定客人情绪,并立刻将这一情况向组团旅行社做了汇报,紧接着小宣联系了冰岛航空公司工作人员询问详情。航空公司有关人员给出的最终答复是航班取消乃因为飞行员罢工,并告知今天确定不飞,具体飞行时间等罢工结束后再通知。

　　于是,领队请航空公司开具了航班取消证明,紧接着再跟中国的组团社汇报,之后安排客人离开候机大厅,取回自己的行李,在外面的值机大厅等候安排。

　　接下去,领队要解决的问题就是客人入住酒店的安排。由于罢工算是不可

167

抗力因素,再加上团队人数多,航空公司是不会为大家安排住宿和交通的。所以国内组团社请德国地接社赶紧安排酒店让客人入住。由于德国当地时间已经是傍晚6点(中国是晚上12点),而且一下子要订16个房间,难度有点大。领队小宣建议中国组团社安排客人在机场附近的酒店入住,但是组团社考虑到成本问题没有这样安排(机场附近的酒店往往比较贵)。在等待近两个小时后德国地接社终于在离慕尼黑机场30公里处订好了酒店。那么,如何去酒店呢?当时德国当地时间已近晚上8点了,想叫一辆大巴非常困难,领队就建议大家打车去酒店。

领队首先询问了德国租车公司包一辆大巴要多少钱,公司答复500欧元,接着领队继续问当地出租车司机,打车到30公里外的酒店是什么价格,出租司机回复60—70欧元。

他一核算:团体共30人,加上行李最多8辆车也够了,总共最多也就560欧元,但可以省下很多时间。而且从上海登机后,客人已经超过25小时没有好好休息,此时已经非常疲惫,因此一肚子怨气。此时领队理所当然地成了出气筒,客人一股脑儿地把气撒到领队身上。经过核算之后,中国组团社同意客人打车去酒店,客人也基本满意。

到酒店后就商议接下去的行程,因为冰岛去不了,所以只能把四天冰岛的行程改到德国。但幸运的是,在慕尼黑的第二天就被告知冰岛航空可以飞了。于是客人欢欣鼓舞,一致同意再飞冰岛并缩短冰岛行程,从原来的四天缩到两天。这样就不会影响从冰岛回德国后接下去的行程,也能将整个损失降到最低。

[评析]

罢工在西方国家为劳资双方沟通意见的一种方式,但在团体旅游行程中,如遇交通运输业员工罢工,则将深受影响。因为团队行程早已经安排好,环环相扣,一处脱节,全程波及受害,故领队需要谨慎处理。

遇到罢工事件时,出境旅游领队应立即联系其他航空公司确保机位,并要求原航空公司给予转乘其他航空公司的证明。否则,应要求原本所搭乘的航空公司给予合理的安排,并保证航班恢复正常后,首先让团队客人乘坐飞机离开。

在境外旅游经常会出现航班由于各种原因,如天气原因(低能见度、低空云、雷雨区、强侧风)、航空管制、机械故障、飞机调配、罢工造成航空公司取消当日航班的情况。特别是罢工属于不可抗力的因素。当地旅行社肯定要给客人安排酒店住宿。至于赴入住酒店的交通费用,有时在境外临时租一辆大巴,并不见得比叫出租车便宜(临时叫车费用往往还要包括司机加班工资、空驶费等),而旅行社考虑到团队的成本问题,当4人合坐一辆出租车的总费用比租用大巴便宜时,领队需要根据自己从目的地国家(地区)得到的最新消息来说服中国组团旅行社进行调整,以最快的速度将客人送往酒店安顿好。案例中,领队最后决定叫出租车就是一个例子。我曾带团从新加坡夜间野生动物园返回"小印度"周边的酒店,发现4人合用一辆出租车要比乘夜间野生动物园专线返回市区便宜。

Flying to the Northernmost Country in the World, Iceland

Mr. Xuan was the tour leader of an outbound tour group to Europe for 21 days. On the morning of May 17th, she led the group to depart from Shanghai Pudong International Airport and arrived at Munich early on the morning of 18th in southern Germany. The itinerary included Germany, Iceland, Luxembourg, Belgium, Czech, Slovak and Austria. The 30 group members came from the same company.

At 2:00 p. m. the group arrived at the Munich airport, ready to take the flight to the capital Reykjavik. The group checked in, got boarding passes, had luggage checked, and said farewell to the local guide. Then they were told that the flight would be delayed for two hours. The group had to wait. Two hours later, the "Delayed" on the flight information board changed to "Canceled", so the guests requested explanation from the airlines. Mr. Xuan immediately began to pacify the guests' mood and in the meantime notified this to the organizer before contacting the airlines staff involved. It turned out that the pilot strike caused the flight cancellation. And the groups were confirmed for no flight that day and the next flight would be notified after the strike.

Then the tour leader asked the airlines to issue a certificate of flight cancellation and reported that to China's organizer before taking the group out of the boarding hall with the luggage.

The next issue was to arrange hotel accommodation for the guests. As to the strike is a type of force majeure and number of guests is big, the airlines would not arrange accommodation and transportation for the group. Therefore, the organizer asked the German local operator to arrange a hotel for the guests. As it was 6:00 p. m. in Germany local time(Beijing time 12:00 p. m.), it would be difficult to book 16 hotel rooms at this moment. The tour leader suggested the organizer arrange a hotel nearby the airport for the guests, but the organizer did not follow this proposal due to the cost(sometimes hotels near the airport are more expensive). Two hours later, the local operator finally booked a hotel about 30 kilometers away from the airport. It would be hard to get a coach to transfer the guests there at 8:00 p. m. in Germany.

The tour leader suggested all of the group members take taxies to the hotel. First they inquired the price for renting a coach and were told 500 euros. Then the tour leader asked the local taxi drivers and were replied 60—70 euros.

After calculation, the total group of 30 people with luggage might need 7—8 taxies with a cost about 560 euros, and it would save much time. By then the guests were very tired after boarding from Shanghai and didn't take a good break for 25 hours and all tried to release their anger toward the tour leader. At last, the Chinese organizer agreed that the group take taxies to the hotel.

Back at the hotel, the group began to discuss about the follow-up of the itinerary. As they could not continue their tour to Iceland, it had to be changed to tour in Germany. Fortunately, they were informed that the original airlines could execute the flight on the second day. The guests became so excited and agreed to continue the tour in Iceland with a shortened schedule from four days to two days. In this way, the loss was minimized.

Comments

Strike is one means of communication between the employees and employers in the west. An outbound tour group will experience tremendous frustration if a strike happens during travel. As the itinerary has been set earlier, failure of any part of the tour may lead to serious problems and deserves a tour leader's careful consideration.

When a strike takes place, the tour leader should contact other airlines immediately to guarantee passengers' seats and request the original airline to issue a certificate for transfer to other airlines. Or he may ask the original airline for necessary arrangement and give the group priority to take the flight after the flights are normalized.

Outbound tours may experience accidents in flights such as: weather (low visibility, low clouds, thunderstorms, strong crosswind), air traffic control, mechanic failure, flight cancellation due to strike. Particularly, strike is one type of force majeure. The local travel agency must arrange the accommodation for the guests. As for the fare for reaching the hotel, sometimes renting a coach may not be cheaper than taking taxies(affected by additional work hours and the return trip cost). But the travel agency, considering the cost of the group, often tends to arrange a coach to transfer guests to the hotel. When there are quite many group members, it always turns out cheaper to take taxies(4 members for each taxi) than renting a coach. By then, the tour leader needs to convince the tour organizer in China to adjust the itinerary based on the latest information in the destination country (region), thus taking the guests to the hotel at the highest speed. The above case tells a typical example. I used to take the guests from the Night Safari, Singapore, to a hotel beside Little India and found out that taking a taxi by 4 was cheaper than taking the exclusive Night Safari line.

机上靠近紧急出口的位置该谁坐？

2008 年春节，某国际旅行社接手一家保险公司奖励员工赴"千岛之国"菲律宾旅游的团队。春节期间，领队人手非常紧张，年轻的小徐担任了此次团队的领队。

该团前几天的行程在当地导游和领队的配合下，相当顺利，团员们也非常开心，尽情享受着由 7100 多个岛屿组成的国家——菲律宾的美丽风景。但在最后一天离开马尼拉时，问题出现了。那天下午，客人按惯例提前 3 个小时来到机场，准备乘坐客机回国。在领队的协助下，客人顺利拿到了登机牌。飞机定于当地时间 11:30 起飞，预计 14:55 到达上海浦东机场。

飞机上，除了机组成员和七八个外国乘客，其余全是从菲律宾旅游回来的中国游客。机舱第 11 排座位左右两边是安全门，座位左边坐的是该保险公司的总经理，右侧为其他团队的客人。乘客坐稳后，过来一位空姐，用一口流利的英语与第 11 排座位上的乘客交谈。但乘客没听懂，空姐就找来领队翻译。空姐的意思为这是应急出口，紧急情况时，需要及时与懂英语的乘客沟通，希望 11 排的乘客和几位外国人换一下座位，以方便沟通。领队听得似懂非懂地告诉客人要换一下位子。右侧的乘客起了身，在空姐的安排下和老外换了个位子，但左侧的乘

173

客没动。空姐上前劝说,但他们就是不起身。"凭什么要我换座,我的登机牌上就是这个座位。为什么要让给外国人!"那位保险公司的总经理愤愤地说道。空姐再次说明情况,他便又大声地反问了一句:"难道你们航空公司就这样歧视中国人吗?"空姐听不懂他的话,但他那愤怒的表情让她感到很尴尬。于是,空姐找来了机长,但机长的劝说还是无用。机长联系了地面的警察,把他带下了飞机,理由是他威胁到了正常旅客的安全。出人意料的是,当这名总经理下飞机后,机上保险公司的20多位乘客也跟着下了飞机。

飞机起飞后,20多位客人滞留在飞机场,该团原订的机票作废,又要延长签证。客人又自费让当地的旅行社代订酒店及用餐,重新买了马尼拉回上海的机票。团员们也付出了巨大代价,第三天才登上飞机回到上海。回国后,保险公司投诉了这家国际旅行社。

[评析]

领队外语水平差是出境旅游服务质量差的重要原因。本案例的发生,保险公司总经理不听空姐劝说,没有调换到合适的位置上就座,这是客人的不对。但是,领队的英语水平差以及对国际航空协会的统一规定不熟悉,或者说根本不了解,是酿成这起事件的主要原因。试想,如果一名职业的领队对飞机的紧急出口的就座规定非常了解,他肯定会在空姐发言之前就对客人做好解释工作。另外,在空姐与客人争执的过程中,领队应该起到翻译与协调的作用,把矛盾弱化。

Who Should Be Seated near the Emergency Exit on the Plane?

In the Spring Festival of 2008, one international travel agency organized a group of staff from an insurance company to visit the Philippines, known as "A Country with Thousand Islands". During the Spring Festival, as the number of tour leaders was very limited, Mr. Xu, a young man, took the role of the tour leader of this group.

In the beginning, with the corporation of the destination's tour guide and leader, the itinerary went smoothly. The tourists were appreciating the beautiful scenery of the Philippines and had a great time. However, on the last day when they were leaving Manila, there was a problem. According to the route, the tourists came to the airport 3 hours ahead of the time to take the flight. With the help of the tour leader, the tourists got the boarding cards successfully. The plane was scheduled to take off at 11:30 a.m. and was going to land at Shanghai Pudong International Airport on 2:55 p.m.

On the plane, besides the plane staff and several foreign passengers, there were only Chinese tourists traveling back from the Philippines. On the left side and right side of Row 11 were emergency exit doors. The general manager of the insurance company was seated on the left. On the other side were the group's other tourists. After they were all seated, a flight attendant came and talked to the passengers of Row 11 in fluent English, but the passengers couldn't understand it. The flight attendant asked the leader of a tour group to interpret that she hoped the passengers in Row 11 could change the seats with a foreigners. Because these were emergency exists, if any emergency happened, they needed to communicate with the passengers who could understand English. The passengers on the left stood up and changed seats with foreigners with the arrangement of the flight attendant. The leader of the insurance company caught the information vaguely and asked his guests to change without clear explanation. The flight attendant persuaded them for a long time, but the guests didn't move. The general manager of the insurance company was indignant. He insisted that there should be no reason to change seats with a foreigner, for the seat number printed on the boarding card was where he was. The flight attendant repeated the reason again. But he shouted loudly, "Is that how you discriminate Chinese?" The flight attendant couldn't catch his Chinese, but the indignant expression of his face made her feel awkward. She could do nothing but find the captain. But what the captain did still didn't work either. The captain contacted the police on the ground. Soon the general manager was taken out of the plane for he had threatened the security of the passengers on the plane. Unexpectedly, when the general manager got off the plane, the other 20 passengers of the insurance company followed him.

The plane took off, leaving the tourists at the airport. The tickets became invalid, and their visas had to be extended. The tourists paid their own money to ask the local travel agency to book the hotel and the meals. They bought the tickets from Manila to Shanghai again. After making great efforts, they finally got on the plane on the third day. When they came back to China, the insurance company made a complaint about the international travel agency.

Comments

The poor foreign language ability of tour leaders is a main cause leading to poor travel quality. In the above case，it was the guest's mistake that the general manager of the insurance company didn't listen to the flight attendant. He refused to change seats with the foreigner. However，the poor English of the tour leader and his unfamiliarity with or even ignorance of the rules of International Air Association was the main reason that led to the occurrence of this case. A professional tour leader who was very familiar with the rules of emergency exit on plane must have explained to the guests before the flight attendant spoke. In addition，in the process of arguing between the attendant and the guests，the tour leader should take the responsibility to interpret and communicate in order to weaken the contradiction.

坐一艘大船去旅行

游轮,是一个大型商场。吃,喝,玩,乐,一样都不少。自助早餐、午餐、下午茶、晚餐和夜宵,一天五餐,中西结合,满足挑剔的味蕾。在甲板上,捧本书,来杯茶或咖啡,惬意。玩的项目是最多的:室外游泳池、健身中心、按摩浴缸、桑拿浴、图书馆。健身课程(有氧气操、伸展运动、舞蹈、踏板操等)还有健身房教练指导。当然日常活动也不少:游戏比赛、寻宝游戏、智力比赛、卡拉 OK、主题派对,更有船长参加的鸡尾酒欢迎会及提供特别菜单的联欢晚会。到了深夜,剧场还有各种音乐和表演。如果愿意,可以日日 high 到极点。

某国际旅游公司资深领队小蔡,通过自己多次带团赴游轮的经历,总结了游轮旅游与其他线路不同的 3 个特点。

首先,游轮能在 6 天或 7 天的行程中,游览两个国家,如:意大利"浪漫号"(Costa Romantica)游轮就能在 5 晚 6 天的时间里,游览两个国家的 3 个城市——日本的福冈、熊本,韩国的济州岛,这是与大部分出境游线路不同的。

其次,乘游轮旅行可以免去一路上的汽车长途跋涉的辛苦,免去飞机在高空的无奈无聊,还可以免去多次更换酒店收拾行李的麻烦。没有 morning call,想睡多久就睡多久,想吃几餐就吃几餐,特别适合老人和小孩出游。在这个连手机信号都没有的世界里人们可以抛开顾虑,远离压力,无拘无束,尽情享受游轮行驶在海上的悠闲时间,同时在海上感受大自然的浩瀚无边、变幻万千。

最后,游轮旅行的性价比确实很高,价格最便宜的内舱房每人只要2999元,加上游轮港务费、游轮服务费、全程领队小费、日本签证费(韩国济州岛免签证),以及上岸费,总花费在5000元左右。

领队小蔡的小孩读小学三年级,小孩同学的家长有知道小蔡是在旅游公司工作的,就让他推荐暑期的旅游目的地,小蔡推荐家长们带孩子游轮旅行并列出了以上的三条理由。这样,10户人家(33人)的甜蜜亲子游轮假期一下就定下来了。因为是在暑假出发,小蔡3月份的时候就在旅游公司订了船位,满足了大部分家庭欲订内舱房间的需求(往往是越便宜的舱位越早才容易订到)。

8月25日,10户人家30多人,浩浩荡荡的一个大团,按预定的行程在上海国际客运码头登上了"浪漫号"游轮。游轮上,每天的节目丰富多彩。孩子们在"思高"儿童俱乐部玩耍,大人们则在一旁的沙发上交流着育儿心得。家长们总结出游轮旅游的一个特点:无论孩子们在游轮上怎样"疯玩",他们最后肯定能找到他们的家(房间)。

在选择下船游览的自选线路时,领队小蔡根据小孩的兴趣,选择了"激情阿苏火山与经典熊本城""畅游太宰府天满宫、九州国立博物馆与购物"及"中文度假区——泰迪熊博物馆与购物"三条线路。当看到世界第一复式活火山——阿苏火山(阿苏火山群产生的火山灰超过了全球其他任何火山,也是熊本"火山国"美称的由来),孩子们激动不已。孩子们也从日本导游口中了解到太宰府天满宫相当于中国的孔庙。当看到坐落于韩国济州岛的泰迪熊博物馆时,孩子们群起欢呼。小朋友不仅拍照,还买回了自泰迪熊问世103年以来世界各地的多种泰迪熊布偶。

6天的行程马上就要结束了,领队小蔡在第五天晚上去团员的各房间巡视的时候,发现小孩都早早地枕着海风睡着了。不知是因为玩累了想回家了,还是小朋友期盼着一觉醒过来又到了一个新的国家(城市)。总之,睡梦中孩子们的脸上都挂着甜美的微笑,也许梦中又见到了一艘更大的船带他们去远方旅行。

[评析]

休闲游轮旅游源于 1835 年。马克·吐温在创作于 1869 年的畅销小说《傻子出国记》中将这种旅行方式巧妙地喻为"巨型野餐"。1904 年,P&O 游轮公司首次推出豪华级游轮短途旅行线路,标志着游轮旅游现代模式的形成。但是从 20 世纪 50 年代开始,乘飞机旅行逐渐兴起,游轮业的发展因此受到打击。70 年代游轮业开始复苏,1977—1986 年间播出的美国电视剧《爱之船》,使游轮旅游充满浪漫色彩。

近年来,游轮旅游不断发展,乘客人数逐年递增。根据中国交通运输协会的数据统计:2013 年乘坐游轮的人数已经高达 140 万人次,而 2005 年才 1 万人次。

中国交通运输协会会长钱永昌曾表示:"据测算,2020 年,游轮市场对我国经济的贡献将达到 510 亿元,成为我国航运业、旅游业的经济增长点。目前,游轮业发展早已达成共识,中国成全球游轮旅游业发展最快的新兴市场。"

领队小蔡是一名旅行社从业人员,能根据旅游市场主体分析法中的人口细分法(根据人口特征中的年龄因素,旅游市场可以分为老年旅游市场、中年旅游市场、青年旅游市场以及亲子市场),以及亲子市场的特点,向周边的朋友推荐游轮旅游,不失为一个很好的销售策略。

游轮旅游在欧美发达国家十分流行,是一种注重享受、亲近自然、贴近海洋的休闲度假方式。随着我国旅游业逐渐发展,游轮旅行也成了时下中国人出游的热选方式之一。游轮不同于普通客轮,它主要以提供游客享乐为目的。游轮行的内容一般包括航线以及游轮设施两个部分。大部分游轮都拥有 5 星设施,包括自助餐厅、游艺厅、健身房、泳池、购物中心、酒吧等,乘坐游轮本身也是旅途的重要经历。

Trip on a Big Cruise Ship

Cruise is like a large mall including activities of eating, drinking, playing and enjoying. Buffet breakfast, lunch, afternoon tea, dinner and night snack make up five meals a day, mixed with oriental and western styles. On board, people feel free to read books, drink tea or coffee. Most activities are held in outdoor swimming pools, fitness centers, massage bathtubs, saunas, libraries, fitness classes with guidance of gym instructors. Of course, there are many daily activities, such as games and competitions, treasure hunt, karaoke, theme parties, the cocktail reception attended by the captain, and gala with special menu. Until the midnight, there are all kinds of music and shows in the theatre. If you like, you can feel high every day.

Mr. Cai, a senior leader of an international tour company had a lot of experiences of tour with cruise ships, and he summarizes three different characters between cruises and other routes.

Firstly, cruise ships can visit two countries in six or seven days, such as Italy Costa Romantica cruise ship. It can also visit three cities of two countries in five nights and six days, namely, Fukuoka and Kumamoto of Japan, Jeju island of Korea. These are different from most outbound tourist routes (general

181

route is one route to one country).

Secondly, traveling by cruise ship is not as hard as by bus, not as boring as by plane, also not as inconvenient as changing hotels several times. Without morning call, you can sleep as long as you want, eat as much as you can. It's very suitable for old people and children. In the world without cell phone signals, people can throw off their worries, be far away from stress, enjoy the time at sea and feel the vast nature.

Finally, the price ratio of cruise travel is very high. The cheapest room only costs RMB 2,999 for one person. With the harbor service fee, tip for tour leader, visa fee of Japan (visa-free of Cheju, Korea) and landing tour fee. The cost of cruise trip amounts to around RMB 5,000 in total.

Mr. Cai's child is a pupil of grade three. The parents of the child's classmate knew that Mr. Cai worked in the tour company, and came to ask him to recommend a tourist destination for summer holidays. Mr. Cai recommended that they travel by cruise ship, and gave them the three reasons above. Then the family's happy cruise trip was set in the winter holidays. Mr. Cai booked the ship's positions in March. This could fulfill most families' requirements of booking the cabin rooms.

On 25th, August, the 10 families got on the Costa Romantica cruise ship. On the cruise ship, there were many kinds of programs. Children were playing in the children club. Their parents were chatting beside. No matter how crazily the children played, they could finally find their families.

When it came to choosing optional tours, the tour leader Mr. Cai picked up three routes of "Asosan and Kumamoto city", "Dazaifu Tenmang, Kyushu National Museum and shopping" and "Jungmun Tourist Complex, Jeju Teddy Bear Museum and shopping". When children saw the world's first resurrection volcanic, Asosan, they were quite excited. Children also learned from the

Japanese guide that the Dazaifu Tenmang equaled to China's Confucian temple. Jeju Teddy Bear Museum located in the Jeju Island suddenly became lively. Children not only took pictures, but also bought many kinds of teddy bears from all over the world.

The 6-day trip was coming to an end. On the fifth night, tour leader Mr. Cai found that all the children had already fallen asleep. He didn't know if they were so tired and wanted to go home, or they wished they would be in a new country when they woke up, but he know the children were smiling happily in the dreams. Maybe they dreamed that they were on a bigger ship for further trips.

Comments

The popular novel *The Innocents Abroad* which was written by Mark Twain in 1869 called the cruise trip a "giant picnic". In 1904, The P & O cruise ship company first launched short trip routes by luxury cruise ship, which marks the form of modern cruise trip. But since the 1950s, travel by plane has become more popular than cruise tour. In the 1970s, the cruise tour started to recover. Between 1977 and 1986, with the American teleplay *The Love Boat*, the cruise trip was full of romantic colors.

Recently, cruise trips are developing. According to the statistics by China Communication and Transportation Association, those who took cruise in 2013 reached 1.4 million person-times, while it was merely 10 thousand person-times in 2005.

The head of the association once said, "It is estimated that the cruise market will contribute RMB 5.1 billion to our national economy by the year 2020, and has become a hot spot of growth in transportation and tourism industry. Currently, it has been commonly recognized in the cruise circle that China is the fastest emerging market of the global cruise industry."

Mr. Cai worked for a travel agency. He could adopt effective methods according to the subject of tourist market's population segmentation and separate the tourist market into old people tourist market, middle age tourist market, young people tourist market and family tourist market. According to the characteristics of family tourist market, he could recommend friends around to specific cruises. It was a very good sale strategy.

Cruise tour is very popular in Europe and America. It is a way of going on holidays close to nature and sea. With the development of our tourism, cruise tour is becoming one of the hottest ways chosen for Chinese people. Cruise ships are different from common passenger ships. Its main goal is making tour experience enjoyable. Enjoying a cruise tour generally includes two parts: enjoying the route and enjoying the facilities of the cruise ship. Most cruise ships own five-star facilities, a buffet restaurant, a recreation hall, a gymnasium, a swimming pool, a shopping mall, a bar, and so on. Taking cruises itself is also an important journey experience.

24 小时内转机的学问

自由奔跑在原野上,激动的心尽情地驰骋……

这就是肯尼亚,一个美丽的东非国家。

2008 年的某一天,有着 5 年领队工作经验的资深领队小王带领 5 名客人去肯尼亚旅游。由于在中国除了广州以外没有直接飞肯尼亚的航班,所以旅行社安排客人在泰国首都曼谷素万那普国际机场转机赴肯尼亚首都内罗毕。

出发那天,客人顺利地从上海飞到了曼谷。在曼谷机场,领队小王为客人办理转机手续时,柜台值机人员对小王说,由于你们 6 人没有提前确认机票,曼谷—内罗毕航段的座位已经没有了。客人听了非常着急,没有座位便意味着得等上几天才能到达内罗毕。因为曼谷到内罗毕不是天天有航班的,且不说要推迟抵达内罗毕,费用也会额外增加,旅游时间亦会缩水。客人顿时焦虑不安起来,纷纷询问领队该如何解决。小王一边劝客人不要着急,一边与机场人员交涉。值机人员告知小王,你们的联程机票没有确认,所以被取消了。听到这番话,小王突然有了灵感,便对值机人员说:"按航空公司的规定,持联程机票的旅客到一中转地,必须在 72 小时之内确认。而我们只是在曼谷机场转机,根本没超过 24 小时,别说是 72 小时了,你的理论是不成立的,你应该为我们安排航班。"值机人员听了小王的解释，觉得非常有道理，于是，值机人员在向主管请示后，将另外 6 名候补客人的机位挤掉，给他们 6 位办理了登机牌。拿到登机牌后，客人们都松了一口气，夸小王真能干，感谢他解决了困难。

等此团回到中国，领队小王与旅行社的计调人员核实发生此情况的原因时发现，原来是航空公司的电脑出了问题，导致了这次意外。

[评析]

领队的资深不一定表现在其走过世界的角角落落，却必然表现在其带团过程中的每一个细节。案例中所发生的这一幕，在航班座位较满的情况下是经常会发生的。机位候补的客人往往早早地等候在办理登机手续的柜台前，等候办理，以争取尽早拿到登机牌。而航空公司的值机人员往往会找出各种理由取消那些没有确认的机位。领队小王敢于与航空公司交涉并最终成功，这些都建立在对所学知识的灵活掌握上，假设小王并不懂"旅客座位再证实"的国际条文，被航空公司值机人员的一句话弄得不知所措，也没有有力的证据去说服值机人员，后果将是什么呢？旅行社将面临的是什么呢？投诉、赔偿……这就说明领队仅仅有良好的服务意识是不够的，本身需要有大量的知识储备，还要能从容冷静地面对并解决困难。工作中 1% 的疏忽会抵消 99% 的努力，会造成无可估量的损失。

美国作家特里·培根、戴维·皮尤所著《赢在细节》中说，面对不断同质化的产品，面对激烈竞争的市场，企业想把自己与竞争对手区别开来变得越来越困难了——至少依靠传统做法是很难做到的。本书作者结合自己多年的咨询经验，在广泛调研的基础上，通过剖析丽嘉酒店、西南航空公司、沃尔沃公司等各具特色的典型企业的成功模式，向读者介绍了一种竞争利器——行为方式差异化。这种差异化即通过长久保持独树一帜的行动方式和企业文化，在经营及与客户接触等各个环节上注重细节，从而形成竞争优势。

Transfer within 24 Hours

Running freely on the plain with a heart soaring ...

This is Kenya, a beautiful country in East Africa.

Mr. Wang was a senior tour guide with at least 5 years' working experience. Once he took 5 guests to Kenya for a travel in the year of 2008. As there was no direct flight to Kenya except Guangzhou in China at that time, the travel agency arranged them for a transfer to another flight in Suvarnabhumi International Airport of Bangkok in Thailand.

On the day of departure, the guests flew from Shanghai to Bangkok. When Mr. Wang helped them proceed to the transfer counter for their connecting flight, the check-in staff informed him that seats on the flight from Bangkok to Nairobi were all full, as they hadn't previously confirmed the air tickets. As there was no daily flight from Bangkok to Nairobi, it meant they had to wait for days till the next flight was available. The arrival time would be delayed. Besides, there would be additional cost and also the schedule of the trip would be changed for the late arrival. The guests were so anxious that they asked Wang for an explanation.

Mr. Wang appeased guests and negotiated with the airport personnel. For a while he was informed by the check-in staff that their joint-way air tickets were cancelled due to their failure to confirm the tickets. It was unacceptable to Wang, and he attempted to negotiate with the check-in staff. According to the rules of the airline, guests have to confirm the joint-way air tickets within 72 hours. However, Wang and his guests had been here for a transfer flight for less than 24 hours.

After negotiation, with the permission of higher authorities, the check-in staff allowed them to check in and gave them boarding cards. The guests were much relieved and appreciated that. After they finished the journey and came back to China, Wang, with his colleagues, investigated into this incident and found that it was the malfunction of computer of the airline that led to the accident.

Comments

The degree of expertise a tour guide needs does not depend on how many places he or she has traveled but on his or her attention to the details during the whole journey. What happened in this case is also what happens often if the flight is fully booked, and the candidates have to wait early in the counter for check-in. But the staff of the airline used to cancel those unconfirmed tickets with proper excuses. The negotiation between Wang and the airline staff was based on Wang's expertise and experience. If he didn't have enough knowledge on the international rule of airline industry, he would be confused by the words of the check-in staff at the airport and would be faced with complaints and compensation claims of the guests.

Good service, full knowledge on and experience in tourism are also the basis of being a good tour guide. It is necessary to be calm when faced with problem and tour leaders should try their best to resolve difficulties. 1% carelessness in the work will result in your 99% efforts in vain. Cursoriness will cause incalculable loss.

In the book *Winning Behavior* written by Terry Bacon and David Pugh，the homogenization of products and the gradually fierce competition make it more difficult for enterprises to be differentiated from their competitors based on traditional ways. This book，based on the writer's years of consulting experience and extensive research，and through the analysis of successful modes of enterprises such as Ritz-Carlton，Southwest Airlines and Volvo，introduces to readers the competitive edge tool called differentiating behaviors. Such differentiation makes the competitive edge of enterprises by persistently keeping the independent type of operation and corporate culture and by paying attention to the details of all the sections of the management and CRM.

在英国，像英国人一样生活 /250

When in Britain, Do as the British Do

入乡随俗，在欣赏了英国街头行为艺术的同时，你也需要付小费

As a local custom, one needs to tip for the
behavioral art on the streets in England

优质的服务源于经验的积累——在越南岘港享用海鲜餐 /254

Service of High Quality Comes from the Accumulation of Experience:
Enjoy Seafood in Da Nang, Vietnam

游客抵达斯里兰卡一家五星级酒店后，服务人员派送休闲食品给他们

Guests are given snack food by service staff
after they reach a five-star hotel in Sri Lanka

[第五篇]
Chapter V
全球导游服务篇
World Wide Tour Guide Services

在中国美术学院学习过的斯里兰卡导游拉吉夫，绝对的南亚风范

Sri Lanka tour guide Rajiv, who studied in China Academy of
Arts, is of pure South-Asian style

作者带团赴台湾时，与台湾导游在野柳地质公园的合影

A photo of the author and a Taiwan tour guide
in Yehliu Geopark

忍耐与等待之后，一切都会好的 /295

Everything Will Go Well after Endurance and Waiting

夏宫由美丽的喷泉、公园、宫殿组成，是圣彼得堡著名的旅游景点

Summer Palace consists of beautiful water fountains,
parks and palaces, a famous scenic spot in St. Peterburg

在阿联酋的旅游车上充当沿途导游 /301

Being a Tour Guide on a UAE Tour Bus

作者在澳大利亚凯恩斯与一日游司机的合影

A photo of the author and one-day-tour driver in Keynes, Australia

在斯里兰卡度蜜月 /307

Honeymoon in Sri Lanka

斯里兰卡导游每天给每位客人准备一朵鲜花，
每天早上游客都会收获这样一个惊喜

The Sri Lanka tour guide prepares a fresh flower for
each guest every day, a surprise for them every morning

一位被洋流冲走的客人得救了 /312

A Tourist Rescued from the Ocean Current

印尼巴厘岛阿勇河漂流惊险刺激，但一定要注意安全

Drifting on Ayung River in Bali Island, Indonesia, is thrilling, but safety is still the priority

游客在马来西亚皇宫前被马咬了一口 /317

A Guest Bitten by a Horse in Front of the Malaysia Imperial Palace

马来西亚皇宫

Imperial palace in Malaysia

[第六篇]
Chapter VI

境外游览享受篇
Enjoyment in Outbound Destinations

法国巴黎罗浮宫内，导游员正在绘声绘色地讲解

The vivid narration of a tour guide in the Louvre, France

作者参加2014年意大利旅游展销会的留影

A photo of the author in 2014 Italy Tourism Fairs

定制"新马"亲子游　　/338

Tailor-made Parent-child Travel of Singapore and Malaysia

新马亲子游中的10位小朋友在新加坡圣淘沙名胜世界的合影

Ten children of a parent-child tour in Singapore and Malaysia
take a group photo in Resorts World Sentosa, Singapore

墨尔本大洋路一日游　　/344

One-day Tour on Great Ocean Road in Melbourne

马来西亚华人在墨尔本经营的长青旅游公司

Extragreen Holidays in Melbourne run by Malaysian Chinese

8位客人的旅游巴士？　　/351

The 8 Visitors' Tour Bus?

英国巴斯街上的观光车绘有多少面国旗，
就意味着车上导游能用多少种语言进行沿途风光讲解

The number of national flags on the sightseeing bus on Bath Street in the UK
indicates the number of languages for presentation of sightseeing

造访澳华历史博物馆 /356
A Visit to the Australian Chinese Museum

作者与澳大利亚墨尔本大街上穿红上衣、戴红帽子的人合影，
他们是旅游服务志愿者，腰包是放置旅游宣传册的

A photo of the author and those with red blouses and caps
on the street in Melbourne.They are volunteers offering service
to tourists and their waist bags have tour safety guidelines inside

瑞士边境购物一日游 /364
One-day Shopping Tour across Swiss Border

意大利旅行社的门市接待处除了出售旅行产品外，还出
售书籍和本地纪念品

The reception service of an Italian travel agency
sells not only tour products, but also books and
local souvenirs

澳洲黄金海岸自由行 /371
Free and Easy Tour to Gold Coast in Australia

十二门徒石位于澳大利亚墨尔本海岸沿线

The Twelve Apostles are located along
the coastline of Melbourne in Australia

在日本自助点餐机上点餐   /377
Order Food by Machine in Japan

在日本的高速公路休息站，有许多餐厅安装自助点餐机，在机器上点完餐后，服务员不久就会将餐食送到您手里
Many restaurants at the rest areas of expressways in Japan are equipped with food order machines, which allow waiters to deliver your order soon

与客人在狮城自由活动一天   /381
A Free Activity Day with the Guests in Singapore

赴新加坡自由行，一定不能忘了参观夜间野生动物园
The Night Safari is a must when you travel in Singapore independently

第四篇

Chapter IV

品牌酒店感悟篇

Perceptions of Famous Hotels

[**本章导读**]

　　旅游者在境外进行观光旅游，其入住酒店的优劣对其能否顺利完成旅游计划有举足轻重的作用。自由行游客和出境游领队应对自己下榻饭店的情况，诸如酒店名称、星级、位置、周围交通设施、酒店内部布局、康乐设施、国际长途电话收费标准、无线网络的使用、周边治安情况等了解清楚。这样才能在享受酒店服务的同时，增长酒店的专业知识。此外，出境游领队也可以借此给客人提供良好的服务。

　　本篇介绍了世界各地的品牌酒店，让读者了解出境旅游入住境外酒店时的要求，以及了解世界各地品牌酒店的服务项目等。

〔Chapter Outline〕

For tourists traveling abroad for sightseeing, quality of hotels plays a pivotal role in the successful completion of travel plans. Both independent outbound tourists and professional tour leaders should get familiar with hotels, such as hotel name, star rating, location, transport facilities, internal layout, recreational facilities and rates for international calls, Wi-Fi service, and its perimeter security situations. They can enrich themselves with hotel expertise while enjoying hotel service, and outbound tour leaders can provide better services for guests.

In this part, through the introduction of famous hotels around the world, the author is trying to let readers know the requirements of staying in world-famous hotels and their service scope.

体验洛桑的酒店服务

翻开瑞士地图，主要的旅游城市包括伯尔尼、苏黎世、卢塞恩、洛桑、日内瓦、因特拉肯等。而洛桑和日内瓦是此次瑞士之行最主要的游览城市。

我们从法国小镇博纳出发，一路嗅着芬芳四溢的葡萄酒香（博纳位于法国东部勃艮第葡萄园区），经过建造于 15 世纪的主宫医院（电影《虎口脱险》里修道院的原型，目前这里已经成为葡萄酒博物馆），中午时分抵达日内瓦，观赏了日内瓦湖上 140 米水柱的大喷泉，以及象征着瑞士钟表生产历史地位的大花钟。

从日内瓦到洛桑 100 公里的路途中，我们参观了瑞士最著名的西墉城堡后，抵达了日内瓦湖畔的瑞士第二大城市——洛桑。洛桑是沃州的首府，位于日内瓦湖畔北部沿岸的中心，和日内瓦、伯尔尼、苏黎世相连接，是通过高速列车到达巴黎的交通中心。大家兴致勃勃地参观了世界上收藏奥运会资料最全面的博物馆——国际奥运会和奥林匹克博物馆。游览结束后，入住位于日内瓦湖畔的洛桑慕温匹克酒店。

一走进酒店，我们就被酒店前台的设计所吸引。前台由三个半月形大理石柜台所组成，每个柜台内可以站立 3 个工作人员。这意味着，前台接待人员在同时接待 3 批客人时，互不干扰，非常人性化。接待小姐在给我们房间钥匙时，特别认真地告诉我们:每个房间均可上网,用户名和密码均已经印制在钥匙卡里的小纸片上。

我进了自己的房间,迫不及待地用手机试着连接网络,却发现不能上网。于是,我拿着手机和小纸片跑到前台询问,小姐微笑地重新给了我一张印有用户名和密码的小纸片。见我依然担心网络连不上,便对我说:"让我来帮你试试。"我将手机交给她。在调试的过程中,手机跳出了中文的界面,小姐俏皮地对我说:"这个我就无能为力了。"我将页面上的中文翻译成了英文。她操作几下以后,手机就能上网了。"谢谢你。"我脱口而出,那位小姐也会心地一笑。

第二天早上,我用完早餐正准备离开时,又碰见了昨晚的那位小姐。她面带微笑地问我:"后来手机能上网吗?"我说:"一直可以上的。"在这样愉快的对话中,我们离开了酒店。

[评析]

有这么一个段子:在国外旅游时,意大利人喜欢寻找晒日光浴的地方,德国人喜欢到处潜水,法国人会问美女多吗,而中国人问得最多的一句话是:哪里有Wi-Fi?

21世纪是互联网的时代,提供智能化服务以及帮助客人使用智能化设施也是提高酒店服务质量的一个方向。不管是在异国他乡,还是在本国的地盘,服务人员如果能帮助客人解决一些智能化设备使用方面的难题,客人就会对这个酒店或目的地留下良好的印象。以上就是"智能化+个性化的服务=优质服务"的案例。

瑞士这个国家除了钟表非常不错,酒店管理也是世界一流的。享誉全球的洛桑酒店管理学院是世界上办学最早、学科最全面的学校。入住洛桑的这家酒店,一下子就有了不一样的感觉。硬件设计简约化、人性化;软件服务亲切主动,让人们不禁感叹瑞士的酒店确实还是与众不同的。

Experiencing Hotel Service in Lausanne

Taking a look at the map of Switzerland, we can see some major tourist cities like Berne, Zurich, Lucerne, Lausanne, Geneva, Interlaken, etc. Lausanne and Geneva were the cities we were going to visit on this trip.

We set off from the French town, Beaune, which is located on Burgundy vineyard in the eastern France. The hospice de beaune, built in the 15th century, the prototype of the Monastery in *La Grande Vadrouille*, has now been turned into a wine museum. Upon arriving in Geneva at noon, we were fascinated by the 140-meter-high fountain and the Flower Clock that represents the quality and status of Swiss watches and clocks.

After the 100 kilometers' trip from Geneva to Lausanne, we visited Chateau de Chillon and finally arrived in Lausanne, the second largest city of Switzerland around the Geneva Lake. Located along the northern bank of the Lake Geneva and connected with Geneva, Berne and Zurich, Lausanne is the capital city of Canton of Vaud. People can arrive in Paris through TGV. We visited the International Olympic Museum and went to Mövenpick Hotel Lausanne.

We were attracted by the design of the reception area upon entering the hotel. The reception area was composed of 3 half-moon-shaped marble desks.

209

Each desk has 3 receptionists, receiving 3 groups of tourists at one time without interfering with each other. It was quite tourist-friendly. The receptionists told us patiently that each room had access to the Internet. The user name and password were printed on a small piece of paper in the room card bag.

I checked in and failed to get access to the Internet. The lady at the reception desk gave me another piece of paper with user name and password on it. I was still worrying about connection failure. She found my worries and help me. The cell phone's language was Chinese, so I switched it into English. She tried a few times. Finally, I got to surf the Internet with my cell phone.

The next morning, I ran into the lady who helped me last night. She asked whether my cell phone was Okay with the Internet. I replied yes. We had a really pleasant conversation.

Comments

There goes a fun saying that Italians like to do sun-bathing, Germans like scuba-diving, French people ask how many beauties, and Chinese people like to ask where Wi-Fi is.

The 21st century is an era of the Internet. Smart devices are widely used. It is a goal for hotels to provide smart services and help tourists with smart devices. If service staff could help tourists solve problems about smart devices, the whole trip would leave a nice impression on tourists. The above case is a great example of premium service = intelligence + personalized service.

Switzerland boasts world class watches, clocks and hotel management as well. The world-renowned Ecole Hoteliere Lausanne is the earliest college specializing in hotel management with the most comprehensive subjects. Staying in Mövenpick Hotel Lausanne gives tourists special feelings. The design of the hotel is simple and tourist-friendly. Meanwhile the service is sincere and active.

在迪拜得到的特殊礼遇

迪拜人一向以擅长建造巨大、醒目的建筑物闻名全球,他们拥有全球最大的人工岛——棕榈岛,位于阿联酋购物中心的世界最大的室内滑雪场,还拥有全球第一家七星级酒店——帆船酒店。迪拜塔的揭幕,又令迪拜人拥有全球第一摩天大楼。如今的迪拜成了不折不扣的奢华的代名词。

当你来到这个沙漠之国,除了体验迪拜一座座奇异别致、创造奇迹的建筑外,购物也是不可错过的畅快体验。迪拜一直推行低进口税及无销售税的政策,历来便有"购物天堂"之称,一线品牌的化妆品、香水、服饰和皮具比国内便宜不少,给不少购物扫货的游客带来极大诱惑。

领队小范带团去了海湾六国(沙特阿拉伯、阿拉伯联合酋长国、阿曼、卡塔尔、巴林、科威特)之一的阿联酋。从杭州经香港转机,飞行了11个小时,终于抵达了阿联酋的第一大城市——迪拜。让人觉得奇怪的是,香港飞迪拜的香港国泰航空航班上的空姐并没有让乘客填写进入阿联酋的入境卡和海关申报单。下了飞机后,客人跟着领队小范沿着"Arrival(抵达)"和"Luggage Claim(行李领取)"的指示牌,很容易地找到了"Passport Control(护照检查)"。领队想这样就可以入关了,手续真是太容易了。就在这时,一位身穿阿拉伯白色长袍的男性工

211

作人员请领队带领整团先去"Visa Collection(签证收集)"处照一下眼膜。照完眼膜后,工作人员就在客人预先打印出的电子签证上盖章。这时客人们拿着盖章的电子签证打印件和护照去移民局才能过关。

过了移民局,客人们各自拿到了自己的行李,出了海关。团员们纷纷议论着,阿联酋这个石油王国与别的国家在入关时真的不一样,不知道往后还有什么特殊的事情会发生。

该团的行程是6天阿联酋之旅。团员们在迪拜足足有4天的游览时间。该团去迪拜的时间是8月份,正值伊斯兰教的斋月。考虑到斋月的特殊性,领队小范和导游露西商量,尽量将最精彩的行程安排在最后面。所以,露西将最后一天(即第五天)的行程调整为:中午在七星级的帆船酒店享用自助餐,晚上登全球最高楼——迪拜塔。领队觉得这样的安排着实让客人期待很多。

客人在阿联酋首都阿布扎比参观了谢赫·扎耶德大清真寺。该清真寺目前规模位列世界第三,是伊斯兰建筑史上的杰作,收藏有世界最大的波斯地毯。扎耶德大清真寺是为纪念1972年建立阿联酋后的第一任总统谢赫·扎耶德而建的。他曾经是阿布扎比酋长国的国王,于2005年去世。阿联酋正是在他领导下逐步发展到今天的。整个建筑群都用来自希腊的汉白玉包裹着,内部装饰金碧辉煌。来到这里,有一种净化心灵的感觉。在阿联酋第三大酋长国沙迦,客人们无不为阿联酋的奢华而震惊。

第5天终于盼到了,客人们上午游览了迪拜的国家博物馆和迪拜河,中午来到了帆船酒店。大家根据领队在行前说明会上的要求,都穿上了休闲风格的服装。但引台小姐将整团客人引入座位时,有3位客人却被挡在了餐厅门外,理由是客人穿的是旅游鞋。这3位客人对此十分恼火。这时,领队灵机一动,将自己的鞋子给一位客人穿上,自己等在餐厅的休息厅,又请导游向司机借了一双鞋,再向餐厅借了一双鞋,客人这才顺利地进入餐厅,愉快地享用这顿丰盛的自助餐。

6天的行程精彩而短暂,客人们回味无穷。

[评析]

　　眼睛中的虹膜是人体器官中组织特征最稳定最不容易改变的部分。虹膜是一种可见且受到保护的结构，它通常不会随着时间的变化而变化，因此是进行生物识别的理想部位。多数情况下，即使人们的眼睛接受过外科手术，虹膜的结构也不会发生变化。即使是盲人，只要眼睛中的虹膜未缺失，就可以使用虹膜扫描仪扫描。玻璃镜片和隐形眼镜一般不影响数据读取，也不会导致读取误差。

　　虹膜扫描仪能够通过对眼睛虹膜的扫描，准确地辨认出所有过境旅客的身份，入境检查人员完全可以根据扫描结果来判断是否要让旅客通过。这个精确的系统在辨认身份上，可谓万无一失。每个人的虹膜，都各有特点。即使是双胞胎，虹膜的特征也不会完全一样。而且虹膜的结构和特征是终生不会改变的，所以它的稳定性要比指纹来得高。人们不可能通过改造虹膜来掩饰自己的身份。

　　一些国际机场在客人进行入境检查时通过虹膜扫描的方式来确认旅游者的身份。由于中东地区经常有恐怖分子的袭击，所以，阿联酋也通过这种方式来确认旅游者的身份。领队应该在出发前告知客人进入阿联酋的必备手续，让客人积极配合，有序地完成入关手续。

　　当你打开帆船酒店的官方网站时，你可以看到网站上就有对用餐客人的着装要求。大意是午餐时，男士要求穿有领衬衫、长裤或者休闲牛仔裤、满帮鞋。女士要求穿套装或者连衣裙、长裙或短裙与较为讲究的便上衣。阿联酋民族服装在这里也是很受欢迎的。如果穿着短裤、汗衫、拖鞋和运动鞋等着装都是不允许进餐厅的。

　　此案例中，虽然领队在行前说明会上强调过赴帆船酒店的着装要求，但由于游客在着装上的随意，如团队中有一位客人在整个旅途中只穿一双旅游鞋，因此无法调换，加上导游在用餐之前没有反复强调，造成了客人存在着无所谓的想法。所以，类似这样的情况，领队应该在旅途中反复提醒客人用餐的着装要求，把话说在事情发生之前。

Special Courtesy in Dubai

It's an accepted fact that Dubai people are well-known all around the world because of the tremendous and splendid buildings they built. The biggest artificial island in the world—the Palm Islands—is made by them; Mall of the Emirates has the biggest indoor ski resort within; and the first seven-star hotel, Burj Al Arab is also located there. The opening of Burj Khalifa Tower gives Dubai people one more No. 1—the highest skyscraper in the world.

Right now Dubai has become a code of pure and simple luxury.

When you pay a visit to this desert country, besides the fantastic architectures, shopping is another lightsome experience. This country promotes low import duty and none sales tax policies, so it enjoys the title of "shopping paradise." Some top brand cosmetics, perfumes, trappings and leather wares are much cheaper. It's a very big temptation for the people to go shopping there.

The tour leader Miss Fan took a tour group to visit one of the six gulf countries—The United Arab Emirates. The 11-hour flight was from Hangzhou to Dubai via Hong Kong. What surprised them was that the airhostess of Cathay Pacific Airways did not ask passengers to fill in arrival cards and customs declaration forms of the United Arab Emirates on the plane. Following the signs of "Arrival" and "Luggage Claim", "Passport Control" was easily found by Miss Fan. She thought doing arrival formalities would be very convenient. Right at that time, a staff member at the airport wearing an Arabian robe took the whole group to go to the visa collection to check the retina. After that, the staff there affixed a seal to your printed electric visa. Finally, the guests passed the passport control with the stamped electric visas and the passports.

After the passport control, the tourists found their own luggage and passed the customs. The United Arab Emirates is really different from other countries. They were wondering what other special things might be waiting for them.

It was a 6-day tour in Dubai. They had a 4-day sightseeing arrangement there. It was August when we went to Dubai and the right time for Ramadan of Islam. Considering this festival, the tour leader Miss Fan and the local guide Lucy decided to put the most wonderful parts of the tour in the end. So the last day in Dubai they arranged a buffet lunch in the seven-star Burj Al Arab Hotel, and climbing the highest skyscraper in the world—Burj Khalifa Tower at night.

The tour group visited Sheikh Zayed Grand Mosque in the capital city of United Arab Emirates—Abu Dhabi. This temple is a masterpiece of Islam construction, ranking No.3 in the world. The temple keeps the largest Persian carpets in the world. They built this temple in order to commemorate the first president of United Arab Emirates—Sheikh Zayed who had this country founded in 1972. He used to be the king of Abu Dhabi, and passed away in 2005. Under his leadership, the UAE developed with a fast speed. All the houses are covered by marbles from Greece and decorated magnificently inside. It's a very good place to retreat your soul. The tour group also visited the third largest emirate of the UAE—Sharjah.

In the morning of the fifth day, the group visited the national museum and

Dubai River and in the afternoon they went to the Burj Al Arab Hotel. According to the requirements of pre-tour briefing, everyone should be in casual style clothing. This time, three people were rejected entry by the usher lady because they wore sneakers. The three tourists were certainly very angry. Seeing this, the tour leader offered a pair of shoes to one of the three guests. She also borrowed another pair from the driver and got the third pair from the restaurant. In this way the problem was solved.

Comments

The iris of the eye is one of the steadiest and the least likely to be changed part of our human organs. The iris is a kind of visible and protected structure, and is the ideal part to do biometrics because normally it won't change over time. In most cases, even your eyes have received surgery, the iris won't change; for blind people if your iris is not missing, the iris scanning is valid; glasses and contact lens generally do not affect the data for reading.

Iris scanners can accurately tell the identities of all the passengers and the customs officers can completely rely on the results to determine whether to let the passengers go through. To use this precise system to identify can be described as a very safe way. Different people have different characteristics about the iris around the pupil. Even for the twins, their irises are not exactly the same. Because the structures and the characteristics will not change in your life, so the stability of iris is much higher than fingerprint. It's not possible for people to conceal their real identities by changing the irises.

Some international airports use the iris scanner to identify the tourists. As the problem of terrorist attacks is serious in the Middle East, the UAE also adopts this way to identify. Before starting the trip the tour leader should tell every guest about the necessary formalities of the UAE, and the guests should cooperate with the tour leader and finish the formalities in order.

When you open the official website of the Burj Al Arab Hotel, you will notice the dress requirements.

In brief, for lunch, gentlemen are requested to wear shirts with collars, long trousers or smart jeans, closed shoes. Ladies are requested to wear suits or dresses, long or short skirts or dressy slacks and tops. The UAE national dress is welcome. For gentlemen, shorts, T-shirts, flip-flops, sneakers, etc., are not allowed.

In this case, the tour leader had already made a statement about the dress requirements of the Burj Al Arab Hotel in the tour briefing, because of the ignorance of dressing taboos. For example, one of the guests had been just wearing the same shoes during the whole trip, so there was nothing to change. But the local guide did not repeat the requests before the lunch. Therefore, the tour leader ought to repeat important things over and over again during the trip.

一套餐厅服务员制服所引发的话题

"绝美锡兰—兰卡 7 天 6 晚世界尽头之旅",行程是从杭州起飞抵达香港,再从香港飞往科伦坡,经停新加坡,总共飞行 8 小时 50 分钟。抵达科伦坡时已经是当地时间 22:40。团队在科伦坡附近住了一个晚上,第二天离开科伦坡前往斯里兰卡东北部的狮子岩。团队在古城波隆纳鲁沃附近的小城哈勃拉那中的 Cinnamo Lodge 度假村住了两晚,客人们被安排入住一幢幢别具特色的小别墅。

入住第一晚的晚餐,客人被安排在游泳池旁的自助餐厅用餐,连领队在内整个团一共 20 人。餐厅经理安排团队用 10 人一桌的西餐桌用餐,共两桌。并告知,入住酒店期间第二天的早、晚餐以及第三天的早餐均安排在同样的餐桌,便于客人寻找。

入住酒店第一天的晚餐,我给客人介绍了自助餐台菜肴的摆放位置并特别介绍了斯里兰卡的特色菜肴——炒饼。用餐期间,客人饶有兴致地谈论着南亚国家酒店餐厅的环境、菜肴的特色。我在一旁参与客人的聊天,用餐的气氛非常好。加之团体中有四五个小孩同行,谈话的内容非常有趣。

第二天早上,团员们仍在这个餐厅用餐,我继续将斯里兰卡的特色早餐圆煎饼介绍给客人。由于大家用完早餐后还要赶去参观波隆纳鲁沃古城,因此大家各自问早安后，没有更多地展开话题。

第二天晚餐时，大家还是在同样的餐厅用晚餐，可能是因为一天的行程比较赶，所以客人个个看上去比较累。用餐时，大家似乎没有聊天的兴致，气氛比较沉闷。这时，我故意将一位服务员叫到身边，问他："为什么今天你们穿的服装与昨天的服务员穿的服装不一样？"男服务员微笑着地对我说："我们的服务人员换了一批，餐厅服务人员服装的要求是每天穿的服装不能与前一天相同。"我及时将我与服务员的对话翻译给了部分客人，客人一下子来了兴趣，都凑过来倾听。这个服务员问我们从哪里来，我说我们来自中国杭州，他憨厚地笑了笑并摇头告诉我们，他没有去过中国。我随即拿出一张印有"三潭印月"图案的一元人民币给他看，告诉他我们的家乡在中国杭州。他听了我的介绍后告诉我，最近越来越多的中国旅游团来到斯里兰卡，他们也开始慢慢地了解中国了。

忽然，这位服务员似乎意识到什么，认真地告诉我，他是一位钱币收藏爱好者，各国的货币都收藏，包括中国在内。我将此段话翻译给客人听后，客人马上拿出各种硬币给服务员，服务员顿觉受宠若惊，连声说"谢谢大家！"

随后，这位服务员又继续为大家服务，而当他经过我们团的餐桌的时候，也总是微笑地点点头，和团友们友好互动。

[评析]

随着出境游价格的不断降低，出境旅游越来越呈现出大众化的倾向。出境游领队在带团的过程中可以遇到社会中各个层面的人。人们谈论的话题五花八门，所显示出来的个性也是千差万别。有些旅游者什么场合都能高谈阔论，有些旅游者总是沉默无语。怎样让团队游客通过出境旅游的机会相互认识，结交朋友，也成了出境游领队带团要考虑的一个问题。

领队可以在大巴上让客人进行自我介绍，这也是领队与团友相互认识并尽快熟悉的好方法。案例中，领队借助第三方的力量，通过领队与服务员的交谈，引起客人谈话的兴趣，同时也加深了客人之间的互动。

旅游除了欣赏各种自然景观，与目的地国家（地区）的居民进行交流也是一项内容,融洽的团内气氛对于旅游团内的每个人来说都是有必要的,领队应通过各种机会尽力去营造这样的团队氛围。

A Topic Started by the Uniform of a Restaurant Waiter

On the first day of "7 Days and 6 Nights Tour in the Gorgeous Ceylon and Lanka—the End of the World," we flew from Hangzhou to Hong Kong and then took the connecting flight to Colomobo which stopped by Singapore. Finally, we arrived at Colomobo at the local time 22:40. Our group lived in Colomobo for one night and the next day we left for the northeastern area of Sri Lanka, Sigiriya. That night we spent in a vacation village called Cinnamo Lodge in Habarana which was near the ancient city, Polonnaruwa. It was really special as our guests were assigned in small villas.

The first dinner after we checked into the hotel was arranged in the buffet restaurant which was beside the swimming pool. We had 20 people in all including the tour leader, so the restaurant manager prepared two tables for us, each table for 10 people. What was more, he told us that the breakfast and lunch of the second day and the breakfast of the third day could be enjoyed at the same tables so that it was easy for us to find.

Before we had the dinner of the first day, I introduced to guests about the place where the buffet was prepared and the special cuisine of Sri Lanka,

Kotthu Rotti. During the dinner, guests were talking about the environment of the hotel's restaurant and the specialties of cuisine. I was talking with guests. Definitely the atmosphere was really good. Besides, our group had 4 or 5 children, which made the talking more interesting.

The next morning, our group members still had their meals at the same restaurant and I introduced them the special local breakfast, Hoppers. Because we were hurrying to visit the ancient city, Polonnaruwa, after breakfast, we just said good morning to each other with no other topics.

We still enjoyed the next day's dinner at the same restaurant and it seemed that all the guests looked tired. Maybe it was because the schedule of yesterday was very busy. Therefore, during the dinner time everyone had no interest in chatting and the atmosphere was tedious. At that time I asked a waiter to come to my place on purpose and said, "Why are the clothes you wear today different from yesterday's?" Then this waiter answered with smile, "We have changed the waiters today and according to the hotel's requirement, waiters' clothes must be different from the previous day." I translated this to my guests and they became interested in that immediately. A lot of guests came to my seat. The waiter asked us where we were from and I told him we were from Hangzhou, China. The waiter shook his head with smile and said he had never been to China before. Then I took out a note of RMB 1 with the picture of "Three Pools Mirroring the Moon" and told him our hometown was Hangzhou. After hearing this, the waiter said that as more and more Chinese tourists came to Sri Lanka, he started to know more about China.

Suddenly this waiter seemed to realize something and told me he was a coin collector who collected every country's coins including China's. When I translated this to our guests, some of the guests gave various coins to the waiter. The waiter felt extremely flattered and continually expressed his gratitude to us.

After that this waiter started doing his work again. Every time he passed us, he smiled and nodded to us.

Comments

The falling price of outbound tour makes outbound tourism have a trend of being more and more popular. Tour leader of outbound tour can meet different people with different backgrounds. Some tourists can be very conversational while some are very quiet. Therefore, how to let tourists know each other and make friends through the outbound tour becomes a problem the leader should take into consideration.

Tour leader can let tourists introduce themselves on the coach during the trip which is a good way to know each other. In this case, the tour leader depended on the third party to attract tourists to be interested in chatting to increase the familiarity among themselves.

Except appreciating various kinds of natural scenery, communicating with local people of the country/region visited is also included in traveling. A harmonious atmosphere is very important to every person in a tourist group and the tour leader should try his best to create this kind of atmosphere.

在垦丁享用瑞士主厨主理的自助餐

　　自 2008 年台湾对祖国大陆居民开放观光旅游,已有 9 个年头。与此同时,台湾陆续对大陆 36 个城市开放了自由行,赴台湾旅游的形式也越来越多。有参加旅行社组织的全包服务的旅行团,有参加自由行的,也有参加自驾游的。总之,台湾与大陆同根同源,语言相通,是许多旅游者的首选目的地。资深领队老余所带的,是一个由一家科技公司高管及其家属组成的 16 人团,团里光 12 周岁以下的小孩就有 5 人。整个行程除客人自理的两餐外,其他如旅游车、酒店、领队及当地导游、景区游览均由旅行社负责安排。

　　从台北桃园机场下飞机用餐开始客人就对团队的菜肴不满,说用餐环境不好、菜肴质量不高等等。团队客人在台北用了 4 次正餐后,再也没有办法接受团队餐了。团长要求领队将后面 4 天在云林县的剑湖山、阿里山、高雄以及垦丁的旅行社安排的正餐全部取消,改成让导游及领队推荐或客人自己点餐。领队在征得组团社的同意后,让台湾导游将后面 4 天的餐费退给了客人。但出于对第 4 天从阿里山游览下山后,没有合适的餐厅与充裕的时间用餐,以及第 6 天在垦丁的夏都沙滩酒店的中式午餐颇为优质这两点考量,领队最终说服客人保留了这两餐的预订。

离开台北后的3天行程中,台湾导游非常用心地给客人介绍台湾的各种美食,带客人去了西门町,介绍了"鸭肉扁"餐厅的粉面、阿宗面线、老牌的日本料理等。但是,在接下来的3天行程中,客人对海鲜情有独钟,连续吃了3顿海鲜。

第5天下午,旅行团抵达垦丁的夏都沙滩酒店。入住后孩子们经不住沙滩的诱惑,在沙滩上听着海边的波涛声,挖着沙坑,踩着浪花,响亮的笑声压根就停不下来。离用晚餐还有3小时左右,领队和导游跑到垦丁大街看是否有适合16人同时就座的大餐厅。一圈走下来觉得没有合适的餐厅,他们又回到入住的酒店,看到酒店的爱琴海西餐厅晚餐供应由瑞士主厨主理的自助餐。领队和导游进入餐厅看了菜肴的品种,发现有北海道空运来的海鲜、现切牛肉、台湾的冬令滋补菜肴,还有适合小孩子吃的比萨之类的食品。最给力的是,1.2米以下的儿童可免费用餐。余领队测算自助晚餐的费用,要比他们前几次吃海鲜更便宜,而且氛围相当好,有菲律宾乐队演唱助兴。于是,余领队向团长推荐了晚餐用自助餐的主意。客人觉得海鲜吃多了,确实也有点腻,认为此建议非常适合他们目前的情形,于是采纳了这个意见。

结账时,导游还用自己的信用卡为大家免了10%的服务费,算下来比前几次吃海鲜还便宜。在台湾享受了如此高性价比且有异域风情的自助晚餐,大家热情高涨,感谢领队和导游的推荐,"这顿自助餐既便宜又非常符合小孩子的口味!"

[评析]

随着网络的发展,自由行这种旅游模式被越来越多的旅游者所接受。旅游者已经从国内旅游自由行拓展到出境旅游自由行。此案例并非完全的自由行。它是因为对旅游团的团队餐不满,临时改成半自由行的模式。

由于客人在境外对用餐环境等不熟悉,职业领队在整个团队运作中有责任在当地导游的协助下替客人找到性价比高、环境优雅且卫生的餐厅,以挽回客人对团队餐不满的情绪,而不是撒手不管。领队除了推荐客人去享用具有当地特色的菜肴以外,价格合适、环境优雅、食品质量有保障、就餐形式多样化的推荐,也是一个职业领队应该做的事情。

Enjoy the Buffet Prepared by a Swiss Chef in Kenting

It has been 9 years since Taiwan opened for sightseeing to Mainland Chinese. Meanwhile, people from 36 Mainland cities have been permitted as individual tourists to Taiwan. Ways of travel in Taiwan become diversified, including tours organized by travel agencies, free exercises, self-driving tours, etc. In short, Taiwan has been among one of the top destinations for Mainland tourists because Mainland China and Taiwan share common roots. Mr. Yu, a senior tour guide, led a 16-person tour group consisting of senior executives of a hi-tech corporation and their family members. In the group, there were 5 children under age 12. The travel agency was in charge of all affairs like arrangement of coaches, hotels, tour leaders and local guides, except two dinners paid by tourists themselves.

Tourists began to complain about the group meals at the very beginning of the trip after they arrived at Taoyuan Airport. They were not satisfied with the food, dining environment, etc. They refused to have group meals after the first 4 meals in Taipei. The head of the group asked to substitute the following group meals (in Jianhu Mountain, Ali Mountain, Kaohsiung and Kenting) with self-ordered dishes or food recommended by the tour leader and the guide. The tour leader asked the guide in Taiwan to refund the expenses of the meals in the following 4 days with the consent of the travel agency. Given the fact that tourists would have no enough time and an ideal place to have dinner upon Ali Mountain on the 4th day, and the fact that the Chinese luncheon provided by Chateau Beach Resort Kenting is quite good, the tour leader managed to talk tourists into having these two meals as originally planned.

In the following three days after leaving Taipei, the tour guide led the group to Ximenting and introduced local delicacies to them, like Yaroubian Noodles, Ay-Chung Noodles, traditional Japanese food, etc. Tourists had three seafood meals constantly for they really loved it.

The group arrived at Chateau Beach Resort, Kenting on the 5th afternoon. Children were fascinated by the beach. They kept laughing along the beach, hearing the sound of the waves, playing with the sea sprays and sand pits. The tour guide and the leader went to Kenting Street looking for a table that could accommodate 16 persons three hours before dinner time. They went back with no proper options. However, they noticed that Aegean Sea Restaurant in Chateau Beach Resort Kenting provided buffet prepared by Swiss chefs. The tour guide and the leader entered to look for more details. The restaurant provided seafood from Hokkaido by air, fresh beef, nutritious Taiwan dishes and pizza. The best news was, kids under 1.2m could enjoy food for free. The tour leader Mr. Yu figured that having dinner here costs less than seafood meals they had had before. Besides, the restaurant would have a Philippines band over in dinner time. He recommended this place to the head of the tour group. Tourists were happy with his recommendation.

When footing the bill, the restaurant cut 10% service fee because of the tour guide's credit card. This buffet cost less than the previous seafood meals.

Tourists were very delighted after having such an inexpensive dinner with exotic flavor. They thanked the tour leader and the guide for their recommendation. "It's quite affordable. Kids liked it."

Comments

With the development of the Internet, independent travel is embraced by an increasing number of tourists. They even travel independently overseas. This case was not entirely a free one. It was changed into semi-free exercise when tourists expressed their dissatisfaction with group meals.

Given the fact that tourists are not familiar with the restaurants overseas, it is tour leaders' responsibility to find affordable and clean restaurants with an elegant dining environment with local tour guides' coordination to console the tourists who are dissatisfied with group meals. A professional tour leader should help tourists find local delicacies and good restaurants with various dining experiences.

第四篇　品牌酒店感悟篇

2015 日本印象两则

　　2015 年的春节,由于日本的境外旅游免税政策、旅游营销、日元贬值,以及人民币近几年基本保持升值状态,国人大量赴日采购日用品,如高档电饭锅和带杀菌除臭、加热、冲洗等功能的马桶盖。由于出境组团旅行社缺少专业的领队,于是我又一次踏上了日本的国土,担任了"日本本州 5 晚 6 天之旅"的领队。虽然是第六次赴日,但是途中遇到的两件事情还是给我留下了很深的印象。

　　印象一:

　　行程的第一天,抵达的是关西日航酒店。航站楼与酒店的建筑是一体的,酒店离机场只有 5 分钟的步行路程。客人可以不出机场,直接步行抵达酒店。酒店周边有小型的便利店,方便晚间抵达的客人。

　　怀着体验机场酒店的心情,次日,客人拿着餐券早早地来到餐厅门口。领座先生给了每一位用餐的客人一张用餐座位卡,卡的一面用日文写着:很抱歉,这个位置已有人使用。卡片的另一面则写着:用餐已经完毕,谢谢。有两位客人拿着这张卡片,不明白是什么意思。我立刻向客人解释:用餐的时候,请将"这个位置已有人使用"这面朝上放在桌上,以防去取餐时,别的客人坐到位置上。用完餐后,请将卡片反过来,让写有"用餐已经完毕"的这面朝上放在桌上,以便服务人员尽快将餐桌收拾好，方便给别的客人使用。这样的一张用餐座位卡方便有效，兼顾礼貌。但是有些客人用完餐后还是忘了将餐牌翻到"用餐已经完毕"这面。我观察到后就替客人去翻了一下卡片。

印象二：

行程第二天，团队从大阪的关西地区前往京都，最后抵达了日本的中部地区。客人入住的酒店在日本中部地区属于房间比较多的一家酒店，入住率几乎是100％。入住客人来自中国、泰国、印尼等国家，以中国团的客人为主。令人诧异的是，客房的门锁使用传统的钥匙，而非采用电子门锁。入住的第二天早上，办理退房手续时，大厅里挤满了人。轮到我的团队退房时，客人陆陆续续将钥匙返还给了总台。总台仅有2名工作人员，非常忙碌。恰巧团里一名客人将钥匙忘在了637房间。他要求我和总台接待员讲一声，让楼层的服务生将房间门打开取出来。当我将此事与总台接待员描述后，总台人员微笑地给我一把637房间的备用钥匙，让我自己去将忘在房间的钥匙取出来。备用钥匙的房号上有一个红点标注着。我马上将备用钥匙交给客人，客人以最快的速度跑回房间将钥匙取回，交给了总台。

[评析]

旅游业的服务质量一直都是人们十分关注的话题。旅游服务质量的构成可以分为硬件和软件两大部分。对于硬件设施的质量各旅游企业均比较重视，也是比较容易达到标准的。但软件的服务质量才是各旅游企业体现其个性，增强企业市场竞争力的关键。在某种程度上，硬件设施的不足可以通过良好的服务质量来弥补，但如果软件质量跟不上，再好的硬件也难以弥补其缺陷。在目前各旅游企业旅游服务的硬件差距越来越小的情况下，旅游服务的软件差距将直接影响各旅游企业的竞争实力。

众所周知，日本服务业中软件的服务是非常精细的。除了我们平时看到的有礼貌、热情好客以外，他们还将软件服务程序化，以防"服务缺陷"的产生。文章中"印象一"就是一个将软件服务程序化的案例。通过让客人配合使用用餐牌,提高服务人员的工作效率。用餐的客人会在比较有序的情形下取餐、用餐,整个餐厅的就餐环境也会感觉比较安静。

文章中"印象二",给客人一把备用钥匙,让客人取回钥匙,虽然谈不上精品服务,但是,日本人做事讲究效率是值得学习的。

Two Impressions of Japan in 2015

During the Spring Festival of 2015, many Chinese went to Japan for shopping, as a mixed result of Japan's tax-free policy to foreign travelers, tourism promotion, yen slump, and the steady appreciation of the RMB. They went after all kinds of home wares, such as luxurious electric cookers, advanced toilet seat covers with functions such as disinfection, deodorization, heating, washing, etc. Since there have never been enough professional tour leaders for oversea group traveling, I set my foot on Japan once again, as the tour leader of "5-day-and-6-night tour of Honshu, Japan." I was my 6th time to Japan and two events left deep impressions on me.

Impression Ⅰ

On the first day, we checked in at Nikko Kansai Airport Hotel. The hotel is integrated with the terminal building, which is only a 5-minute walk from the terminal. Passengers can walk straight to the hotel upon arrival without leaving the airport. Convenience stores can be easily found around the hotel, bringing convenience to passengers who arrive late at night.

The next morning, tourists in our group went to breakfast early with their vouchers. The usher gave each of us a seat card, which had "Sorry, Seat Taken" on one side and "Meal Finished, Thanks" on the other. Two tourists didn't quite understand how it worked, so I explained to them. They could use the "Sorry, Seat Taken" side while they were leaving for food, in case other people might take the seats while they were away. When the meal was finished, turn the side "Meal Finished, Thanks" up to remind waiters to clean the table for other customers. We could find convenience, efficiency and politeness in the design of the simple seat card. Some tourists forgot to turn the card to the side of "Meal Finished, Thanks"when leaving, so I helped turn them up.

Impression Ⅱ

On the second day, we went from Kansai Area to Kyoto and finally we arrived at central Japan. We checked in a hotel which had a great number of rooms. Its occupancy rate is often nearly 100%. Tourists here are from all over the world, such as China, Thailand and Indonesia. Chinese tourists particularly favor this hotel.

The rooms in the hotel were equipped with traditional door locks rather than electronic ones. The next day morning, we found the lobby quite crowded. There were only two receptionists dealing with customers' checking-out. One of my tourists happened to leave the key in Room No. 637. He wondered if the staff could take care of it. I talked with the receptionist about this. She smiled and gave me a spare key with a red mark on it. I passed it to the tourist. He went back to his room, got his key and gave the spare one back to the hotel.

Comments

Travel agency quality has always been a hot topic among tourists. It is comprised of "hardware" and "software". Travel agencies pay great attention to the facilities, which can be standardized easily. However, it is the "software" service that demonstrates travel agency's competitiveness. Great service may make up for modest facilities. Given the fact that all travel agencies currently provide great facilities, service would determine their market competitiveness.

As we all know, the service in Japan is of high standard. Besides their politeness and hospitality, they have particular processes to ensure service quality and avoid service defect. Impression I is a typical example of systematical service. The restaurant improved the staff's working efficiency by giving customers seat cards. In addition to that, all customers had their food in an orderly and quiet manner.

In Impression II, preparing a spare key for guests in advance is another great example of great services. Though it is not good enough to let guest fetch the key, the pursuit of high efficiency is worth learning.

越南岘港酒店赠送的礼物：越南米粉、滴漏壶……

　　游走过许多地方,也欣赏过一些名山名水。这一回却非常想去岘港——这个被美国《世界地理》杂志评选出的"人生必到的 50 个景点"之一。《世界地理》赞其为:阳光地带,现代文明与自然的完美结合,世界著名的六个海滩之一。

　　当包机抵达越南中部最大的海滨旅游城市岘港时,已经是越南时间凌晨2：30,大家从飞机上下来时,都睡眼惺忪,有一点饿,但又觉得能够倒头就睡是最美的事情。抵达岘港银岸国际酒店时,中国领队以最快的速度将房间钥匙分到各位客人的手中,并强调:大家将行李安放在房间后,可以凭钥匙牌赴一楼餐厅品尝一碗鲜美无比的越南米线。大家被这一深夜特别安排所打动,都想赴餐厅品尝一下越南的特色小食——米线。

　　走进餐厅,穿着越南国服"奥黛"的女侍应生,端上一碗碗热腾腾的越南米线给客人。顿时,大家乘坐"红眼航班"所带来的疲倦都被驱走了。凌晨品尝过一碗小小的米线后,再去睡觉,胃感到无比舒适。

　　根据行程的安排,当日 15：00,大家集合在酒店大堂,前往会安。从岘港市到会安镇的路上能从车窗外,看到广袤无垠的稻田、莲叶层叠的荷塘、波翻浪涌的大海……一路上导游介绍着越南"四大苗条":国土苗条、房屋苗条、道路苗条、女性苗条。

国土苗条：越南国土形状为细长的 S 形,南北长 3000 多公里,最窄的地方只有 50 公里。

房屋苗条：越南实行土地私有制,百姓建造房子按门面宽度计费,一般宽 2 到 3 米,但是纵深可以长达 20 多米,高度在 2 到 5 层,所以看起来特别"苗条"。

道路苗条：越南没有高速公路贯穿,南北只有一条沿着海岸线的国道,宽度刚好可以并排开两辆车,显得非常拥挤、缓慢。所以越南人经常调侃说:"在我们越南摩托车跑得比汽车快,汽车跑得比火车快。我们也有高速公路和高铁,道路两边的树长得比路高就是'高树公路',公路比铁路高叫'高铁'。"

女性苗条：越南女性身材非常苗条,特色服装"奥黛"把女性的曲线展现得淋漓尽致。

说着说着,团队很快抵达了被联合国列入世界文化遗产的古镇——会安。

秋盆河环绕着小镇会安,到处停泊着彩旗飘飘的小船。早在 16 世纪,此地为占婆国对外贸易港口,与马来西亚古城马六甲一起成为东南亚最重要的商埠,也是越南最早的商埠。几百年来,一批批华人到此繁衍生息,形成了独特的华人社区——店铺、会馆和庙宇聚集在一起,丰富多彩的中国传统文化得以在此根植。

走着走着,团队中的几位女孩看到了能做"奥黛"的裁缝店。越南女子习惯在正式场合穿着国服"奥黛"。这是越南女性独特的传统服饰,通常用丝绸类质料裁剪,款式类似中国的旗袍。上衣是长衫,自腰间以下开有高叉,下身配同花色的宽松长裤,不论蹲坐、骑车都非常方便。

会安的"奥黛"完全由纯手工制作,客人可以根据自己的喜好挑选布料,然后裁缝会给你量体裁衣。"奥黛"最大的特点就是能够百分之百地展示出女性的曲线美。一般缝制一套"奥黛"需要 3 到 5 个小时,如果你时间不够也可以选择成衣,裁缝会根据你的身材改小或改大,费用根据布料材质的不同大约在 30 万到 3 兆越南盾不等,折合人民币为 100 到 800 元。"奥黛"颜色有很多种,但越南女性偏爱白色。这时再戴上用棕榈树叶做的斗笠,微风拂过,白衣飘飘,必然能吸引众多爱美的眼球。听着导游的介绍,几个女孩下决心一定要做一套穿穿。

很快就要结束 3 晚 5 天的越南岘港之旅了。由于回程的航班需要在第 5 天凌晨起飞,导游告诉我们,晚上等大家退了房间后,酒店特意准备了几个地方供大家选择休息:其一,大堂的休息室,供游人阅读;其二,一楼娱乐城内有贵宾休息区及免费茶水,最让人惊喜的是客人临出发前可以在前台领取一只滴漏壶——会安人喝咖啡时喜欢用的。杯中先放好炼乳之类,杯上放一种器具,让过滤后的咖啡一滴一滴往下漏,比福建的工夫茶耗的工夫还多。喝一杯,便是半日休闲。

虽然只是 3 晚 5 天的行程,但越南米线、会安古镇、"奥黛"服装制作、滴漏壶,给大家留下了深刻的印象。岘港,这个幸福指数世界排名第五的越南第二大港口城市,真让人羡慕。

[评析]

在东南亚海岛游中,相比巴厘岛、普吉岛等热门海岛,越南岘港还不为人所熟知。许多旅游者可能还没有游览过越南北部的河内和南部的胡志明市,却先来到越南中部古城——岘港。所以,如何将目的地国家(地区)的文化传递给旅游者并让游客留下深刻印象,是旅游中间商——旅行社开发出境游产品中所要重视的问题。

以上案例,是旅行社与酒店合作谈判的结果。一方面,推出"东方夏威夷"岘港的游览,需要旅行社的配合。而旅行社为了争取到更多的客源,与航空公司合作加开"红眼航班",将优惠价格提供给客人。同时,酒店为争取更多的客源,为乘坐"红眼航班"的客人提供诸多方便。如提供 24 小时开放的餐厅,深夜及凌晨提供越南小食——米线,客人临走时赠送越南工艺品——滴漏壶。既宣传了越南的传统文化,又传递了一份浓浓的旅途爱意。这是旅游业三大支柱行业——旅行社、酒店、航空公司战略合作的结果。

The Gifts from Da Nang Hotel in Vietnam: Vietnamese Rice Noodles, Drip Pots ...

I have traveled to many places and viewed some famed mountains and lakes. But this time I wanted to go to Da Nang, which has been selected as one of the top 50 attractions one must visit in his life by *World Geography*. And it is praised by this magazine as a perfect combination of modern civilization and nature, and is one of the six most beautiful beaches.

It was 2:30 a.m. already when the group arrived in Vietnam. All of them were sleepy and hungry. But they felt much better when they thought they could sleep immediately. The Chinese tour leader assigned key cards to guests quickly, and stressed that everybody could put their luggage in their rooms first, and go downstairs to have a bowl of special Vietnamese rice noodles for free with the key card.

When we sat in the restaurant, the waitress dressed in Audrey served delicious Vietnamese rice noodles for us. It was very thoughtful of them. Having had rice noodles, we fell asleep, feeling warm and comfortable.

According to the itinerary, at 15:00 on the same day, we gathered in the lobby to go to Hoi An. On our way there, we were able to view the vast extension of paddy fields, dense lotus leaves in the haw thorn, rough sea from the bus windows. Along the way, the tour guide was introducing four slims, that is, slim homeland, slim houses, slim road and slim women.

Slim homeland: The Vietnam homeland is an elongated S-shaped stretch over 3,000 km from north to south, and the narrowest place is only 50 km wide.

Slim houses: Vietnam practices private ownership of land. Vietnamese build houses charged according to the width of the facades. A house is generally 2—3 meters wide with a depth of 20 meters and a height of 2—5 layers, which looks particularly slim.

Slim road: Without expressway, Vietnam's land runs from the north to the south through one national road along the coastline. The width of the road can just accommodate two cars side by side. It is very crowded and slow. Vietnamese often joke about the Vietnamese motorcycle: It runs faster than a car, the car runs faster than a train. We also have "highways" and "high-speed rails". As the trees on both sides of the road are higher than the road, hence the name highway. And the railway is higher than the regular road, hence the name "high-speed rail".

Slim women: Vietnamese women are very slim. Audrey, a local costume, can well demonstrate women's nice figures.

The group soon arrived at Hoi An, which has been listed as world heritage site by the UNESCO.

The town of Hoi An is filled with parked boats, with flags fluttering everywhere. Early in the 16th century, the area used to be a foreign trade port. Along with the ancient city of Malacca Malaysia, Hoi An was Southeast Asia's most important commercial port. It was the first commercial port in Vietnam. Groups of Chinese came thriving here, forming a unique Chinese community with shops, club houses, temples and so on.

We were walking along the street, and saw a tailor shop that could make "Audrey." Vietnamese women used to wear national dress on formal occasions. "Audrey" is a unique traditional costume, usually made of silk and is similar to China's cheongsam. The upperpart is a long skirt, open from the waist, and the lower part are pants with loose trousers, suitable for squatting, sitting and cycling.

Audrey in Hoi An is totally hand made. The customers may choose their favorite cloth and have the tailor make the Audrey for them according to their sizes. The feature of Audrey is that it may perfectly reflect the beautiful female curve. It takes 3 to 5 hours to make an Audrey. You may also choose the ready-made garment if you have little time. The tailor will amend the garment according to your size. The charge ranges from 300 thousand to 30,000 billions Vietnamese Dongs, about RMB 100 to 800. There are different colors available and the white ones are the most popular among female Vietnamese. With the bamboo hats, female Vietnamese pass by and the breeze kisses their Audrey. Many people are attracted by the beautiful scene. Hearing the tour guide's introduction, some girls decided to have an Audrey.

The 3-night-and-5-day trip to Da Nang, Vietnam, would soon come to an end. The return flight would take off in the early morning of the fifth day. The local guide told us on the fourth day that when group was checking out in the evening, the hotel would prepare a few places for people to rest. One was the lobby lounge for visitors to read; another was the first floor entertainment park. The VIP seating area and free tea were available. The most amazing part was that guests received a drip pot at the front desk. The first cup places the condensed milk and there is only one tool on the cup. Let the coffee filtered drop by drop down through the leakage, more efforts are made than Fujian Gongfu tea. Drinking a glass means half-day leisure.

Although it was only 3 nights and 5 days, the Vietnamese rice noodles, Hoi An ancient town, Audrey clothing production and drip pots left a deep impression on everyone. It is really admirable that as the second largest port city in Vietnam, Da Nang's happiness index ranks fifth in the world.

Comments

Compared to the popular islands such as Bali, Phuket in Southeast Asia, Da Nang in Vietnam is not well known. But now many tourists would first come to the ancient city of central Vietnam, Da Nang directly. So how to promote the culture of the destination to tourists? This is what travel agencies should pay attention to.

The situation of the above case was the result of the negotiation between the travel agency and the hotel. The introduction to the "Oriental Hawaii" tour of Da Nang took a travel agency to travel there in order to win more tourists. In cooperation with the airlines, additional "Red Eye" flights with a lower price were offered to guests with hotels for more tourists. Guests took the "Red Eye" flight were provided with a lot of Vietnamese snacks-rice noodles, and they were given Vietnamese handicrafts, drip pots, before departure. It not only introduced the traditional culture of Vietnam, but also conveyed a deep sense of love. This was due to the efforts of three pillars in tourism industry, that is, travel agencies, hotels and airlines.

澳大利亚酒店的"不速之客"

澳大利亚地处南半球,年平均气温为 22—23℃,相比较其他同纬度的地区, 它的气候更为宜人。迷人的景色,丰富的旅游资源,得天独厚的地理环境和独特 的自然景观,每年都会吸引无数中国人慕名前往。于是,中国的春节,也成了澳 新线的旅游旺季,机票、酒店、导游、地接都十分紧张。

2015 年春节期间,领队小孙带领一个中国旅游团前往澳大利亚,开始"澳大 利亚＋凯恩斯 8 日游"。由于春节团队众多,地接社没有足够的中文导游,就派 了一个留学生来带团。留学生显然业务不熟,以致让客人产生了一些不满的情 绪。在布里斯班,团队入住在郊外一家度假村,酒店由各幢连体别墅组成,周围 是大片的树林,自然环境优美。留学生导游把客人送到后也没有说注意事项就 走了。领队直到进入房间后,才在电视旁边的一张小告示牌上看到如下提醒: "The sensitive ecosystem in the tropics determines that we share our environment with a number of different creatures including ants, geckos and a variety of insects. May we suggest you avoid leaving food on benches and keep your door closed in an effort to keep these unwanted creatures out……(热带地区敏感的生 态系统决定了我们要和大量不同的生物共享大自然,如蚂蚁、壁虎和各种昆虫。

为了避免这些'不速之客',我们建议您不要在长椅上留下食物,保持门窗紧闭……)"于是,领队在之后查房的时候便告知客人:"不要把门窗敞开通风,也尽量不要在房间里吃东西,如有开封食物一定要扎紧。"

可就在提醒过后没多久,一位女性游客跑到领队房间大喊,要求换房间。询问后才得知,原来她入住后竟发现房间里有蜥蜴。于是领队便亲自去房间确认,当看到客人的房门和窗户都敞开着时,才恍然大悟。由于正值旅游旺季,酒店并没有空余的房间了,值班经理也安慰客人:"蜥蜴是人类的好朋友,不会伤害人。"可客人还是坚持要换房间,无奈,领队把自己的房间换给了客人。第二天大清早,领队小孙被一声惨叫惊醒,跑过去一看,原来是团里的一位客人房间桌子上爬满了体型庞大的热带蚂蚁,吸引蚂蚁的是桌子上几包开封的食物,而蚂蚁的队伍一直排到露了一条缝的窗户。小孙赶紧把食物扔进了户外的垃圾桶,一场虚惊才算告终。

车上,小孙再次和大家解释了澳大利亚的生态环境:一般靠近森林的宾馆时常会有小动物来光顾,但这些动物不会伤害人。他再一次告诉客人,在澳大利亚,请不要在房间里留下食物残渣并要随时关好门,以防这些"不速之客",希望大家入乡随俗。游客们对此都表示能理解。

[评析]

澳大利亚是一个非常重视生态环境保护和建设的国家。在有序高效的管理体制下,整个澳大利亚就像个生态乐园,享有"骑在羊背上的国家""野生动物的世外桃源""珍奇植物的王国"等美称。

在机场,澳大利亚海关和检疫部门对入境旅客检查非常苛刻。在澳大利亚可以感受到人类与各种动植物共享大自然的乐趣。

澳大利亚昆士兰州地处热带,各种动物较多,为了避免一些游客的误解,酒店会有告示牌告知注意事项。而由于文化差异,中国游客喜欢开门窗通风等生活习惯常引来被澳大利亚人视为"好朋友"的蜥蜴、蚂蚁等。案例中的领队小孙,就做好了相关的说明和提醒。虽然当地导游业务不熟,但小孙一看到酒店的告示牌后,就通过查房再次提醒客人。虽然还是发生了意外,但客人还是表示能够理解。

"Crasher" in an Australian Hotel

Australia is located in the southern hemisphere and the annual average temperature is between 22 ℃ and 23℃. Compared with the climates of other regions of the same latitude, its climate is more pleasant. Enchanting views, abundant tourism resources, unique geographical environment and splendid natural landscape attract millions of tourists from China every year. As the Chinese Spring Festival is the peak tourist season to Australia and New Zealand, air tickets, hotels and tour guides at that time are in short supply.

During the Spring Festival in 2015, the tour leader Sun was leading a Chinese group to Australia. It was a 8-day tour of Australia and Keynes. Because there were lots of tours during the Spring Festival, the local travel agency did not have enough Chinese tour guides and sent an overseas student to handle the tour. Obviously, the overseas student was not familiar with tour guide's job, which made tourists a little annoyed. In Brisbane, the group checked into a suburban holiday village. The village hotel was composed of the conjoined villa, surrounded by big trees with beautiful natural environment. The overseas student left the hotel immediately without informing the group members of matters needing attention. When the tour leader came into room, he saw the notice on a small billboard beside TV.

"The sensitive ecosystem in the tropics determines that we share our environment with a number of different creatures including ants, geckos and a variety of insects. May we suggest you avoid leaving food on benches and keep your door closed in an effort to keep these unwanted creatures out ... "

When tour leader checked rooms, he told tourists to close windows, try not to eat in rooms, and close the openings of package food.

Shortly afterwards, a female tourist ran to the tour leader's room and asked to change a room because there was a lizard in her room. Then the tour leader went to check her room and found that windows and doors were open. During the peak tourist season, the hotel did not have any vacant room. The hotel manager comforted her, saying that lizard was our friend and it would not hurt humans. However, the tourist insisted on changing her room. As a result, the tour leader changed his room with hers. On the second day's morning, the tour leader was waked up by a scream. He ran to see what had happened, only to find big tropical ants crawling on the table in one of tourist's rooms. It was the open package food that attracted those ants. The tour leader quickly threw the food into the dustbin outside.

In the coach, the tour leader explained to tourists about the ecological environment of Australia. Usually there were some animals which would visit rooms when the hotel was near forest, but the animals would not hurt. He reminded the tourists again that they should close doors and not leave food in rooms. And he hoped tourist could do in Rome as Romans do. The tourists showed their understanding.

Comments

Australia is a country which attaches great importance to ecological environment protection and construction. Under orderly and efficient management, Australia is like an ecological playground and enjoys reputations as a country riding on the sheep's back, a wildlife sanctuary and an exotic plant kingdom.

At the airport, the Australian customs and quarantine departments check entry passengers very strictly. In Australia people can enjoy the joy of sharing nature with various animals and plants.

Queensland is located in the tropics with a lot of animals and insects. In order to avoid misunderstanding from some tourists, hotel will show you matters needing attention on the billboard. Due to cultural differences, Chinese tourists like to open doors, windows and eating snacks, which could easily attract lizard, ants and so on. In this case, the tour leader Sun did some explanation and reminders. Although the local tour guide was not familiar with his work, the tour leader compensated by doing some additional work. Therefore, when some problems occurred, tourists could understand.

出境游领队的护照与另纸签证分开后……

马来西亚是一个自然资源非常丰富的热带国家,全年适宜旅游。纯净的海滩、奇特的海岛、原始的热带雨林以及现代化建筑组合成马来西亚独特的文化。赴马来西亚,你可以在诗巴丹潜水观看海底美景,也可以在国家清真寺感受马来国的信仰,可以在热浪岛沙滩享受日光浴,在国家公园探秘原始丛林,还可以在吉隆坡、沙巴、兰卡威、槟城等旅游城市感受不同城市的魅力。

出境游领队小王带领着一行 20 人的旅游团队赴马来西亚一国游览。团队从上海出发,经过 5 个多小时的飞行,终于到达马来西亚的吉隆坡国际机场。正当大家对这次马来西亚充满欣喜与期待时,发生了一件不太顺利的事。

领队小王带领全团人员准备入关,在给移民局官员查看护照和团队签证时,被告知不能入境。小王感到疑惑不解:护照和团队签证都有,为什么还不能入境?随后移民局官员向领队解释道:由于领队的护照和团体签证的另纸分离了,而且领队的护照有破损的现象,故暂时不能入境。领队小王有些着急,团队还没有完全进入目的地国家,就出现了问题。小王此前并不知道护照与另纸分离及护照破损发生的严重性。随后小王被移民局官员带入移民局办公室。移民局官员问小王为何护照少一只角,小王解释道:将另纸签证撕下来时,订书机上的订书针将护照撕破了一只角。尽管理由似乎十分合理,但移民官还是打电话给马国驻上海领事馆询问小王所带的团体人数、计划旅游的城市等资料。全部资料核实通过后,才让领队及团队成员一个一个地通过移民局关口。

至此,领队小王心里的石头才落下来。

[评析]

从专业素养方面来看,案例中领队没有认清另纸签证的含义和它的作用。另纸签证,通常只是一张有签证效用的纸质证明,使馆签发时会将其附在团中某一位团员的护照上(通常是领队的护照上),而其他团员的护照上面并没有任何签证的印记。也就是另纸签证必须和护照同时使用,才能通过目的地国家的移民局。因此,此团中领队对出入境等相关工作的专业知识掌握不够,不清楚另纸签证相关规定,才导致理所当然撕开签证分别交与移民局这样的后果。

从护照规范管理方面来看,《中华人民共和国护照法》有针对性的规定:一是护照具备视读机械功能和防伪性功能;二是任何组织和个人不能非法扣押护照,也不得伪造、变造、转让、故意损毁护照。因此,护照上储存着个人信息,能够被识读。若护照被损毁,如案例中领队无意中把护照损坏,从而导致个人信息可能无法识别,那么护照作为个人在国外的身份证明这一功能就无法正常发挥作用,而移民局方面就无法正常给予通行。由于护照不完整存在许多潜在问题,如身份无法识别、护照造假等,因此,移民官需将领队暂扣,与使领事馆联系,进一步对其进行身份调查与核实。

When the Passport and the Other Paper Visa of the Tour Leader Were Separated ...

Malaysia, a tropical country with abundant natural resources is suitable for traveling all year around. It has clean beaches, unusual islands, primitive tropical rain forests and modern architectures. In Malaysia, people can watch undersea scenery when diving in Sipadan, get familiar with religion when visiting national mosques, enjoy sunbath at Redang beach, explore virgin jungle in national parks and experience the charm of different cities, such as Kuala Lumpur, Sabah, Langkawi and Penang.

The tour leader Mr. Wang led a tour group of 20 guests to Malaysia. The group set out from Shanghai. After 5 hours' flight, the group landed at Kuala Lumpur International Airport in Malaysia. Suddenly, an unexpected incident happened.

Mr. Wang was very confused when he was told they were not allowed to enter the country when he showed the passports and the group visa to the customs officer. The customs officer explained that the passports and the group visa were separated and there was a piece of broken paper on the tour leader's passport, so the group could not enter into the country. Mr. Wang was a little worried about the problem. Later, he was brought into the immigration office. The officer asked why part of Mr. Wang's passport was missing. Mr. Wang explained that when the other paper visa was taken off from the passport, the stapling nail tore off part of the passport. Reasonable as it seemed, the officer still called the Malaysia consulate in Shanghai to check the number of group members, itinerary, and the cities to visit. After all the information was checked, Mr. Wang and his group were allowed to pass the customs.

Mr. Wang finally felt relaxed.

Comments

From the point of professional quality, in the above case, the tour leader did not realize the meaning and function of the other paper visa. The other paper visa is normally a paper certificate for visa. When the embassy issues the other paper visa, it will attach the visa to one of group members' passport (usually on the tour leader's). And there is no sign on any other group member's passport. The other paper visa must be used together with the passport when passing the customs of the destination. In the case, the tour leader lacked knowledge about immigration and didn't know much about the other paper visa. Therefore, he tore off the visa from his passport and caused the problem.

From the view of passport regulations, the Passport Law of the People's Republic of China provides: First, the passport has mechanical function of vision, read and security; second, any organization or person can not detain illegally or forge, change, transfer, destroy the passport on purpose. Therefore, the information on the passport can be read. If the passport is destroyed, just like in the above case, then the personal information could not be read. The passport, as an ID card used abroad, cannot function normally. The immigration office thus cannot allow people with a broken passport to pass. Because the broken passport may cause many potential problems, such as the ID failing to be identified, the forge of the passport, etc. Therefore, the immigration officer had to detain the tour leader in the case, and investigated his ID with the consulate.

在英国，像英国人一样生活

2016 年冬,经过长达 10 多个小时的长途飞行,我们终于来到了曾经的"日不落帝国"。这真是一个令人着迷的国度。在英国,除了伦敦,有限的时间内,还值得一去的必须就是爱丁堡了。行走于这两个城市,你既能遇见英格兰的优雅,又能体验苏格兰的风情。而为了更接地气地游玩,我们在爱丁堡这一站,选择了酒店式公寓的住宿方式。

骑士公馆是一家距离爱丁堡城堡只有 10 分钟步行距离的公寓住所,外表并不出众,就如同普通居民住宅,但是装修风格温馨大方,内部设施一应俱全,从普通酒店都有的各项设备到酒店式公寓套房特有的起居室、厨房间、洗衣机加烘干机,更不用说各种生活用具,使你在居住期间真是如同在家一般自在方便。而令人印象最深刻的就是它的英式管家服务了。在我们到达前,公寓管理人员就通过电子邮件的方式和我们联络,询问我们的到达时间,是否有特殊的需求。当获知到达时间后,也会及时地反馈给我们他们的工作时间,以及万一过了工作时间,我们该如何自己入住的细节。

到达骑士公馆,已经是当地时间晚上 10 点多,走进大堂后,公寓的前台经理就热情地用他刚学的中文和我们打招呼,带领我们去预订好的套房。套房的大门上居然还有住客的名牌，非常有意思。经理说，这样就不怕找不到自己的房间了。虽然当时已经快到下班时间，但是前台经理带我们到房间后，还是细心地给我们讲解了房间各种电器设备的使用方法，时刻注意我们是否理解。同时他一再强调如果他语速过快，一定请打断他并再次询问他，因为苏格兰英语和英格兰英语还是不太一样的，但是事实上他的口音和语速都非常棒。临走时，经理照顾到我们是外国人，初到异地，可能会不适应，还半开玩笑地对我们说，虽然他马上下班了，但是如果有问题，可以通过各种方式联系到工作人员，所以请不要感觉被"遗弃"在公寓里了。此外，这家酒店公寓的迎宾篮也是丰富异常，考虑到我们是中国人，还贴心地准备了香港的公仔泡面，里面的其他零食饮料到离开的那天都还没吃完。在这里居住的几天，我们真的感觉如同在家生活，没有一丝不方便，唯一不同的是，我们多了一个非常棒的英国"管家"。每天，他会帮忙处理好包括房间卫生在内的一切家务，在你进出公寓时，适度又热情地寒暄，时刻注意你的需求。

[评析]

管家起源于法国，完善在英国。细节就是一切，从过去到现在，英式管家就是家政服务的典范。培训一名合格的管家绝非易事，几乎囊括所有的知识门类，充满大量细节。而作为管家，除了职业技能外，还要求有主动服务意识。英式管家的职责是对每位雇主进行细致分析，提供特色照顾。他们不仅要想到如何实现客人的想法，更应提前预估主人的期望，早做安排。难怪乎林语堂先生将英式管家和中国厨子、日本老婆并列为梦想生活的必备因素了。

而英国的酒店式公寓引入了这个概念和模式，虽然不能和真正的英式管家服务相提并论，但可以说这也是酒店服务的一项特色。

When in Britain, Do as the British Do

After over 10 hours' flight, in the winter of 2016, we finally arrived in Britain, the once "Sun Never Sets"empire. It is an amazing country. People say if you are tired of London, you are tired of life. We didn't believe such words until we arrived here. In Britain, if you have limited time, then besides London, you have to go to Edinburgh. You may enjoy the elegant England as well as the stylish Scotland in the two cities respectively. When we arrived in Edinburgh, we chose a serviced apartment hotel to experience local customs.

Knight Residence is a serviced apartment, about a 10-minute walk to the Edinburgh Castle. With a plain appearance, the apartment had decent and comfortable inner decoration with complete facilities, including washing machine and drier, making you feel at home. The most impressive about the apartment was its British butler service. For example, before our arrival, the manager e-mailed us about our arrival time and special requests if any. When he learned that we might arrive quite late at night, he told us in detail how to check in if they were not available at late night.

On the night we arrived at the apartment, it was already over 10:00 p.m. The manager at the front office greeted us warmly in Chinese he just learned and led us to our reserved apartment. There was a label on each door with one of our names. The manager explained that by doing this we would not get lost. Though it was almost time to be off duty, the manager still explained carefully to us how to use the facilities in the room. Meanwhile, he paid attention to whether we could follow him or not. And he emphasized if he spoke too fast, did interrupt him as there were many differences between England accent and Scotland accent. In fact, his speed and accent were just fine and clear to us. Upon his leaving, considering we were foreigners, he comforted us that we could feel free to contact their staff in time of trouble. Besides, there were many snacks in the welcome basket, including Chinese instant noodles. We really felt like staying at home when we were there. The manager arranged everything well for us and greeted us every time we were back.

Comments

Butler originated from France but perfected in Britain. Detail is everything. From past to now, the British butler has been a classic model in housekeeping field. It is very difficult to train a qualified butler. The butler courses include various kinds knowledge and details. A qualified butler should have a strong service sense as well as professional skills. The responsibilities of a butler include analyzing the needs of the employer in detail and provide special services. A butler should not only meet the demands of the employer, but also foresee the employer's expectation and make certain arrangements. No wonder Mr. Lin Yutang described dream life with a British butler, a Chinese cook and a Japanese wife.

The British serviced apartment introduces the butler concept into their management. It is not real butler service, but a kind of hotel service.

优质的服务源于经验的积累——在越南岘港享用海鲜餐

越南岘港人口约 80 万,为越南中部最大的深水港口及商业中心。由于位置良好、港口条件佳,自古以来就是重要的国际港口与转运站,非常繁荣。此外,岘港曾是强大的占婆王国的首都,现今市区和近郊还留有占婆时期的遗迹。如今,随着海滨旅游资源的进一步开发,岘港已经成为越南著名的海滨城市。

莺飞草长的 4 月,我带着 30 位客人,乘坐越南航空班机从杭州出发到越南岘港旅行。我们 21:15 准时起飞,飞行时间为 3 小时左右,越南时间比北京时间晚一个小时,旅行团到达越南岘港的时间是当地时间 23:45。一落地,一股闷热潮气扑面而来。出了海关见到导游后我就带领着客人乘坐大巴赴酒店入住。

赴岘港的团队旅行以休闲为主,行程非常轻松,基本没有太多的景点需要参观,出发之前大多数客人都做过攻略。现今的岘港已经几乎没有军事基地的风貌了。港内停泊着大型渔船,市场里喊价的声音此起彼落,让人感觉这是一个明亮、有朝气的城市。海鲜很美味,而且价格实惠。所以,抵达后的第一个晚上,一部分客人就来邀请领队吃海鲜。岘港的海鲜一条街是最有名的品尝海鲜的地方。我们一行叫了几辆出租车去了那里。从我们住的皇冠酒店到那里,每辆车的花费是 6 万越南盾(折合人民币不到 20 元)。我们一行找到了岘港当地一家有名的海鲜馆，里面品种多，有螃蟹、虾、鱿鱼、贝类等。当地的蘸料是一种叫作鱼露的调味品，是一些鱼发酵做出来的酱，中国人习惯了将醋和芥末作为调料，还是不习惯把鱼露作为调料。幸好我事先有准备，把带来的醋和芥末拿出来给大家食用。尽管部分团友认为鱼露咸咸的还有一股发臭的味道，但是他们还是想尝试鱼露。大家吃完海鲜，沿着沙滩返回了酒店。

第二天，一位客人告诉我说他肚子好像吃坏了，身体很不舒服。我恍然大悟，他吃了海鲜，喝了冰啤酒，可能肠胃适应不了吧。他说想去买点药来吃，要不太难受了，可是导游告诉我们买药根本不可能，要去找医生开过处方，方可买药。而且，我们没有当地医保，药价也很贵。团里有位客人说他带了一些治拉肚子的药，我了解清楚药效说明之后，让这位拉肚子的客人吃了一些，让他好好休息。别的团友告诉我他吃了很多鱼露。

几天后，客人终于好起来，我也算是松了一口气。

[评析]

在日常的工作中积累经验是服务业从业人员必备的基本素质，而将日积月累的工作经验服务于客人，也是从业人员的一种美德。

领队带团赴海岛国家旅游，尤其在吃海鲜的地方，一定要准备醋或者芥末，这样不会让肠胃难受。对一些肠胃不好和患有"三高"的客人，一定要提醒他们适量食用，注意不要与冰啤酒一起享用。案例中，领队考虑得非常周全，将中国人的饮食习惯与东南亚人的饮食习惯的不同细化到调料，值得从业人员效仿。

工作经验包含很多方面，依照领队的经验，由于进入越南岘港是采用落地签，所以出发之前领队就帮每位客人填写好入境卡，以方便到达岘港机场之后办理入境手续。此外，喝了埃及、土耳其酒店的水容易拉肚子，领队出发时，可在行李中带热水壶，帮助客人在酒店烧热水喝，以防拉肚子。

Service of High Quality Comes from the Accumulation of Experience: Enjoy Seafood in Da Nang, Vietnam

Da Nang, Vietnam, has a population of about 800,000 and is the largest deep-water port and commercial center in the middle of Vietnam. Because of its good geographical position, and as a port with good conditions, it has been an important international port and transfer station since ancient times and was very prosperous. In addition, Da Nang was the capital of the powerful Kingdom of Champa and now there are still remains of Champa period in the city and suburb. Today with the further development of coastal tourism resources, Da Nang has become a famous coastal city of Vietnam.

In April, I led 30 guests and took a flight of the Vietnam airlines to Da Nang from Hangzhou. The plane took off on time at 21:15 and the flight time was about 3 hours. Because the time in Vietnam was one hour later than in Beijing, the group's arrival time was 23:45, local time of Da Nang. The stuffy moist air came immediately when we arrived there. When I came out of the customs and met the tour guide, we went to the hotel to check in.

The group tour visiting Da Nang was to focus on recreation basically and the route was very relaxing and there were not many scenic spots to visit. A lot of tourists had made detailed travel strategies before they started off. Today's Da Nang has lost its style as a military base. There were large fishing boats anchoring in the port. Loudly bargaining filled the market. It was a bright and lively city. Seafood was very delicious, the price was affordable. On the first night, some tourists came to invite me to have seafood with them. Da Nang Seafood Street was one of the most famous places to taste seafood and we went there by taxi. Every taxi cost 60,000 dong (less than RMB 20) from our hotel to there. We found a famous local seafood restaurant with various kinds of seafood such as crabs, shrimp, squid and shellfish. The local condiment was called fish sauce which was made from the fermentation of some fishes. Chinese are used to eating vinegar and mustard as condiments and they still do not get used to the fish sauce as a condiment. Fortunately, I had prepared in advance and brought out the vinegar and mustard for everyone to eat. Although some group members thought fish sauce was salty and had a stinking smell, they still wanted to try some. Having finished this meal, we returned to the hotel along the beach side.

The next day, a guest told me that he seemed to have a stomachache and his body was very uncomfortable. I suddenly realized that it was because he ate seafood, drank ice beer. He said he wanted to buy some medicine to take. But the tour guide told us that it was impossible because you must have doctor prescription before you buy medicine. Another guest told me that he had the medicine to treat stomachache. After I made its instructions clear, I told my guest to take some medicine and have a rest. Other group members told me that he ate a lot of fish sauce.

After several days, this guest became better and I felt relieved.

Comments

Accumulating experience from daily work and using the experience to serve guests are basic qualities of staff in service industries.

Tour leaders should prepare vinegar or mustard if he leads a tour group to visit island countries, where you can eat seafood because vinegar or mustard can make your stomach feel comfortable. Besides, tour leaders should remind people who have stomach troubles, hypertension, hyperglycemia and hyperlipidemia that they should eat at a moderate amount and do not eat seafood and ice beer at the same time. In this case, the tour leader took the different eating habits and condiments between Chinese and Southeast Asian into consideration and it is worth following.

Work experience covers many aspects. For example, according to tour leader's experience, he should help every guest fill out arrival cards before they start off. In Da Nang, Vietnam, visa-on-arrival applies and thus it is convenient for them to go through entry formalities. In addition, it is easy to have loose bowels when you drink water in Egyptian and Turkey hotels. The tour leader should carry a kettle to help guests prepare hot water to drink and prevent them from having loose bowels.

第五篇

Chapter V

全球导游服务篇

World Wide Tour Guide Services

[本章导读]

目的地导游服务是衡量旅游服务质量高低的重要标杆，始终居于旅游综合服务的中心地位、主导地位。目的地导游的服务意识与服务质量直接影响着游客的旅游消费行为，进而关系到相关地旅游业的持续发展。同时，高质量的目的地导游服务对整个旅游线路的顺利完成有举足轻重的作用。旅游者在世界各地游览时，会遇到不同教育背景、不同个性、不同人种的导游，他们所展示出来的导游服务也各有特色。旅游者在享受境外导游服务的同时，也同样能感受到异国的风情。

本篇通过记叙作者在目的地国家（地区）的旅途见闻等，旨在介绍全球各地导游的精品服务，并开阔读者的眼界。

[Chapter Outline]

When traveling in a destination country/region, tour guide service is an important indicator of tourism service quality. It has always been the critical part of the comprehensive tourism service. Not only the consuming behavior of tourists but also the sustainable development of local tourism is influenced by tour guides' service and service quality. Meanwhile, to fulfill the itinerary successfully highly depends on the tour guides of the destinations can provide good services. When traveling around the world, tourists will encounter tour guides with different educational backgrounds, characters and races, which will lead them to offer guiding services with different styles. Tourists will be greeted with exotic atmosphere while enjoy the guiding services from tour guides of destinations.

In this chapter, based on the previous outbound travel experiences, etc., the author has selected some premium services offered by tour guides around the world, with the aim of assisting tourists in evaluating guiding services properly and broadening their horizons.

比较讲解：让斯里兰卡的历史更容易被理解

无尽的海滩，永恒的废墟，好客的人们，成群的大象，迷人的海滩，低廉的价格，有趣的火车之旅，著名的红茶，诱人的食物……我们可以继续说上一天一夜。

2014年暑假，我有幸担任了杭州招商国际旅游公司"微笑兰卡5夜7天游"旅游团的领队。全团连领队在内的20名团员均是杭州本地人，其中包括4名中学生，4名大学生。

旅游团搭乘7月23日的航班从杭州出发，抵达香港后再从香港经新加坡，最后抵达斯里兰卡的首都科伦坡。尽管是转机，但是从航班提供的机上亚洲美食，以及在香港转机、新加坡经停的短暂休息等方面来说，客人还是感到相当满意的。

来机场迎接我们的导游名叫 RAJIV KANATHIGODA，中文翻译为"达尔克"，他让我们大家称呼他"小达"。巧合的是，小达曾在中国留学13年，在南京师范大学学习汉语，在中国美术学院学过设计，在杭州住过几年，2010年回到斯里兰卡后，他开始从事导游工作。小达和我们真有缘分，他见到杭州的旅游团显得格外热情，与客人的交流自然又亲切。

旅游团行程的第二天上午，我们参观了平纳瓦拉大象孤儿院。这座大象孤儿院建于 1975 年,主要是收养无家可归的、落入陷阱受重伤的、脱离群体迷途的、因战火负伤的及患病的幼象,现共有 70 头左右。目前世界上有两所大象孤儿院,分别在斯里兰卡和肯尼亚。下午,大家游览了拥有 1500 年历史的著名狮子岩古城。小达介绍道:狮子岩古城是弑父篡位的迦叶波一世(477—495)建在岩石上的王宫遗址。狮子岩坐落在葱郁的丛林之中,其建造水平和历史意义让人称奇,登上狮子岩后所能欣赏的绝美景色同样让人惊叹。这块红色的岩石离地有 600 英尺,像一头雄狮俯视天下。在狮子岩上,曾经有 500 幅壁画,现在只剩下 19 幅。

我发现导游在讲解年代的时候,大学生和中学生都没有反应。这时,我在旁边给团员补充了一句:477—495 年这段时间相当于中国的南北朝,团员点头表示理解。

行程的第三天,我们赴波隆纳鲁沃古城游览。这里是斯里兰卡中世纪时的国都。团员们看到了几代国王修建的壮观的宫殿遗迹。神殿、佛牙寺、砖砌的佛塔等建筑遗址无不体现了几何之美,而从婆罗门教遗址可以看出印度文化的影响。在整个讲解中,我又补充了波隆纳鲁沃古城的年代相当于中国的宋朝。团员们也慢慢开始有了对比的习惯。

行程已经过了三天,在酒店用自助餐的时候,我告诉导游小达,在讲解斯里兰卡的历史时,最好能把斯里兰卡与中国做一个对比。这样,游客理解起来比较容易。

斯里兰卡丰富的文化遗产,分布在西古城阿努拉特普拉、东古城波隆纳鲁瓦和中古城康提所形成的三角地带,故称"文化三角"。行程的第四天早上,在大巴上我对团员解释道:"西古城阿努拉特普拉没有包含在行程中,东古城波隆纳鲁瓦我们已经游览过了,今天我们即将游览康提,那里的佛牙寺是康提最著名的朝圣地,始建于 15 世纪,因供奉佛祖释迦牟尼的佛牙而享有盛名,也是康提最重要的景点之一。"经过导游和领队的重复讲解,团员们慢慢对斯里兰卡的历史有了清晰的认识。

[评析]

境外导游的中文水平因不同国家的导游所学中文的途径不一样或练习的方法不一样而有所差异。例如：案例中小达的中文是在南京师范大学学的，按理说水平应该是不错的，但相比小达的旅行社老板——韦先生，就有差距了。显然，韦先生的中文字正腔圆。而某些导游是在斯里兰卡的大学学的中文，他们说话，游客往往听不懂。东南亚国家接待中国团的导游往往是华侨的第三、第四代，他们的中文受上一代华侨的影响较多，加上赴东南亚国家的出境团相对比较多，与中国人的交流相对比较流畅。

南亚国家首先从地理位置上来讲比东南亚国家更远离中国，诸如印度、斯里兰卡，都是近年才有旅行社组团赴这些国家旅游，当地的中文导游严重缺乏。当旺季到来时，连导游都不够用，就很难提出更高的要求了。

进行目的地景点及游览途中的导游讲解，是当地导游的最主要的工作。领队应监督当地导游完成这项工作。领队在导游的讲解过程中，应给予协助。如果导游对其中的部分内容讲解不清，或导游因可能会涉及的人名、地名的中文翻译的差异而产生误解时，领队在旁可轻声向导游进行提醒。在导游未讲解或者讲解完毕的时候，领队应向游客做一些补充解说，特别是对一些历史知识，最好能把目的地国家（地区）的与中国的做一个对比，让旅游者更容易理解。

Tour Guiding by Comparison, Making the History of Sri Lanka More Easy to Understand

Endless beach, perpetual ruins, hospitable people, clustered elephants, beautiful beach, low prices, funny train journey, famous black tea, enticing food ... we can continue talking about Sri Lanka for one day and one night.

During the summer in 2014, I was honored to be the tour leader of the group "Smiley Lanka Five-Day-and-Seven-Night Trip" organized by Hangzhou Merchants International Travel Company of China. The 20 group members, including tour leader were all local people of Hangzhou. This group also included four middle school students and four college students.

This group started on July 23rd from Hangzhou to Hong Kong and then from Hong Kong to Colombo, the capital of Sri Lanka via Singapore. Guests were satisfied with the Asian food provided by the airlines of Dragonair and Cathay Pacific of Hong Kong and the short break in Singapore Changi Airport.

The name of our tour guide who came to Colombo Bandaranaike International airport to pick up us is RAJIV KANATHIGODA and in Chinese it could be translated into Daerke. He let us call him "Xiaoda" and coincidentally he had studied in China for thirteen years. He used to study Chinese in Nanjing

Normal University and studied design in China Academy of Art and also lived in Hangzhou for several years. He went back to Sir Lanka in 2010 and started his work as a tour guide. He seemed extremely enthusiastic when he met the group from Hangzhou.

The schedule of the second morning for this group was to visit Pinna Vala Elephant Orphanage. This Elephant Orphanage was built in 1975 for adopting your elephant that were homeless, wounded by traps, lost with group, injured by wars or got sick. There were 70 elephants in all and this orphanage is one of the only two elephant orphanages in the world. The other one is in Kenya. In the afternoon, we visited the famous ancient city of Sigiriya Lion Rock with 1500 years history. The ancient city of Sigiriya Lion Rock was the relic of imperial palace built on rocks by Gayepothi(477—495)when he killed his father to gain crown. This Sigiriya Lion Rock is located in lush forest. Its standard of construction and the meaning of history impressed us a lot. Tourists were surprised at the wonderful scenery after getting on the top of this rock. This rock is 600 feet high and looks likes a lion overlooking the world. It was said that there were 500 murals on Sigiriya Lion Rock, but now only 19 murals are left.

I noticed that the college students and middle school students in my group had no responses when the tour guide was explaining the historical time. So I added that 477—495 year corresponded to the Southern and Northern Dynasties in China. Tourists nodded to show their agreement.

On the third day of the itinerary we went to Polonnaruwa,an ancient city for visit. It was the capital of Sir Lanka in the Middle Ages. The tourists appreciated the grand palace relic built by generations of kings. Shrines, Asgiri Mahanayake, brick pagoda and other building remains showed the beauty of geometry. From Brahmanism site we could read the influence of Indian culture.

I also added that the age of Polonnaruwa corresponded to the Song Dynasty in China. Gradually the group members were accustomed to this kind of comparison.

I told Xiaoda when explain the history of Sir Lanka it was better to make a comparison between Sir Lanka and China, which would make it easier for tourists to understand.

The rich historical and cultural heritages of Sri Lanka are located in the triangle zone between Anuradhapura in the west, Polonnaruwa in the east and Kandy in the middle. The zone was called "Culture Triangle". On the morning of the fourth day I added explanation to the tourists that the western ancient city, Anuradhapura was not included in our plan and we would went to the middle ancient city Kandy, as we had already visited the eastern ancient city, Polonnaruwa. Asgiri Mahanayake, the most famous pilgrimage site in Kandy, was constructed in 15th century and was famous for enshrining and worshiping the teeth of Shakyamuni Buddha. It was also one of the most important scenic spots. With the detailed explanation of the tour leader and tour guide, the group members were clear about the history of Sri Lanka.

Comments

When it comes to outbound tourism, tour guides of different countries have different levels of Chinese proficiency because they learn and practice Chinese in different ways. For example, in this case, Xiaoda learned his Chinese in Nanjing Normal University and it seemed that his Chinese proficiency was good. However, when compared with that of Xiaoda's boss, Mr. Wei. Xiaoda's Chinese was not that perfect. Mr. Wei's Chinese is better with clear articulation and a mellow tune. However, some tour guides learned their Chinese in the colleges of Sir Lanka and it is really hard for tourists to understand. The tour guides of Southeast Asian nations are usually the third or fourth generation of overseas Chinese, and there are many outbound tourist groups going to Southeast Asian nations, so these guides can communicate with Chinese people fluently and easily.

Geographically, South Asian nations such as India and Sri Lanka, as the destination countries of the tourist groups arranged by travel agency in recent years are further from China than Southeast Asian nations. The number of local guides in those countries is limited. The Chinese-speaking tour guides in these countries can never meet needs in peak tourist season.

Tour guides play the most important role in explaining scenic spots of the destination and views on the way. Tour leaders should supervise tour guides to complete this work and offer proper help to him when the tour guide is explaining. If the local guide is not clear about some parts of content or translates some names of people and places improperly, the tour leader can remind him softly. Before or after tour guide's explanation, the tour leader can make some supplementary instructions, especially the history of the destination, it's better to compare between China and the destination to make it easier to understand.

宝岛最温馨的记忆——金门高粱酒

"亲爱的贵宾,宝岛台湾马上就要到达了,请各位……"

4月中旬的某一天,当我从杭州出发,途经香港,在台湾长荣航空公司的班机上听到这则广播时,心情无比激动。台湾——这个在课本里出现过的,我听说过无数次却没有到过的地方,今天终于可以见到它的真面目了。

一提到台湾,人们总会在前面加上"宝岛"二字。这个美丽的岛屿从飞机上看形似一片芭蕉叶,它北临东海,西对台湾海峡,东对太平洋,南端是巴士海峡,其得天独厚的旅游资源,举世少有。虽然面积只有3.6万平方公里,却横跨亚热带与热带,再加上地壳板块运动造成复杂的地形,高山、丘陵、盆地、平原、纵谷与海岸等地貌应有尽有。高耸的山岳也将温带生态带入宝岛,让旅游者在短短的旅程中就能见识到温带、亚热带、热带三种各具特色的自然生态。

我们的行程共有8天。前三天天气一直不错,团员们参观了台北"故宫博物院"珍藏的文物,特别欣赏了镇馆之宝——"翡翠玉白菜"和"肉形石"。其形态逼真,大家都啧啧称赞。其间,团员们还兴致勃勃地在珍珠奶茶发源地——台中,品尝了地道的珍珠奶茶及味道鲜美的新竹米粉。

第三天,团员们游览了如诗如画的日月潭。日月潭位于台湾中心唯一不临海的南投县,是台湾最大的淡水湖泊。此趟旅行在这里也到达了最高潮。到了第四天,旅游团从台南驱车前往阿里山,途中天气还是好好的。我们品尝了阿里山高山茶。午后,忽来的大雨加冰雹让我们在阿里山森林游乐区的行程遇到了不小的麻烦,山路减慢了我们的步速,狂风大雨把我们的雨伞也变成了摆设,大家全部被淋湿了。我们跟着台湾导游小熊从阿里山森林游乐区回到车上的时候,他突然转身说要临时买样东西,让我领队先把游客领上车,当时让我十分不解。过了几分钟小熊回来的时候,他的手里多了一瓶金门高粱酒。接下来他的行为让我颇为感叹。导游小熊一边对因大雨受到影响的行程做解释,安抚游客,一边拿出一次性纸杯把酒倒上分给游客喝。金门高粱酒历史悠久,口感清香,余味悠长,同时有祛风除湿、活血通络的功效。刚爬山下来又被雨淋湿了的游客,这样喝一杯是再适合不过了。导游的这份热情周到的服务感动了参团的游客朋友。

[评析]

酒是用来安抚及馈赠游客的。买酒给游客品尝,这是一个极为普通的行为,但何时何地买酒大有学问。案例中,台湾导游的灵活应对,以及对酒的药用知识的了解,让我们深切体会到了台湾旅游业"服务为先"的先进理念。

大陆与台湾的文化同根同源。导游的服务行为及理念的执行是否完美,会直接影响到两岸民众的情感。换句话说,台湾优质的服务会让更多的大陆同胞赴台湾旅游,也能使两岸民众的交流更加畅通。

Kinmen Kaoliang Liquor, the Warmest Memory in Taiwan

"Dear passengers, we will arrive at Taiwan in no time, please ... "

One day in mid April, hearing the broadcast on the flight from Hangzhou to Taiwan via Hong Kong, I became excited. I could see Taiwan, the place I had seen on the textbooks and I had heard for so many times, with my own eyes!

People always call Taiwan "treasure island", since it possesses unique and rare tourism resources. Viewing from the airplane, it looks like a banana leaf facing the East China Sea on the north, Taiwan Strait on the west, Pacific Ocean on the east and Bashi Channel on the south. Covering an area of 36,000 square kilometers, it goes across the subtropical and tropical zones. Besides, the plate movements contribute to the varied complex topographies like mountains, hills, basins, plains, valleys and coasts. The towering mountains bring temperate ecosystems to Taiwan. So tourists could enjoy three different natural ecologies of the temperate zone, subtropical zone and tropical zone with their respective features.

Our trip would last eight days. The weather was good for the first three days. We appreciated cultural relics in "Palace Museum" in Taipei. Claimed as the treasures of the palace, the "Jadeite Chinese Cabbage" and "Cooked-pork-like Stone" were our focus. Their lifelike shapes and colors amazed us deeply. During the trip, members of our group tasted the authentic pearl milk tea in Taizhong—the birthplace of its kind and the delicious Xinzhu rice noodles.

On the third day, our group members visited the picturesque Sun-moon Lake which is located in central Taiwan's Nantou County which is the only one not by sea. It is the largest freshwater lake in Taiwan. On the fourth day, the weather was good while we were on our way from Tainan to Alishan. But after we tasted the Alishan high mountain tea, it changed to a sudden heavy rain and hail, making our trip in Alishan forest a difficult one. The mountain trails slowed our pace; our umbrellas malfunctioned due to the strong wind and heavy rain. Everyone was soaked.

Then we followed the local guide from the Alishan Forest recreational areas back to the bus. He suddenly turned and said to me that he wanted to buy something and asked me to get on the bus with the travelers first. After a few minutes, he came back with a bottle of Kinmen Kaoliang liquor. He comforted the travelers for the inconveniences caused by the heavy rain. At the same time he took out disposable paper cups and poured the liquor for the tourists.

Kinmen Kaoliang liquor is one of the treasures with a long history. With the functions of dispelling wind-evil and eliminating wetness, it is perfect for the travelers who just climbed down the mountain and got wet in the rain. His hospitable and thoughtful service moved all the travelers.

Comments

Wine usually serves as a gift to thank and comfort travelers. So buy wine for your customer is a very common behavior. But when and where to buy is a big issue. In this case, the local guide's flexibility and quick response, his knowledge of the medicinal functions of wine，taught us a lesson about Taiwan's "service first" concept in tourism industry.

Taiwan and the mainland are the same root. The guide's service quality greatly influences the relations between the two sides. In other words，the high quality service of Taiwan guides will leave a positive impression on mainland travelers，and promote the heart-to-heart communication between people on both sides of the strait.

热气球怎么未能升空？

　　澳大利亚昆士兰州北部的凯恩斯是一座充满魔力的海滨城市，也是前往世界奇观大堡礁的必经之路。这里接近赤道，四季如春，背倚高山，四周郁郁葱葱，拥有世界最大的活体珊瑚礁群景观、原始雨林风光、迷人的海岸线、宝石般的岛屿、银色沙滩及蓝色海洋，所以凯恩斯素有"热带首都"之誉。

　　在"澳凯 8 日游"的行程中，凯恩斯正好处在整个行程的中间，也是整个行程的精华所在。从悉尼飞往凯恩斯的当天，旅行团就游览了被列为世界自然保护遗产的库兰达热带雨林公园。团员们在热带雨林中与考拉拍照，观赏了 40 多种奇特的热带水果，学习了如何抛掷回力标和射箭，如何吹奏迪吉里杜管，还聆听了土著人最质朴的歌声，欣赏了他们最原始的歌舞。同时，团员们乘坐水陆两用军车穿梭于热带雨林中的密林激流之间，在林深叶茂、枝缠藤错之中聆听天籁之音。晚餐时，团员们谈论着白天的精彩旅游，憧憬着第二天乘坐"太阳恋人号"游轮去大堡礁观光。

　　这时，凯恩斯导游过来向客人推荐第二天的自费旅游项目，乘坐热气球观景——随着热气球在房顶、田园上空飘行，可以看到天边缓缓升起的太阳，观赏袋鼠进食，远眺白天游览过的库兰达热带雨林公园，在如此宽广辽阔的空间，大口大口呼吸新鲜空气,尽情享受这难得的美好时光!客人听了导游的描述,都非常想参加此项活动,但导游告诉大家,若要参加此项活动必须在第二天清晨4:00起床,4:30离开酒店赴乘坐热气球的地点。团员们商议后,决定参加此项自费活动并将费用交给了导游。导游收完了钱,和旅游公司确认人数后告知客人,大家乘坐热气球的自费活动将被安排在第二场。由于场次的不同,乘坐热气球的时间和所观赏的内容就有了很大的变动,第一场是安排在清晨5:00多看日出并观赏袋鼠进食,以及俯瞰库兰达热带雨林公园。第二场要早上8:00才能坐上热气球观看凯恩斯的城市全貌及俯瞰库兰达热带雨林公园。但无论参加哪场活动的客人都得清晨4:30离开酒店。

团员们觉得早上4:00起床,要等到8:00才能坐上热气球,而且也不能看到日出与袋鼠进食,不太合理。商议之后决定取消该自费项目。当领队告诉导游这一决定时,导游表示已经订好的活动项目是不能取消的,而且也无法退回乘坐热气球的费用,示意游客必须参加。游客表示不理解,导游之前根本没有讲到热气球活动有两场,现在甲、乙双方的合同还没有实施,怎么会不能退款呢?导游打电话给当地的旅游公司,旅游公司的计调人员在电话的那一端告诉导游不能把钱退给游客。这时,领队接过电话,告诉计调人员:不管怎么说,由于导游没有把旅游产品介绍清楚,所以客人的取消是合理的,退款是必须的,今天不退,客人回到中国也会要求退的。到时,我们中国的组团社还会从团费中扣除这笔费用,但这给游客留下的是什么印象呢?

同时,领队立刻打电话至中国的组团社,要求组团社打电话给凯恩斯的地接社,迫使他们以最快的速度将款项退还给游客。经过领队与导游长时间的协商,在参加"热气球"活动的全体游客的坚持下,导游终于同意全额退款。

第二天,游客们兴致勃勃地乘坐"太阳恋人号"游轮去大堡礁观光。从水下和水面上观赏美丽的珊瑚礁、各色鱼类、海龟、巨蚌等。一天的兴奋,使游客们慢慢忘却了"热气球"事件。第三天,团友们就要离开凯恩斯赴澳洲第三大城市——布里斯班。考虑到因热气球项目的取消,导游可能会承担一定的损失,领队在第二天晚餐时,关于"热气球"事件向游客做了解释,提出希望参加热气球项目的客人能给予导游一定的现金补偿。于是，领队拿出一个空信封，传递给游客，游客理解了领队的用意，一个一个地将信封传递下去。导游拿到这个信封后，感谢之意溢于言表。就此，因热气球自费项目导致的尴尬得以终止。

[评析]

本案例中的导游对此自费项目并无体验，在介绍前也没进行细致的了解（这一点，是在发生了争端以后，从领队和导游的交谈中得知的）。所以，导游在向客人推荐"热气球"这个自费项目时，未能做到具体翔实，从而导致游客的误解。事实上，导游在介绍第一场热气球活动时，应该以看日出和袋鼠进食为卖点；第二场则应该以观看清晨城市全貌作为卖点，进行宣传。这样的话，游客在交纳费用之前，会有一个明确的选择，就不会导致后续事件的发生。因此这场争端的导火线，是导游对旅游产品的不熟悉。

领队带团出境，所具有的一个重要职能就是对旅游产品的诠释，决不能因为是第一次或者从未去过某国而不去关心或者不去介入旅游者与导游的纠纷。设想，如果领队能在出团前，对将有可能出现的自费项目进行了解，并在导游收款之前替导游对这两场热气球活动做个补充解释，那争端也许就不会发生。出境领队的另一个重要职能就是协调。领队虽然自身对产品没有做充分的了解，但始终以大局为出发点，在与当地旅游公司、导游进行协商后，退还给了游客自费项目的费用，缓和了游客的情绪。随后，又进一步向游客们做出说明，使游客愿意向导游支付一定的赔偿，化解了导游与游客之间的矛盾，起到了导游与游客之间的桥梁作用。

旅游产品是个整体概念，它是由旅游资源、旅游设施、旅游服务和旅游商品等多种要素组成的。其特征是旅游服务成为旅游产品构成的主体，其具体展示主要有线路、活动和食宿等方面。

推销旅游产品要从以下几个方面着手。第一，对游客会前往的旅游设施、将享受到的旅游服务及所要购买的旅游商品进行充分的了解。第二，推销时做到诚信、具体。第三，在带团过程中做好协调工作，使行程更加顺畅，使服务得以完善。

Why Doesn't the Hot Balloon Lift Up?

Located in the north of Queensland, Australia, Cairns is a magic seaside city, and also a must way to visit the world wonder, the Great Barrier Reef. As the city is not far from the equator, it is like spring all the year round. Leaning against high mountains, its scenery around enjoys a luxuriantly green scape. Cairns also possesses the biggest living coral reef group in the world, original rainforest scenery, charming coastline, diamond-like islands, the silver beach, and blue sea. Therefore, Cairns enjoys the reputation of a "tropical capital".

During the 8-day visit to Australia, Cairns is the essence of the trip. On the day after our flight from Sydney to Cairns, the group visited the Kuranda tropical rainforest park that has been listed as the world natural conservation heritage. The group members took photos with koalas, viewed more than 40 kinds of peculiar tropical fruits, learned how to play the boomerang, how to shoot an arrow and how to play the dean jiri du tube, listened to the simplest songs of the natives, and appreciated their primitive songs and dances. Meanwhile, the members took amphibious military vehicle, zigzagging in the thickest woods and fierce streams, and enjoying the celestial voice in the branch-bounding and deep leafy forest. During the dinner, the tour members chanted about the wonderful trip in the daytime, and longed for next day's visit to the Great Barrier Reef by the cruise named Sunlover.

Just at that moment, a Cairns guide came to recommend an optional project, viewing from a hot balloon. As the hot balloon flies over the roofs and fields, visitors can view the rising sun smiling to them, observe kangaroos dining, overlook the Kuranda tropical rainforest park, take a gulp of breathing in this vast place and fully enjoy the good time! On hearing the guide's description, all the members wanted to experience it. But the guide told them that if they were going to take part in this trip, they had to get up at 4:00 a.m. the next morning and leave hotel at 4:30 to the place where they could take the hot balloon. After discussion, the tour group members decided to take this activity at their own expense. The guide took the money and count the number of customers. But after he confirmed the number of tourists with the local tourism company, he told the group that their trip would be arranged in the second session. There were great differences between different sessions. The first session would be at 5:00 and the visitors could see the sun rising, watch the kangaroos dining, and overlook the Kuranda tropical rainforest park, while the second one would be at 8:00 for tourists to take the hot balloon to look at the whole city and have a bird's view of the Kuranda tropical rainforest park. Visitors of both sessions should leave the hotel at 4:30.

Hearing that, the group members thought that they had to get up at 4:00, and wait until 8:00 to take the hot balloon without seeing the sunrise and kangaroos, dine. So they decided to cancel this activity. When the tour leader told the guide about this, he was informed that this part of the tour could not be canceled and refunded, indicating that they had no other choice but take part in the activity. The customers were confused, because the guide hadn't mention

第五篇 全球导游服务篇

279

that there were two sessions of this activity before. Now that contract between the two sides had not been executed yet, why couldn't they ask for a refund? The guide called the local tourism company and the tour planner of the company told the guide that the money couldn't be refunded to the customers. At the moment, the team leader took the phone and told them that in any way, it was the guide that didn't introduce the project clearly, so the customers' cancellation was reasonable, and the refund would surely be made. If they could not get the money back now, they would ask for refund after going back to China. At that time, the travel agency who organized the group would deduct it from the group's total payment, and then what would be the impression left in the customers' mind?

In the meantime, the team leader called the Chinese travel agency immediately, and asked the latter to call the local agency in Cairns, urging them to return the fare. After a long negotiation between the team leader and the guide, and thanks to the persistence of all the customers that took part in the activity, the guide finally decided to give a full refund.

The next day, the group members took a trip on the Sunlover Cruise to visit the Great Barrier Reef in high spirits, appreciating the beautiful coral reefs, the various kinds of fishes, sea turtles and big clams from both underwater and above the water. After a whole day's excitement, all the customers gradually forgot the hot balloon event. On the third day, they were leaving Cairns to the third biggest city of Australia, Brisbane. Considering the cancellation of the hot balloon activity might cause some loss to the guide, the tour leader suggested that the customers who had wanted to joined this project give some cash as a compensation to the guide. He took out an empty envelope and passed it to the customers. The customers showed their understanding by putting money into the envelope and passed it one by one. The guide was really grateful when he received this envelope. So far, hot balloon issue was solved properly and successfully.

Comments

The guide in this case didn't have any experience of this optional project, neither did he have a detailed knowledge before (this information is known during the talk between the team leader and the guide after the conflict). So when the guide suggested the optional hot balloon project to the customers, his introduction was not detailed and accurate, and that led to the customers' misunderstanding. In fact, when introducing hot balloon project, the guide should take viewing the sunrise and the kangaroos dining as the selling points of the first session and appreciating the whole city in early morning as the selling point of the second session. If so, the customers would have a clear view before they paid the fees, and the subsequent events wouldn't have taken place. Therefore, the conflict was caused by the tour guide's unfamiliarity with the tourism products.

One of the important functions of a tour leader is the familiarity with tourism products. It is not allowed to disregard or stay away from the conflict between the visitors and the tour guide, by the excuse of first coming or never been to the destination country. If the leader had had a brief knowledge of the optional projects before the group went abroad, or gave a complementary explanation on the two sessions of the hot balloon project before the tour guide charged, the conflict in the case may not have happened. Another important function of an outbound tour leader is coordination. Though the leader didn't have a good knowledge of the products, he bore in mind the overall interests of his group all the time, and demanded refund for the customers after negotiating with the local travel company and the guide, alleviating the customers' unpleasantness. After that, he further explained to the customers and made them willing to pay some compensation to the guide, dissolving the contradiction between them. In this case, the tour leader acted as a bridge, connecting the customers and the guide.

Tourism product is a whole conception，and consists of many factors such as tourism resources，tourism facilities，tourism services，tourism commodities and so on. Among these tourism services is the main ingredient and is shown in the forms of routes，activities，accommodation，etc.

Selling a tourism product can be done from these aspects. First，the guide should have an overall，detailed and accurate understanding of tourism facilities and services that the customers will have，and the commodities the customers will buy. Second，when the guide recommends a tourism product，he should be honest and detailed. Third，the guide should coordinate well in the course of leading the tour group，making the trip successful.

在甲米，踩到海胆后

　　提起泰国，这个 1988 年向中国公民开放的旅游目的地国家，中国国内的旅游者首先想到的旅游城市可能是曼谷、帕提亚，或者普吉岛。最近，"普吉＋甲米"的行程越来越受到中国旅游者的追捧。甲米岛在泰国的南部，与普吉岛隔海相望。甲米拥有 30 多个离岛，是安达曼海岸边最美丽的地方。这里有温暖而干净的沙滩，有远离世俗的慢节奏生活，可谓无处不美景，无处不浪漫。这里的沙滩各具风情，而每一片沙滩面积都不大，不会互相打扰，因此能安静地分享同一片海景。甲米的海并不是一望无际的，时常可以看到近前的大大小小的岛屿。小岛附近的海水呈绿色，然后依次是浅蓝色、水蓝色、深蓝色。

　　今天是"普吉＋甲米 4 晚 6 天豪华团"的第三天行程，许多客人直接换好了泳装，披着当地最有特色的纱笼从酒店出发，因为第一站就是乘快艇前往度假天堂——珊瑚岛，这是欧美人最爱的日光浴天堂！珊瑚岛能让游客感受到南国岛屿的活力。一旦去那儿，游客就会为它的清新美丽深深着迷，这里有清澈湛蓝的海洋、洁白如雪的沙滩，以及让你敞开心扉的多项水上活动。

　　客人王女士虽然年纪大了些，可是心态依然很年轻，但出于安全和身体考虑，她选择了最安全的海底太空漫步。别的客人也根据自己的身体情况选择了不同的水上活动项目。领队和导游安排好了所有客人的水上项目时间,才在沙滩椅上坐下来休息,并帮客人照看他们的衣物,但没能坐上 5 分钟,就听到团员大喊领队小程。导游和领队闻声就朝着人群走去,只见王女士满脸的痛苦。"阿姨,你这是怎么了?"领队小程焦急地问道。王女士好像痛得没法说话了,只能指指脚。原来,王女士看见大海太兴奋了,把刚才上岛宣布的注意事项全给忘了,虽然这个岛风景怡人,但是有些区域有很多海胆,王女士一不小心踩到了海胆。

海胆又名"海刺猬",胆壳布满棘刺,一般约 1—2 厘米长,1—2 毫米厚,呈圆锥形。棘刺本身中空及易碎,断掉的棘刺可以再生长出来,而有些海胆的棘刺末端有毒囊。王女士不小心走进了海胆区,踩到了海胆,幸好这里的海胆是无毒的,可是踩到海胆相当痛。"怎么办?用针挑出来吧。""不,我们还是应该上医院。"围观的人七嘴八舌地出着主意。领队小程也很紧张,这事可真棘手。小程对王女士说:"阿姨,这个海胆刺是空心的,而且你脚上可有一大片,挑出来也要费不少工夫。但如果不及时处理,你会发烧,脚也会很肿,哪儿都去不了。如今只有一种办法,就是当地人用的土办法,用比较硬的拖鞋底拍您的脚,直到把这些刺都拍碎了,然后您再吃点消炎片,过两天就好了,也不会发烧,只是拍打的时候非常疼。"这时,边上围观的人又七嘴八舌议论开了,有些人赞同,有些人反对,认为还是要去医院。领队小程压力很大,这事要是处理不好,到时可都会怪自己。看王女士还在犹豫,小程又对她说:"阿姨,我是一名专业领队,这件事情上请您相信我的专业知识及长久以来的带团经验,当然最后的选择权在您手上,您可以选择去医院,也可以选择用土方医治。"这时导游已经从餐厅拿来了醋准备消毒,并告诉王女士领队的方法是正确的,只是真的很痛,不知道阿姨能不能忍。后来王女士在她先生的陪伴下强忍着痛被拖鞋拍打了好一阵,直到刺都被打碎了,其间还不断用醋消毒。

两天之后,王女士脚上的碎刺已经不见了,她也可以走路了,只是脚还有一些肿,但慢慢走路没问题,阿姨脸上又露出了花一般的笑容。

[评析]

从旅行者向旅行公司咨询开始,到旅游合同履行完毕为止,都是旅行社履行告知义务的阶段。告知义务的履行必须贯穿于旅游服务全过程。在签订旅游合同阶段，旅行社必须将旅游目的地的固有情况告知旅游者，由旅游者决定是否参加旅游；在旅游合同的履行阶段，领队、导游在服务的每一个环节上都要告知旅游者注意事项，确保旅游者人身财产安全。

案例中王女士由于看到大海一时比较激动，忘了导游、领队在上岛前宣布的注意事项。尽管领队、导游已经履行了告知义务，但客人在旅游活动中还是出了问题。领队在处理该案例时果断、快速。导游也是当机立断，较好地解决了发生的难题。

履行告知义务必须针对不同的旅游产品。常规线路有常规线路的提示和说明，非常规线路有非常规线路的警示和提醒，不能千篇一律。所以领队、导游在出团之前一定要做好功课，不但要预测到可能会发生的问题，而且要想好解决问题的方法。

After Treading on a Sea Urchin in Krabi

Thailand was the country as a tourist destination to open to Chinese citizens in 1988. The tourist cities in Thailand at that time were Bangkok, Parthia and Phuket Island. However, in recent years, the trip of "Phuket Island and Krabi" has become more and more popular among Chinese tourists. Krabi is located in the south of Thailand, facing with Phuket Island across the sea. With more than 30 offshore islands here, it is the most beautiful place on the Shore of Andaman Sea. In addition, you can enjoy the warm and clean beach and a slow pace of life here. Everywhere is beautiful and everything is romantic. Each beach here has its own enchanting scenery and they can share the same sea scenery without disturbing with each other because of the small area of each beach. The sea of Krabi is indeed not endless and sometimes you can see a few small or big islands above sea water. The color of the sea nearby is green and then light blue, water blue and dark blue progressively.

It was the third day of the deluxe group of four nights and six days in Phuket Island and Krabi. Most people started off from hotel in swimsuit or in the special local sarong. They would take a yacht to the first scenic spot, Coral Island—a paradise resort, and a paradise of sunbath which is the most favorite to westerners. Coral Island is a warm island that you can feel the vigor. You will be obsessed with its fresh and beautiful scenery once you visit there. And you can feel free to choose the various kinds of water sports there.

One of our guests, Mrs. Wang was a senior citizen, but she had a young heart. In consideration of security and her body condition she chose spacewalk under the sea activity. Others also chose different water sports according to their body conditions. After arranging water sports for tourists, the tour leader and the tour guide sat on beach chairs for a short rest and took care of all luggage of tourists. Suddenly, they heard tourists yelling for help. They immediately went to see what had happened. When they got there, they saw Mrs. Wang's face was full of pain. The tour leader asked her anxiously, "What is wrong, Mrs. Wang?" Mrs. Wang felt so painful that she could not even speak a word and just only pointed to her foot. What happened was that Mrs. Wang was so excited when she saw the beautiful sea that she forgot all the matters needing attention. Although this island is very enchanting, there are a lot of sea urchins in some districts. And Mrs. Wang treaded on a sea urchin.

Sea urchin is called "sea hedgehog". Its shell is full of thorns which are 1—2 cm long, and 1—2 cm thick and it looks like a conical. Thorns are hollow and fragile and can re-grow if they are broken. There are poison sacs on the bottom of thorns for some kinds of sea urchin. Mrs. Wang stepped into sea urchin area carelessly. Fortunately sea urchins here are nontoxic. However, treading on sea urchins caused much pain. "How to deal with such a thing? What about picking those thorns out by needle?" "No, we should go to hospital." People started to suggest. The tour leader, Mr. Cheng, was a little nervous because of this troublesome thing and she told Mrs. Wang that those thorns were hollow and it would take a lot of time if she tried to pick them out as those thorns covered a large area. However, if she did not deal with it immediately, she would have a fever and her foot would get swollen and thus she could go nowhere. Now there was only one way and that was a local method. It was patting her foot with the hard sole slipper until all the thorns were broken. Afterwards, Mrs. Wang should take anti-inflammatory. Then she would recover after two days and not get a fever although it was painful when her sole was patted. Having heard this method, people expressed their opinions again. Some agreed with using this local method and some did not agree and insisted going to the hospital. Mr. Cheng, the tour leader, suffered huge stress because if she could not handle it well she would be to blame. Realizing Mrs. Wang's hesitation, Mr. Cheng told Mrs. Wang that she was a professional tour leader to be trusted because she had professional knowledge and a lot of experience. Of course, Mrs. Wang could make her own choice. At that time, the tour leader came back with vinegar for disinfecting and told Mrs. Wang this method was correct but it was really painful and he did not know whether she could stand it or not. Later, accompanied by her husband, Mrs. Wang bore the pain with difficult when patted by the slipper for a while until the thorns were all broken. At the same time, her foot kept being disinfected by vinegar.

After two days, the thorns in Mrs. Wang's foot were already gone and she could walk slowly although her foot was still a little swollen.

Comments

Travel agency should perform the duty of informing all the way till it has finished performing the contracts. When signing the travel contract, travel agency should tell tourists about the situation of tourist destination and whether participation in traveling is determined by tourists themselves. In the period of performing the travel contract, the tour leader and the tour guide should inform tourists of points for attention at every stage of providing service to ensure their personal and property safety.

In this case, Mrs. Wang was so excited at the beautiful sea that she forgot the points of attention which the tour guide and the tour leader had said before. Although the tour guide and the tour leader had already performed the duty of notice, guests still had trouble. Luckily, the tour leader handled this problem immediately and decisively with the proper help from the tour guide.

In addition, performing the duty of notice must fit in with different tourist products. Conventional routine has its own points for attention and instruction different from unconventional routines. Therefore, the tour leader and the tour guide should be well prepared, forecast problems may happen and think out solutions before departure.

当伊朗导游的讲解与网上看到的内容一样时

　　伊朗是具有近五千年历史的文明古国。波斯是伊朗的古名。公元前 6 世纪，波斯帝国盛极一时，成为世界上第一个地跨亚、非、欧三大洲的帝国。波斯帝国的兴盛及多民族文明的交融，造就了波斯民族文化的多样性。

　　马汉航空开通了上海飞德黑兰的航线，从而省去了赴伊游客中途转机的时间，同时也催热了伊朗文化之旅。2014 年 7 月，笔者有幸担任了"面纱后的波斯：伊朗 12 日探寻之旅"的领队。旅途中，有欢喜，有惊奇，有疑虑，也有一点点小遗憾。但无论如何，客人们都觉得不虚此行。作为领队，笔者有一点感悟，以飨读者。

　　行程的第三天，旅行团来到了著名的格列斯坦宫（Golestan Palace），"Gole"是"花"的意思，因此格列斯坦宫意为"花之皇宫"。这座王宫从卡加王朝到巴列维王朝都为王室居住地，是一座集华丽的宫殿、宁静的水池及优美的花园为一体的王宫。后来，我们又看了若干个不同时期的王宫，基本都由这三个元素组成。在波斯人的心目中有一种说法：有水、有花园、有庭院的地方就是天堂。

　　走进王宫，首先映入眼帘的是一个长长的水池，一溜儿喷泉，两旁鲜花盛开，绿树掩映，那干热的天气也变得令人愉快了。水池尽头就是一座宫殿。它是开放式的,在水池的另一头就能远远看到宫中的宝座。这是一座类似汉白玉雕刻的宝座,两侧各由三位服饰不同的女子驮着。据说这表示波斯帝国疆土开阔,统辖着各族人民。令人不解的是,这样沉重的宝座为什么要让女人来驮?宝座的台阶下蹲着两只狮子。狮子两旁各有个精灵模样的人站立。

这座宫殿无论是外表还是内饰都很华丽,最令人印象深刻的是外墙上的彩釉瓷砖,内部晶莹闪烁的镜面镶嵌装饰,以及精细的石膏雕花。卡加王朝开始的装饰元素主要就是这三个——马赛克、镜面和石膏,都是比较经济的材料,但工艺很考究,看上去富丽堂皇。据说主要是因为到了卡加王朝,已进入半殖民地半封建时期,北面被俄国人控制,南面被英国人控制,波斯帝国日渐式微,而国君却只顾自己享乐。特别是卡加第四任国王纳赛尔丁,他很亲西方,喜欢西方的艺术。这座宫殿就有不少西方元素:比如一般的波斯瓷砖或马赛克装饰的花纹以几何图形和花草为主要图案,可这座宫殿外墙上的瓷砖却常常可以看到西方的油画。波斯宫殿的颜色以蓝色为主,而这座宫殿外墙颜色非常艳丽,据说也是国王的品位偏西方所致。

伊朗导游非常认真地带领游客参观宫殿内的陈设、装修,讲解着那些他认为的独特之处。但是,尽管伊朗导游事先强调过,请先跟着他,听完讲解,然后再自由活动。但是,一部分游客还是惊叹于园内美不胜收的景色,慢慢脱团,管自己拍照去了。该伊朗导游也算是半个"中国通"了,他了解中国游客的行为模式。但是忍了许久之后,他还是在去宫内一个参观点的途中,半开玩笑半认真地询问了两个会讲英语的团友:为什么不愿意跟着他听解说呢?本来,他只是随便一问。但是两位团友的回答,却让人诧异。他们直接说:"你讲的,网上都有,我们看过了。"虽然也是开玩笑的口吻,但是在大庭广众之下,还是让伊朗导游十分尴尬。

事后,作为领队试图想缓解下气氛,但导游还是十分愤懑,好在他的职业素养较好,继续讲解下面的景点。

[评析]

据伊朗媒体报道,2014年3月至6月,赴伊朗旅游的外国游客数量较去年同期增长 21.5％,其中很大一部分来自中国。伊朗马汉航空已开通上海、广州直飞德黑兰的航班,北京飞德黑兰也在 2014 年 10 月 30 日首航。受直飞航线开通、旅游配套设施不断完善等因素影响,像伊朗这种传统意义上的小众目的地国家被越来越多的中国游客关注。客户群从旅游经验丰富、对文化旅游感兴趣的高端客户逐渐扩大到大众游客。

  导游在伊朗、土耳其、埃及这些中东国家属于社会地位较高的职业。导游只负责讲解工作,而在机场、码头等地接送游客的工作则由导游的助理来完成。因此,他们的导游服务理念和中国不太一样。在导游讲解时,对旅游者倾听的要求非常高,一是因为认真倾听是对导游讲解服务的尊重,二是因为他们的汉语有时不是非常流利,旅游者不认真听讲,导游的情绪会受到影响。所以,领队在带团过程中,一定要控制住团队人员的流动,尽量不要让客人离团。另外,出境游领队有义务提醒游客在对境外导游开玩笑时,要收敛一点。毕竟不同国家之间存在文化差异,若引起误解与不悦,绝对不是一件小事情。

When What the Iranian Guide Said Was What You Saw on the Internet

Iran is an ancient country with a history of almost 5,000 years. It was called Persia in the ancient times. In the 6th century BC, the Persian Empire dominated and became the first empire which crossed Asia, Africa and Europe.

The rise and decline of Persian Empire and the fusion of ethnic culture are the reasons for the variety of Persian national culture.

It has saved the time of taking a connecting flight and triggered Iranian cultural tour upsurge since Mahan Air opened new routes between Shanghai and Teheran. In July 2014, I was lucky to be the tour leader of "Persia Wearing a Veil: 12 Days Exploring Tour in Iran". The journey was accompanied with happiness, surprise, confusion and a pity. All the guests thought it was a worthwhile trip. As a tour leader, I had some insights, which I could share with readers.

On the third day of our trip, we went to the famous Golestan Palace. "Gole" means flower, so Golestan Palace means Flowery Palace. The palace was the residence of the royal family from the Qajar Dynasty to the Pahlavi Dynasty. This is a gorgeous palace with quiet pool and beautiful garden. Other palaces we visited later which were built in different periods were also composed of water, garden and court yard. In the eye of the Persian, a paradise is like this.

When we came into the palace, we first saw a long pond, a row of fountains, trees and flowers on both sides, which made the dry and hot weather pleasant. At the end of the pond was a palace. It was an open palace and you could see the throne from distance at the other end of the pond. The throne was carved by white marble and there were three women in different clothes supporting the throne on each side. It implied that the Persia Empire had a large territory and dominated people of all nationalities. But we wondered why this heavy throne had to be carried by women. Under the bench of the throne were two lions. Lion was the symbol of authority like that in China. On each side of these two lions stood a man who looked like a spirit.

This palace was gorgeous both inside and outside. What impressed us most

中国公民出境旅游服务质量解析

was the exterior wall decorated with colored glaze ceramic and mosaic tiles, glittering mirror and delicate plaster carvings. The decorative style of the early Qajar Dynasty was embodied by three elements: mosaic, mirror and plaster. The economical materials, with delicate craftsmanship created a grandeur atmosphere. It was said that the Qajar Dynasty was a semi-colonial and semi-feudal society. The northern part was controlled by Russia while the southern part was controlled by England. The Persia Empire became weaker and weaker because the emperor just considered his own enjoyment. The forth emperor, Naser al-Din Shah Qajar, favored Western countries and their arts. So this palace had a Western style. For example, usually the patterns of Persian ceramic tiles or mosaic decoration were mainly geometric figures, flowers and grasses. However, you can see Western oil painting on the ceramic tiles of the Palace's exterior wall. The main color of Persia was blue, but the color of the exterior wall was very colorful.

The Iranian guide led the tourists to visit the furnishings and decoration of the palace and explained its unique parts. Although the Iranian guide emphasized that tourists should follow him first and then they could have free time after listening the explanation, there were still some tourists leaving the team to take photos. Noticing this, the Iranian guide asked two tourists who could speak English about the reason why some tourists did not want to listen to him. The answer was that what the tour guide said was exactly the same as the information on the Internet. The tour guide was very embarrassed.

After this, the tour leader tried to relax the atmosphere, but the guide was still very angry. Fortunately, he continued to guide us to the following scenic spots, showing his professional attitude.

Comments

As the Iranian media reported, from March to June in 2014 the number of inbound tourists had increased 21.5% compared with a year ago and most of them were from China. Iranian Mahan Air has already opened routes directly from Shanghai and Guangzhou to Teheran. The first flight from Beijing to Teheran started on October 30th, 2014. Because of the opening of direct fight routes and the improving of tourism facilities, once unpopular destination countries like Iran has been drawn attention to by more and more Chinese people. The customer group has been expanding from high-end customers with rich experience and great interests in cultural tourism to those general tourists.

Tour guide is an occupation with high social status in Middle East countries such as Iran, Turkey and Egypt. Tour guides in Iran are responsible for delivering tourism attractions' commentary. Picking up and dropping off tourists is the job of tour guide's assistant. Therefore, the concept of tour guide service is different from that in China. When a tour guide is explaining a scenic spot, tourists should listen very carefully. Because your attention not only shows your respect to the tour guide, but influences the mood of the tour guide. In a word, tour leader should notice the group and try his best to keep the members together. In addition, tour leader should remind tourists to be careful when making jokes with foreigner tour guides, since we have different cultural backgrounds which could possibly cause misunderstandings and unpleasantness.

忍耐与等待之后，一切都会好的

　　现在六七十岁的中国人，基本都会对俄罗斯这个国家怀有特殊的感情，因为他们在年轻时代时是哼着《莫斯科郊外的晚上》去幽会，读着列夫·托尔斯泰的《战争与和平》入睡的。现在，这群共和国的同龄人基本都已经退休了，其中很多人都非常想去俄罗斯旅游，造访莫斯科的革命圣地——红场，参观莫斯科的心脏和历史发源地——克里姆林宫。

　　8月中旬，笔者带着一个年龄均在60—70岁的老年人团队，共37人，从上海出发，经由迪拜到莫斯科，到达时间为当地时间晚上11：40（飞机比预定的时间晚到50分钟左右）。在莫斯科谢列梅捷沃机场办完了所有出关手续以后，已经是当地时间半夜一点多了，而让笔者非常着急的是没有看到来机场接机的莫斯科导游。机场外面下着雨，有些风，温度也有点低。我打电话给莫斯科导游，电话一直没人接。时间在等待中一分一秒地过去，莫斯科机场的风越来越大，上了年纪的客人开始有些不安了。我联系国内组团旅行社的操作人员，操作人员给莫斯科地接社经理打电话，而经理打电话给导游也始终没人接，之后莫斯科地接社经理给了我大巴的车号。快半夜两点了，老年游客开始烦躁，埋怨机场外风大天冷，围着笔者要求在机场附近就近住宿，一切费用由组团社承担，若不尽快安排,就拨打大使馆电话进行求助,并且拍摄了现场的视频。团里一个律师还扬言回到中国后要与组团社打官司。我安抚好客人的情绪后,前往机场停车场,查看一辆辆车子,其中确实有一辆大巴。我前后敲车门敲了5分钟左右,司机才开门。核对了旅游团团名、人数及导游姓名后,发现这辆车上的导游与司机就是来接我们团的。由于航班的延误,导游与司机在车里睡着了。而导游一不小心将手机调成了振动模式,因此,地接社经理与领队给她打电话也没有听见。相互进行了短暂的交流后,我立刻引领游客登上了大巴。

导游上车以后,首先向客人道歉。然后,她向大家介绍道,她的中文名字叫白雪,是在中国的齐齐哈尔学的中文。客人问她为什么不在北京学习,而要到齐齐哈尔去学。"那儿的学费比北京的便宜。"她回答道。当老年客人听到这个开场白后,不悦的表情转变成苦笑。接着她又介绍道:到俄罗斯来旅游要学会两件事,一件事是忍耐,另一件事是等待。学会忍耐与等待之后,一切都会有的,面包也会有的。客人听到这些话,笑了起来。因为,苏联电影《列宁在1918》里就有这样的台词,而车上的老年游客差不多都看过这部电影。车上的气氛顿时变得轻松起来。

抵达酒店入住休息已是凌晨4点多。第二天,通过团队餐加菜等方式,客人也慢慢地原谅了导游,大家沉浸在莫斯科旅游的兴奋当中。

[评析]

出境旅游时,由于客源国与目的地国家(地区)存在时差,有时,从中国飞往目的地后,往往会是深夜或凌晨。若碰上航班延误或出关速度慢等,目的地国家(地区)的导游往往会回大巴车休息一下。由于是深夜或凌晨,导游与司机在大巴车上休息时,很容易睡着。

案例中,丰富的带团经验告诉出境游领队,目的地国家的地接社已经派出了导游与司机,而电话没有人接,很有可能是导游与司机在车上睡着了。领队通过查看停车场,终于找到了导游与司机。出门在外,什么事情都会发生,全靠领队的睿智。

中国公民出境旅游服务质量解析

导游的劳动是极富创造性的脑力劳动,山河依旧,人物常新。不同游客的文化素质、兴趣爱好、身份等各不相同,游览的时间安排也不同,导游应根据情况繁简适宜,满足不同的游客的需要。因此,能否根据客人的特点和现实情况做好开场白至关重要。常见的导游开场白形式可以归纳成概要式、请教式、自我褒扬式、临场发挥式和提问式等五种形式。所谓临场发挥式需要导游灵活机智,随机应变能力强。而自我褒扬式就是一方面要对客人有个正确的评估,另一方面对自己的水平也有准确的定位。案例中,俄罗斯导游所采用的方式就是临场发挥式与自我褒扬式的完美结合,导游根据所接待客人的年龄,就能揣摩出游客的喜好,运用幽默的语句,一下子拉近了导游与客人之间,中国与俄罗斯之间的距离。

Everything Will Go Well after Endurance and Waiting

Many Chinese in their sixties and seventies have special affection for Russia. When they were young, they sang the song *The Evening of the Moscow Outskirts* when dating and read *War and Peace* written by Leo Tolstoy before sleeping. Nowadays these people have already retired and most of them are eager to travel to Russia, to visit the revolutionary shrine in Moscow—Red Square—the history cradle and the heart of Moscow, Kremlin, and so on.

In the middle of August, I took a group of 37 people aged from 60 to 80 to visit Russia. It was 23:40 (50 minutes later than scheduled time) after we arrived in Moscow from Shanghai via Dubai. After finishing all the formalities at Sheremetyevo Airport in Moscow, it was about 1:00 a.m. But what worried me was the local guide who was supposed to pick us up did not appear. Outside the airport, it was raining. The wind was blowing and the temperature was a bit low. I called the local guide in Moscow but nobody answered the phone. With time passing by and the wind becoming stronger, some aged members started to feel upset. Then I contacted the operator of domestic travel agency who called the manager of local agency in Moscow. Later the manager called the local guide but there was also no answer. The manager then told us the license number of the coach which was arranged to pick us up. It was almost 2 a.m. when the elder became fretful and complained about the heavy wind and cold weather. They asked me to get accommodation near the airport which would be paid by domestic travel agency. If I did not arrange this immediately, they would called the embassy for help. To make things worse they had shot video of this situation and there was a lawyer among the group who said he would prosecute the domestic travel agency when he returned to China. After comforting them I went to the parking lot to look for our bus one by one and finally I found it. I knocked the bus gate for about five minutes and at last the driver opened the door. I checked the name of both the group and the local guide, and the number of group members with driver and finally I was sure that this driver and guide were the ones picking us up. Because the flight was delayed, they fell asleep in the bus. The local guide carelessly put her phone into vibration mode. That was why she did not answer the phone when I and the manager called her. After a short communication with each other, I led the group to get on the bus.

After the local guide got on the bus, she made an apology to guests. Then she introduced herself that her Chinese name was "Baixue" and she learned

Chinese in Qiqihar. Guests asked her why she learned Chinese in Qiqihar instead of Beijing. "The tuition in Qiqihar was cheaper than Beijing," she answered. After hearing this, the travelers' facial expressions turned from displeased to good. Later she told them that people should learn two things when traveling in Russia, enduring and waiting. After that you would have everything like bread. When guests heard this, they began to smile because this sentence appeared in the Soviet Union film *Lenin in 1918* which most of these elders were familiar with. The atmosphere in the coach became relaxing.

It was over 4 o'clock when we arrived at the hotel. The next day guests gradually forgave the local guide after adding extra dishes for guests'meal by local guide. Everyone enjoyed themselves in the excitement of traveling in Moscow.

Comments

Because there is time difference between your own country and the destination, it may be at midnight or early in the morning when you fly from China to your destination. Besides, because the flights are often delayed and it takes long time to go through the customs, the local guide usually chooses to take a short break in the bus. It is easy to fall asleep at midnight or early in the morning.

In this case, as the tour leader, I, with rich experience predicted that the local guide and driver might have fallen asleep since the local agency in Moscow had already arranged for the guide and driver and they did not answer the phone. So the tour leader knocked the doors of the buses in the parking lot one by one and finally found the local guide and driver. As a matter of fact, everything could happen during the trip and how to deal with problems depends on the wisdom of tour leaders.

The work of a tour guide is a creative one. Different tourists have different education backgrounds, hobbies, identification and usually different traveling plans.

Therefore，tour guide should act differently according to different situations to meet the needs of different tourists. In addition，it is very important to make an opening remark according to the characters of tourists and situation. There are five types of opening remarks：inductive profile type，consulting type，self praise type，impromptu-speech type and Q&A type. Impromptu-speech type requires tour guides to be flexible and adaptable. Self praise type requires tour guides to possess correct assessment of tourists and himself. In this case，the local guide in Moscow combined self praise type and impromptu-speech type perfectly. She could predict tourists' hobbies according to their age and spoke in a humorous way，which close the distance between tour guide and tourists，as well as China and Russia.

在阿联酋的旅游车上充当沿途导游

　　某年的春节,笔者带着 12 名客人踏上了"阿联酋 6 天之旅"的旅程,从上海乘阿联酋航空公司的国际航班直飞阿联酋第二大城市——迪拜。迎接我们的导游是一位来自山东某职业技术学院的学生,来迪拜做交换生期满后,拿着工作签证继续在迪拜的一家旅行社打工。春节期间阿联酋很缺中文导游,所以她有了临时担任导游的机会。

　　从机场到早餐餐厅的路途中,迪拜的街景吸引了团员,客人们不停地向导游发问,导游却回答不上来。客人们开始抱怨起来,我立刻将客人的这份不满告诉了导游,导游表示会尽量多介绍一点。

　　早餐后,客人们兴致勃勃地参观了朱梅拉海滨浴场及朱梅拉海滨酒店,在那里沐浴了阳光、海风,体验了度假休闲情趣并拍照留念,还参观了朱梅拉清真寺。之后的行程是前往阿联酋首都阿布扎比,在旅游车上导游对客人说:"从迪拜到阿布扎比的车程是两个小时,途中大家可以在车上休息一下。"接着就一屁股坐了下来。我看到客人脸上出现了不满意的表情,觉得这样下去客人一定会爆发。

　　其实之前,我就听说迪拜的导游水平参差不齐,且春节期间严重缺乏中文导游。在此团出发之前,我看了客人名单表,团员中有大学教授、企业家,还有一些中学生。那时我就已经对迪拜的景观介绍做了准备。此时一看情形不对，我拿起了麦克风先将迪拜的景观——世界最高楼迪拜塔、世界唯一的七星酒店帆船酒店、壮观的谢赫·扎耶德大清真寺、最大的人造棕榈岛等做了一个总的介绍，又将世界三大宗教的教义、建筑形式等做了阐释，特别是对伊斯兰教习俗做了详细的介绍，因为阿联酋人的信仰是伊斯兰教。

很快团队抵达了中东最大的清真寺——谢赫·扎耶德大清真寺，这也是世界第三大清真寺，可容纳四万名信徒。这是拥有世界最大地毯及最多吊灯的清真寺，其建筑华丽壮观、无与伦比、令人惊叹。之后前往人工岛参观了民族村，了解了阿联酋的历史。

下午入住酒店后我们安排客人在阿布扎比自由活动。晚上我们将团队集中起来用晚餐时，团员中一位私营业主动情地对我说："要是从迪拜到阿布扎比的路上你不给我们讲解的话，我们一定会要求换一个导游，好在你娓娓道来，让我们忘了换导游的事情。"

[评析]

中国旅游团在境外游览时，地接社所派的导游人员一般都是由当地的华人来担任，可能是当地的中国留学生、移民的后代等，甚至有些是刚刚从国内到达当地去谋生还没有站稳脚跟的冒险者，当然也有部分当地人讲着非常不地道的汉语为中国旅游者担任导游。案例中，这位导游就是在迪拜学习过两年，现在拿着工作签证的劳务输出人员。这些人因为没有经过系统训练和严格考核，不能很好地掌握导游讲解服务方式和技巧。他们的讲解大多数是自己的成长史、自己家族的发展史，或者东拉西扯，为卖自费项目做铺垫。而对旅游车经过的街景、标志性建筑等旅游者感兴趣的话题他们几乎一概不知。这些问题在东南亚地区尤其明显。

沿途讲解这种导游服务适用于城市观光。进行沿途讲解时，导游应该向来自客源国的游客介绍本地马路名称的演变和起名原因及方位和特点、街道两旁标志性建筑、商业街布局、树木绿化及街景、本地奇闻逸事、城市发展前景等。总之要紧扣沿途景观,引出游客感兴趣的话题,使游客始终有一种求知的满足感和兴奋感。

类似情况许多领队人员都或多或少遭遇过。避免游客不满的行之有效的方法就是领队人员担起当地导游的讲解任务,其实这个也是不难做到的。

随着出境旅游的发展,"领队兼导游"这个概念将进一步深入人心。领队人员应该努力学习目的地地区和国家的相关旅游知识,做好文化交流工作。旅行社降低成本,领队提高收入,对游客的服务更加贴心——这样的好事情何乐而不为? 不过有一点也很重要,就是确保自己的"领队兼导游"工作符合当地的法律规定。

Being a Tour Guide on a UAE Tour Bus

I took a group of 12 members heading to the UAE for a six-day trip during a Spring Festival. We flew with Emirates Airline from Shanghai to Dubai, the second largest city in the UAE. The local tour guide we met was a Chinese girl from a vocational college in Shandong. She was an exchange students staying in Dubai. With a working visa in hands, she worked in a local travel agency after finishing her study there. Since Dubai lacks Chinese tour guides during the Spring Festival, she was asked to work as a tour guide temporarily.

On the way from the airport to the restaurant for breakfast, the guests were attracted by the street scene. They kept asking the tour guide questions, while the answers given by the tour guide couldn't make the customers feel satisfied. The guests later started to complain about the tour guide when they reached the restaurant. I passed their words to the tour guide right away. And she stated she would try to introduce more to the guests.

After breakfast, the guests visited Jumeirah Beach and Jumeirah Beach Hotel, where they enjoyed the sunshine, sea wind, the feeling of real holidays and took a lot of pictures. They also visited Jumeirah Mosque. Later the group got on the bus heading to Abu Dhabi, the capital of the UAE. On the bus, the tour guide said to the group, "It would take two hours from Dubai to Abu Dhabi, so we can take a break on the trip." Then she just sat down by herself and ignored the customers. I sensed that the customers were not happy about the service and I also realized that they would definitely make complaints about it.

By the way, I looked through the guests' personal information before departure. Some of them were professors in universities, some were entrepreneurs, and a few of them were students still in high schools. Thus, I prepared a lot of information about the UAE in advance. So I took the microphone and started the introduction of the attractions in Dubai, such as Dubai Tower which is the highest building in the world, Burj Al Arab Hotel, which is the unique seven-star hotel, and the most luxurious mosque Sheikh Zayed, which is the biggest man-made Palm Island. After that, I also made a description of the three major religions in the world, the typical architectures, as well as the traditional culture of Islam which I put a few more words on since the people out there believe in Islam.

The group soon reached the biggest Mosque in the Middle East, Sheikh Zayed Grand Mosque, which is also the third largest Mosque in the world. It can house 40,000 believers once. The building and design is splendid and incomparable. It also impressed the tourists with its largest carpet as well as the most numerous drop-lights in the world. Later they visited an ethnic village on the man-made island to learn about the history of the UAE.

After the guests checked in the hotel, they had free time activities in the afternoon in Abu Dhabi. In the evening when we gathered for dinner, a guest who was a private business owner came up and said to me, "if you didn't share the stories with us on the way from Dubai to Abu Dhabi, we might ask to change the guide. Fortunately, the great commentary you delivered on the way really took our minds off that and we enjoyed it very much."

Comments

In an outbound travel, most of the local tour guides are Chinese people living there for a while. They could be Chinese students studying abroad, offspring of immigrants, etc. Some of them are even explorers who have just arrived. They could also be local people with a primary Chinese language level. In this case, the tour guide studied in Dubai for two year before she became a migrant worker with a working visa in hands. These people don't have any training of tour guiding or pass related examination. Therefore, they have no idea of how to guide tourists. Normally, they just simply talk about how they grew up, their family history, or something else to make guests buy stuff. However, they also have no idea about the landscapes or landmarks along the way. These situations are quite common in Southeast Asia.

Introducing the landscape along the way is very suitable for enjoying the view of the city. When conducting an on-the-way commentary, tour guides should introduce the local street names, their locations and characteristics, the landmarks, the whole environment of the cities, local anecdotes, as well as the development of the city. Anyway, it's important to make the guests interested and excited.

The above case might be encountered by many tour leaders. In order to make guests feel satisfied, it's important for tour leaders to be well prepared before departure, which is not difficult at all.

With the development of outbound tourism, the idea of acting as a leader and guide at the same time is becoming more popular. So it's essential for tour leaders to work harder to learn more about tourist destinations to become a leader and guide. It would certainly help travel agencies lower cost and raise the income of tour leaders. Therefore, they can deliver excellent service to their guests. So why not? But it is also very important to make sure that your position as a leader and guide will not violate local legal practices.

在斯里兰卡度蜜月

　　打开世界地图,你会在印度的东南方找到一个形似泪滴的岛国,这就是斯里兰卡。800 多年前,马可·波罗将它描述为"世界上最完美的岛屿"。

　　从一脉相承的高跷钓鱼人,震撼的出海观鲸,到充盈着温情与欢笑的大象孤儿院,被称为"印度洋之泪"的斯里兰卡,有着太多值得期待的旅游体验。

　　笔者担任"微笑兰卡 7 日游"领队期间,印象最深的就是每到一个入住的酒店,迎宾小姐就会端上一杯冰镇饮料,有些酒店还会提供一些当地的零食。每天早上,当你乘坐旅行社大巴外出游览时,导游的助理就会奉上一朵鲜花,每天的品种都不同。路上、大街上的行人都会朝你微笑。怪不得斯里兰卡国家旅游局对外宣传的广告用语为:微笑的兰卡。

　　我所带的团队加上我共计 20 人,其中,13 名客人是组团旅行社连锁门市部的一名销售员的直客,4 名大学生和一对年轻的夫妇分别是某两家旅行社转交给这家组团社的客人。在机场与客人见面交谈时,我发现这对年轻的夫妇刚刚结婚,特地选择了斯里兰卡作为蜜月旅游地。我心想你们选对了地方,来南亚的斯里兰卡度蜜月真是特别合适。

　　行程的第二天,旅游团在斯里兰卡著名的狮子岩附近的城市——哈勃拉那一家名为 Cinnamo 的度假村入住两个晚上。行程的第三天上午,我们游览了斯里兰卡的第二大古城波隆纳鲁瓦,下午安排游客回酒店休息或自由活动。我和导游商量了一下,请酒店送一个水果篮给这对来度蜜月的新婚夫妻,酒店经理微笑着表示同意,并告诉我下午会派人将水果送到这对夫妇的房间。

晚上 7:30 是约定团队用自助餐的时间。客人们都精神抖擞地来到餐厅用餐。我见到这对夫妻时,他们并没有表现出任何喜悦和谢意。无奈之下,我只能问他们下午在房间是否收到酒店送去的水果篮。小夫妻告诉我没有。但是他们马上意识到可能是因为他们下午在房间睡觉的时候房门上挂着"请勿打扰"的牌子,服务人员没敢打搅他们,所以才没有送水果篮。了解了情况后我透过导游请服务人员晚餐后再将水果篮送去房间。

第二天早上用早餐时,年轻的夫妇告诉我,昨晚他们收到了酒店送来的一大篮水果,他们和 4 位大学生一同分享了。虽然已事先知道了,但是同样要向我和导游表示感谢。

[评析]

送鲜花水果给旅游者,是旅游业比较常见的表达殷勤好客的一种方式。但是,怎么也想不到,客人门上挂着的"请勿打扰"的牌子,将酒店服务人员拒之门外。案例中的领队一心想给客人一个惊喜,忽视了这个事情发生的可能性。如果领队在客人回房间的时候,能给这对夫妇一个暗示,告诉他们,某个时段酒店服务人员可能会来房间,可能这种情况发生的概率就会小很多。还好领队追问了这对新婚夫妇并知道了事情的原委,从而及时进行了补救。

另外,这对新婚夫妇是以散客拼团的形式,加入组团社的团队中的,而组团社所派出的领队,却表现出对所有客人一视同仁的服务态度,没有使拼团的散客产生因为他们是别的旅行社拼过来而享受到的服务就会逊色一点的想法。

Honeymoon in Sri Lanka

Opening up the map of the world, you will find an island that looks like a teardrop to the southeast of India. It's Sri Lanka which was depicted as "the Perfect Island" by Marco Polo 800 years ago.

Fishermen on stilts, sailing out for incredible humpbacks and the elephant orphanages filled with sentiment and laughter, Sri Lanka is full of overwhelming sceneries, described as "Tears of Indian Ocean".

As a tour leader, I once took a travel group for the "Smiley Lanka Seven-Day Trip" to Sri Lanka. There were a few things that really impressed me. Whichever hotels we stay in, we were greeted with iced beverage. Some hotels would bring some local snacks for guests. Every morning when you boarded the coach, the assistant of the tour guide would provide different kinds of flowers for guests. Everyone walking on the street smiled at you. No wonder Sri Lankan national tourism administration uses "Smiley Lanka" as the slogan for tourism advertising.

There were 20 members in my group, and 13 of them were organized by a salesman who worked in the branch office of the organizing travel agency. The rest of the members were 4 college students and a young couple, who were transferred from their original agencies to the current one (the wholesaler). Chatting with the guests at the airport, I found out the couple was newly married and wanted to spend their honeymoon in Sri Lanka. "You two made the right decision." I said to myself, "It is a perfect place for honeymoon."

On the second day, the group stayed 2 nights at Cinnamo resort in Harbarana, a city close to the famous Sigiriya Lion Rock in Lanka. The next day, we paid a visit to Polonnaruwa, the second largest ancient city in Lanka. In the afternoon, we went back to the hotel for free activities. Consulting with the tour guide, I decided to ask the hotel to prepare a fruit basket for the newly married couple. The hotel manager agreed, and told us the basket would be delivered to the couple's room in the afternoon.

At 7:30 p. m., it was time for the group to have a buffet dinner. The guests entered the dining room full of energy. But the couple didn't have any appreciation and thankfulness on their faces. I asked them if they had received the fruit basket from the hotel this afternoon. They said no. Suddenly they realized that they had probably put "DO NOT DISTURB" sign on while taking a nap in the afternoon. The waiter didn't knock the door so as not to wake them up. With this in mind, I arranged a waiter with the help of the guide to deliver the basket again after dinner.

The next morning during breakfast, the couple told us they had received a fruit basket last night from the hotel. They shared the fruits with four college students. Although knowing the surprise in advance, they still expressed the heart-felt gratitude to the tour guide and me.

Comments

Sending flowers and fruit to guests is a common way to show hospitality in the tourism industry. Surprisingly, the guests had DO NOT DISTURB sign on to lock out the service. The leader wanted to impress the guests，but he overlooked the possibility that things like this would happen. If the leader had given them a hint in advance，it would be better. Fortunately the leader made up for it after knowing the reason.

The newly married couple joined the group-organizing travel agency （wholesaler） as individual travelers. The tour leader treated them fairly，which made the guests feel at home.

一位被洋流冲走的客人得救了

"普吉岛4晚6天"的行程马上就要启程了。资深领队小冯的心情依然无比激动。因为他即将带领一个19人的旅游团赴泰国普吉岛旅游,生活在陆地上的人总是对大海有种向往和憧憬。每一次出发前他都会认真地做好出发前的旅游准备工作。

前三天的行程在领队的带领下进行得非常顺利。行程的第四天是这样安排的:上午游览被泰国政府规划为国家公园的小PP岛及大PP岛,活动的内容包括游览天涯海角情人沙滩、天堂游泳池、国家珊瑚保护区,海上浮潜,与热带鱼同游,以及面包喂鱼等。团队在大PP岛午餐后,乘坐快艇到皇帝岛(Racha Yai)享受月光、沙滩及畅游海上的服务。Racha在当地语言中是"皇帝"的意思。与普吉岛其他热门或不那么热门的景点相比,皇帝岛算是一个非常新的面孔。但是自从被推出以来,它便以其精致而绝美的景色、纯净无污染的海水与沙滩、相对独立的地理位置以及奢华的配套服务,得到了不少品位高雅的游客的青睐,其中尤以欧美游客为甚。

冯领队宣布完海边游玩的注意事项及集合时间后,团员们分头开展各自的活动,部分团员游泳,部分团员浮潜。活动完毕的集合时间是下午3点,3点过后，团员们陆续回到了海边指定的集合点。这时，冯领队发现在领队、导游规定的海上活动范围之外，一名游客挥动着一只手，有求救的意思。冯领队脑子里立刻蹦出的想法是不管他是否是我团队的客人，救人要紧。于是，他马上要求船工将快艇开到那位呼救的客人那里，泰国的船工二话没说，以最快的速度开到了游客的身边，将他救了上来。船工回到岸上，冯领队立刻将500泰铢给了船工，作为对船工的感谢。这时，这位被救上来的客人一再对领队和船工表示感谢。仔细一核对，这位客人确实是冯领队团体中的客人。领队问他怎么回事，客人说他也不知道，不知不觉就被洋流冲得那么远了。

此团结束游览回杭后，被求的游客特地赠送了一面锦旗给小冯领队以示感谢。

[评析]

海岛（诸如巴厘岛、长滩岛、济州岛、塞班岛等）的旅游项目一般都有浮潜这一项，由船方根据当天天气和海域的稳定性决定客人浮潜的区域。客人往往要穿着救生衣、戴着面罩下水，其实这还是有一定技术难度的。在放客人下水前需要跟客人说明浮潜的区域，以防意外的发生。

《中华人民共和国旅游法》第八十条规定：旅游经营者应当就旅游活动中的下列事项，以明示的方式事先向旅游者做出说明或者警示：（一）正确使用相关设施、设备的方法；（二）必要的安全防范和应急措施；（三）未向旅游者开放的经营、服务场所和设施、设备；（四）不适宜参加相关活动的群体；（五）可能危及旅游者人身、财产安全的其他情形。案例中的冯领队，在看到有人招手的瞬间，马上想到让船工出海营救，想到的并不是"是不是自己的客人"，而是"要把他救回来"。这是责任心和职业道德的表现。出境游领队最基本的工作之一就是保证客人的安全，在每次解散客人以后就应该做到随时点清人数。

A Tourist Rescued from the Ocean Current

The senior tour leader Mr. Feng was still very excited for he was going to lead a group with 19 tourists for the trip of "4 Nights and 6 Days in Phuket". People who live inland always have aspirations and expectations for ocean. Every time Mr. Feng would be prepared very well before departure.

The first three days went smoothly under the leadership of the tour leader. The agenda for the fourth day was: In the morning, the tourists would visit the Thailand national parks—Phi Phi Le and Phi Phi Don. The activities were visiting Lovers' Beach at Edges of World, Paradise Swimming Pool, national coral reserve, and sea snorkeling, swimming with the tropical fish, feeding fish with bread, etc. The group enjoyed moonlight, beach and went sea swimming on Racha Yai Island after having supper on Phi Phi Don. "Racha" means "Emperor" in the local language. Comparing with other hot or regular scenic spots in Phuket, Racha Yai is a new one. But ever since it was launched, it has been very popular with many tourists, especially with the tourists from Europe and America, for its beautiful and fine scenes, pure and non-polluted sea and beaches, relatively independent location and luxurious services.

After Feng announced the dos and don'ts as well as the gathering time, the tourists in the group were scattering for their own entertainments. Some were swimming and some were playing sea snorkeling. The gathering time was 3 p. m. As the time was approaching, the tourists came back gradually. At that time, the tour leader Mr. Feng noticed that a tourist was out of the range told by the tour leader and the guide. The tourist was waving his hand for help. Immediately, what came to his mind was to save the life no matter whether he was or was not his guest. So, Mr. Feng asked the boatman to drive the speedboat to the tourist. They rescued the tourist and went back to the sea shore. Mr. Feng gave 500 Thai Baht to thank the boatman. At that time, the guest who was rescued thanked again and again to the tour leader and the boatman. Later, Mr. Feng found out that the tourist was one of the guests in his group. And the tourist couldn't explain why he was floated so far away by the ocean current.

After the group completed their trip and went back to Hangzhou, the tourist sent a silk banner to thank the tour leader.

Comments

When tourists travel on an island (such as Bali, Boracay Island, Jeju, and Saipan Island, etc.), the travel agencies always offer tourists sea snorkeling as a gift. Then shipman will decide the snorkeling area according to the weather and ocean calmness. The tourists are required to wear life vests and masks when they come in water, and it has some difficulties for some tourists. The tour leader should claim sea snorkeling area before letting tourists enter the sea in case any accidents would happen.

According to the 80th provision of the Tourism Law of the People's Republic of China the travel agency operators should inform or warn the tourists clearly about the following items in the travel activities: 1. how to correctly use relevant facilities

and equipment; 2. necessary safe protection and emergency countermeasures; 3.
the operating, service field, facilities and equipment which are not open to the
tourists; 4. people who are not suitable for certain activities; 5. other cases that
may put the tourists in danger. The tour leader（Mr. Feng）in the above case
thought about rescue with the boatman's help as soon as he saw somebody waving.
His thought of the rescue rather than considering whether the tourist was or was not
his guest represents the sense of responsibility and career morality of a tour leader.
One of the basic jobs for a tour leader is to ensure the safety of guests. After every
dismissing, the tour leader should count the number of guests from time to time.

游客在马来西亚皇宫前被马咬了一口

出境旅游团在赴马来西亚的旅游行程中，必定有一项参观马来西亚皇宫的安排。马来西亚国家皇宫坐落在吉隆坡的一座小山丘上，虽没有其他大国的皇宫建筑的宏大气派，却有着皇宫一如既往的辉煌与庄严。在平常的日子，皇宫并不对外开放，所有的游客只能在皇宫门口欣赏皇宫的华丽。

皇宫门口是由一扇并不是很宽敞的铁门与旁边的小岗亭和小门洞组成的。仅仅就这一小片风景，就已让游客迷恋不已。铁门是用黑色作底色，配有金色装饰物，典雅大方，严肃中透出一种高贵。在铁门侧边的岗楼和岗楼旁的门洞中，各有一名哨兵站岗。岗楼中的哨兵身穿白色上衣、绿色前裙的制服，手持长枪；门洞中的哨兵，则身穿红色上衣、黑色长裤，胯下骑一匹黑色高马，威风凛凛，常常吸引无数镜头。另外，不时在门口还会出现一排扛枪哨兵供人们拍照留念，闪闪的长枪在阳光的照射下与皇宫金顶遥相辉应，分外亮丽。

某旅游团中的丁先生一家三口与骑马哨兵合影留念。和其他游客一样，需要和马保持 1.5 米以上的距离。当时，丁先生的儿子站在前面，夫妻俩在后面，不清楚是有人抚摸了马匹致其受惊，还是其他原因，场面陷入混乱，那匹马冲上前就咬住了丁先生的胳膊。丁先生的左臂被咬伤，并有两处破皮出血。领队在第一时间询问了受伤情况，丁先生告诉领队："我从来没被马咬过，好疼的，手上的肉好像被火烧一样。"

领队告诉丁先生：这匹马是很金贵的纯种马，对人的伤害小，并且下一个景点就有医院。丁先生夫妇想：伤情不重，再说也就拖延几个小时，就同意去下一个景点医治。结果到达下一景点时才知道那是一个赌场内部的小医务室，不仅语言不通，而且没有基本的医疗设备和材料。后来，在当地华侨的帮助下，医务人员才给丁先生注射了破伤风针。

第二天，丁先生一家找到了马来西亚当地导游，一方面要求帮助联系马的主人，另一方面要求寻找医院注射狂犬疫苗。中午 12 点整，丁先生才得到救助，接种了狂犬疫苗，但是对方拒绝联系马主人。

发生这件意外以后，回到杭州的丁先生开始持续 8 个月的维权，并要求旅行社赔偿 9000 元。但是相关部门认为丁先生被马咬一事纯属意外，客人并未购买保险，最后，组团的出境旅行社愿意给出 1650 元的赔偿。

[评析]

丁先生一家在拍照前，马来西亚导游事先提醒过注意事项。而客人被马咬纯属意外，在拍照前，出境游领队应该再次提醒客人为了自身的安全时刻警惕，处处小心。在旅游者出发旅行前，旅行社工作人员应该不断提醒游客旅游时应购买意外保险。案例中，只因丁先生没有购买意外保险，所以在要求赔偿 9000元时，旅行社最终只愿补偿 1650 元。

被马咬伤也需要接种狂犬疫苗。疫苗接种越早越好，最佳时间是被咬伤后48 小时之内。被咬后，为了降低风险，应马上使用肥皂水或大量清水对伤口进行冲洗。如在野外一时找不到水源，甚至可以用人尿冲洗，随后再设法找水源。注意几点，要快，伤口清理要彻底，伤口不可以包扎。由此可见领队需要掌握一些急救知识，把游客的人身安全放在第一位。

A Guest Bitten by a Horse in Front of the Malaysia Imperial Palace

Visiting the Malaysia Palace is a must on the itinerary when traveling in Malaysia. Located on a hill in Kuala Lumpur, the palace is not as big as others but is still splendid and solemn. On ordinary days, the palace does not open to the public and tourists can only enjoy the grandeur of the palace in front of its gate.

At the gate of the palace, there is an iron gate which is not so wide, a small watch booth and a door way. The iron gate is black and has golden decorations, which is elegant, noble and solemn. Near the watch booth and the door way were two soldiers. The one in the sentry box is wearing a white coat and green skirt with long spear and the one in the door way is wearing a red coat and black trousers, riding on a tall black horse with power and prestige. They attract lots of cameras. Besides, there is a line of soldiers who carry guns. People may take photos with them. The sparkling guns under the sunshine reflect the golden roof of the palace nearly.

Mr. Ding and his family members were taking photos with the handsome bodyguard and the horse. Just like other tourists, they kept a distance of 1.5 meters with the horse. At that moment, the son of the family was standing in the front and the couple was standing behind. Out of nowhere, the horse suddenly got frightened. The situation was out of control. The horse rushed forward, bit Mr. Ding, and ran away. Mr. Ding was bitten on the left arm. The tour leader inquired Mr. Ding about his wound immediately. Mr. Ding told the tour leader that he had never been bitten by a horse. It was very painful, and the flesh of his arm was like on fire.

The tour leader told Mr. Ding that the horse was a very expensive pure blood horse, which did little harm to human body and that there was a hospital in next scenic spot. Mr. Ding thought of the wound was not so serious, so he agreed to get cured later. But it turned out that the hospital was only a small clinic inside a casino without basic medical treatment equipment and materials. Besides, there was language barrier. Later, with the help of local overseas Chinese, Mr. Ding got the injection of tetanus.

The next day, the Dings requested the local Malaysian guide look for the horse owner and get the rabies vaccine in the hospital. At 12:00, Mr. Ding was injected the rabies vaccine. But the local guide refused to contact the horse owner.

After the accident, Mr. Ding started his 8 months long right claim after he was back to Hangzhou. He asked the travel agency for the 9,000 *yuan* compensation. But relevant department believed that the horse bite was an accident and the guest did not buy relevant insurance. At last, the organizing travel agency paid 1,650 *yuan* as compensation.

Comments

The Malaysian guide had warned before the Dings took photos, and the guest bitten by the horse was totally an accident. Before taking photos, the tour leader should remind his guests again, and the guests should also take care of their own safety. The staff in the travel agency should encourage their guests to buy accident insurance before departure. In the above case，Mr. Ding didn't buy the accident insurance，so he only got 1,650 *yuan* as compensation，not 9,000 *yuan*.

If anyone gets bitten by a horse，he or she should take the rabies vaccine. Rabies vaccination should be injected as soon as possible. The best time should be within 48 hours after bitting. And if people cannot go to the hospital immediately，soap water and a large amount of clear water can be used to wash the wound to reduce the risk. If it is in the wild and there is no water beside，the human urine can be used to wash the wound. And then try to find the water source. There are some tips：first，the wound should be dealt soon and completely；second，it should not be bound up. The tour leader should also have command of some first aid knowledge and always put guests' safety first.

第六篇

Chapter VI

境外游览享受篇

Enjoyment in Outbound Destinations

　　旅游者参加出境旅游的终极目的，是为了享受在境外国家或地区的实地旅游过程。在办理出入境手续、乘坐飞机等烦琐的程序后，抵达想要游览的目的地国家（地区），就是为了体验在境外游览观光、住宿用餐、购物逛街等。

　　本篇把作者在目的地国家（地区）游览的各景点作为切入口，来介绍目的地国家（地区）各景区的历史沿革、风土人情、禁忌、礼仪习俗等。通过文字描述，让读者有身临其境之感。

[Chapter Outline]

The ultimate goal for tourists who take part in outbound travel is to enjoy the on-site travel experiences in outbound destination countries/regions. After completing the complicated steps like exit and entry, taking a plane, and various inspections, tourists finally arrive in destination countries/regions. Then, it is time for tourists to fully experience the authentic enjoyment of sightseeing, accommodating, dining and shopping.

With tremendous outbound travel experiences, the author tries to introduce the history, local customs, taboos, etiquettes and practices of some destinations. Besides, the descriptive words will present readers the vision of being there.

享受着欧洲导游的车上讲解

在"德法意瑞"的行程安排中,第一天从上海乘飞机前往法兰克福。第二天早上在法兰克福市区观光半天,包括罗马广场、歌德故居和保尔教堂,之后,安排了一个小时的自由活动时间。因此,团队在 11:00 才离开法兰克福市区,经过卢森堡,最后到巴黎市区。从法兰克福到卢森堡有 280 公里的路程,直到下午两点才抵达卢森堡,团队在这里吃了午餐。足足三个小时的车程,大家都在车上非常专注地听导游的讲解。

还在法兰克福酒店享用早餐时,有一位客人说,早餐的奶酪特别好吃。于是,导游就从欧洲人普遍喜欢的奶酪开始讲起。大约公元前 3000 年,随着奶牛被引入欧洲,人类开始制作奶酪这种集营养和美味于一身的食品。苏尔美人记载了大约 20 种软奶酪,是奶酪存世的最早证明。从此,奶酪就在人们的宠爱下被不断推广、创新,同时也成为欧洲生活与文化的重要组成部分。接着,导游又告诉我们:对于奶酪制造工艺真实出现的时间我们却只能猜测,最可能的理论是大约公元前 10000 年,山羊和绵羊被家养,早期的牧人开始利用变酸的牛奶分离出凝乳和乳浆,再经过沥干、成型、干燥、凝固就可以变成一种简单而有营养的食物。由于牛被家养的时间明显晚于山羊和绵羊,所以牛奶奶酪比羊奶奶酪晚两三千年。接着导游又给我们介绍了德国食品中最有名的香肠和火腿。

食品专题讲完后,导游开始给我们讲解德国的历史,包括德国的城市同盟、宗教改革、德国的 1848 年革命、德奥同盟和三国同盟、德国革命爆发与纳粹党、法西斯统治、德国分裂与德国统一。从古代史、近代史到现代史、当代史,导游娓娓道来,让客人在不知不觉中上了一堂有关德国甚至欧洲的历史课。

快要到达卢森堡时,导游又给我们介绍了这个大公国。导游说,卢森堡有一点法国味,有一些西班牙味,也有一点德国味。这是因为它的地理位置很特殊,历史上曾多次被欧洲其他国家占领,这些国家不但留下了他们的文化,还留下了不少历史遗迹。这让所有的客人对卢森堡都十分期待。

[评析]

欧洲旅游往往是大巴旅游。大巴旅游的优点是旅行社出发前都已经把路线安排好了,旅游者不需要做攻略,也不需要为酒店预订等犯难。但是,往往由于国家与国家,景点与景点之间的距离较长,客人乘坐大巴的时间也较长。所以这就要求导游能够在大巴上讲一些历史文化典故。做到这一点需要导游平时的知识积累。而讲解时,也讲究技巧,从旅游者感兴趣的或摸得着、看得到的开始讲解。案例中,导游先从入住酒店的早餐开始讲,从吃的奶酪、香肠,延伸到德国的历史,娓娓道来,丰富了游客的旅途。

Enjoying On-the-coach Interpretation of a European Tour Guide

According to the itinerary of the Germany, France, Italy and Switzerland tour, the group went to Frankfurt on Day 1. The next morning, the group had a tour to downtown of Frankfurt including Roman Forum, Goethe-Haus, Paulskirche. After that, they had one hour free time. The group set out for downtown of Paris from Frankfurt via Luxembourg at 11:00 a.m. It was 280 kilometers from Frankfurt to Luxembourg. The group had lunch in Luxembourg at 2:00 p.m. The group spent 3 hours in the coach, listening earnestly to the interpretation of the tour guide.

The European tour guide started by talking about the breakfast in the hotel in Frankfurt. One tourist liked the cheese very much. The guide began to talk about cheese. It was about 3,000 BC that people began to make delicious and nutritious cheese with the introduction of milk cows. Sumerian recorded about 20 kinds of soft cheese. Since then, cheese has been promoted and improved and become an indispensable part of European life and culture.

Then the guide told us that by theoretical guessing, cheese making probably started in 10,000 BC when sheep and goats were raised at home. The early shepherds began to extract curd and whey from sour milk. Then after draining off, shaping, drying and congealing, a simple and nutritious kind of food was formed. Cow was raised at home much later than sheep and goat. Therefore, cow cheese occurred two to three thousand years later than sheep cheese. The guide also introduced the famous German sausage and ham.

After the introduction to food, the guide began to talk about German history including City Alliance, Religious Reform, Revolutions of 1848 in the German States, Dual Alliance, Triple Alliance, German Revolution in November 1918, the Nazi Party and fascism, Germany's secession and unity. These events covered ancient, modern and contemporary history. The guide gave a lesson of German or even European history to the tourists in a natural way.

Upon arriving in Luxembourg, the guide told about the Grand Duchy. Luxembourg embodies French, Spanish and German culture. Because of its special geographical location, it was occupied by other European countries for several times throughout the history, forming its unique mixed culture. The few words aroused the tourists' high expectation of the tour in the country.

Comments

Package tour in Europe usually travels by coach bus. Compared with free tour, package tour has its own advantages. The travel agency has set routes, arranged guides, transportation and accommodations well. Considering the long distances and long breaks between countries or historical sites, the guide should talk more about history and culture, etc. It requires great knowledge. An experienced tour guide usually starts with things that are visible or touchable to tourists.

In the above case, the guide started by talking about food, the cheese. Then he moved on to German and European history which really enlightened the journey.

米兰自助一日游

我曾赴意大利米兰开会,借此我们一行在米兰进行了米兰自助一日游。

米兰最值得游览的要算米兰大教堂了,它是世界上最大的哥特式建筑,是世界第二大教堂,仅次于梵蒂冈的圣·彼得教堂。教堂坐落于米兰市中心的大教堂广场,长 158 米,最宽处 93 米,塔尖最高处达 108.5 米,总面积 11,700 平方米,可容纳 4 万人。米兰大教堂在宗教界的地位极其重要,著名的《米兰赦令》就从这里颁布,使得基督教合法化,成为罗马帝国国教。达·芬奇、布拉曼特曾为它画过许多设计草稿,达·芬奇为这座建筑发明了电梯,拿破仑曾在这里加冕。此外,米兰大教堂也是世界上雕塑最多的建筑和尖塔最多的建筑,被誉为大理石山。

我们从下榻的酒店提供的地图上看到 Duomo(意大利文为"教堂"的意思)旁就有一个地铁站,但是我们不知道入住酒店周边是否有地铁站通向教堂,于是询问了酒店总台热情洋溢的意大利小伙子。他告诉我们从酒店门口坐电车会更方便,无须去找离酒店较远的地铁站。小伙子告诉我们,如果我们准备坐电车,他这里就可以买票。大家觉得小伙子传达的信息靠谱,决定乘电车进行米兰自助一日游。我们在总台买了赴教堂的来回电车票(来回票会优惠一点),小伙子还告诉我们从酒店到教堂共 14 个站,到时候车上会报站名的。我们一行迫不及待地离开了酒店,坐上电车来到了米兰大教堂。

下了电车,一眼就看到了教堂的正门。教堂正面被 6 个巨大的方柱分隔出 5 扇铜门,每扇铜门上分有许多方格,每个方格内雕刻着教堂历史、神话与圣经故事。位于正中的最大的铜门于 1906 年完工,重 37 吨,描绘的是圣母玛丽亚的一生。正面的方石柱上刻有几十幅大型浮雕和上百个人物像。

我们来到了教堂的内部,弯曲线条装饰的彩绘玻璃窗,让人觉得非常震撼,绝对不可以错过。

走出教堂的内部,我们来到了大教堂广场左侧的维托里奥·伊曼纽尔二世拱廊,这座 19 世纪下半叶建造的玻璃圆筒拱形隧道是世界上最早且最雅致的购物商城。维托里奥·伊曼纽尔二世拱廊履行了大量的社会职能。它是城市的中心,位于大教堂和斯卡拉歌剧院之间。拱廊和大教堂一样呈十字形,顶上装有彩色玻璃棚,地面是用大理石铺成的马赛克图案。拱顶边上的绘画分别代表了欧洲、亚洲、非洲和美洲。巨大的拱形建筑富丽堂皇,长廊内有装潢考究的古奇、托德斯及路易·威登这样的品牌服装店。麦当劳对面历史悠久的萨维尼餐厅漂亮而有活力。拱廊内到处挤满了人,里面的石桌及可以品尝到高价咖啡的餐馆和酒吧吸引了许多路人。我们在拱廊内的一家咖啡馆喝了咖啡,吃了冰淇淋,作为暂时的休息。我们看到许多人站在拱廊中心,噢,原来是大家围着中心圆顶下地面上黄道带的金牛座图案,据说站上去转个圈能带来好运。路人热心地为我们示范,但也说不上缘由。无论如何,凑这个热闹的人想必不少,以至于金牛身体的某个地方被磨出一个锥形的深坑。

到了午餐时间,我们沿着河道行走的时候看到了一家比萨店,人群熙熙攘攘,突然产生了应该去尝一尝意大利比萨的想法。涌进餐厅点了比萨和别的意大利菜肴,品尝比萨后觉得和中国烹制的比较,中国的比萨确实更加油腻一点。

午餐后,沿着长廊走,游览了城堡、斯卡拉歌剧院和布拉雷美术馆,我们感觉一天的游览非常满足。晚餐后,我们又坐上回程的电车回到了入住的酒店。

[评析]

散客旅游(full independent tour)简称 FIT，又称自助或半自助旅游，在国外称为自助旅游。它是由旅游者自行安排旅游行程，零星现付各项旅游费用的旅游形式。随着中国经济的腾飞，"90 后""00 后"的年轻一代外语水平普遍提高，越来越多的年轻人进入了散客旅游的行列。而散客旅游是否能顺利进行，与目的地的管理是密切相关的。

目的地管理组织全面负责目的地综合体各元素的协作与整合，以及目的地营销。目的地管理组织以不同的组织规模和类型分布在世界各地，已存在至少100 年的历史。许多目的地管理组织属于政府机构，一些则是半官方性质。

目的地综合体和目的地产品是相似的概念。每一目的地拥有两个产品组成部分：吸引物和基础设施。吸引物是吸引游客来目的地的关键，如米兰的大教堂、米兰的拱廊等。良好的基础设施是必需的，以支持和保障目的地内安全愉快的旅行。如：米兰的地铁、电车等公共交通设施的车票均相通，而且，连酒店也出售电车、地铁票，极大地方便了旅游者的观光出行；大街上到处都有公共自行车供旅游者租赁；充足的住宿和餐饮设施满足了游客需求。

意大利是欧洲"文艺复兴"运动的发源地，但丁、达·芬奇、米开朗琪罗、拉斐尔、伽利略等文化与科学巨匠对人类的进步做出了无可比拟的巨大贡献。意大利丰厚的文化艺术遗产是国家的瑰宝，也是旅游业的源泉。得天独厚的地理位置和气候条件、四通八达的海陆空交通网、完善的配套服务设施，以及渗透在人民生活各个层面的文化气息，每年都吸引三四千万外国游客前往意大利。旅游业因此成为意大利国民经济的支柱之一。

One-day Full Independent Tour in Milan

I had an opportunity to attend a meeting in Milan, Italy this February. Therefore we, who attended the same meeting, organized a one-day full independent tour in Milan.

Milan Cathedral is the most worthy visiting place. It is the biggest Gothic architecture and the second largest in the world, only smaller than Saint Peter's Church in Vatican. Milan Cathedral is 158 meters long and 93 meters wide at its most and is located in the Cathedral Square, at the center of Milan City. The highest tower is 108.5 meters. The Cathedral occupies 11,700 m^2 with the capacity of 40,000 people. It enjoys high reputation in religious field. The famous Edict of Milan was issued here, which legalized Christianity which became the national religion of the Roman Empire. Numerous design manuscripts left by Leonardo da Vinci and Bramante make it more splendid. Napoleon was crowned here and da Vinci invented an elevator for the building. Milan Cathedral has the most statues and towers and is known as Marble Hill.

We found that there was a subway station near the Duomo (church in Italian) from the map provided by the hotel where we stayed, but we didn't know whether there was a subway station near the hotel. Therefore, we inquired the ebullient young Italian man at the front desk who told us that it was more convenient to take a tram to go to the Duomo and we could buy tram tickets from him. We believed him and decided to enjoy the one-day tour in Milan by tram. We bought the return tickets for it was cheaper. The young man went on telling us there were 14 stops from the hotel to the Duomo and the announcements of stops would be heard on the tram. We left hotel immediately and headed for Milan Cathedral by tram.

When we got off the tram, we saw the front gate of the Cathedral, 6 giant square pillars with 5 bronze doors. There were lots of panes on every bronze door. And in each pane was the church history, mythologies or biblical stories. The largest bronze door in the middle was completed in 1906, with a weight of 37 tons, describing the life of Virgin Mary. The square stone pillar in the front were dozens of large carved reliefs and hundreds of portraits.

Then we entered into the Cathedral. The stained glass windows with the curves were astonishing. People should never miss them.

Walking out of the Cathedral, we arrived at the Vitorio Emanuel II Arcade on the left side of the Cathedral Square. The splendid glass arcade built in the end of the 19th century was the earliest and most elegant shopping mall in the world. The Vitorio Emanuel II Arcade carried out lots of social functions. It is the center of the city, between the Cathedral and La Scala Opera House. Like the Cathedral, the Arcade was shaped like a cross. Above was the stained glass shed and down on the ground was the mosaic pattern made of marbles. The paintings on the edges of arch represent Europe, Asia, Africa and America. The giant arcade is so beautiful and imposing. Inside it are finely decorated Gucci, Tod's and Louis Vuitton. Opposite the McDonald's is the historic Savini, beautiful and energetic. People are everywhere. Stone tables, restaurants with high-price coffee and bars attract many visitors. We stopped by a café to have a rest, enjoying the coffee and ice cream. We noticed a lot of people standing at the center of the arcade. Oh, they were around the pattern of Taurus of zodiac on the ground, just under the central roof. It was said if people stood there and turned around, good luck would come. A passer-by set an example for us, but he didn't know the deep reason why people were doing so. However, there must be many people who believed the saying, because there was a deep taper hole in the Taurus.

At lunchtime, we saw a pizza shop when we were walking along the river. It was crowded there. Why not taste the pizzas made in Italy? So we did. After tasting the pizza and other Italian dishes, we thought the Chinese pizza seemed greasier.

After lunch, we went to the Castle, the Scala Opera House and the Brera Art Gallery, feeling very satisfied. After dinner, we came back to the hotel by tram.

Comments

Full independent tour, short for FIT, also is named self-service or half self-service tour. It is called Independent tour in foreign countries. It is a kind of travel form that the tourists arrange their own travel agenda and pay their travel expenses individually. With the fast development of Chinese economy, the post-90s and post-00s generations have better command of foreign languages, so more and more young people join into the FIT. Whether a good and perfect travel can be completed or not is closely related to the management of destination.

Destination management is the management of cooperation, concordance and marketing in the destination. The destination management organizations scatter all over the world in different scales and types, enjoying at least 100-year history.

Many destination management organizations belong to government and others are semi-official.

Destination complex is similar to destination product. There are two products to compose one destination complex: attraction and infrastructure. Attraction is the key to attract tourists, such as Milan Cathedral, the Arcade. Good infrastructure are the necessities to support a safe and pleasure trip in the destination. For example, the subway and tram in Milan use the same ticket system and hotel in Milan sell the subway and tram tickets, making the sightseeing in Milan more convenient. Meanwhile, the public bicycles are available everywhere in Milan to tourists. Accommodation and restaurants should also meet tourists' need.

Italy is the home of European Renaissance. Great cultural and scientific masters like Dante, da Vinci, Michelangelo, Rafael, and Galileo, etc., made huge contributions to human progress. The abundant culture and art heritages in Italy are not only national treasures, but also the source for tourism development. The advantaged geography and climate, convenient transportation, completed service infrastructure, accompanied with tourism resources as well as the cultural connotation deep in the lives of Italian attract 30—40 million tourists to Italy. Thus, tourism becomes one of the pillars of Italian national economy.

定制"新马"亲子游

2014 年农历新年前的腊月廿一日,在新加坡历史最悠久且最富声望的大学——新加坡国立大学的文化艺术中心门口,有一群 12 岁左右的儿童及其家长,正在聚精会神地欣赏一些艺术品,包括中国画、西洋画等。其中,一位小朋友看到艺术中心的楼梯上写着这样一句格言:Everything has beauty, but not everyone sees it.(一切都是美丽的,但不是每个人都能看得到的。)他正用心地把它拍摄下来,并认真地向一位家长请教这句话正确的英文翻译。在一旁引领我们的新加坡导游石小姐不无羡慕地说,现在越来越多的中国家长带着小孩来新加坡和马来西亚旅游,但同龄的孩子聚在一起旅游的情况很少见,除非是以学校交流的名义,由老师带着学生一起来。

一位家长自豪地告诉石小姐:这 10 个小孩在幼儿园时是同学,现在在不同的小学念书,其中一位小朋友的爸爸在旅行社工作,每年都会组织一到两次亲子游活动。这样做的目的,一方面是给孩子提供一次交流的机会,交流不同学校的学习内容。另外一方面,因为现在多是独生子女,家长有意识地让他们从小建立友谊,等他们长大了,万一遇到什么困难,也可以多些朋友商量。

接着,这位家长还告诉了导游此次亲子游的特色:行程比传统"新马 5 日游"

多一天自由活动的时间,让大家有充分的时间去新加坡的环球影城和夜间动物园游玩;饮食方面将东南亚的特色娘惹食品中的代表菜——叻沙、海南鸡饭等包含在内,而逛马来西亚吉隆坡的亚罗街夜市时,可品尝到黄亚华烧鸡翼及烤沙爹,可谓丰富多彩。

另外,针对一些饮食不合小孩的胃口的问题,要求每户人家额外准备一些钱交给团长,用于必要时的加菜。最重要的是,因行程包含三宝山、三宝庙、三宝井这些历史遗迹,大家要求让马来西亚的地接社派一位对历史了解深入的导游,给小朋友们讲解郑和下西洋的相关历史。此外,小朋友们还对热带植物有兴趣,于是大家还要求在行程中安排参观马来西亚布城农业遗产园。

行程中,旅行社特别安排了参观新加坡华人移民最早聚居和工作的地方——牛车水。导游向小朋友介绍:19 世纪初,从中国广东、福建来的华人越来越多,大部分人就住在现在的牛车水区。于是,几年之后,这片地区被划为了华人居住区。在当年,新加坡还没有自来水设备,全市所需要的水,都得用牛车自市郊运到市中心,再由市中心转往市内各地。由于华人聚居区位于中心地区,于是这片以牛车载水来供应用水的区域就被叫作牛车水区。现在的牛车水区,算是市中心的繁华地区之一,不到牛车水就不能算到过新加坡。经过导游的介绍,小朋友了解到一百多年前华人在此处谋生的艰难。

游览完新加坡,大家又兴致勃勃地赴马来西亚游览了。

[评析]

低龄化是近年来境外亲子游的趋势。去哪儿网曾发布针对出境亲子游细分市场的第一份调查报告——《2013 年出境亲子游调查报告》。报告显示,有 62% 的家长计划在孩子 0—5 岁时就开始带孩子出国旅行。75% 的家长表示自己愿意每年带孩子出国玩 1—3 次,近一半的家长选择 5 至 7 天的出境亲子游。超过三分之一的家长在 2013 年带着孩子出国玩。最受家长欢迎的选择为马来西亚、泰国、新加坡、日本、韩国、美国、欧洲、澳大利亚、马尔代夫等。其中,休闲度假游以 86% 的高比例成为家长最常选择的亲子游方式,热门玩法包括海岛游、乐园游、观光游、文化游、游轮游、美食游等。

调查还显示,影响家长做出决定的主要因素依次为安全性、孩子是否喜欢、出游时间是否合适、趣味性、费用、服务是否周到。可见,相比费用,家长更关心安全。

"旅游私人定制"是现在国外非常流行的旅游方式,也越来越受到国内消费者的追捧。根据旅游者的需求,以旅游者为主导进行旅游行动流程的设计。在不少人的概念里,"旅游私人定制"往往与奢华连在一起,笔者认为:私人定制实际上就是"量身定做",即根据客户的要求来设计一些特殊的旅游产品。案例中,旅游者的需求就是让孩子们多看一点,多了解一点。所以,"新马亲子游"的行程,只是在旅行社传统的"新马5日游"的行程中,在新加坡增加一天自由活动的时间,安排参观新加坡国立大学及新加坡南洋理工大学等额外内容。符合小学生的"学中玩,玩中学"的特点。在安排这个特色行程时,旅行社销售人员从领队、导游、用餐、参观景点都做了精心的安排。考虑到一路上的餐饮小孩会不适应,就从团费中预留出一部分款项用作加菜的费用,这一做法非常灵活,值得学习。同时,"定制亲子旅游"推翻了"上车睡觉,下车拍照,被导游牵着鼻子走"的传统跟团游方式,打造出"顾客有需求,我们就来设计"的全新理念。

Tailor-made Parent-child Travel of Singapore and Malaysia

On the 21st of the 12th lunar month before the 2014 new year, at the main entry of the Cultural and Artistic Center in Singapore's oldest and most prestigious university, National University of Singapore, a group of 12-year-old children and their parents were enjoying the works of art including Chinese painting, oil painting and so on. Among them, a little kid noticed a motto on the stairs to the Art Center: Everything is beautiful, but not everyone sees it. The kid took a picture of this motto and also seriously consulted a parent for right English translation. Singapore tour guide Miss Shi said with admiration, "Now more and more Chinese parents took their children here for trips. But children of the same age together are few, unless the students are led by teachers in the name of school communication."

One of the parents proudly told Miss Shi that the ten kids are actually kindergarten students now studying in different primary schools. One of the little kids has a father working in the travel agency. Every year, parent-child activities are held. The purpose of doing so was to give their children a chance of communication. On the other hand, because there was usually only one child in the family, so parents consciously let them set up a kind of emotional contact, when they grow up. If they meet with difficulty, they can get more friends' help.

Then, the parents told the tour guide about the feature of the parent-child travel—there was one more day free time in Singapore than the traditional "5-day tour". So everybody had more time to go to the Universal Studios and Night Safari during the whole trip. The diet focused on South East Asia special Nyonya food, Laksa, Hainanese Chicken with Steamed Rice included in the trip. Plus around Aro Street—the night market in Kuala Lumpur of Malaysia, everybody could taste Huang Yahua roast chicken wings and satay.

In addition, if the diet was not to child's appetite, every household gave some extra money to the head for adding food when necessary. The most important was visiting Bukit China, Sam Po Keng Temple, Hang Li Po Well and other historical relics. Therefore, Chinese tourists demanded a guide to explain the history about Zheng He's Expenditure to the children in the group, making the children slowly began to understand history. Considering children's interest in tropical botanical knowledge, a trip to Putrajaya Agricultural Heritage Park in Malaysia was arranged.

During the trip, travel agency arranged a visit to the Chinese immigrants in Singapore's first live and work places, China town. The tour guide said to kids, at the beginning of the 19th century, more and more Chinese from Fujian and Guangdong lived there. Then, after a few years, the division was treated as the Chinese residential area. In those years, Singapore had no tap water equipment. The city's water needed to be transported from suburb to downtown by cattle carts. As the Chinatown was located in the center, so the cattle car water supply area was called Chinatown, also known as the Chinatown of Singapore, Now the Chinatown District is one of the bustling downtown areas, so the trip was a must when in Singapore. After the guide's interpretation, children began to understand that more than a hundred years ago, how difficult Chinese in Singapore made a living.

Done with Singapore visit, everyone would be in the best of spirits to visit Malaysia.

Comments

To travel overseas at a younger age has become a trend in recent years. The website Qunar issued the first report on overseas parent-child tour in 2013. The report shows that 62% parents are willing to take their children of 0—5 years old to travel abroad. 75% parents plan to take their children to travel abroad once or three times per year. Nearly 50% parents investigated plan to have parent-child tour for 5—7 days each year. More than one third of parents took their children to travel abroad in 2013. The most popular destinations for parent-child tour are Malaysia, Thailand, Singapore, Japan, South Korea, America, Europe, Australia, Maldives and so on. Leisure tourism has become the most welcome way of parent-child tour, occupying a high proportion of 86%, which includes island tour, amusement park tour, natural scenery sightseeing, cultural tour, cruise tour and gourmet tour.

The report also shows that the main factors affecting parent-child tour are safety, children's interest, fun, cost and service. Compared with the cost, safety is the top priority of parents in their decision.

"Tailor-made private tour" is now very popular in both foreign and domestic tourism markets. "Tailor-made private tour" aims to design itineraries mainly according to the demand of tourists themselves. In the eyes of most people, this new way of traveling is closely related with luxury. This author, however, considers "tailor-made private tour" as a special tourism product that is designed to cater to the very needs of clients. In the above case, the travelers' needs were leading children to see more and learn more. As a result, the itinerary in the case adds one free day in Singapore for children to visit National University of Singapore and Nanyang Technological University. The arrangement was suitable for children to learn from playing and to play in learning. Besides, the travel agency sales persons were very considerate in the arrangement of scenic spots and meals. For example, some fund was deducted from the total group fee in the very beginning and reserved for adding dishes along the way to give children more tasty food. This was very flexible and is worth learning from. Finally, "tailor-made parent-child travel" in the case came up with a new concept of designing itineraries according to traveler's needs, overthrowing the traditional package tour mode of "sleeping in the coach, getting off to take photos, and being taken by the nose all the way by the guide".

墨尔本大洋路一日游

8 月底正值澳大利亚冬末春初。一天中午,墨尔本市中心的斯旺斯顿大街熙熙攘攘,我们沿着斯旺斯顿大街由北向南行走,快要到 Lt Bourke 街时,看到沿街一家挨着一家的旅行社,门面上分别用中文写着"长青旅游公司""长城旅游公司""宏城旅游公司"及"羊城旅游公司"等。

带着好奇,我们走进了马来西亚华侨经营的长青旅游公司。销售小姐向我们介绍,旅游公司正在推出周末特价优惠活动,"大洋路一日游"原价为 69 澳元,周末特价优惠,只要 45 澳元。她还补充说,如果我们参加墨尔本的三大经典"一日游"线路——大洋路和十二门徒岩石、菲利普岛观神仙企鹅归巢、疏芬山淘金古镇游,旅游公司可以给优惠套餐价,即在原价的基础上减 26 澳元。听了销售小姐的介绍,我们真想马上报名参加墨尔本的三项旅游活动,只可惜其中的一项活动已经在刚到墨尔本时参加过了。于是,我们兴奋地报了周末"大洋路一日游"的活动。

周六早上 8 点半,我们在旅行社与我们约定的集合地点,即旅行社的门口坐上了赴"大洋路"旅游的大巴。大巴可以乘坐 50 多人,车上好不热闹。游客大部分是华人,而让人感到好奇的是团里还有 3 位来自美国的学生,他们在中国学习过汉语,这次因为价格便宜,加上可以听听中文讲解,所以参加了这个团。

大巴首先越过墨尔本西门大桥,我们欣赏到了菲利普港湾沿岸的风景。一路上导游向我们介绍了大洋路的概况:大洋路位于墨尔本西南,在 20 世纪 80 年代初对游客开放,是维多利亚州最著名的观光点。它是为纪念参加第一次世界大战的士兵修建的,参与建设的人也包括许多参战老兵,共有 3000 余人为此付出了艰辛与汗水。这条路于 1919 年开始动工,1932 年全线贯通。大洋路沿着维多利亚州西海岸蜿蜒伸展,带给游客壮丽的海洋风光和许多海滩活动。旅游车经过了吉朗市——维多利亚州的第二大城市,这表明旅游车真正开始进入全长约 300 公里的海滨公路。谈笑间,旅游车停在了写有 Great Ocean Road(大洋路)几个单词的剃刀鲸岛拱门下,我们可以拍照。

之后继续赶路。我们的午餐安排在位于山脚下的美丽的小镇阿波罗湾。这里的海鲜新鲜无比,餐馆众多。导游特别向我们推荐了一家希腊人开的餐厅,每人 9 澳元,自选 3 样食物。味道果真不错。

午餐后,大巴继续沿着全世界风景最壮观的车道——大洋路滨海观光车道前行。一路上,导游向我们介绍了零星的沉船遗骸、古老的渔村、茂密的内陆树林。3 点左右终于到达了雄奇的十二门徒岩石。十二门徒岩石实际上是经过亿万年的风化和海水侵蚀后矗立在太平洋上的独立礁石,好似耶稣的十二门徒在听课。由于大自然的不断侵蚀,目前,能看到的礁石只有 7 块了。这些垂直距离高达 45 米的古老岩层与大陆相对而立,形成了众多壮丽奇绝的峡谷与岩壁景观。

在导游的推荐下,我兴奋地乘坐直升机观赏了洛克阿德峡谷、风洞和伦敦桥等。从空中往下看,陡峭的悬崖、美丽的沙滩、温柔的海风、晶莹的海水、神秘的石灰岩——大自然的神秘与壮美一览无遗。

4 点左右,我们起程回墨尔本市区。望着车窗外南太平洋汹涌的波涛和车窗前维多利亚州起伏的山峦,我想"大洋路一日游"是路途最崎岖、最壮美、最绮丽的奇幻之旅。

澳大利亚的"一日游"旅游产品始于20世纪70年代,80年代开始形成规模。以悉尼和墨尔本两个城市"一日游"的产品为例:位于澳洲的东南部的、新南威尔士州的首府悉尼,除了市区观光外,其他景点如著名的蓝山、邦迪海滩均离市区比较远;悉尼还可以延伸一个到首都堪培拉"一日游"的产品。墨尔本的三大"一日游"线路——大洋路和十二门徒岩石、菲利普岛观神仙企鹅归巢、疏芬山淘金古镇游——也离市区较远,加上澳洲部分本地人也不愿意开车旅行,这样就促使"一日游"首先在国内市场迅速成长起来。

在旅游淡季如冬季,旅游机构适时推出买一送一、折扣促销的手段来吸引世界各地的旅游者。周末推出特价,希望能薄利多销,以量取胜。比如案例中的墨尔本长青旅游公司推出周末"大洋路一日游",在69澳元的基础上给予45澳元特价。这使得淡季也能出现每天发3团,每团50人以上的盛况。

同时,旅行社往往会让旅游者购买2—3项"一日游"的产品,它会提供多一点的优惠给顾客。游客参团达到10人或者15人以上会给予更多优惠,以鼓励游客团购。此外,旅游公司极力推荐网上购买"一日游"的旅游产品,这样游客可以得到更多的优惠。

随着越来越多的国家对中国公民开放自由行,参加当地"一日游"的旅游活动对中国游客来说,是一个非常好的选择,既可以让自己的时间安排比较自由,又能参与旅行社精心策划的旅游项目。

One-day Tour on Great Ocean Road in Melbourne

Late August was the end of winter and the beginning of spring in Australia. One day at noon, we were walking from the north to the south on Swanston Street, a busy street in the center of Melbourne. When we were getting to Lt Bourke Street, many travel agency stores came into our sights. Their façade read "Evergreen Holidays", "Great Wall Travel Company", "Guangzhou Travel Company", etc.

Out of curiosity, we entered the Evergreen Travel Agency, run by some Malaysian Chinese. The saleswoman told us that they were having a Big Sale Weekend. Through her introduction we knew one day tour for Great Ocean Road used to cost 69 Australian dollars, but it only charged 45 Australian dollars for the weekends. She also added if we chose the three classical tours in Melbourne—visiting the Great Ocean Road and the Twelve Apostles, seeing penguins on Philips Island and visiting Sovereign Hill gold-seeking village, we could get a discount package price which would be 26 Australian dollars cheaper than the original price. Hearing the introduction, we eagerly wanted to register for the three tours in Melbourne. But it was a pity that we had already visited one of them. In the end, we decided to join the one-day tour on Great Ocean

Road.

At 8:30 Saturday morning, we gathered at the place which the agency appointed, and then got on the bus to the Great Ocean Road. The bus held more than 50 passengers, and the majority are Chinese. What surprised us was that 3 American students who had learnt Chinese in China also joined this group. The reason was that they thought the price was cheap and they could have the chance of listening to guide commentary in Chinese.

Our trip started by crossing the Simon Bridge in Melbourne where we could appreciate the sea view along the Port Phillip Bay. On the way, our guide made a brief introduction to the Great Ocean Road. It is located in the southwest of Melbourne, and was listed as the National Park in the early 1980 when it opened to tourists. Since then it had been the most famous scenic spot in Victoria. It started to be built in 1919 and was completely finished in 1932 in order to honor the soldiers joining the First World War. About 3,000 people, among whom there were also many retired soldiers, took part in the construction. The road stretches along the western bay of Victoria and brings visitors the spectacular ocean view and great fun of beach activities. The bus got to Geelong, the second biggest city in Victoria. A few minutes later, the driver parked the bus beside an arched door with the words "Great Ocean Road". We got off the bus and took photos there.

After that we continued our trip. Our lunch was arranged at a beautiful little town named Apollo Bay located at the foot of a mountain, where there were many restaurants and seafood was super fresh. Our guide recommended a restaurant owned by a Greek family to us. Each person could select 3 kinds of food by spending 9 Australian dollars. I must say they were really tasty.

After lunch, the bus continued to run on the most spectacular avenue in the world, Great Ocean Road. On the way, our guide introduced the remains of the sunken ships, the ancient fishing villages and the lush inland forest. At 3:00 we finally got to the Twelve Apostles, which were actually stones shaped by air-slaking and sea water and now erected independent on the Pacific Ocean. They looked like the twelve apostles of Jesus listening to him. Because of the constant erosion of nature, we could now only see seven of them. These age-old stones with 45 meters height stood against the land like a forever company, which had formed a lot of unique and astonishing views.

Under the recommendation of our guide, I excitedly got on a helicopter to have a bird's eye view of Loch Ard Gorge, Blowhole and London Bridge. Looking from the sky, the sharp cliffs, the beautiful beaches, the shining sea water and the mysterious limestone were quite clear. I could feel the tender sea wind and the beauty of our great nature.

At around 4:00 p. m. we started to go back to downtown of Melbourne. Looking out of the window, I could see the surging waves on the South Pacific Ocean and the ups-and-downs of Victoria mountains. The one-day tour on Ocean Road was the most adventurous, spectacular and wonderful journey.

Comments

The tourism products of one-day tour in Australia started from the 1970s and became mature in the 1980s. Take the one day tour product in Sydney and Melbourne as an example. Sydney, the capital of South Wales, located in the Southeast of Australia, not only has attractions in downtown but also has many other attractions far away from the downtown like Blue Mountain and Bondi Beach. And it can also have the product of one-day tour to Canberra. The three biggest lines, visiting the Great Ocean Road and the Twelve Apostles, seeing penguins on Philips Island and visiting Sovereign Hill gold-seeking village, are also far away from the downtown. In the condition that some local people in Australia don't like driving on their own to travel, one-day tour products grow fast in the local market.

In the low season such as winter, big sales and many promotion products will be used to attract tourists from all over the world. Agencies will offer special prices on weekends in order to have more tourists and get more profit, just like the Evergreen Holidays in this case. They also offered a one-day tour to Great Ocean Road at a discounted price of 45 Australian dollars on the basis of 69 Australian dollars. During this promotion period, they could have a very good business. Every day they could set out 3 groups with 50 passengers.

At the same time, many travel agencies will let the passengers buy two or three one-day tour products together, so that they can provide much more discount to the passengers. Some travel agencies even have the promotion policy to encourage group purchases. When the number of passengers reaches more than 10 or 15, they can get a more favorable price. In addition, the travel agencies highly recommend the passengers to buy one-day tour products online where they can get bigger discount.

With more and more countries opening to Chinese citizens, choosing one-day tours locally will be an ideal way to have more freedom in schedule planning and enjoy the well-planned tourism activities.

8 位客人的旅游巴士?

当俄罗斯、芬兰、冰岛、英国豪华游的行程进行到第 8 天时,旅游团从冰岛的首都雷克雅未克飞往英国第四大城市格拉斯哥。客人下了飞机后,领队发现英国境内安排的旅游车是带有行李箱的 16 座小型巴士,与旅游合同上的要求不符。领队小陈和英国导游核对了双方的行程计划,领队手上的确认单是 28 座的车,而导游想当然地认为 8 个人的团队使用 16 座的车也够了。小陈立刻打电话向公司汇报了这一情况。

没过多久,英国的接待社 Titi Tata 旅游公司驻上海代表处的蔡先生马上打电话向领队解释:由于英国正在举行"爱丁堡艺术节"和"诺丁汉狂欢节",用车特别紧张。换车难度较大,成本也较高,言语中流露出希望领队能谅解的心愿。领队心想,客人目前是没有很强烈的反应,但是如果没有明显的弥补措施,万一客人对接下来的行程,特别是对用车不满意的话,很可能会被投诉。于是,领队在电话里跟蔡先生商量,决定采取以下措施来弥补用车没有达到预定要求的不足:其一,将白天乘船游伦敦泰晤士河的游览项目改成夜游,因为泰晤士河的夜景比白天的美丽多了;其二,在格拉斯哥—爱丁堡—曼彻斯特—伦敦的大巴旅游途中,增加游览历史最悠久的大学城——牛津城的项目,这也解决了行程松散的问题；其三，在伦敦市中心增加一次西餐的安排。

领队让客人尽量把行李安放在车后的行李箱里，以腾出车厢内的空间，让客人在远途旅行时坐得舒服些。客人们最终忘记了"旅游车"的插曲，高高兴兴地离开了伦敦，结束了愉快的欧洲之旅。

[评析]

案例中所出现的问题责任在谁当然重要，但分清责任的同时，更要紧的是找到弥补的办法。领队凭着多年实践经验，以及出发前对旅游目的地及线路的充分了解，在处理以上案例中所出现的问题时，一方面和英国旅行社协商，另一方面又注意到客人的需求，真正起到了弥补服务的作用。

随着旅游者个性化需求的日趋突出，越来越多的旅游企业开始实施差异化战略。差异化战略的本质是创造一种可识别的、与竞争对手有区别的特殊服务。此案例也可以认为是弥补服务朝差异化服务转变的一个典范。领队对这一案例的处理方法是套用了导游带华东线客人不满意时所采用的弥补方式。案例中增加的牛津城游览项目，相当于苏州至杭州的路上增加了游览乌镇的项目；夜游泰晤士河相当于夜游上海的黄浦江；享用正宗的伦敦西餐相当于品尝杭州风味或上海"梅龙镇"风味美食。领队这样做的目的是培养顾客的忠诚度，提高旅游企业长期盈利的能力。

旅游业内有句俗语：$100-1=0$。其含义是旅游过程中，一切都很完美，出现一点纰漏，就会影响客人对整个活动的评价。这就要求我们旅游从业人员在为游客提供服务时必须坚守基本原则"关注＋专业"。

The 8 Visitors' Tour Bus?

A luxurious tour of Russia, Finland, Iceland and England consists of the flight from Reykjavik, the capital of Iceland, to the fourth biggest city of England, Glasgow, on the eighth day of their trip. After the group got off the plane, the tour leader found that the tour bus was a 16-seat mini one, which was different from what was agreed on the tour contract. Then Mr. Chen, the tour leader, checked the confirmed travel schedule with the British guide, finding that the arrangement on Mr. Chen's confirmation sheet was a 28-seat bus. It was the local guide that took it for granted that it was enough to use a 16-seat bus for 8 people. Mr. Chen immediately called his company and made a report about the case.

After a while, Mr. Cai, who was from the Shanghai representative office of British travel agency Titi Tata, called Mr. Chen and explained the buses were very short-supplied because of the ongoing Edinburgh Festival and Nottingham Carnival. It would be very difficult to provide another bus. He hoped the team leader could understand this situation and settle for this. The team leader thought if no obvious remedies were taken next, and if the customers got dissatisfied with the following trip, especially the bus, they would probably lodge a complaint. Therefore, the leader discussed with Mr. Cai on the phone and reached an agreement to take the following steps to remedy the situation:

1. Cancel the day visit to the Thames on ship and arrange a night visit instead, because the night view of the Thames is much better than that in the daytime.

2. Arrange a visit to Oxford city during the bus trip of Glasgow/Edinburgh/Manchester/London, which could not only fill the loose schedule but also enable the customers to see the earliest university town in the world.

3. Arrange a western-style meal in the downtown of London.

During the whole journey, the team leader managed to place the luggage in the trunk to save space and let them feel more comfortable in the long trip. The customers all forgot the "bus event" and left London happily, putting an end to the pleasant European trip.

Comments

There's no doubt that it is important to make clear who should be responsible for the problem, but to find a solution is more important. Based on the rich practical experience and a good knowledge on the destination and the trip route, the team leader negotiated with the British travel agency and at the same time noticed the customers' requirement when dealing with the problem mentioned above, making up the deficiency of service indeed.

As the personalized needs of the customers become more and more outstanding, more and more travel agencies begin to take a differentiation strategy, whose essence is to create a recognizable special service different from the rivals. This case can also be taken as a mode of changing from remedying service to differentiation service. The team leader's way in dealing with this case is an imitation of the guide's behavior when the customers got dissatisfied during an

Eastern China tour. The added visit to Oxford city is equal to the added visit to Wuzhen town during the trip from Suzhou to Hangzhou; the night visit to the Thames is equal to the night visit to Huangpu River in Shanghai; having an authentic London meal is equal to having a taste of Hangzhou local food or Shanghai "Meilong County" flavor. The purpose of the team leader to do so is to develop the loyalty of customers, and improve the company's ability for long-term profit.

There is an idiom in tourism circle: $100 - 1 = 0$. It means that during a trip, though everything is perfect, a little deficiency will affect the customers' evaluation of the whole journey. Thus, the basic principle that we tour operators should obey is: attention + professionalism.

造访澳华历史博物馆

在一个冬日周末的早晨,澳洲墨尔本街头寒风凛冽。我们计划去参观校友即香港理工大学墨尔本校友会副会长刘彦汝女士特别推荐的一个博物馆——澳华历史博物馆。

早上 10:00 我们从入住的海港公寓酒店出发,乘坐免费的城市环线电车经过 3 个站点后在斯旺斯顿大街下车。在斯旺斯顿大街口,我们找不到前往博物馆的路了。这时,一位穿着印有"Melbourne Visitor Center(墨尔本游客服务中心)"醒目红色制服,背着一个装有地图和各种小册子的小包的志愿者上前来问我们是否需要帮助。我们跟这位志愿者讲我们要去澳华历史博物馆参观,但不知如何走。这位志愿者非常热情地给我们指了路,并问我们是否需要墨尔本地图,我们感激地告诉他已经有了。

于是,我们沿着斯旺斯顿大街,继续往北走,到了小博街街口,便看到了带有浓郁中国色彩的墨尔本唐人街。我们继续往里走,便到了澳华历史博物馆。

澳华历史博物馆是一座 5 层高的西式小洋楼。博物馆门前有一对巨大石狮。该馆入口处有一条金光闪闪、威武雄壮的中国巨龙。地下一层陈列着各种造型的龙,展现出龙的传人的精神。馆内分设四个展厅,一楼为陈列大厅,中间摆放着一条色彩鲜艳、栩栩如生的绸制巨龙,起名为"墨尔本大龙"。每逢春节,当地的华人青年舞龙队就会舞动着"墨尔本大龙",投入街头欢庆节日表演队伍的行列。博物馆的二、三、四、五楼是展览厅,陈列着当年华人开采金矿的照片、澳洲各华族同乡公馆的锦旗,以及澳华名人返回中国各地观光和旅澳华人欢度春节活动的照片等。馆内还长期展出被誉为世界第八大奇观——秦始皇陵兵马俑的复制品。

博物馆的接待小姐是来自中国台湾的新移民,她用软绵绵的普通话向我们介绍,自19世纪40年代开始,广东、福建沿海一带数以万计的中国人为谋生,先后以契约华工等身份进入澳大利亚垦荒、淘金。这些移民先驱在澳大利亚从事最繁重、最艰苦的劳动,并饱受种族歧视和雇主的盘剥与虐待,有不少人不堪忍受劳苦与折磨而客死他乡。华人移民为当地的经济、文化发展和社会繁荣付出了血与汗、力量与智慧,成为澳大利亚光荣的拓荒族之一。在第一块金矿被发现之后的6年里,维多利亚的华人人口最高达4.2万人,他们中的大多数来自中国广东省的四邑一带。当笔者一次猜对接待小姐的原籍是台湾台南时,她觉得非常惊讶。我告诉她,现在两岸的交流变得越来越频繁,我们对台湾及台湾居民的了解日趋增多,我可以根据你讲话的口音来判断你来自哪里。接待小姐感叹道:"是啊,毕竟都是同根同源的中国人。"

在参观期间,我们正好看到了一群澳大利亚小学生在老师的带领下参观博物馆。接待小姐告诉我,澳大利亚是个移民国家,第二次世界大战以后,有歧视的移民限制政策开始松动并在1972年得到最终解除,华人移民队伍随即逐渐成长起来。在多元文化的背景下,澳洲学生了解各国文化是有必要的,当然包括中国文化。

接待小姐还兴奋地告诉我们,博物馆工作人员还经常承担带领团队游览华埠历史古迹、中药店、茶肆、酒楼,带游客到中餐馆用餐等各项服务工作。他们也常组织汉字书法示范、中国民族乐器演奏及中国武术表演等活动。博物馆开展这些延伸增值服务,深得澳洲社会的好评。

我深深敬佩为中华文化的发扬光大而做出贡献的澳洲华人。

[评析]

澳大利亚联邦政府对旅游业高度重视。从 2004 年起,仅用于旅游推介的经费每年都在 2 亿澳元以上。各州政府和领地政府一年的旅游促销经费也高达几亿澳元。各旅游企业和协会每年在组织、宣传及推介方面投入的总费用与政府的大致相当。

笔者采访了墨尔本旅游局所属"墨尔本市委员会"的旅游营运总监 Ellena Ly 女士,她告诉我们,墨尔本游客服务中心由当地政府全额拨款,于 2002 年 10 月正式对游客开放。该中心的员工每年招聘两次,均是经过考试的志愿者,大多数是在校大学生及退休教师、护士。志愿者们还会在周末走上主要街区进行旅游宣传册分发等活动。每年约有 90 万人次来该中心咨询。它是个一站式服务点,当你走进墨尔本游客服务中心,即可一次得到维多利亚州和墨尔本的所有旅游信息,包括免费宣传册、地图及活动清单;此外还提供纪念品,以及住宿和游程预订服务。游客也可以直接向该游客中心的旅行社预订各种旅游线路。在墨尔本有五处这样的游客服务中心。这些与澳大利亚联邦政府及州政府在旅游业上的投入是分不开的。

案例中,笔者在墨尔本的一条南北方向主要大街——斯旺斯顿大街所遇到的志愿者就是墨尔本游客服务中心派出的。这些志愿者被称作城市大使。年长的志愿者把这项工作看作接触社会的好时机,他们往往有着良好的学历和工作背景,或者曾经在旅游相关行业工作过。而年轻的志愿者往往把这份工作看作练习英语或让世界各地游客了解墨尔本和澳洲的好机会。笔者在伯克街购物中心的墨尔本游客服务站见到的两位志愿者:一位是曾在香港国泰航空工作过的空姐,已经 83 岁了,但思维敏捷,反应迅速;另一位是来自越南的留学生,正在墨尔本大学读书。

修建澳华历史博物馆纪念华人历史功绩的建议,是一位受人尊敬的澳大利亚人首先提出的。他就是维多利亚州旅游局主席东·邓斯坦。这位澳大利亚人认为,华人在澳大利亚历史长河中所扮演的角色太重要了,应被澳大利亚社会所了解。1984年,他倡议在墨尔本唐人街这一具有历史意义的地方建造澳华历史博物馆,用来搜集、研究和展览澳大利亚早期华人的历史遗物,使之成为一个独特的旅游景点。邓斯坦先生的倡议立即得到各华人社团、墨尔本市政当局及维多利亚州政府的响应和支持。州政府捐款24万澳元,随即在唐人街内购得一栋建于19世纪90年代的旧货仓大楼作为馆址,经过一年多的装修、筹备,澳华博物馆于1985年11月正式对外开放。由所在国政府出资创办华人历史博物馆,这在全球还是首次。

A Visit to the Australian Chinese Museum

It's a cold windy weekend morning in winter Melbourne. We was going to the Australian Chinese Museum. It was recommended by Mrs. Liu Yanru, my school mate in Hong Kong Polytechnic University as well as the chairman of alumni association in Melbourne.

At 10:00 in the morning we set out from Harbor View Apartment Hotel where we stayed. We took the free city loop-line electric bus to Swanston Street, 3 stops away. But at the crossing of the Swanston Street we totally had no idea of where to go. Just at that time, a volunteer in an outstanding red uniform with three words "Melbourn Visitor Center" asked whether we would need any help. We told him that we were going to the Australian Chinese

Museum, but we didn't know the way. The warm-hearted volunteer showed us the way and asked whether we would need a Melbourne map. As we already got one, we politely declined but expressed our great thanks to him.

We kept walking to the north along Swanston Street. When we reached the crossing of Litter Bourke, we saw a typical Chinatown. After walking into the street, we finally arrived at the museum.

The Australian Chinese Museum was a five-storey western style building. In front of its gate, there were two stone lions. At the entrance of the museum, we saw a giant glittering golden Chinese dragon full of power and grandeur. On the first floor of the basement, there displayed many beautiful Chinese dragons in all kinds of shapes, which symbolized the traditional spirit of Chinese people. The museum was divided into four exhibition halls. The exhibition hall on the first floor displayed a bright colorful and vivid giant dragon made of silk whose name was "Big Melbourne Dragon". Every year in the Spring Festival, the local Austrlian Chinese youngsters do the performance on the street with "Big Melbourne Dragon". From the second floor to the fifth floor were the exhibition halls showing pictures taken at the time when Chinese mined gold, flags and data of Chinese communities in Australia, as well as pictures of Australian Chinese celebrities taken when they traveled in China and celebrated Chinese New Year in Australia. The museum also displayed the duplicate of the eighth world wonder, Terracotta Warriors.

The receptionist of the museum was a new immigrant from Taiwan. She introduced the history of Chinese in Australia in mandarin with her sweet accent. Starting from the 1940s, hundreds of thousands of people living in the coastal area of Guangzhou and Fujian constantly came to Australia to mine gold and develop virgin soil as contracted Chinese labor. These immigrant pioneers did the most backbreaking work and had to suffer from racial discrimination as well as the exploitation and abuse from employers. Many of them couldn't tolerate the torment and died in this country far away from their hometown. These Chinese immigrants made their contribution to the development of local economy, culture and social prosperity. They are one group of glorious developers. The discovery of the first golden mine changed everything. The number of Chinese people once reached 42,000 in the following 6 years. Most of them came from the villages of Guangdong province. I guessed the receptionist's ancestral home was Tainan in Taiwan. She was quite surprised that I got the right answer after the first guess. I told her that nowadays the communication between mainland China and Taiwan had become more and more frequent, and we were getting to know more about Taiwan and residents in Taiwan. I could recognize where she comes from by her accent. The receptionist said emotionally, "It's true. After all, we were born to be Chinese."

We happened to see a group of Australian primary school students who were learning the history under the guidance of their teachers. The receptionist told me Australia was a country of immigrants, the restrictions with discriminations started to be loose and were finally removed in 1972. From then on, the number of Chinese immigrants grew steadily. So for this multi-cultural background, it's necessary for Australian students to know the cultures of different countries, including Chinese culture.

The receptionist also told us excitedly that the museum staff had been always taking tourists to Chinese historic sites, Chinese medicine shops, tea houses and restaurants. They also did the performance like Chinese calligraphy, Chinese national instrumentals as well as martial art. All these services they did had been well appraised by Australian society.

I deeply admire Australian Chinese who made great contribution to develop

Chinese culture and make it known to the world.

Comments

The Australian government is concerned about tourism industry. The states have been spending more than 2,000 million AUD on advertisement of tourism since 2004, and the state governments spend billions of AUD in promotion. Meanwhile, the tourism enterprises and the associations in areas spend as much as the government to do the organizing, advertising and marketing work every year.

I interviewed Ms. Ellena Ly, the director of tour operation in City of Melbourne Committee. She told us Melbourne Visitor Center was founded by the entire fund from local government and was opened to the public officially in October, 2002. The staff in the center would be recruited twice a year. The volunteers who passed the test were mainly college students, retired teachers and nurses. The volunteers would distribute tourism brochures on main blocks on weekends. Every year there're about 900 thousand people coming to the center for consulting. It is a one-stop service station where you can get all the information about Victoria State as well as Melbourne through free brochures, maps and activities schedules. Besides, they also offer souvenirs, and accommodation and tours booking service on the internet. Visitors can directly book various tours of travel agencies through 5 visitor centers in Melbourne. The tourism centers are mostly boosted by the investment of tourism industry from Australian Federal Government and the state governments.

In this case, the volunteer we met on Swanston Street was dispatched by Melbourne Visitor Center. These volunteers were called City Ambassadors. The elderly volunteers regard this job as an opportunity to get in touch with the society. They are well-educated and have outstanding working experience, and some of them have done jobs related to tourism. While to young volunteers, they are more likely to regard this job as a good chance to practice English or a way to introduce

Melbourne to tourists from all over the world. I met two volunteers at shopping mall on the Bourke Street. One of them was an elderly lady who had once worked as an airline stewardess for a Hong Kong Airline. The other was from Vietnam who was now studying in Melbourne University.

The idea of building a museum to illustrate the contribution made by Chinese immigrants was first proposed by a distinguished Australian, the former chairman of Victoria State Tourism Bureau, whose name is Don Duhstan. This native Australian thought Chinese people played an important role in the long history of Australia, and they should be known by Australian society. In 1984 he proposed to build the museum in Chinatown, a place full of historical meanings. They collected the historical remains and did research on them, and displayed treasures in the museum. In this way, the museum became a unique attraction. The proposal from Don Duhstan was supported by the Chinese communities, the Melbourne government and the Victoria State government. With 240 thousand AUD donated by the state government, they purchased an old storage house established in the 1890s as the museum's site. After one year's preparation and decoration, it was officially opened to the public in November, 1985. This was the first try in the globe that a foreign government invested on the construction of a Chinese historical museum.

瑞士边境购物一日游

2014 年 2 月,笔者有机会赴意大利的米兰开会,还获得了一次意外的旅行机会,那就是在瑞士边境购物一日游。

赴意大利米兰之前,一同前往的同伴就在网上查询了米兰附近有哪些直销商场。查询的结果是,从米兰驱车两小时,大约 50 公里,就会抵达瑞士小镇卢加诺的郊外(接壤意大利米兰及瑞士边境),那里有一家名为门德里西奥"狐狸镇"厂家直销中心的商场。而且,旅游者可以在米兰当地的旅行社门店柜台购买边境购物一日游的车票。

我们一行人乘坐从杭州经由香港转机赴米兰的班机,抵达米兰已是早上。稍作休息后,我们就坐上出租车直奔网上搜索到的米兰大教堂附近的 Agenzia Viaggi 旅行社,购买了 20 欧元一张的大巴票。午饭后,我们在下午两点之前就早早地等候在发车的集合点。与我们一样准备去购物的游客来自世界各地。

两点整,司机点好人数后,开着高大宽敞的欧洲大巴带我们奔赴瑞士的小镇——卢加诺。一路上,我们看到了雪山,经过了意大利北部的城市——科摩,一个半小时后,我们一行就抵达了门德里西奥"狐狸镇"厂家直销中心。

门德里西奥"狐狸镇"厂家直销中心,占地面积达 27000 平方米,包含 160 多家精品店,拥有250个主要品牌,国际品牌全年3折至7折,是物美价廉的购物天堂。当我们走进去后,就看到了一本小册子上写着以上介绍。和美国、法国的厂家直销中心不同,卢加诺的"狐狸镇"是一座四层的大厦而非购物村,各种商品的价格用欧元和瑞士法郎标价。欧元在瑞士也是通用的。不过你在付款的时候,如果想支付欧元,一般要特别告知,不然都是以瑞士法郎结算的。

我们购买了瑞士军刀等特色商品,在付款时,商场的营业员热情地告诉我们,所购买的商品可以在本商场退税,而且可以马上拿到退税款。我们按照营业员的要求填写了退税表,支付完货款后,按照营业员所指的方向,到退税窗口,将退税表、护照、信用卡交给了工作人员。之后工作人员告诉我们,退税款已经在信用卡里。但是,当你离开这里回米兰路途中,司机会在瑞士与意大利的边境停下来,在边境的海关盖一个章,然后你将此退税单放入一个邮箱就可以了。

晚上7点钟,我们又坐上了原来的大巴,半小时左右司机停下了车,引领我们到边境的海关办公室,大家鱼贯而入,盖了章并将退税单放入邮箱。司机清点了人数,将大家送回米兰市区。

[评析]

1970年起,欧洲的一些服装和日用品加工企业开始利用工厂的仓库销售自己的订单尾货。1988年以后,去工厂直销店购买商品的顾客越来越多,于是,有不少工厂便把自己的直销店开在一起,逐步形成了具有购物中心性质的工厂直销购物中心。但那时的"狐狸镇"一般都是真正的工厂直销店,大多远离城市,功能单一,虽然以名牌和低价吸引顾客,但仍然没有形成有规模的销售。

兴起于20世纪70年代的品牌直销购物中心作为一种零售业态,因销售名牌过季、下架、断码的商品,受到了追求最佳性价比的消费者及急于寻找另类销售平台的品牌厂商的极度欢迎。很快,品牌直销就在世界品牌云集的欧洲大陆风行起来。在发展商的深度参与后,一些品牌直销商家逐步发展成拥有自身品牌价值的连锁集团。"狐狸镇"就是在这种情况下成长起来的一个品牌直销国际连锁零售集团,已在全球23个地区开设了品牌折扣店,年营业额超过98亿欧元并持续成长。

与旅游购物不同的是,购物旅游的主要出游目的为购物活动,也就是说,旅游者将购物看成旅游决策的主要原因。这种情况下,购物旅游已经被提升到与观光、度假等旅游产品并列的地位。

20世纪80年代突然出现加拿大公民跨越边境到美国购物旅游的热潮,造成了美加两国贸易关系中加拿大赤字的情况。这个事件说明了两个问题:其一,购物已经成为旅游动机的引发因素;其二,跨境购物旅游不仅会对目的地国家(地区)产生影响,对客源地国家(地区)也会产生影响,并引起连锁反应。

意大利与瑞士是邻国,在进行购物旅游合作时做得相当完美。米兰是著名的旅游目的地城市,每年都有几百万的旅游者前往,而瑞士的"狐狸镇"已经有40年以上的历史,在全球都很有名。米兰在输送客源给瑞士的同时,也增加了自己的入境旅游人数。人们在米兰旅游之后,不会错过赴瑞士边境进行购物旅游的机会。

非欧盟国家的旅游者赴欧洲旅游,比较麻烦的事就是退税,而"狐狸镇"将退税的步骤做得非常人性化。一般的退税步骤是旅游者离开欧盟国家时将已购买的商品拿到机场出示给海关人员查看,盖章后,才能拿到退税款,但"狐狸镇"却将这些步骤简化,旅游者购物后马上可以拿到退税款,这也是方便旅游者的一种有效做法。

One-day Shopping Tour across Swiss Border

I got an unexpected opportunity to have a day shopping on the Swiss border while attending a meeting in Italy in February, 2014.

Before going to Milan, one of my companions had searched for outlets near Milan. Her search result showed that the Mendrisio Foxtown Factory Outlet was near Milan, about 50 km away, in the suburb of Lugano, Switzerland. It needed a two-hour drive. What's more, tourists might buy one-day border shopping tour ticket in one of the local travel agencies in Milan.

We took the flight from Hangzhou to Milan, transferred in Hong Kong. We arrived in Milan in the morning. After a short rest, we took a taxi to Agenzia Viaggi Travel Agency which we found on the Internet and was near the Milan Cathedral. We each bought a 20-euro bus ticket. After lunch, we waited at the gathering point early before 2:00 p.m. The tourists who had the same travel plan with us were from Middle-east, Asia, Africa and so on.

After counting the number of tourists, the driver took us to Lugano, Switzerland in a huge and spacious bus. On the way there, we saw the snow mountain, and passed by Como, a northern city in Italy. After an hour and a half, we arrived at the Mendrisio Foxtown Factory Outlet.

The Mendrisio Foxtown Factory Outlet occupies 27,000 m^2, including over 160 boutiques and 250 major brands. The international brands are 30%—70% off all year round. According to the brochure we got when entering the outlet, here is the shopping paradise for tourists. Different from America and France, the Foxtown Factory Outlets in Lugano is a four-story mansion, not a shopping mall. Prices are in euro and Swiss franc. Euro is acceptable in Switzerland, but people should mention it if they want to pay with euro, otherwise the goods will be paid in Swiss franc.

We bought some featured commodities such as Swiss Army Knives. When we paid the list, the shop assistant warmly told us those goods may have duty refund and we could get the money in the outlet immediately. We filled the duty refund forms with the help of the shop assistant, paid the money, went to the duty refund window, and handed in the forms, passports and credit cards to the staff. The staff told us that the money had already been put back in our credit cards. When people were on the way back to Milan, the driver stopped and got the same stamps at the border customs. Then people should put the duty refund forms into a mail-box.

We got back at 7 o'clock in the evening. The driver stopped after half an hour and led us to the customs office on the border. Everybody went in, got the stamps and put the duty refund forms into the mail-box. The driver counted the number of tourists and sent us back to the downtown of Milan.

Comments

Some clothes and commodities processing enterprises have started to sell the surplus goods in factory stores since the 1970s. After 1988, more and more customers went to the factory stores to buy goods. Therefore, many factories set up their direct stores nearby and then formed a kind of shopping center combining factories and stores. But at that time, the foxtowns were normally factory stores and far away from the city. Their function was very simple and single. Though the brands and low price attracted some customers, the sales scale was not formed.

Outlet, started in the 1970s, is a retail form, selling outdated brand goods, size-shorted goods and off-the-shelf commodities. It is very popular with the customers who want quality goods with low price. It is also popular with brands merchants who seek for another sales platform. Soon, the outlet becomes more and more popular in Europe. After the participation of developers, some merchants in outlet gradually have developed into a chain group with their own brand value. And Foxtown is one of these international chain retail groups. The Foxtown has set up brand discount stores in 23 countries and regions all over the world with annual sales over 9. 8 billion euros and it still is developing.

Different from the shopping activities during sightseeing and vacation, shopping tourism means the tourists mainly focus on shopping activities, which indicates that the tourists' shopping desire decides their travel plan. In such case, shopping tourism is a travel product, the same as sightseeing and vacation, etc.

In the 1980s, Canadians suddenly went across the border, bought goods and travelled in America, which led to the Canadian deficit in Canada-America trade relationship. It explains two things: first, shopping becomes the trigger of traveling; second, cross-border shopping tourism not only affects the destination country, but also the source country, and then results in the chain effect in politics, legislation, economy and society.

Italy is the neighbor of Switzerland. They have perfectly cooperated with each other in shopping and tourism. Milan is a famous travel destination. Every year, millions of tourists go to travel in Milan, while the Foxtown in Switzerland has an over-40-year history, and is famous all over the world. Milan sends customers to Switzerland and meanwhile promotes the inbound tourism. People will not miss the border shopping in Switzerland when they travel in Milan.

One of the troubles for the tourists from non-EU countries is duty refund. Foxtown makes the process very convenient for people. Generally speaking, the tourists can get their duty refund when they leave the country, show the goods to the customs officers at airport, get the stamps. But Foxtown settles the trouble. The tourists can get their refund as soon as they complete their purchase. It is really very convenient for tourists.

澳洲黄金海岸自由行

2012 年 7 月末,笔者再一次造访澳洲第六大城市——黄金海岸,体验颇丰。

我们一行 7 人从凯恩斯乘飞机抵达昆士兰州首府布里斯班国际机场认领行李时,正在为乘坐何种交通工具赴离布里斯班 80 公里以外的黄金海岸发愁。突然发现,行李转盘旁就有一个购买"空中火车"赴布里斯班市区和黄金海岸的购票处。商量过后我们买了每张 12 澳元的火车票,按照售票员指引的方向坐上了赴黄金海岸的接驳火车。

一个半小时后,我们抵达了处在地球南回归线上的黄金海岸,入住了黄金海岸冲浪者天堂附近的沃特马克酒店。冲浪者天堂是黄金海岸的旅游中心。在酒店的不远处,就有一家华人开的"旅游预订中心",入口处的广告上写着预订项目,包括主题公园、精彩活动、酒店住宿、美食推荐、购物指南、房产投资等。走进预订中心,大家一下子被琳琅满目的宣传册子吸引住了,无法定下来选哪一条旅游线路。此时,在一位叫詹妮弗的店员的推荐下,我们一行 7 人决定参加"热带雨林四驱车一日生态游",内容包括赏鸟、品酒、追踪野生动物等。

次日早晨,按照约定的时间,导游兼司机,澳洲人纳贝尔,开着公司的越野车,准时来到酒店门口接我们。我们在纳贝尔的引领下,乘着超大马力的四驱无穷;在被列为世界自然保护遗产的雷明顿国家公园里,了解雨林生态,探索动植物奥秘。一日游的行程还包括欣赏手工艺品,在酒庄免费品酒,寻找野生的树熊、袋鼠、火鸡,观赏稀有的野生鸟类等。

一日游的内容让我们觉得值回票价,澳洲人纳贝尔对澳洲的了解很全面,特别是其丰富的植物知识,加上他周到、热情的服务,让大家对这家旅游预订中心的选择更有信赖感。于是,结束一日游后,我们让纳贝尔把我们送回旅游预订中心,续订了接下来的旅游项目。由于第三天下午我们就要离开黄金海岸赴悉尼,因此第三天的安排是上午黄金海岸环城运河游,下午1:00乘坐巴士回布里斯班机场。和第一次一样,我们支付了全部费用,手中拿到了预订中心给的旅游券和发票。

第三天上午,我们按照旅游券上的时间乘船游览了黄金海岸运河,下午1:00我们在沃特马克酒店等候预订的车子赴布里斯班机场。但过了1:00还不见巴士过来,我们急了,马上打电话给预订中心。詹妮弗告诉我他们会马上与车行核实到底是怎么一回事。在我们不断的催促下,巴士在1:35才抵达我们等候的酒店。

驱车行驶了1小时20分钟,我们终于抵达布里斯班机场,恰好赶上了飞往悉尼的飞机。

[评析]

随着对中国公民开放自由行的旅游目的地国家和地区不断增多,越来越多的中国人加入了自由行的行列。一般自由行的旅游者在出发之前都会做好攻略,包括预订好来回机票(特别是国际段)以及在各国城市入住的酒店,但其他项目往往会随机在当地预订。案例中预订的一日游、半日游以及乘坐的车辆,其实都不是这个预订中心自身固有的旅游产品。确切地说,它只是预订中心,囊括了跟旅游相关的所有内容,包括房产等,而不是旅游公司。供应商提供旅游产品给它,它来代理销售探险旅游、游船、汽车服务项目,预订中心也没有自己的导游。

所以,自由行旅游者一定要寻找声誉好、品质好的预订中心。案例中,送机场的巴士没有按时来接客人,到底是接受预订的职员詹妮弗忘了向巴士公司预订,还是巴士公司内部调度出了问题,我们不得而知。试想,如果在旅游旺季(黄金海岸的最佳旅游时间是 9 月至次年 5 月,那时会吸引无数游客来观光度假)忘了向汽车公司订车,临时再订的结果一般是一车难求,况且款项已经全部付清,再退也有难度。

在国外旅行寻找华人预订中心预订旅游产品时,会发现他们与顾客签的条款往往是单方面保障他们自身利益的,可以说是霸王条款,一旦出现违约,客人的利益很难得到保证。

另外,接受预订的詹妮弗告知我们,从黄金海岸市区到布里斯班机场的车程是 1 小时 5 分,但实际行驶用了 1 小时 20 分钟,幸好我们在做预订时按照经验给自己多留了一些时间,正好与预订的巴士迟到的半小时和实际路程多花费的一刻钟抵消。因此,自由行的旅客赴国外机场、车站等一定要留出足够的时间以应对突发事件,譬如工人罢工、游行、交通堵塞、临时更换登机口等。

Free and Easy Tour to the Gold Coast in Australia

In the end of July in 2012, I visited the Gold Coast in Australia again. It was still impressive to me.

The seven of us arrived by plane from Cairns at Brisbane International

Airport, the capital of the State of Queensland. While claiming our baggage, we started worrying about which means of transport to take to go to the Gold Coast, which was 80 km away from Brisbane when suddenly we found a ticket office next to the baggage carousel selling tickets for the Air Train going to downtown of Brisbane and the Gold Coast. After consultation, we bought the Air Train tickets for 12 AUD each, got on the train to the Gold Coast effortlessly in accordance with the direction of the conductor.

One and a half hours' ride took us to the Gold Coast on the Earth's Tropic of Capricorn. We stayed at Watermark Hotel near Surfers Paradise on the Gold Coast. Surfers Paradise was a tourist center in the Gold Coast. Not far from the hotel, there was a travel reservation center run by Australian Chinese, whose advertisement at the entrance said it provided services including reservations of theme parks, exciting activities, hotel accommodation, food recommendation, shopping guiding, and real estate investment. Walking into the reservation center, we were all of a sudden attracted by many brochures there. It was hard to choose. At the recommendation of a clerk named Jennifer, we decided to take the "One Day Eco-tour to Tropical Rainforest by Four-wheel," which includes bird appreciating, wine tasting and wild animal tracking.

The next morning at the agreed time, Nabel, our Australian tour guide and driver, came to the front of the hotel with his off-road vehicle to pick us up. Under the guidance of Nabel, we rode on the super-powered four-wheel drive deep into Mt. Tamborine, probing the secluded tropical rainforest. We hand fed wild rainbow bird at the O'Reilly's. What a great fun! At Lamington National Park, the world natural heritage conservation, we explored the rainforest ecosystem and the mysteries of plants and animals. The day trip also included appreciation of arts and crafts, free wine tasting at the winery, looking for wild koalas, kangaroos, turkeys, and appreciating rare species of wild birds.

The day trip was really worthwhile. Nabel's comprehensive understanding of Australia and his rich knowledge on plants in particular, coupled with his thoughtful and friendly service, won our trust in this travel reservation center. Thus, after the day trip, we asked Nabel to take us back to the reservation center to book our next tour. As we were leaving the Gold Coast for Sydney on the afternoon of the third day, the arrangement for that day included Gold Coast canal tour around the city in the morning and transfer to Brisbane Airport at 1:00 p.m. Like the first time, we paid all the fees to the travel reservation center and got our tour vouchers and receipts.

On the morning of the third day we toured the canal of the Gold Coast by boat in accordance with the time on the travel voucher. At 1:00 p.m, we were waiting at Watermark Hotel for the bus we booked to take us to Brisbane Airport. But the bus didn't show up when it already passed 1 o'clock. We called the travel reservation center. Jennifer told us that they would check with the dealer to see what had happened. With our constant urging, the bus arrived at the hotel where we were waiting at 1:35.

After an hour and twenty minutes' driving, we finally arrived in Brisbane Airport, just early enough to catch the plane to Sydney.

Comments

As Chinese citizens are granted to traveling as individual tourist in more and more countries and regions, lots of Chinese people have started to join independent travels. Normally, individual travelers would collect certain information about the journey they are about to have, book flight tickets (especially the tickets for international flights) and make hotel reservations. For the part of sightseeing, they can make reservations in any local places. In this case, one-day tour, half-day tour and hiring a tour bus were not the tourism products of the travel reservation center. It was just a booking center dealing with travel related business, or real estate, etc. Suppliers provided them with tourism products. The travel reservation center sold the adventure tour, cruises and bus service as an agent. It didn't have tour guides of its own. So it's important for individual travelers to find a booking center with good reputation and high quality. In this case, the bus didn't show up in time to pick up the guests at the hotel. Whether it was because Jennifer, who accepted the reservation, forgot to hire the bus or because something went wrong in the bus company, we would never know. Imagine, if the people working at a booking center forgot to hire the bus in peak season, it would be very hard to get one temporarily (the best season for the Gold Coast is from September to May, it attracts millions of vacationers from all over the world). Besides, the payment had been made in full. It wouldn't be easy to refund.

When groups travel aboard and look for booking centers (tourism companies) to book tourism products, they would find that the contracts signed by both sides are often only for the benefit of tourism companies. They are in a way imparity clauses. In case of default, it would be hard to safeguard the rights and interests of the customers.

Furthermore, Jennifer told us it would take an hour and five minutes to drive from downtown of the Gold Coast to Brisbane Airport. It actually took an hour and 20 minutes. Luckily, out of our experience, we gave ourselves more time when making the reservation. It just offset the delay of the bus and a quarter for driving. Therefore, it's necessary for individual travelers to set aside enough time to get to places like airports, bus stations just in case of emergency, such as strikes of workers, parades, traffic jam, change of boarding gate, etc.

在日本自助点餐机上点餐

2015 年春节，笔者又担任了"日本本州 5 夜 6 天超值之旅"的出境游领队，踏上了日本国土。旅游公司设计的 6 天行程采用飞机往返套票。所以首尾两天我们几乎都在搭乘飞机和办理酒店住宿，剩下的 4 天行程被安排得满满当当。

行程次日早晨，客人离开关西地区赴大阪游览。午餐后又马上赶到日本的古都——京都，去游览金阁寺、八坂神社和祇园艺伎花见小路等名胜风景。下午 5 点左右，京都的行程结束。当晚，团队被安排在距离京都车程约两小时的名古屋住宿。

日本导游向我提出了很好的建议，从京都到名古屋的路途中没有适合旅游团就餐的餐厅，不如在高速公路休息站将餐费发给客人，客人不仅可以想吃什么就买什么，也可以体验一下在日本自助点餐机上点餐的乐趣。晚上 6 点左右，拿到餐费的客人（特别是孩子）直奔自助点餐机，照着点餐程序选餐、等号、取餐。客人在品尝日本餐食的同时，也参与了其乐无穷的用餐体验。

行程第 5 天的东京一日游，上午的安排是秋叶原电器街自由购物及参观浅草寺，下午的安排是自由购物，行程中旅行社只安排午餐，晚餐由客人自理。

早餐过后，客人们都坐上了赴东京市区的旅游大巴。笔者在大巴上问导游午餐的用餐地点。导游回答我，我们团体人数比较多，没有合适的场地吃团队餐，还是发钱给客人吧，让他们自行解决。我驳回了导游的提议，建议给大家安排团队餐。因为我觉得团队旅游偶尔有一次发钱给客人，让客人感受一下异域的餐饮文化还是可以的，但次数多了，客人会感觉麻烦。况且，组团旅行社给客人午餐和晚餐的标准是不一样的，午餐是 1080 日元，晚餐是 1500 日元。客人若觉得 1080 日元不够吃，可能会投诉。最后我们选择了在浅草寺旁的一个日式餐厅吃日本定食。

中午，客人在餐厅边吃午餐边跟我讲："这是日本之行的最后一顿团队餐了。日本餐食做得很精细，非常不错。小孩子们在一起玩了四五天也有感情了，今天的这顿餐结束后，我们就得自行活动了。"言语中显得非常珍惜大家在一起用餐的机会。

[评析]

2014 年以来日本游热度一直不减，从出行方式来看，跟团游仍是赴日旅游的主要方式，第一次出游日本的游客仍以团队游为主。

职业出境游领队在实际带团中的作用，包含许多方面，诸如带领旅游者完成登机，办理出入境等手续；提供语言翻译服务等。其中调控行程使团队顺利运行和监督导游服务是领队不能忽视的两项重要工作。案例中，领队从不利于保持团队的整体性及午、晚餐的标准不同，易引起客人的不满两点出发，最终制止导游第二次发钱给客人自由用餐的行为。

境外导游从业人员素质参差不齐。即使同一个导游在不同的工作时间内，也有不同的状态体现。领队的这一做法堵住了导游试图想偷一点点懒的动机，来确保团队的正常运行。

Order Food by Machine in Japan

During the Spring Festival in 2015, I went to Japan as a tour leader for "the Great Value Trip to Honshu, Japan (6 days)". Round-trip air tickets were booked for this trip by the travel agency, and therefore the first and last days were taken by airport check-in, flight and hotel check-in. We had a tight schedule in the other 4 days.

The tour group went to Osaka after leaving Kansai Region on the second day. After lunch, we went to Kyoto, the ancient capital of Japan, to visit such places of interest as Kinkakuji, Yasaka Shrine, and the Hanami Street in Gion with geisha dreams, etc. We finished our tour in Kyoto at around 5 p.m. and drove about 2 hours to Nagoya for the night.

The tour guide in Japan suggested that since there was no ideal place to have dinner between Kyoto and Nagoya, the tourists could get refund for the missed meal and order whatever they want from machine. All the tourists, especially the kids, rushed to the machines at dinner time, ordering dishes, waiting for the numbers. They had fun using the machines and having Japanese food.

We visited Tokyo on the 5th day. Sensoji Temple and free shopping in Akihabara Electric Town were scheduled in the morning and free shopping in the afternoon. The travel agency paid only for lunch.

After breakfast, all the tourists were on the bus to downtown of Tokyo. I asked the guide, "Where are we supposed to have lunch?" He said, "It's difficult to find a dinning place for such a large group. Give them money and let them decide." I declined his advice and demanded the guide to arrange a group meal for them, because the tourists may feel bothered if they have to look for restaurants on their own all the time. Besides, the lunch fee is 1,080 yen which is less than that for dinner, which is 1,500 yen. If the tourists fail to have a nice meal with 1,080 yen, they may complain. Finally, we had bento in a Japanese restaurant near the Sensoji Temple.

One of the tourists chatted with me during lunch time. This was the last group meal. Japanese food was great. It was well-prepared. Children made friends with each other over the past few days. We would have to do the rest of the tour on our own after this dinner. We surely value the opportunity to have lunch together.

Comments

Trips to Japan have been hot since 2014. Most people tend to take package tours, especially for those who go to Japan for the first time.

Professional outbound tour leaders play a key role in many aspects (helping tourists with boarding, entry and exit procedures and being an interpreter, etc.), among which team coordination and supervision of guides' work are the most significant. In this case, considering that the dissolution of the group would damage the group's integrity and the price difference between lunch and supper may easily lead to dissatisfaction, the leader stopped the guide from letting the tourists have meal on their own for the second time.

The qualities of overseas tour guides vary. A guide's working attitude may also vary in different times. In the above case, the leader prevented the guide from being lazy and ensured the smooth running of the tour by his proper intervention.

与客人在狮城自由活动一天

　　每一个去过新加坡的人都会时不时地想念它的好：安全、便利、舒适、丰富。从多年前闻名于世的"Garden City"（花园城市）到如今正在悄然蜕变的"City in the Garden"（花园里的城市），这片动人的岛屿从未停止过勾画理想家园的美妙蓝图。无论你是美食粉、购物狂、设计迷还是酒店控，都可以在新加坡找到和自己对味的城市元素。它的"小"让我们得以收获更多的当地体验，它的日新月异让我们常来常往，兴致益然。坐在保存完好的老巴刹里吃一份沙爹烤肉，高耸入云的现代派商务大厦甘做背景，与其说我们喜欢去新加坡旅行，不如说我们热爱去新加坡过一段日子。

　　浙江中青旅出境游领队小余所带的一个"新加坡4晚5天亲子团"有一天自由活动的时间，团员可以感受一下新加坡人的生活。这个团共计24人，其中有10个放寒假的六年级小学生。由于此团是亲子团，领队在出发前就向该团队的团长询问自由活动时的需求，得到了统一的答复：自由活动的一天统一安排游览环球影城及夜间动物园。

　　自由活动安排在抵达新加坡的第二天，余领队出发前就在地图上查询了所住酒店大富酒店，与新加坡名胜世界及夜间动物园有些距离。在抵达新加坡的第一天,余领队就自行前往酒店附近的"小印度"地铁站进行了巡视。回来后和酒店前台的接待员核实了线路,确定了出游路线:先从"小印度"地铁站出发,乘地铁到港湾站下车,然后换乘轻轨至圣淘沙,游览完了圣淘沙名胜世界里的环球影城等地,再乘坐地铁至多美哥站转至宏茂桥,然后转公交 138 路至夜间动物园。

到了第二天,余领队就信心十足地带领了连小孩在内的 24 人团队,从"小印度"地铁站出发。领队先让每个小孩尝试着自己购买地铁票,等到了港湾站又让小朋友试着用英语与柜台内的马来人对话购买轻轨票。最后,终于到达了圣淘沙名胜世界。在那里,环球影城是小孩的首选,不论大人孩子都会向往"变形金刚"和"木乃伊复仇记",小朋友守着时间点观看史瑞克和马达加斯加企鹅"真人秀",再加上全球首个《遥远王国城堡》的 4D 电影,不知不觉一天就过去了,大家却还感觉意犹未尽。

晚饭后,24 人在余领队的带领下,乘坐地铁及公交共花了一个小时,从新加坡的南面到达了西北面——新加坡夜间动物园。新加坡白天炎热,夜间凉爽,因此,不少野生动物都是在夜间更加活跃,夜间动物园将 1200 多种动物按地理位置分成不同区域:喜马拉雅丘陵、印度次大陆、东南亚雨村、非洲稀树大草原、南非洲彭巴斯草原……刻意调整过的灯光和自然星光接近,既能让游客看清又不会让动物们不安。

结束了夜间动物园的游览,已经是晚上 11 点多了,动物园门口有通往市区主要站点的专线车,而如果是按 4 人乘坐一辆出租车来计算,费用几乎差不多,但出租车的行驶速度比在各主要站点停靠的大巴快多了,因为出租车既不停靠也不绕圈行驶。于是,领队将团体按人数分配好,让他们全部坐上了出租车。大约半小时后,所有的团员都抵达了饭店。就此,狮城的一天自由活动圆满地画上了句号。

[评析]

由于出境旅游者越来越年轻化,"80 后""90 后"的客人完全是拿着护照自己出去玩。所以一些旅行社会把境外的旅游产品,尤其是东南亚的产品打得足够"碎",像自由行搭配一日游或半日游,再如细到一顿餐或者几个小时的租车服务。另外,部分旅行社将进一步跟东南亚各个国家的旅游局合作,更多地开发一些小而精的景点和线路。

案例中,新加坡4晚5天的行程属于半自由行旅游产品。针对该类行程,旅行社会派遣领队服务客人,但仅有一天自由活动时间,其余时间旅行社还是有行程安排的。自由活动时,领队不一定要跟随客人一起活动,但出行的注意事项领队还是需要和客人讲清楚,诸如,交通工具的乘坐、酒店的地址、游览区内的门票价格及营业时间等。考虑到该团是亲子团,如此多的小孩一起出行的安全最为重要,因此领队主动承担起组织集体一日游的任务。从赴景点的线路设计到交通工具的安排,从景点内适合小孩玩耍的项目到用餐的地点等细节,都做了精心的策划。该领队的专业性还体现在,行程的第一天他就去考察了地铁站并与酒店总台接待员核实了交通线路。显而易见,这样的线路设计让小朋友既体验到了新加坡地铁(包括中途中转地铁)与公交,也省了不少花费。客人在哪里,领队的服务就必须跟到那里。

《中华人民共和国旅游法》对旅行社行业的影响是明显的,旅行社行业洗牌也是必然的,尤其是对于做东南亚市场的旅行社来说,不遵纪守法,不按常理出牌必将被淘汰。只有这样,旅行社才可能一步步抛弃低价竞争,回归到"产品为王、服务为王"的宗旨上。

A Free Activity Day with the Guests in Singapore

Everyone who has been to Singapore would miss this beautiful city, miss its safety, convenience, comfort and richness. The city that used to be well-known as Garden City has been gradually changed to City in the Garden. This amazing island has never stopped sketching the blueprint as an ideal home. You can always find a perfect place for yourself whether you are a foodie, a shopaholic, a design freak or a hotel weirdo. The small size of the city amazes us so much that we can plunge in at the city's deep end. The way she changes with each new day interests us most. When we sit in the well preserved Lau Ba Sat, having Satay right behind the tall buildings, it seems more like living in Singapore than just a trip with passion.

Yu, a tour leader from CYTS, took a family group to Singapore for 5 days and 4 nights. It contained a whole day of free time for the purpose of experiencing the real lives of Singaporeans. The group consisted of 24 people, among whom there were 10 kids in grade six on their winter vacation with their parents. In light of the family group, Yu asked the leader about free day activities ahead of time. The guests reached a consensus that they would arrange for a visit to the Universal Studio and the Night Safari on that day.

The free day was arranged on the second day in Singapore. Before departure Yu checked the distance from Hotel Grand Chancellor to Resorts World Singapore and to the Night Safari respectively on map. He headed to the Little India metro station for a quick tour by himself. After returning, he checked with the hotel receptionist to make sure the route, which was taking metro from Little India metro station to the harbor, and then transferring to LRT to Santosa, after visiting the Universal Studios in Resorts World Santosa, taking metro to Dhoby Ghaut and changing to Ang Mo Kio, then switching to the bus No.138 to the Night Safari.

On the second day, Yu hit the road with the group of 24 members, kids included. They set out at Little India. Yu tried to let the kids buy their own tickets. After arriving at the Harbor, he let them talk to Malays to buy tickets for the light rail. Finally, they reached Resorts World Santosa. The Universal Studios was the best option for the children. "Transformers" and "Revenge of Mummy" were suitable for people of all ages. The kids waited to watch the reality shows of *Shrek* and the penguins of *Madagascar*. Other than that, the movie *Far Far Away Castle* out there was regarded as the first 4D version. After a long day staying at Santosa, everyone was too delighted to leave.

After dinner, 24 people took public transportation for one hour under the leadership of Yu from the southern part to the northwest of Singapore, the night zoo. Singapore has hot days and cool nights, which is why lots of wildlife animals come alive at night. According to geographical locations, the zoo divided the 12,000 animals into different regions: Himalaya foothills, Indian subcontinent, rain village in southeast village, African Savanna, the pampas in South Africa, etc. The artificial lights were similar to the starlight, so the guests could see through the scenery, and the animals wouldn't feel uncomfortable about them.

It was 11:00 p.m. when they finished the tour in the zoo. There were shuttle buses to the downtown. But if they put 4 people in a cab, the cost would be pretty much the same. Besides, taxies are faster than the buses, because they neither stop at any place nor drive in circles. The tour leader divided them into groups of equal number for the cabs.

After a 30-minute drive, the group reached the hotel. So the free day in Singapore called a perfect end.

Comments

With more and younger people choosing outbound travel for their vacations, the generations born after the 1980s and born after the 1990s would just bring their passports and go abroad by themselves. So some agencies roll out their products with more details, such as individual travel with one-day or half-day tour, a meal or even vehicle service for a couple of hours. In addition to that, agencies would cooperate with tourism bureaus of the countries in Southeast Asia to develop small but excellent destinations and tourist routes.

In this case, the itinerary of 4 nights and 5 days in Singapore was a half independent travel. The travel agency assigned a tour leader for the tour. It only had one free day. The other days had travel schedules planned by the travel agency. On the free day, tour leaders don't have to stay with their guests all the time, but they still should provide information of certain items for the guests, such as public transportations, hotel address, entrance fee and business hours of attractions, etc. Considering that this was a family group, the leader proactively took on the responsibility for the free day tour to ensure the safety of kids traveling in a group altogether. From the tour route design to the arrangement of public transportations, from the places proper for kids in attraction to the restaurants, the tour leader did everything with careful planning. Checking the metro stations and making sure the route with the hotel receptionist on the first day demonstrated his professionalism. Apparently, the route helped the kids experience the real public transportation in Singapore, and also saved lots of money. As long as tour leaders are with their guests, they should serve the guests' hearts and souls all the way.

The Tourism Law of the People's Republic of China certainly has a prominent affect on tourism industry. Some travel agencies are bound to be eliminated in the competition, especially for those focusing on Southeast Asia markets. If the agencies are unruly and don't observe laws and disciplines, they will definitely be knocked out. Only in this way can travel agencies get rid of low price competition, and bring back the tenet of "the products first, service upmost".

[第七篇]
Chapter VII

领队服务智慧篇
Service Art of Tour Leaders

菲律宾长滩岛，海天一色

Baracy Island, the Philippines, combines the sea with the sky

海滩边深水区的警示牌你看得懂吗？

Do you understand the warning in the deep water zone by the beach?

宝岛冬至暖人心　　/409

Travelers Soothed by Early Celebration

of Winter Solstice in Taiwan

24小时营业的台湾诚品书店会让你流连忘返

Taiwan Eslite Bookstore opening around the clock will make you enjoy and forget to leave

菲律宾之旅 = 亲子 + 旅游　　/414

The Philippines Tour = A Parent-child Travel

孩子们在菲律宾为其中一位的家长过生日

A birthday party organized by children for a child's parent in the Philippines

"瑕疵" 得来的肯定　　/421

The Perfect Imperfection

瑞士军刀多种多样，是游客喜欢的纪念品之一

Swiss army knives with many varieties are one kind of the tourists' favorite souvenirs

飞机迫降安克雷奇机场 /425
Emergency Landing at Ted Stevens Anchorage
International Airport

新西兰基督城机场行李领取处
Baggage claim at the airport of Christchurch, New Zealand

这样的安排才代表了沙巴旅游的真正水平 /431
Such an Arrangement Represents the True Level of Sabah Traveling

斯里兰卡的半自助游十分受中国游客喜爱，图为斯里兰卡的世界文化遗产——狮子岩
Semi-self-help trip in Sri Lanka is popular among Chinese travelers, and the picture
is the Lion Rock, a World Heritage in Sri Lanka

品尝到了巴黎华人制作的盒饭 /435
Try Take-away Made by Chinese in Paris

法国巴黎的一家普通中餐厅
An ordinary Chinese restaurant in Paris

杭州旅游团南非约翰内斯堡历险记 /439

A Hangzhou Group's Adventure in Johannesburg, South Africa

作者与南非儿童合影

A photo of the author with children from South Africa

台中、福州、温州的特殊接驳 /446

Special Transfers in Taichung, Fuzhou and Wenzhou

台湾高雄一所中学的门口

The entry of a high school in Kao-hsiung, Taiwan

夜色中的台北"故宫博物院"
Night view of "Palace Museum" in Taipei

泰国酒店电梯前的标志：榴梿不准带入客房
There is a sign at the elevator in a hotel in Thailand，"No Durian"

一对上海夫妇被"请"下飞机　1465

Forced to Get off the Plane—an Experience of a Shanghai Couple

中国国际航空公司的空中服务
Air China Flight Attendants' service

象牙可以购买与送人吗？　1470

Can Ivory Be Bought and Sent to Someone as a Gift?

除非有特殊与必要的用途，要带象牙回中国是不可能的
Except for special and essential use,
it is impossible to take tusks back to China

在香港免税店购物　1476

Shopping in a Hong Kong's DFS

香港的某一家免税店，免税品琳琅满目
A duty-free shop in Hong Kong offers a variety of products

帅气的新西兰皇后镇流浪艺人在弹奏风琴

A handsome street performer is playing the organ

"歌诗达"邮轮是一艘流动的五星级酒店

The Costa is a mobile five-star hotel

这里是讲授传奇爱情故事的地方——英国贝尔法斯特泰坦尼克号博物馆

Titanic museum in Belfast, the UK, a place for telling a legendary love story

在斯里兰卡俱乐部召开行前说明会 /498
Orientation at Sri Lanka Club

作者与英籍斯里兰卡司机的合影
A photo of the author and a British Sri Lanka driver

译，或者不译，这是一个问题 /504
To Translate or Not, This Is a Question

阳光下的伊朗老人
A senior Iranian in sunshine

第七篇

Chapter VII

领队服务智慧篇

Service Art of Tour Leaders

[本章导读]

　　出境游领队是全权代表组团社带领旅游团出境旅游，督促境外接待社及其导游履行合同约定，实施游览计划，并为游客提供出入境等相关服务的人员。

　　出境游领队是 21 世纪年轻人比较向往的职业之一。借助这份职业的特性，领队可以带领旅游者周游世界，在给旅游者提供优质服务的同时，也能接触全世界各种各样的人，实现"不花钱即可周游世界"的梦想。

　　出境游领队是整个出境旅游团队的核心，因为团队运行过程中的所有环节与衔接需要合理的组织与安排，这都需要领队来完成。

　　本章通过介绍出境游领队在境外提供给客人的各项优质服务，让旅游者全面了解旅行社领队的职责与义务。

[Chapter Outline]

An outbound tour leader is a person who leads a tour group to travel abroad as a representative of the tour organizing agency that supervises and prods the outbound travel agencies and tour guides to fulfill the contracted itinerary and provides related services like exit and entry inspections.

The feature of this occupation allows an outbound tour leader to realize the dream of "traveling globally for free" while guiding tourists around the world and to have interactions with varied people all over the world when offering premium travel services for them. Therefore, outbound tour leader is one of the most attractive occupations to young people in the 21st century.

Outbound tour leader is the core of an outbound travel team because he or she is the link of the chain, conducting management and arrangement properly.

By presenting a wide range of premium services offered by outbound tour leaders to guests, this chapter tries to fully introduce tour leaders' responsibilities and obligations to tourists.

"红眼病"的传染性变弱了……

说起菲律宾，人们一定会说它是"千岛之国"。菲律宾所蕴藏的独特魅力，确实来自那 7000 多座大大小小的岛屿。这其中的 2000 多个岛屿有名称。它们如同一颗颗美丽的明珠星罗棋布于万顷碧波之中。即使你每天去一个岛，也要近20 年才能玩遍。人们纷纷涌向这些岛屿度假、休闲，度过一个完美的假期。

资深领队小徐所带的团进行的是菲律宾（马尼拉、长滩）5 晚 6 天之旅。行程的安排是客人从首都马尼拉进出，期间在曾被《孤独星球》旅游书评选为全世界最美沙滩之一的长滩岛入住 3 个晚上。宽松、休闲的行程，既让客人通过游览首都马尼拉了解菲律宾的殖民历史，又让客人在世界知名的休闲旅游度假胜地感受西太平洋的魅力。

长滩岛魅力无穷：热闹的集市、绚丽的夜景、神秘的 SPA、high 翻天的酒吧。在长滩岛团员们进行了诸多海上活动：乘着螃蟹船出海、海上垂钓、珊瑚花园浮潜、海底漫步，还有品尝岛上海鲜烧烤午餐，以及海边烤乳猪晚餐——整头猪放在炭火上慢慢烤制，现出炉的乳猪色泽焦黄、肉嫩皮香，蘸上当地特有的调料，回味无穷。

行程第 5 天早上 10:00，团员们随领队先乘坐半小时的海上渡船，而后又乘了一个半小时的旅游巴士,抵达卡里波机场,准备乘坐飞机离开长滩岛,飞往马尼拉。就在卡里波机场办理登机手续的时候,两位团员被值机人员发现患有红眼病,不能登机。怎么办?如果不能乘坐飞机,那么,第6天从马尼拉回上海也就不可能了。而团体旅游签证只有7天,签证即将到期,长滩岛这个地方也没有中国驻菲的领事馆,延长签证也不方便,况且客人的语言沟通也成问题。如果领队留下来陪这两位客人,那另外的30位客人又该怎么办呢?于是小徐与值机人员商量,值机人员说除非导游带客人去城里的医院开出患者已经过了高发期,已经可以登机的证明,才可以办理登机手续。于是,领队请导游带客人去离机场最近的医院做检查,自己先帮客人办理登记卡及行李托运,让别的客人在一旁稍作休息。

半小时后,导游带着这两名客人回到了机场,手里拿着医生刚刚开具的证明,上面用英文写着"红眼病发病10天,传染性变弱,不要与人握手,不要使用他人的毛巾,回国后继续治疗"。见这两位客人办好了登机手续,所有的客人都为这两位客人松了口气。在飞机起飞前25分钟,全体团员登上了飞往马尼拉的航班。

第6天,团员们准备乘坐马尼拉飞往上海的航班回国。领队和导游为大家办理登机手续,出了菲律宾的移民局,过了安检,准备登机。在机场广播乘客可以登机时,机场检查登机牌的工作人员又发现了这两位患红眼病的团员的异常,便让他们在一旁等候,并用英语问他们一些问题。这时,领队心里又开始犯愁了:地陪早就与客人告别了,万一上不了飞机……于是,领队走上前去问客人要来前一天从医院开具的证明副本,出示了证明后,工作人员终于放行,让客人登机了。

至此,菲律宾之行总算画上了一个圆满的句号。

[评析]

红眼病,临床上称传染性结膜炎,又名暴发火眼,是一种急性传染性眼炎,以春夏季节多见,通常伴有发烧等症状,病程为1—2周。当患者患病超过1周,并无发热时便可参加旅游活动。

　　该案例中两位客人患有红眼病，领队在出发前并不知晓，所以，才出现了案例中所发生的那一幕。幸好在办理从长滩岛赴马尼拉的乘机手续时，被值机人员发现了红眼病，并让两位客人赴医院检查。如果没有医院的那一纸证明，在马尼拉机场怎么上得了飞机呢？所以，在旅途当中领队发现客人患有"红眼病"或其他传染性疾病，应该立刻让客人在国外的医院就医，以便在最短时间里使客人病情好转。

　　另外一种情形是客人在出发前告诉旅游公司或领队自己患有红眼病（或其他传染病）。此时，旅游公司或领队应该规劝客人尽量不要参加旅游活动。至于在旅游费用的退还上，应尽量帮客人争取多一点的退款，让客人少一点损失。如果客人执意要参加旅游活动，那一定要医院开证明，至少是证明疾病传染性大幅减弱，而且，要让客人签字保证，万一进出关被拒绝入境或出境，其后果自负。

The Infectivity of "Pinkeye" Has Weakened

　　People call the Philippines a "thousands islands country", with more than 7,000 islands, big or small. More than 2,000 of them have names. Each like a bright pearl as the decoration of the Pacific Ocean. And it is said that it will take almost 20 years to enjoy one island only in one day. People all around the world come to have their happy holidays there.

Mr. Xu was a senior tour leader. This time his group was in the Philippines for 6 days and 5 nights. Starting from the capital city Manila, they would spend three nights in Boracay. This island has been praised by the famous tourism book series *Lonely Planet* as one of the most wonderful bund in the world. It was a light-hearted and casual journey aiming to make tourists know about the colonialism history of the Philippines as well as the charm of West Pacific Ocean.

The charm of Boracay was endless: busy streets, brightly-lit night, mysterious spa and exciting pubs. And the group had a lot of activities at sea, such as sailing in the crab boat, sea fishing, snorkeling in the coral garden, having roast seafood as lunch, and enjoying roast suckling pig as supper.

On the fifth morning of the journey, the group started at 10:00 a.m., and finally arrived at Kalibo Airport after half an hour's ferryboat and half an hour's bus. When they were checking in, two members were found with "pinkeye" so that they were banned to board the plane. If they could not board, the arrangement of going back to Shanghai on the sixth day would be impossible. The validity of the group visa was only seven days. Besides, there was a language problem. But the tour leader could not leave here for this. Then the check-in staff told them the only solution was taking them to the hospital in the city to get a demonstration to show the two were able to board the plane. The guide led the two guests away and the tour leader did check-in for the group.

After half an hour, the guide and two members came back with a paper of demonstration, which said "The disease has lasted 10 days. The infectivity has weakened. They should continue to be treated when going back to China." Then after check-in, all the members felt happy for the two. And the group boarded the plane to Manila 25 minutes before it took off.

On the sixth day, the leader and the guide did the check-in for the group when they were at the airport. Everything was OK when the group was told to get aboard. But the two members had the same problem again. And then the leader remembered that the copy of the hospital demonstration was in their hands. The two guests showed the paper to the airport staff.

Thus, the journey in the Philippines came to a happy end.

Comments

"Pinkeye" is an infective disease, which frequently happens in spring or autumn, and usually is accompanied with fever. It can last 1—2 weeks. And the patient can be engaged in tourism activities as usual when he has caught it over a week and has no fever.

In this case, the two members got pinkeye. But the tour leader didn't know it before they started. When they checked in at kalibo airport, fortunately, they were told to go to the hospital to get a demonstration to show that there was no problem of them. This demonstration paper helped them solve the trouble again at Manila Airport. So if tourists are found with disease like "pinkeye", they should be sent to a hospital as soon as possible.

Another case that may happen is the tourist may tell the travel agency that they have "pinkeye" or other diseases. If so, the company ought to persuade them not to attend the activity. As to their cost which should be refunded, it's better to let them suffer the least loss. But when they insist to take the activities, they must get the demonstration to show there is no problem to get on with others. And they should write down identification that they should take responsibility individually. In this way, the tourists themselves can get ready for the problems that may take place in their journey.

许多到过印尼巴厘岛的游客感慨,参加过阿勇河漂流,才算真正了解巴厘岛。阿勇河全长约 11 公里,流经 22 处急流点,两岸均是原始森林的景象。漂流由专门水上教练陪同,一般橡皮艇上乘坐 3—5 名游客。河流在深窄的峡谷中奔腾,两旁是热带雨林,藤蔓密布,椰树成荫。整个线路上,迎面而来的景观,忽而是茂盛的树林,忽而是辽阔的田野,忽而是阴森的蝙蝠洞,忽而是美丽的瀑布,变幻无穷,令人赞叹不已。

领队小宣所带的旅行团参加巴厘岛阿勇河漂流活动。领队和其中一组游客乘坐一艘皮筏艇,皮筏艇上坐 4 位客人、领队及教练,共 6 人。

当漂流开始大约不到 10 分钟,就来到第一个转弯处,小宣看到前方有艘皮筏艇在转弯处搁浅——船上的人正努力使皮筏艇下水。但不幸的是小宣一行的皮筏艇一下冲到了那艘皮划艇上面,从而侧翻,最后 180 度翻转。此时小宣船上 6 人全部落水,其中两个人在落水瞬间被大水冲走,皮筏艇教练就本能地去追那两个被冲走的游客,剩下两名女游客和小宣被压在了皮筏艇下面,皮筏艇就像一个大锅盖重重地把 3 个人扣在了水下。

此时,女游客惊慌失措,不停大叫。小宣用身体不断撞击皮筏艇,试图将其顶开,但是根本没有任何作用。小宣意识到想要活命就必须要从皮筏艇下面出来。于是小宣使劲往水底游,并且刚好抓住皮筏艇一边的绳子,从另一边钻了出来。此时,小宣看见两名女游客还在水下被皮筏艇压着,并且还在被急流冲得打滚。小宣立刻回去拉皮筏艇,他顺着绳子钻到皮筏艇下面,想把其翻开,但是没有着力点,加上大水不断的冲击,小宣根本站不住脚。后来他就直接跪下来,跪在水底一块大石头上面,然后使劲往水流前进的方向推皮筏艇。终于皮筏艇被推掉了,两名游客当时就浮起来,而后被冲了下去,此时小宣也瞬间失去可以支撑的物体,被水冲了下去。那时候小宣只觉得他的脚被无数块大石头划过,最后右脚背重重打在了一块大石头上,刚好这时教练用船桨把小宣拉了上去。小宣刚坐上皮筏艇就看到那两名游客就漂在旁边,于是就把她们也拉上来了。

大家到达终点,医疗队伍马上过来,为团员们消毒上药。巴厘岛地接社经理和漂流公司经理把他们送到医院进行检查和治疗。诊断结果是 4 位客人都只是皮外伤,配了一点止疼药和消炎药。领队右脚背骨轻微骨裂,需要好好休养,不能频繁走动。所幸的是 5 个人都没有出现更大的危险。

[评析]

《中华人民共和国旅游法》第六章旅游安全的第八十条规定:旅游经营者应当就旅游活动中的下列事项,以明示的方式事先向旅游者做出说明或者警示:(一)必要的安全防范和应急措施;(二)可能危及旅游者人身、财产安全的其他情形……

该案例为我们留下了深刻的经验教训。首先,作为领队,在遇到危急事情的时候一定要保持冷静,绝对不能慌张。本案例中,假如领队不能游泳,或者没有想到从船底游出来,那么领队和另外两名游客有可能遇到更大的危险。第二,在玩漂流等有风险的娱乐项目时,一定要求自己和客人严格按规定穿戴救生衣和安全帽,万一落水时能多两重保障。案例中,领队和 4 名客人都被大水冲出五六米远才被救起,但是头部和上身都没有受伤,这就是安全帽和救生衣起的作用。第三,在出发前必须认真学习活动规则并在活动过程中听从教练指挥。此次落水也有一部分原因是听错了教练的命令。教练说让大家往右边划,他大声喊"这边这边",而大家却听成了"左边左边",所以大家都往左边划了,结果船就翻了。第四,在发生意外事故的时候,一定不能慌张,而要冷静下来寻求庇护。

A Thrilling Scene of Rafting on Ayung River of Bali

Many tourists who have been to Bali in Indonesia signed and said that people did not know well about Bali until they experienced the Ayung River rafting. The Ayung River is about 11 km long and has 22 sharp turns, with changeable scenery on its banks. Escorted by a water coach, 3 to 5 tourists are on a rubber boat. The river rushes into the valleys, and tropical rain forest is along the river. The vines are stretching and the coconut trees are growing on the banks. On the route, there are changeable and amazing scenery: flourishing forests, vast fields, gloomy bat caves and beautiful waterfalls.

The tour leader Mr. Xuan, along with his tour group, participated in the rafting. The tour leader, 4 tourists and a water coach were on the same rubber boat.

In no less 10 minutes, the boat was coming to the first turn. The tour leader saw a boat stranded there and the passengers were trying to make it go. Suddenly, Xuan's boat rushed into that stranded one but unfortunately was on top of that. The boat was turned upside down. Therefore, 6 passengers on the Xuan's boat fell into the river. 2 passengers were suddenly swept away by the torrent. Out of instinct, the coach immediately chased the tourists being washed away. The other 2 female tourists and the tour leader were under the rubber boat, like under a heavy pot cover.

At that time, the female tourists were screaming and yelling while turning around in the water. The tour leader hit the rubber boat constantly, trying to push up the boat away, but failed. The tour leader realized that if they wanted to survive, they had to swim down and come out from the edge of the boat under water. Therefore, he swam toward the bottom of the river, grabbed a rope tied to one side of the boat and came out from the other side. The tour leader found that the 2 female tourists were still under the boat in the river, rolling in the water. He came back and tried to pull the rubber boat away. He came to the underneath of the boat along the rope and tried to turn it up, but he could not find a standing point in the water. Then, the tour leader knelt down on a big rock, pushed the boat toward the flow of the river and finally he succeeded. The 2 tourists floated up but were rushed away by the water, so did the tour leader who lost his support. The tour leader felt that he was hit by lots of rocks and his left foot was hit badly. Just at that time, the coach dragged the tour leader with a paddle. As soon as the tour leader was in the boat, he saw the 2 female tourists and then he rescued them as well.

The medical team was waiting at the destination. When everybody arrived there, the team came up, sterilized the tourists and did necessary treatment. The managers from the local travel agency and the drifting company sent the group to the hospital for examination and treatment. The diagnosis showed the 4 tourists had just bruises, and only needed some pain killers and anti-inflammatory drugs. The tour leader had a little bone crack on his right foot and needed rest. Fortunately, the 5 persons suffered no serious injuries.

Comments

The Tourism Law of the People's Republic of China describes in the 80th article, Chapter 6 on traveling safety: The tourism operators should offer a clear explanation and warning to tourists in advance concerning tourism activities: 1. necessary safe prevention and countermeasures; 2. other situations that may put the tourists' body and possession at risk ...

The above case taught us a lesson. First of all, the tour leader should keep calm in any emergencies. If the tour leader didn't think of swimming out from the underneath of the boat, he or the other 2 tourists may be in bigger trouble. Second, when participating in programs with risks, like rafting, the tour leader must set up strict rules on tourists and himself, like wearing the life jackets and safety helmets according to regulations and then they can get dual safety in case of falling into the water. In this case, the tour leader and the tourists were rushed away 5 or 6 meters by the water when they got rescued. But they did not get hurt on their heads or upper bodies because of the life jackets and safety helmets. Third, before departure, everybody should learn about activity rules carefully and follow the order of the coach strictly. The accident in the above case was partly caused by people mishearing the order form the coach. When the coach said "this side, this side", the tourists thought it as "left side, left side", so they tried left side and the boat turned upside down. Fourth, when the accident happens, people should not be panic. Keep calm and find a way out.

宝岛冬至暖人心

2008 年 12 月 15 日上午，厦门航空的 MF885 航班腾空而起，首次由杭州起飞，朝着祖国的宝岛台湾飞去。与此同时，台湾地区的中华航空执飞的 CI7989 航班已经越过海峡，飞抵杭州萧山国际机场，成为首次从台北起飞直航抵达杭州的航班。历史将铭记这一天，2008 年 12 月 15 日。这一天，杭州和台北，首次从各自的方向伸出巨手，在空中紧紧相握。

在这极具历史性的一天，领队小丁带领浙江地区的 17 位客人赴宝岛台湾游览。客人们都难以抑制激动的心情，翘首以待即将开始的 7 日环岛之旅。然而在客人们拿到机票的那一刻，大家的脸顿时都阴了下来：明明出团通知单上写着回来的那一天是于 13:00 抵达杭州的，可现在机票上显示的却是 19:00 才能抵达，晚饭都赶不上了。12 月 21 日可是冬至日，按照传统，冬至之夜全家欢聚一堂，可现在说好的冬至日团聚餐泡汤了。大家找来一旁的小丁理论，十几位客人你一句，我一句。小丁就任凭客人七嘴八舌地说了个痛快，让大家把心里的气尽情地出一出。渐渐地，客人们也都静下来了。由于两岸直航才刚刚开通，航空公司的运行还并不成熟，因此会出现航班时间不准确这一情况。小丁向大家说明了事情的缘由，并保证到了台湾一定会做出补偿，让大家满意。尽管小丁给了保

409

证,可客人们心里还都感觉闷闷不乐的。

一抵达台湾,小丁便赶紧与当地导游说明了这一情况。在她的沟通下,当地导游给了一个方案,让大家提前一天在台湾过冬至,也就是行程第六天在用餐时为大家加上台湾的金门高粱酒和芭乐汁,过一个台湾风味的冬至。还有,行程最后一天,由于台北回杭州的航班延迟到下午起飞,所以,上午有一段自由活动的时间。领队和导游决定把这段空闲时间也利用起来,免费为客人安排游览台湾唯一的火山公园——阳明山,那是一个山高谷幽、云山雾海、鸟语虫鸣的天然游览胜境。小丁将这一方案告知了客人,客人听了,心里的那些不愉快立刻烟消云散了,都表示非常满意,感动与温暖涌上心头。

7日的环岛之旅让客人们领略了台湾自然风光的无限魅力,同时"早到"的冬至晚餐也让大家感受了宝岛台湾浓浓的风土人情。

[评析]

作为一名领队,时常会遇到计划临时变更的情况,此时灵活应变的能力便是决定团队顺利进行旅行的关键。同时,领队与人沟通的能力也是至关重要的:与客人交流,与当地导游合作,都要求领队具有很好的交际能力。在带团过程中,领队和导游是一个不可分割的整体,双方只有进行很好的合作,才能保证一切顺利进行。

案例中,领队小丁与台湾导游共同商讨的方案,即提前过冬至日,既满足了客人吃团圆饭的要求,又让其体验了台湾过冬至的习俗。此外,还安排了游览最为知名的阳明山。虽然飞机延迟起飞了,但是合理的安排让客人觉得在台湾的每一分钟都利用了起来。领队小丁就凭借自己的能力让出发时客人的不满与抱怨化成了最后的认可与满意。尽管错不在她,她也任凭客人对她抱怨。尽管大家都乱成了一团,她还是有条不紊、灵活应变,换来了客人最后的肯定。

Travelers Soothed by Early Celebration of Winter Solstice in Taiwan

On the morning of December 15th in 2008, Flight MF885 from Xiamen Airlines took off for the first time from Hangzhou to Taiwan. At the same time, Flight CI7989 from China Airlines in Taiwan had already overflown the strait, and arrived at Hangzhou Xiaoshan International Airport, marking the first flight from Taiwan to Hangzhou. December 15th of 2008 would be written into the annals of history, since it's the date when Taiwan and Hangzhou joined their hands in the sky for the first time.

On that special day, the team leader Ms. Ding took 17 travelers from Zhejiang to Taiwan for a 7-day trip. All the travelers were so excited that they couldn't wait to start the trip. However, at the moment when they got the tickets, their faces changed from sunny to overcast. What was going on? The problem was that the arrival time of the return flight should be 13:00 on December 21th, but the time written on tickets was 19:00. That is to say, they couldn't have the reunion dinner with their family on December 21th, the festival of winter solstice, which was very important for all Chinese. Immediately, the travelers rushed to Ms. Ding to complain about this unexpected change. As an experienced team leader, she kept silent initially, allowing the travelers to release their emotions as much as possible. Then, when they calmed down, Ms. Ding began to explain that since the direct cross-strait flight had just been established, the flight schedules were not as accurate as expected. That was the reason for the change of the arrival time. Though Ms. Ding had promised to compensate the travelers when they arrived in Taiwan, they were still depressed.

On reaching Taiwan, Ms. Ding told the local guide about what had happened. After discussion, the local guide came up with a solution: They could celebrate the solstice festival in Taiwan one day earlier on the sixth day of the tour, to experience the Taiwan style winter solstice festival by tasting the local Kingmen Kaoliang liquor and guava juice. Moreover, as the departure time would be delayed to the afternoon, the group would have some free time in the morning. Ms. Ding and the local guide would offer travelers a free visit to the unique volcanic national park—the Yangming Mountain which was a natural sightseeing resort with unspeakable beauty. When the travelers got the news from Ms. Ding, their unpleasant emotions cleared away. They were happy with the arrangements.

The 7-day trip in Taiwan impressed travelers not only by the fascinating natural beauty but also by a deeper understanding of local customs by the early-coming dinner of winter solstice.

Comments

As a tour leader, he or she encounters temporary itinerary changes from time to time. On this occasion, quick and flexible response is the critical element to keep the trip moving on. Besides, communication skills are also very important when interacting with travelers or cooperating with the local guide. During the trip, team leaders and tour guides should unite and work together to make everything go smoothly.

In the case，Ms. Ding and the local guide worked together to meet the travelers' requirement of having a winter solstice dinner，and offered an opportunity for them to experience the winter solstice customs of Taiwan by celebrating the festival earlier. Additionally，visiting the Yangming Mountain which was known for flowers and hot springs made travelers feel they didn't waste one minute in Taiwan，though their flight was delayed. Ms. Ding turned the complaint and dissatisfaction into acclaim and satisfaction through her interpersonal competence. Though it was not her fault，she bore the complaints. Though it was in a mass，she still kept everything well-organized. Flexible response and effective communication helped her win the final affirmation and praise from the travelers.

第七篇 领队服务智慧篇

菲律宾之旅＝亲子＋旅游

2011 年 7 月 21 日晚上 8:00 左右,在菲律宾马尼拉阿基诺国际机场的移民局,一个由 20 名成人、10 位 10 岁左右的小孩组成的亲子团,正在移民局的柜台办理入境菲律宾的手续。显然,家长们为了锻炼孩子们的英语水平,故意让孩子们走在入境到达柜台的前面,独立办理入境手续。与小孩进行了"Where are you from?(你从哪里来?)""I am from China.(我来自中国。)""Do you come with your parents?(你和你的父母一起来吗?)""Yes,they are behind me.(他们在我后面。)"诸如此类的对话后,移民官员啧啧称赞这群来自中国小孩的英语水平,并微笑地对小朋友说:"Welcome to the Philippines!(欢迎来到菲律宾!)"此时,站在孩子们后面的家长们也会心地微笑着。

这是一个由 10 个家庭组成的"亲子学习旅游团",小朋友们是幼儿园的同学,家长们是因孩子而有缘相识的好朋友。我既是亲子团的领队又是其中一位孩子的家长。那么,这个团是如何成形的呢?

我孩子同学的家长都视我为"旅游专家",所以,当孩子结束了小学三年级的学业,准备进入四年级时,想听听我的建议:去哪里既能玩耍又能增长知识。我个人建议参加菲律宾亲子学习旅游,理由有三点:

第一，菲律宾曾经是西班牙和美国的殖民地。因此，赴菲律宾旅游既能让小孩了解作为亚洲国家的菲律宾的历史，也能看到殖民时代所留下的欧式建筑，例如：建于 1581 年的马尼拉大教堂，位于马尼拉市中心的罗哈斯滨海大道，面对马尼拉湾的黎刹公园等。同时还能游玩拥有世界七大美丽沙滩之一的长滩岛。

第二，菲律宾的官方语言是英语，所以，孩子们赴菲旅游，也是一个在英语语言环境中学习英语的好机会。所以，前面文章中所写到的场景，就是我们在出发前已经让孩子们学习了很多常用旅游英语对话的结果。

第三，我让旅行社联系菲律宾马尼拉当地一所小学，开展交流。

就这样，"旅游专家"的建议一下子被家长们采纳了，菲律宾（马尼拉、长滩）5 晚 6 天的行程成形了。

考虑到本次活动的主体是孩子，我还特意召集了所有的团友（孩子和家长），在一户团友家中召开了"旅游行前说明会"，仔细解释了旅游行程，提出了旅游中需要注意的事项，让 10 个小孩出发前完成一些常用旅游英语的背诵，包括了出入境关卡、飞机上、移民局、水果市场、餐厅、入住酒店等场景的常用英语对话，并将这些英语对话印在出团通知单的小册子上。菲律宾盛产水果，有关水果的单词占了较大比例，桃子、葡萄、西柚、椰子、红毛丹、榴莲……孩子们学得不亦乐乎。这不仅给行程的顺利开展带来了帮助，也让小孩通过旅游学习英语，家长们非常高兴看到这一幕。我还对孩子们说，要是学不好这些英文就拿不到签证，也就是不能出国旅游。这也是孩子们异常努力的一部分原因，他们都希望能和伙伴们出去游玩。

旅途中，在与家长们的交流中，我意外地发现团里有位家长在出游的第 5 天过生日，作为领队，我很想让这位家长在国外度过一个难忘的生日。于是，我从行程的次日就着手准备。虽然事先这位家长表示不用太张扬，我用了一个特别的方式让这次生日晚餐过得愉悦无比。当团员从长滩岛飞回马尼拉用晚餐时，大家觉得晚餐的座位排列跟平时有点不一样，我将过生日的家长和所有的孩子安排在中间的桌子旁，然后把孩子们的父母安排在两边的桌子旁，并特意为每桌加了两个菜。所有的孩子都显得异常兴奋，期盼着早点吃上蛋糕，这 10 个差不多 10 岁的孩子围着这位家长唱生日歌、吃蛋糕,把气氛推向高潮。加上一旁家长们的助兴,这位家长感动得眼眶湿润,并动情地说:"有这么多可爱的孩子给我庆祝生日,我真的感到非常开心。"

[评析]

20 世纪 90 年代初,"学习旅游"(study tour)在前往欧美各国、日本等国的出境旅游中就相当普遍了。来华的旅游团团员会参加诸如学习中国历史、中国民族乐器、中国书法等带有中国特色的学习项目。笔者在 20 世纪 90 年代就担任过许多美国学习团的导游兼翻译,这些学习团中既有成人学习团又有学生学习团(有时往往是家长随学生一起来,既能旅游,又能照看孩子)。

目前,境外学习旅游项目,往往是留学机构组织的比较多,而旅行社操作较多的是亲子游。"学习 + 旅游"的模式应该是一个很大的市场,旅行社可积极开拓。

为团友庆祝生日,本来是一件非常简单的事情,但如何在人生地不熟的环境将庆祝活动安排得当,则大有学问。该案例中,笔者抓住了该"亲子团"儿童多的特点,让十个孩子坐在一个家长旁边,既可以让家长开心,又可以让孩子借此机会感谢家长的养育之恩。

所以,领队在带团过程中,临时巧妙设计各种活动流程,也能为旅行社产品平添色彩。

The Philippines Tour = A Parent-child Travel

At about 8:00 p.m. of July 21, 2011, in Manila Airport, a parent-child group consisting of 22 adults and 10 children were doing the entry procedure at the immigration counter. The parents wanted to give their children a chance to practice English, so they intentionally put their children in front of them to do the procedure independently. The immigration officer asked questions and the children answered. They had the dialogues such as: "Where are you from?" "I am from China." "Do you come with your parents?" "Yes, they are behind me." The immigration officials praised these children for their English, and said to the children with a smile: "Welcome to the Philippines." Seeing this, the parents standing behind them also smiled happily.

This was a "parent-child study tour group" consisting of 10 families, whose children were kindergarten classmates. And I am not only a group leader but also a father of a child among them. I felt gratified when I saw my child doing a good job. You may wonder how this group came into being. Let me tell you.

The parents of my child's classmates regarded me as a "tourism expert". When the children were going to enter the fourth grade, they asked me to give some advice about the travel destination. They wanted to go to a place where children could play and learn. Considering primary school is a time to build the foundation for future learning, I recommended the Philippines with reasons as follows:

Firstly, the Philippines used to be the colonies of Spain and America. Therefore, traveling in the Philippines not only enables children to understand the history of the Philippines, but also allows them to see the European architectures left from the colonial era, for example, Manila Cathedral built in 1581, Roxas Boulevard located in the Manila downtown, Rizal Park facing Manila Bayand and so on. At the same time, they can play on Boracay Island, one of the world's seven most beautiful islands.

Secondly, the Philippines are the third country with most English speakers, whose official language is English, so traveling in the Philippines is really a good chance for children to learn English in an English environment. The scene mentioned in the beginning of the article is the result of preparation the children had made before we set out.

Thirdly, since most of the children were at the same age, I asked the travel agency in Manila to contact a local primary school to do an exchange with the children.

As children were the focus of this travel, I gathered all the group members (parents and children) in a family to hold a pre-tour briefing. I announced the travel itinerary and some notices, and I gave homework to the children, that is, reciting some commonly-used English dialogues which could be used at the customs, immigration department, fruit market, restaurant, hotel, and on the plane. All these sentences were printed on brochures. As the Philippines have a variety of fruits, so there were many words about fruits in the brochure, such as peach, grape, grapefruit, coconut, rambutan, and durian ... The children learned these words with joy. This preparation could not only make the travel easier, but also help the children learn English faster. The parents were very happy to see their children have a keen interest in learning. I told the children if they couldn't learn these English words well they were not allowed to get a visa, which meant they couldn't go abroad. It stimulated the children to learn hard, because they all wanted to go abroad with their friends.

Through on-the-way communication, I found the fifth day of our travel was the birthday of one parent in the group. As the group leader I really wanted to let the parent have an unforgettable birthday abroad. So I started to prepare for the birthday party. Though the parent told me not to make it a grand one, I still made this birthday party extraordinary. When the group members were going to have dinner, they found the arrangement of the seats was different from the usual. I arranged the parent to sit in the middle of the tables and be surrounded by all the children. And I ordered 2 more dishes for each table. All the children were very excited to see this, and they couldn't wait to eat the cake. Around the parent, the 10-year-old children began to sing the birthday song, and the other parents all joined them. We were singing songs and eating the cake. It was really a fantastic night. To the parent, it was really a pleasure to have a birthday party with so many lovely children.

Comments

In the early 1990s, study tours became popular as an outbound travel mode in Europe, America, and Japan. The groups coming to China would learn programs of typical Chinese characteristics, such as China's history, traditional instruments and calligraphy. I was a tour guide and interpreter for some American study groups at that time. Some were adult groups, some were children group, and sometimes the parents came with the students, so that they could travel as well as take care of the children. The Philippines travel was based on this idea.

At present, study tours are organized mostly by overseas study agencies, while travel agencies operate more parent-child tours. "study + travel" mode has a great potential. Travel agencies can combine both of them to develop the market.

To hold a birthday party for one of the group members is not a big deal. But it is really something to plan it well according to the condition abroad. In this case, the author caught the characteristic of parent-child tour, and made the 10 children sit around the parent. In this way, the parent would enjoy the talk with these innocent children. What's more, the children could take this chance to thank the parents for bringing them up.

Therefore, when a tour leader leads a group, a wise design of activity will make the service of the travel agency much more impressive.

"瑕疵"得来的肯定

　　近年来,泰国、新加坡、马来西亚3国游一直是一条很受欢迎的旅游线路。某旅游团在"新马泰"旅游行程中,第一站是曼谷,行程包含驱车前往参观国家观光局指定的珠宝展示中心,欣赏闻名世界的红蓝宝石,并可购买一些红蓝宝石纪念品这一项。当天下午,有一位团友在车上把领队小范叫到了她身边,告诉小范,在汽车转弯的时候,在夕阳斜射下,她发现刚买的红宝石戒指上有一条细细的裂纹。这位团友很紧张,怕自己买的是质量有问题的红宝石。这时,小范解释道:这一条不是瑕疵,而是红宝石的"生长纹"或叫"结晶核"。该女士情绪稍稍平复,但还是有些担心。领队小范就又安慰说:"如果您还是不放心的话,我们在行程的第5天还会回曼谷,到时我陪您再去商店确定一下,到时您还有疑惑,可以让店家给您退还。"听了这话,该女士才安下心来,不停地感谢领队。

　　第5天,领队在不影响行程的前提下,提早去了景点,在珠宝店关门前陪同该女士去了那里。当他们到达门口时,场面让该女士有点出乎意料,几十个销售员在门口欢迎该女士。

　　领队协助该女士向老板说明了情况,老板也对这一情况做了详细说明,还拿出一枚价值人民币75万元的红宝石戒指让该女士看,上面也有"生长纹"或者说

421

"结晶核",这让该女士彻底放心。最后该女士很满意地戴着她买的红宝石戒指离开了商店。

事情处理完后,领队小范陪同该女士回了饭店。她对领队感激万分,觉得领队很专业,对珠宝颇有研究,也很佩服领队。在随后的行程中,该女士很配合领队的工作。团内的其他游客在购物时也会让领队帮自己把把关。

回国后,该女士写了一封信给旅行社,表扬领队素质高,服务态度好,知识丰富,以后去旅游就点名让这位领队带队。

[评析]

领队要把一个团队带好,取得客人的信赖,除了有较好的带团技巧外,还要有很广的知识面。客人会提出各种问题,所以,领队要有终身学习的观念,不断地充实自己,从而给客人提供满意的服务。要是此案例中,领队说不出"生长纹"这三个字,客人也许不会如此相信领队。

一个小小的知识点,很有可能在不经意的时候就用上了,甚至可以解决很大的问题。以上案例就能说明这一点。

The Perfect Imperfection

When it comes to overseas travel, destinations in Southeast Asia like Thailand, Singapore and Malaysia have always been a popular outbound tourist route for the past few years.

There was a bunch of tourists taking part in a tour group following the route to Southeast Asia. Their first destination was Bangkok. According to the itinerary, they first visited the world's biggest gem gallery designated by the local government, and then admired the world's famous ruby produced in Thailand. Some tourists purchased rubies as souvenirs.

That afternoon, a group member called the tour leader Fan over, and claimed that the ruby she had bought had a crack in it, and she noticed it under the sunset. She was quite nervous, fearing that the ruby had quality problems. The tour leader explained to her that the crack was neither a flaw nor a quality problem. It's called a growth line. These words helped her erase a lot of worries. But she was still nervous about this imperfect gem. Fan comforted her, and said, "Ma'am, we will head back to Bangkok on the fifth day. And I would like to accompany you to the mall to confirm the gem. If you are still not completely satisfied, you can return it." The lady seemed relieved after hearing his words and constantly expressed her gratitudes to the tour leader.

On the fifth day, in order not to delay the trip, the tour leader went alone with the lady early. When they arrived at the mall, there were lots of shop assistants greeting them at the door.

The leader assisted the lady to ask for clarification. The boss explained the details about the crack and also showed her another ruby with the same flaw which cost RMB 750 thousand. In the end, the guest left with satisfaction. After that, they returned to the hotel. The lady felt grateful for having Fan as their tour leader, and the leader also impressed her with his professionalism as well as his knowledge of jewelry. In the following days, the lady complied with the leader quite well. In addition to that, other guests also asked him for advice when it came to shopping.

After the group returned home, the travel agency received a compliment letter for Fan from that lady, praising his professionalism, good service attitude and rich knowledge as well. And she would love to have him as the tour leader for her future trips.

Comments

Having good skills of tour guiding is a necessary way to gain customers' trust. Other than that, a wide range of knowledge is also very important. Guests would ask any kinds of questions. Thus, lifelong learning is encouraged for tour leaders, to provide satisfactory service for guests. In this case, if the leader hadn't pointed out "growth line", the guest might not have trusted him that much.

The case tells us that knowledge might be useful at any time. Sometimes it could solve big problems.

飞机迫降安克雷奇机场

　　从上海飞往芝加哥的航班已进入夜间休息状态。突然机舱广播响了起来，空中乘务员在询问乘客中是否有医务人员，机上有人需要医疗服务。广播播放了两三次，但没引起大家的特别注意。飞机继续飞行了约一小时，机上广播再次响起，通知大家由于特殊原因，飞机即将在阿拉斯加州的安克雷奇机场降落，请所有乘客携带好随身行李，准备下机，随即机舱内的灯光也全部亮起。机上乘客逐渐从睡梦中醒来，才得知由于机组人员身体出现异常状况，飞机必须在安克雷奇紧急降落，并且将在安克雷奇过夜。航空公司会安排新的机组人员过来，在第二天上午重新起飞，前往芝加哥。

　　当时，出境游领队小陈和他的22人团队也在这个航班上，他们此行的目的地是芝加哥，然后从芝加哥转机前往迈阿密，在罗德岱堡港口登上皇家加勒比游轮展开为期8天的东加勒比海上游轮之旅。本来他们在芝加哥转机的时间就不宽裕，现在如果再耽误一个晚上的话，无论如何赶不上第二天游轮的登船时间了，而游轮是不会因为23名客人未登船而等候的。但是既然飞机要紧急迫降，只能先下了飞机再做安排了。

　　当所有乘客都通过海关检查进入安克雷奇机场大厅以后，机场人员要求所有乘客在大厅等待安排。工作人员开始分发饮料、点心等。领队小陈一边安抚团队客人的情绪，跟他们说明情况，安排他们拿取饮料和食品，一边立即和国内组团社的计调人员联系。组团社相关人员得知信息以后，表示将立即和航空公司联系，尽快安排其他航班前往迈阿密。

与此同时，机场人员也开始安排当晚的酒店住宿。当时团里就有客人表示说要去酒店休息一下，因为大家都很疲劳。但是领队小陈表示大家要在机场等待组团社的消息，一旦买到票，要立刻登机，否则从机场到酒店来回路途耽误时间，可能会赶不上飞机。在等待国内消息的同时，领队小陈也联系了机场的工作人员，说明团队必须要在第二天中午赶到迈阿密的情况，希望他们能给予协助。机场也非常配合地安排了相关人员帮忙查看从安克雷奇飞往迈阿密或者从其他城市中转前往迈阿密的机票。但是一方面时间比较紧，另一方面有 23 个空位的航班也确实很难找，所以一时间没有找到合适的航班能立刻离开安克雷奇。这个时候游客开始不耐烦起来，有人表示要先去酒店休息，等买到机票再回机场；有人表示肚子饿，要先去吃点东西。领队小陈一边安抚客人的情绪，一边再次联系国内旅行社。组团社表示正在寻找空余的机票，让领队无论如何不能带客人去酒店，不然一旦买到机票，可能赶不回来登机。随着时间的推移，客人也越来越急躁，甚至有几位开始大声斥责航空公司不负责任，工作人员服务不给力，以及领队不安排大家去酒店休息等。当时机场的工作人员看到乘客的表现，虽然语言不通，但也感觉到了他们的不满，当即表示既然你们这么无礼，我也不愿意继续为你们联系机票了。所以领队小陈一边要跟机场工作人员解释沟通，一边又要安抚客人越来越激动的情绪，真可谓焦头烂额。

就在这时，国内的电话来了，表示已经买到了从安克雷奇前往盐湖城的机票，然后从盐湖城转机到迈阿密。而此刻离航班的登机截止时间只有 40 分钟了。于是领队小陈带领整个团队，在工作人员的协助下，通过绿色通道，最终顺利地登上飞机。

［评析］

出境旅游中，会发生各种突发事件，客人对此会感到不满。有时，旅游者往往只从自身出发,来要求周边的服务人员。作为一个出境旅游团的主心骨——领队,应该做到心中有数,掌握大局。案例中,如果领队没有主见,听从客人的要求,那岂不是无法准时转机去迈阿密了? 有时,在带团过程中,无论客人情绪多么激动,领队一定要保持冷静,根据自己的带团经验坚持自己的做法还是非常有必要的。

另外,在国际旅游中,转机时间如果超过 4 小时,通常可向航空公司领取饮料券;如果超过 6 小时,则可领取餐券或点心券。转机时,要留意登机门号码是否临时变更,因此,要随时查看电子屏幕上的资讯。

Emergency Landing at Ted Stevens Anchorage International Airport

On the night flight from Shanghai to Chicago, an announcement broke the silence in the aircraft. "Attention, please. We have someone on the flight that needs medical help. If there are any medical personnel on the plane, please inform the crew." The announcement didn't catch passengers' attention even after repeated several times. An hour later, the flight announcement informed the passengers that the plane had to make a forced landing at Ted Stevens Anchorage International Airport, Alaska, due to some special reason, and asked all of the passengers to take their belongings and get ready to get off the plane. All lights of the cabin came on. The passengers awoke out of their dreams and got the news that one of the crew had an unspecified medical condition, so the captain had to make an emergency landing. All the passengers had to wait until the airline arranged for another crew schedule for the flight to Chicago, which meant the guests had to stay in Anchorage till the next morning.

Chen, a tour leader and his 22-member group were on the flight. The destination of their trip was Chicago, and they were going to transfer to Miami for an 8-day eastern Caribbean cruise on Royal Caribbean's at Ft Lauderdale. They only had little time for layover in Chicago. Now if they had to spend one night in Anchorage, there would have no way for them to get on board in time. Besides, it would be impossible for the cruise to wait for a group of 23 people. But the aircraft was forced to make an emergency landing, and all of the passengers had to get off the plane first and make alternative plans afterwards.

When all passengers walked into the Anchorage airport lounge after passing through the customs, the crew asked their guests to wait for the arrangement in the hall. Meanwhile, they started to distribute drinks and snacks. Chen began to comfort his guests, explaining the situation patiently and arranging food and beverage for them. In the meantime, he also reached out to the tour operator from the group-organizing travel agency so that the operator would help them contact the airline to arrange another flight to Miami immediately.

At that moment, the crew started to arrange for accommodation. Some guests wanted to take a rest in the hotel first, since everyone was really tired. Chen suggested they stay at the airport waiting for the news about the flight, therefore they could be boarding immediately after getting the tickets, while heading back from the hotel to the airport would only be a waste of time. When waiting for the news, Chen also got in touch with the airport staff and hoped they could give some assistance. The ground crew checked the flights for him right away. Unfortunately, they couldn't find any suitable flight, which was partly due to the time, and partly because it was hard to get a flight with 23 vacancies.

The guests began to lose their patience. Some required going to the hotel while others complained they were hungry. Chen had to comfort them constantly, and contacted the agency again. The operators said they were still looking for the flight for them and notified Chen the guests had to wait at the airport. As time went on, however, the guests became much more impatient. There were a few of them starting to yell and complaining the airline acting irresponsibly, and the tour leader refused to take them to the hotel. Seeing this, the airport staff said to Chen that they were not going to continue to assist them with the flight tickets because of the guests' inappropriate behaviors. Chen had to explain the situation to the crew, while comforting his guests at the same time. He almost got burned out by the two sides.

Thankfully, the phone call from the agency came at the very moment. The operators got them the flights, which required transferring from Salt Lake City. At that moment, the group only had 40 minutes before boarding. Chen took the guests going through the green channel with the help of the airport staff. Finally, they managed to get aboard in time.

Comments

Guests would come across any type of emergencies during outbound trips, which would make them feel depressed. And they often have requests or the service staff. Accordingly, tour leaders should absolutely be clear in mind of the working procedures. In this case, if the leader had followed the instruction of the guests, none of them would have caught the flight in time. Consequently, tour leaders should always keep calm when problems crop up, because it's essential for them to keep working in their own ways based on practical experience.

In addition, passengers who participate in an outbound trip can ask for drink coupons if their connecting time reaches 4 hours, and meal or snack coupons for more than 6 hours. Meanwhile, they should also keep an eye on gate numbers which might be changed at any time. It is vital for passengers to check the information on LED displays at airports every now and then.

这样的安排才代表了沙巴旅游的真正水平

　　沙巴位于马来西亚东部婆罗洲的北端。对崇敬大自然的旅游者来说,这里是马来西亚之旅中最令人心动的一站。2015年春节,出境游领队小瞿所带的"马来西亚沙巴5日游"海岛旅游团带着这样的憧憬出发了。

　　第一天抵达酒店已经是后半夜了,接机路上导游介绍了马来西亚沙巴的概况、入住酒店周围安全情况等,也讲了行程第三天"一日游"的安排,讲解非常专业周到,但导游丝毫没有提到行程第二天的自由活动如何安排。因为按照双方旅行社协议,导游不得主动兜售自费活动项目。

　　第二天团员们差不多中午才起床,领队小瞿和部分团友一起逛街、吃海鲜,并建立了整个团队的微信群。在与客人的交谈中,领队发现基本上所有的团友因为平时工作忙,春节假期才有时间出来度假,并没有对沙巴旅游做详细的了解。客人们只知道在沙巴可以去红树林看萤火虫,去美人鱼岛看海水等,但不知道怎么去,因而很多游客都在打听第四天的自由活动该干什么或者抱怨没事可干。

　　第三天的"一日游",客人们乘船前往东姑阿都拉曼国家公园,先上马穆迪岛,观看五颜六色的热带鱼,畅游蔚蓝大海。岛上的游人比较多,风景很一般。

下午的活动是市区游览和自由购物。此时,领队就把团友的信息反馈给导游,建议导游通过讲解,促使团友询问自费项目的情况。同时,领队也表示团友有问题尽量找地陪解决。这样,通过团友询问和地陪的介绍,成功地在第四天安排了美人鱼岛浮潜和红树林看长鼻猴和萤火虫,晚上在渔村的水上餐厅享用晚餐,同时观赏渔村文化舞蹈表演。所有的团员对当天的安排十分满意,觉得这样的安排才代表了马来西亚沙巴旅游的水准,觉得不虚此行。

[评析]

　　初次出国或旅游经验不足,尝试着去冒险、寻找自我,但又怕一时无法适应环境或语言能力较差,只能参加旅行社推出的半自助旅游,即旅游产品包括出国机票、机场接送、一日游等。案例中的沙巴 5 日游,只含一个"一日游"项目,其余均为自由活动。此类旅游既能保持自助旅游的简单性即自主性,又能大大降低自由行的风险。

　　团员的需求、动机、目的和兴趣等是多变的,且有很大的差异。所以,了解团员的意见有时也不是一件容易的事。中国游客由于旅游经验不足、语言不通等问题,还是很想参加旅行社设计的半自助游行程的。而领队是服务流程中最常接触游客,并为游客竭诚服务的人员。因此,领队应该主动把握机会,从团员表现出来的态度来了解其内心深处的想法。案例中的领队就是能揣摩到客人态度的变化,及时将客人的意图传递给导游。通过导游的讲解,满足了客人的意愿,团员和旅行社获得了双赢。

中国公民出境旅游服务质量解析

Such an Arrangement Represents the True Level of Sabah Traveling

Sabah is located in the north of Borneo, Malaysia. It is the most exciting stop during a Malaysia trip. The tour leader Mr. Qu and his group set off on their 5-day Sabah trip in the Spring Festival, 2015.

The group checked in the hotel after midnight. After picking up all the tourists, the local guide did a brief introduction to Sabah, said a few words about the 3rd day's schedule with very professional manner and also a few notices on safety. However, he did not mention any plan in day 2 as he was not allowed to promote self-financed activities according to the agreement.

Most tourists got up late till noon in day 2. Some of them went shopping, had meals with Qu and established their WeChat group. Qu learned in their free chat that most tour members had almost no idea about Sabah as they were quite busy with their work. All they knew was that they could go and watch fireflies in Mangrove Forest and the beautiful sea in Mantanani Island. They even had no idea about how to go to those places. Many tourists were complaining about having nothing to do or what they were supposed to do with the free tour in day 4.

On day 3, all tourists went to Tunku Abdul Rahman Park by sea. They set foot on Mamutik Island to see the colorful tropical fish in the beautiful ocean. Then they went to the downtown area to go shopping and sightseeing in the afternoon. Qu told the guide that the members wanted to have more fun in Sabah. He suggested the guide do a brief introduction to various activities to arouse their interest. Finally, they managed to add new arrangements, including snorkeling in Mantanani Island, watching proboscis monkeys and fireflies in Mangrove Forest, having dinner in a floating restaurant and viewing an evening performance with fishing village culture. All tourists were more than satisfied with day 4. They thought such arrangements represent real Sabah and their money finally paid off with these arrangements.

Comments

It is suggested that tourists with few outbound traveling experiences and poor language abilities choose semi-self-help trips that normally include a single ticket, airport pick-up and a one-day trip. In this case of Sabah traveling, it only has one-day activity with 4 free days left. Semi-help-trips allow tourists to make their own decisions. They also greatly reduce risks in free exercise.

Group members have different traveling demands, motivations and interests, which are constantly changing. Therefore, it is difficult to accommodate all the opinions. Chinese tourists with few traveling experiences or poor language abilities tend to choose semi-help-trips. The tour leader, who is frequently communicating with them, should get information by observing their attitudes and behaviors. The tour leader in the above case had surely gotten tourists, attitudes and demands. Finally, he fulfilled tourists' wishes. Both the tourists and the travel agency have benefited from his arrangements.

品尝到了巴黎华人制作的盒饭

　　由法国、意大利、瑞士这分别属于西欧、南欧和中欧的 3 个国家组合的旅游线路,被认为是欧洲深度游的经典线路之一。通常,入境法国后会在巴黎住两晚,第三天早上游览巴黎后,再前往法国小镇博纳。欧洲导游表示,由于午餐后从巴黎出发的时间稍晚,司机又是新手,如果团队在前往博纳途中再安排晚餐,那么赶到酒店时司机的用车时间可能要超标。导游接着说:"我手头确实有两家餐厅可供选择,其中一家离博纳比较近,不需要绕路,但是餐厅周边的环境似乎不是很安全,而去另一家餐厅稍微需要绕一点路,但更安全。"停顿了一下,她又说:"那要不然我们退餐费给客人,让客人自行解决吧。"作为领队的我心想,整个行程共有 10 天,行程的第三天就要退餐,不太好,况且,每人只有 6 欧元餐费可退,有时连买一个汉堡都不够。于是,我问导游,离酒店最近的餐厅车程是多少。她说骑摩托车来需要 20 分钟左右。我提议是不是可以让餐厅送盒饭过来。这个提议立刻得到导游的肯定——"这是个好主意"。客人也表示,他们愿意尝一尝这家法国华人制作的盒饭。导游即刻打电话给餐厅进行沟通,餐厅表示他们已经准备好了 34 人团餐的食材,他们很愿意为团队制作盒饭并送餐。

　　于是,当我们抵达了博纳的酒店后,用车时间并没有超标。半小时后,餐厅送餐人员将热气腾腾的 34 份中式盒饭送到酒店。大家开心地吃着晚餐，表示这样的晚餐适合中国人的胃，既省时又方便。

［评析］

在欧洲驾驶大巴，通常用车时间不能超过 12 小时，且中间每隔 2—3 小时要停下来休息。一般车上都装有记录器，警察会对司机在一周内的驾车记录进行检查。

新手司机往往会有超时的情况出现。为此，有时导游会退餐费给客人以缩短司机开车时间。这就需要领队来掌握退餐这一情况。偶尔退一次餐费，客人吃一个汉堡，也许会觉得很新鲜，但如果行程中有两次以上的退餐情况，客人就很容易产生意见。案例中，笔者想到用送餐的方式，既避免了用车超时问题的产生，也免除了向订餐餐厅退餐的尴尬，同时也让客人品尝到了巴黎华人制作的盒饭，多了一项旅游饮食的体验。

Try Take-away Made by Chinese in Paris

The trip to France, Italy and Switzerland, which respectively belong to Western Europe, Southern and Central Europe, is a combined route and is considered as one of classic travel routes of in-depth travel. We stayed 2 nights in Paris after entering France. On the third day morning, after visiting in

Paris, we took a coach to the French town Boehner. The European tour guide said it was a little late when we left Paris after lunch and the driver was new. If we had dinner on the way to Boehner, it would be an overtime drive. Then the tour guide said that there were two restaurants we could choose from. One was near Boehner but the peripheral environment was not very safe. The other was a little far but safer. Later, she suggested returning meal fee to the tourists. As the tour leader, I thought the tourists could only get 6 euros back which was not enough for one hamburger. I asked the tour guide how far is the nearest restaurant from the hotel we were going to arrive at and suggested a take-out service from the restaurant. Both the tour guide and the tourists agreed. Then tour guide called the restaurant immediately. The restaurant had prepared the food and would love to carry the meals to the hotel.

Later we arrived at the hotel in Boehner, it was not overtime for the driver. Half an hour later, the restaurant sent the food to the hotel. Everybody ate happily and was satisfied with this kind of dinner. It was convenient and saved time.

Comments

In Europe, coach drivers usually can't drive continuously for more than 12 hours, and during driving drivers should stop to have a rest every 2 to 3 hours. Generally the coach is equipped with a recorder, and the police will check the driving record every week.

Based on the above situation, new drivers are likely to do overtime driving. To prevent this from happening, sometimes the tour guide would return meal fee to the tourists to save time. At that case, the tour leader should handle this situation properly. Sometimes get returned meal fee and eat a hamburger is new to the tourists. However, if returning meal fee happens too often, the tourists will be

第七篇 领队服务智慧篇

annoyed. In this case, the tour leader thought out another way, that is, letting the restaurant package meals and sends the meals to the hotel, which not only saved time but also avoided embarrassment of cancelling the meal. At the same time, it gave tourists a chance to have a taste of Chinese take-out made by Chinese in Paris.

杭州旅游团南非约翰内斯堡历险记

2011 年 11 月 3 日,"南非阿联酋 9 天游"的旅游团在南非结束了所有的游览行程,正乘坐旅游巴士前往约翰内斯堡机场,准备离境回国。当时旅游大巴上共有 32 人,其中包括 29 名游客,一位浙江中青旅的领队,一位当地导游和一名当地旅游巴士司机。全团人员从约翰内斯堡市中心的一家商场出来后,取道布鲁玛区欧内斯特·奥本海默大街,前往机场。

当地时间晚 7 点左右,就在旅游大巴开往机场的途中,从大巴的后面传来了警笛声。司机注意到后面跟上来一辆闪着警灯的平民车,车内的警察示意让他们停车,车上的游客觉得很奇怪,但不懂当地语言,也就没有注意,以为只是例行检查。在大巴停下后,几个穿着警察制服的男人登上了旅游大巴。这时,坐在最前排的领队和两位游客发现,几个穿警服的男子全都手拿枪械。有三个看似警察的人上车就问司机关于团队的情况、要去的地方,并要求司机出示证件,然后开始检查司机和客人的证件。通过这些"警察"的言行,领队和游客很快就明白了一个事实:他们遇到了抢劫。

女领队首先对劫匪进行了劝阻。这个身材高挑的姑娘,开始并没有被吓到。但是,接下来的一幕,不得不让这位女领队感到恐惧。因为其中一位持枪劫匪伸手对着女领队的脸就是狠狠一巴掌,其余的男性客人被电棍电击。这一个巴掌,却把领队"打"镇定了。看到劫匪的粗暴行为,以及回想以前发生的抢劫事件,她首先想到的是游客的安全。劫匪们都有枪,所以绝对不可以激怒劫匪,否则游客们可能有生命危险。

女领队很快反应过来,她用英语和劫匪尽心交涉,她告诉劫匪:"请不要动手,我们会主动把值钱的东西交出来,请你们不要伤害任何人。"对于劫匪来说,最重要的就是钱财,但是他们没有想到的是,眼前这位女领队却利用他们听不懂中文,对游客进行了"教育"。女领队转身对游客解释了整个情况,让他们不要惊慌,现在最重要的是人身安全,尽量配合劫匪。但是她同时告诉游客,把自己的护照、现金和贵重物品放好,尽可能把自己装杂物、零食的袋子交给劫匪。这个提示很重要,因为客人中不少人之前刚刚在购物点购买了钻石。但是坐在大巴最前排的两名乘客和领队本人,因为形势紧迫只得将所有的东西如数交出,其中包括他们的护照被一并洗劫。而坐在旅游巴士后面的游客,迅速将护照藏了起来,绝大多数贵重物品也没有被抢走。一些游客甚至把自己的包主动递给劫匪。不过,这些包里大多都是些水果、衣服等不值钱的物品。

匆忙中,劫匪无暇仔细检查袋子里面的具体内容就走了。最后在清点损失时,共有16位游客被劫走了财物,包括钻石1颗,现金近20万。包括领队在内的3位成员被抢走了护照。

随后,女领队拨打了报警电话,并通知旅游公司相关负责人。中国驻南非共和国大使馆和驻约翰内斯堡总领馆对此事也相当重视,非常关心杭州的这些游客。

当地时间11月3日晚9点,未被抢走护照的27位游客按原计划搭机回国,护照被抢的领队跟两位游客滞留在南非机场。在使领馆的帮助和浙江省公安厅的配合下,女领队和另外两名游客的护照,在4个小时内补办完毕。当地时间11月4日晚,滞留的领队跟两位游客搭机回国。

[评析]

导游、领队作为旅游公司的文化使者和形象代言人,是旅途中一道亮丽的风景线。在旅途中会遇到各种突发事件,导游、领队在对突发事件的有效预防和及时有序处理的过程中也为旅游公司树立了良好的品牌形象。

案例中,旅游公司派出的女领队遇事镇定、反应灵敏。否则,不仅游客的贵重物品可能会被洗劫一空,而且可能会发生伤亡的悲剧。领队的专业知识和语言能力在这次事件中发挥了很大的作用。领队良好的语言能力帮助她在第一时间理解劫匪的意图。同时,领队掌握的专业知识能够使她及时地做出正确的行为,提醒旅游者以人身安全为重,并用不值钱的物品打发劫匪,因为劫匪没有这么多的时间去检查行李袋里的物品。此外,领队用流利的英语与劫匪交流时能够适时地转移匪徒的注意力,让旅游者能够有充分的时间来整理自己的东西,最大限度地降低旅游者的损失。

相信大家一定都知道南非,它是一个危险与美丽并存的地方。

旅游业是当前南非发展最快的行业之一,是南非第三大外汇收入和就业部门。2009年到南非旅游的外国游客达990万人次。但南非也是世界上犯罪率最高的国家之一,犯罪形式主要是持刀枪抢劫及施暴、强奸等。2004年共有22名华人在南非被害,2005年又有近10名华人惨死在犯罪分子的枪口下。2006年新年伊始,居然有4名华人在不到一个月时间内相继被杀害。很多人会觉得虽然南非很美,但是治安太差就不愿前往旅游。其实在了解该国国情和知道生活在这个国家的一些最基本的安全常识后,还是能将不安全程度降至最低的。

以下是一些建议性防范措施:

1. 尽量结伴而行,不要单独行动,一切活动遵循"团队进,团队出"原则;

2. 贵重物品、宝石饰品、名牌服装要保管妥当,最好不要外露;

3. 避免出入特定居民区和无人的街道、场所;

4. 日出前、日落后,尽量少出门;

5. 最好使用信用卡或旅行支票,避免在公共场所兑换外币或出示大量现金;

6. 建议每位游客身上都留点"救命钱",一般20至50美元的金额比较合适。分开放在几个不同的口袋里,以防被一网打尽。救命钱可以让你在遭遇抢劫或其他各种困境时及时有效地求救，比如打辆车、打个公用电话；

7. 每位游客必须熟记中国大使馆及当地警方的联系方式。

A Hangzhou Group's Adventure in Johannesburg, South Africa

On the 3rd of November, 2011, a group just finished the "9-day Tour in South Africa and the United Arab Emirates". After they came out from a shopping mall in Johannesburg, they took a bus to the Johannesburg airport to depart. All together there were 32 people on the bus: 29 tourists, a tour leader of Zhejiang CYTS International Travel Co., Ltd., a local guide from South Africa and a local driver. They were driving on the Ernest Oppenheimer Avenue.

It was local time 7:00 at night. They suddenly heard the sound of siren on the way to the airport. The driver noticed that a private car with a police warming light on it was behind. The "police" inside the car gestured for them to stop. The tourists on the bus felt weird. But since they were in a foreign country, and they couldn't understand the local language, they thought it was kind of routine check. The bus stopped and some men dressed in police uniform got on the bus. The tourists sitting in the front soon realized that these "policemen" were with guns. The three police-looking men asked the driver about the situation of the group and where they were going. They ordered the driver and the tourists to show their driving license and passports. By the words and behavior of these "policemen", the tour leader and the tourists soon realized they were meeting a robbery.

The tour leader, a tall slim girl, was not frightened at the first moment. But what happened in the next terrified her. One of the robbers mercilessly slapped on her face, and the male tourists were all shocked by the electric batons. This slap made the tour leader calm down. Recalling the rude behaviors of the robbers and the robberies happened, she had the first thought to ensure the safety of the tourists. The robbers were all armed, so the tourists definitely couldn't annoy them at the risk of loosing their lives.

The tour leader came up with an idea. She tried to negotiate with the robbers, and she promised that the tourists would hand in the valuables if the robbers would not hurt anyone. She knew the robbers couldn't understand Chinese, so she turned around to the tourists and spoke in Chinese pretending she was interpreting the robbers' request. She explained the whole situation and told them not to be panic. She asked the tourists to obey the robbers. Meanwhile, she told them to keep the passports, cash and valuables well. She suggested that the tourists give the robbers bags of snacks or other things. This hint was a key point, because many of the tourists had just bought some diamonds. The 2 tourists sitting in the front and the tour leader had already handed in all the valuables including their passports. The other tourists sitting in the back all hid their passports quickly. Most of their valuables were not robbed. Some of the tourists even handed in their bags to the robbers initiatively. Surely, they were all bags of clothes.

The robbers were in a hurry, so they didn't take time to examine what the bags contained. After the robbery, the tour group checked the loss. There were

16 tourists getting robbed. The lost properties included one diamond and nearly RMB 200,000. The passports of the 2 tourists sitting in the front and the tour leader were also taken away.

Then, the tour leader called the police, and informed relevant people in the travel agency. Embassy of People's Republic of China in South Africa and Chinese consulate in Johannesburg paid great attention to this incident. They were very concerned about these tourists from Hangzhou.

At local time 9:00 p.m. the third of November, the 27 tourists who had passports flied back home. The 2 tourists and the tour leader whose passports had been robbed had to stay at the airport. With the help of the embassy and the Zhejiang Province Public Security Department, they got their passports 4 hours later and then took a flight back to China on the night of the fourth of November.

Comments

Tour guide and tour leader are spokespersons of travel agencies. During a trip they will meet with different kinds of emergencies. Effective prevention and quick reaction are good for the brand building of travel agencies.

In this case, the tour leader kept calm and reacted quickly. Otherwise, the tourists might be robbed of all the valuables, or be killed by the robbers. The professionalism and the capability of language of the leader played a very crucial role. A good capability of language let the tour leader acknowledge the purpose of the robbers. Meanwhile, her professionalism of a tour leader enabled her to respond immediately and correctly. She told the tourists the most important thing was to ensure safety, and they could use valueless things to satisfy the robbers, because the robbers didn't have time to check all the things. What's more, the tour leader negotiated with the robbers with fluent English, which was a strategy to earn more time for the tourists to deal with their belongings, they could hide the valuables to reduce their loss.

I believe you all know something about South Africa. It is a place where danger and beauty coexist.

Tourism is one of the fastest growth industries in South Africa. In 2009, the number of tourists in South Africa reached 9. 9 million. Meanwhile, South Africa is one of the countries with the highest rate of crime. The main crimes include robbery of treasure and cars, as well as violence. In 2004, there were 22 Chinese people getting murdered, and in 2005, around 10 Chinese people were shot by the criminals. So many people think it is a beautiful country, but they also think it is too dangerous to travel in South Africa. If we want to travel in South Africa, we can try to ensure our safety by knowing the country's basic situation and some common senses.

Here are some suggestions of preventive measures:

1. Go with company, don't walk alone. All activities should be done in a group.

2. Keep the valuables, jewelry and brand clothes well.

3. Avoid walking in certain residential areas, empty streets and places.

4. Don't go out before sunrise, as well as after sunset.

5. Use credit card or traveler's checks. Avoid showing a large amount of cash in public places.

6. Put money in different pockets to save you in emergency. 20—50 dollars is OK. These money can allow you to make a call or take a car when you are robbed or in other tough situations.

7. Every tourist must know how to contact the Chinese embassy and the local police.

台中、福州、温州的特殊接驳

夏天的一个傍晚,台湾台中清泉岗机场的广播里传来一则消息:因受台风的影响,台中至福州的航班要延误3小时。这下可急坏了出境游领队小陈,他带的一个28人团队,从台中飞往福州后,紧接着从福州转乘动车回温州。如果没有延误的话,团队从下飞机到入关拿行李,需花40分钟车程抵达火车站。如果按照提前30分钟进火车站,团队接驳的时间也最多只有20分钟。

领队手上拿着一叠动车票,他将所有团员都集合起来,给团员们开了一个简短的会议。领队告诉团员,目前台中飞往福州的航班准备延误3个小时,此类航班延误属于不可抗力,航空公司是不需要负责的。而团队就很被动,一定赶不上动车了,买好的动车票也没办法退,损失全由自己承担。因为这是当天福州到温州最后一班车,这样就变成要在福州住一晚,这个费用也是需要游客自理的。领队话音刚落,团里就像炸开了锅,各种不满意和难听的话都爆发出来,甚至有些不明事理的客人提出要领队全权负责,他们的理解就是:我是跟着你领队出来的,你就要负责,钱我们是不会出的。

这时,领队全然没有理会这些情绪激动的客人,他找到了团里比较有号召力的几位团员,邀请他们和领队一起去航空公司交涉。当然领队知道其实即使这样争取,获得赔偿的机会也不大。如果没有合理的理由,航空公司是不会来承担损失的。就在领队和几位客人与航空公司交涉的时候,其他客人也加入了进来,场面又一次炸开了锅。但此时领队却离开吵闹的人群,只身找到了航空公司主管。他向主管讲述这个团行程中的实际困难,希望航空公司考虑实际情况,能给予一些帮助。主管在请示了上级领导后,答应在抵达福州后,给团队安排一辆车,连夜将团队送回温州,车程时间是5个半小时。领队表示感谢,并请航空公司的主管先不要将这个消息告诉客人,由领队向客人宣布。

与此同时,部分客人还在和航空公司争吵,其实这样的争吵是无意义的,航空公司明确告诉团员,天气原因所造成的延误没有赔偿。

领队又一次召集了客人并告知:"今天的延误属于天气原因,航空公司不给予赔偿。大家自己刚刚也试着维权过了,但也没有结果。现在的情况是:等我们飞到福州,已经没有可以回去的动车了;如果是在福州住宿,费用自理。现在我已经和航空公司谈妥,航空公司准备派一辆车送我们回温州,车程大约需要5个半小时,这是我尽我的力量为大家争取的最好办法了,如果你们觉得不能接受或者你们有更好的办法,去和航空公司协调后,也请告诉我。也请你们不要用拒绝登机或者一些更无理的要求来威胁航空公司和旅行社。如果你不登机,航空公司视作你自动放弃,取消你的登机资格,那么接下来所有产生的费用都将由你自行负责。"领队讲完后,停顿了好久,客人也沉默了好久……最后,客人还是按照领队的意图登上了飞往福州的班机。

尽管这个团比原定计划晚到温州,但一切顺利,所有客人都跟着团回来,也没有让公司增加额外费用,领队成功了。

[评析]

旅游者在旅游终结阶段的一般心理特征是兴奋,那是因为旅游活动即将结束,马上要回家了,又可以见到亲人和朋友,回到熟悉的生活圈子,也可向他们讲述旅游的所见所闻,同大家一道分享旅游的快乐。所以,此次案例中所有客人都挤到航空公司的柜台前与工作人员交涉,实属正常。此时领队应该平复大家的情绪。

在出境旅游中,航班延误是司空见惯的事情。有时,不影响下一航班(船次)的接驳,游客还是能够理解的。但如果对下一次接驳有影响的话,事情就难办了。

领队在处理案例中所遇到的问题时,找到团队里面讲话比较有分量的人一起与航空公司交涉。这样的做法,既能够让客人的代表看到领队的努力表现,也让客人中的代表感受到处理过程中的艰难之处。案例中,经过领队与航空公司的交涉,航空公司也并不是完全不理会客人,而是以用一辆大巴将所有的客人送往最终目的地温州的方式,圆满解决了这一事情。

另外,当航空公司做出弥补措施时,领队要求将这一决定的宣布权归领队所有,这也体现了领队在处理这类专业事件时的技巧,领队在客人中的威信就彰显出来了。

Special Transfers in Taichung, Fuzhou and Wenzhou

On one summer evening, Taichung Ching-Chuang-Kang Airport announced that the flight from Taizhong to Fuzhou would be delayed for 3 hours due to the influence of typhoon. Hearing about this, the tour leader Mr. Chen got very worried because he had to lead his 28-member group to Fuzhou from Taichung, and then transfer from Fuzhou to Wenzhou by train. If there were not any delay, they would have to get off the plane, go through the customs, claim the luggage and took about 40 minutes to get to the railway station. Because they had to get to the train station 30 minutes in advance, so there would be only 20 minutes for transfer.

The leader got all the tourists together and told them the bad news briefly that the flight from here to Fuzhou would be delayed for 3 hours because of the typhoon, so they couldn't make it to get on the train from Fuzhou to Wenzhou, and the airline would not compensate for this because it was an event of force majeure, and they had to stay in Fuzhou for one night and pay by themselves. The whole group was in an uproar at the bad news. Some tourists even said the leader should be totally responsible for this. Their reason was quite simple—you were the leader, you should be responsible and you should pay the extra fee.

The tour leader did not take much time to explain to those hysteric tourists. Instead, he picked up some tourists who seemed to be group leaders to negotiate with the airline together. He knew that the airline would not make any concession without legitimate reasons. When they were negotiating with the airline, some other tourists also got in, the situation seemed to be out of control again. So the leader left the clamant crowd and went to see the executive of the airline alone. He explained the situation and their difficulties to the executive and asked if they could offer any help. The executive of the airline then reported to his superior and promised to the leader that they could offer the group a bus to take them from Fuzhou to Wenzhou that night and it would take about 5.5 hours. The leader showed his gratitude and asked the executive not to tell the tourists about the news, and he would tell them by himself.

At the same time, the tourists were still arguing with the airline though it was meaningless. The airline announced again there would be no compensation for any delay due to bad weather.

The tour leader then got the group together again, telling them it was the bad weather that had caused the delay and the airline would not offer any compensation. The situation was that there would not be any train to Wenzhou when they got to Fuzhou and they had to pay by themselves if they would stay in Fuzhou for one night. And just then, he had got an agreement with the airline that they could offer a bus to take them to Wenzhou that night, and it would take about 5.5 hours. That was the best solution he could get and please let him know if any tourists had any better ideas. Please do not threaten the airline or the tour agency. If you do so, the airline would cancel your ticket and you should pay all your cost after that. There was a while of silence after that. Finally, all the tourists got on the plane from Taichung to Fuzhou.

The whole group got back to Wenzhou later than the previous schedule. But what's important was that everything went well, without any extra cost for the travel agency. The leader made it.

Comments

Near the end of a tour, generally speaking, tourists are excited because they will get home soon to their daily lives. They can share their stories and happiness during the trip with their friends and relatives. So it is not easy for them to keep calm. In this case, it is not unusual for them to get together to argue with the airline clerks. The tour leader then should help them cool off.

Flight delay is quite common in outbound travel, and it's much easier for tourists to accept the situation when it does not influence next flight to transfer.

In this case, the tour leader asked some tourists who had appeal for the others to negotiate with the airline together with him. By doing so, the tourists could see his effort as well as the difficulties. Also, in this case, the airline did offer some help to the group by sending a bus to help the tourists get to their final destination,

Wenzhou，which made a happy ending.

What's more，when the airline promised to help，the tour leader asked to announce this news by himself，which assumed his authority in the group.

第八篇

Chapter VIII

文明出行综合篇

Civilized Traveling Behaviors

[本章导读]

　　伴随中国人出游人数的不断增加,中国游客在旅游过程中表现出来的礼仪修养缺失行为层出不穷。一些旅游者在境外游览中表现出来的"不懂礼仪、不守秩序、喧哗吵闹"的不文明行为,引起了国内外舆论的关注和批评,严重影响了中国礼仪之邦的形象。这些不文明行为既是中国公民本身的陋习所造成的,也是旅游者不了解目的地国家和地区的文化与本土文化的差异所造成的。

　　本篇通过笔者出国、出境时的亲身感受,告诉读者出境旅游应注意的事项,遇到各种文化差异时,应如何处理与解决由此导致的问题。

[Chapter Outline]

With the increase of Chinese outbound travelers, numerous improper manners appeared among Chinese tourists when they travel to outbound destinations. Their uncivilized behaviors such as the poor manners, violation of public order, shouting and arguing loudly have aroused public concerns and criticism both at home and abroad, which has seriously affected China's international image. Both the bad habits of Chinese citizens and the lack of understanding of the differences between their own culture and the cultures of destinations lead to these undue behaviors.

By sharing the personal experiences of outbound travel, the author tries to tell readers what should be highly concerned, and how to deal with and solve problems when encountering culture conflicts.

在台北"故宫博物院"柔声细语

赴台湾旅行,无论是随团旅游,还是自由行,到台北"故宫博物院"参观是必不可少的。台北"故宫博物院"馆藏的 65 万余件珍贵文物,让参观者目不暇接。在所有的文物当中,最值得观赏的三大件文物是台北"故宫博物院"的镇馆三宝:"东坡肉形石""翠玉白菜""毛公鼎"。

当你走进博物馆时,你会感觉被黑压压的人群挤得透不过气来。你可以看到在远处有人举着一块牌子,牌子上写着:请大家柔声细语讲话。当参观的人群看到这个牌子的提醒后,自然而然地将讲话的声音放轻了,而这些举牌的工作人员,往往是来自台湾一些高校的志愿者。

如此这般提醒,让游客感觉特别温馨。同样的提醒,使用了不同的语气,让人们感受到了中国文化的博大精深、中国语言的委婉细腻。如果将提醒语改成"请勿大声讲话",其感觉一定没有像台北"故宫博物院"的提醒语那样的贴心、温馨。而在这样的提醒下参观,游客的讲话声音自然变得很轻了。

[评析]

文明旅游和国民素质是密切联系在一起的。实际上,民众素质的提高也是需要有引导的。以上案例,就是人的素质随着好的引领而提升的展现。目前政府开始高度重视"文明旅游"这项内容,这是一个非常好的开端,由此还能将中华文化的内涵发掘出来。通过旅游特别是出境旅游这个渠道,可以将中华文化传播到世界的每一个角落,让五千年的历史和中华民族的文明展现在世界的舞台上。

聚沙成塔,集腋成裘。点点滴滴的小事凝聚起来,就是一个民族的风格,一个国家的形象。对旅行中种种"不拘小节"的行为,我们再也不能漠视了。中国素有文明古国、礼仪之邦之称,国之大,不仅在于人口众多,更在于文化泱泱,文明灿烂。无论是作为东道主,还是作为观光者,每个人都要从我做起,从每一天做起,让每一条线路、每一个景点都成为传播文明、传递关爱的文明纽带。

Speak Softly in "Palace Museum" in Taipei

"Palace Museum" in Taipei is a place people should visit no matter you are with a group or in a self-guided tour. Over 650,000 precious treasures on display make visitors fully satisfied. Among those precious treasures, there are three highlights in the collection: Dongpo Pork Cube Shaped Jade; Vegetable Shaped Jade and Duke Mao Tripod.

When you enter the museum, you will feel suffocated by the big crowd. But you can always see people holding the sign "please speak softly" in the distance among the crowd. When visitors see the sign, they will lower their voice. The people who hold those signs are volunteers from Taiwan universities and colleges.

Such kind of signs makes visitors feel comfortable. Same reminders, different tones. The euphemism in Chinese is where the charming of Chinese culture lies. If the reminders on the sign are changed into "don't speak loudly", it may make visitors less comfortable. With this kind of reminders, the visitors are willing to speak softly and keep their voice down.

Comments

Civilized travel is closely related with citizens' quality. In fact, citizens' quality needs guidance. The above case shows a good example. People's quality will change according to surroundings. It is a good beginning for our government to pay attention to "civilized travel". Chinese culture will be expanded with the media of travel. The five-thousand-year history and Chinese culture will be shown on the world stage.

Every little makes a mickle. So does the civilization. Little by little, it forms a nation's style and a country's image. We can no longer neglect the unpleasant trifles in travel. China has been appraised as a nation of etiquette. A big country not only counts on its population, but also on its culture. A host or a visitor, you should be strict with yourself everyday on every travel route in every scenic spot. Those tour routes and scenic spots will become cultural links to spread civilization and love.

小孩无意中摸了泰国导游的头

你知道到达泰国之后需要注意哪些当地的风俗习惯吗？如果不注意的话，可能会给别人和自己带来很大的尴尬和麻烦。

某年夏天，笔者带着旅游团来到了普吉岛。普吉岛是泰国南部岛屿，位于安达曼海。首府普吉镇地处岛的东南部，是一个港口和商业中心。普吉岛是泰国最大的海岛，也是泰国最小的一个府，因其迷人的风光和丰富的旅游资源被称为"安达曼海上的一颗明珠"。因自然资源十分丰富，普吉岛有"珍宝岛""金银岛"的美称，主要矿产是锡，还盛产橡胶及各种海鲜和水果。由于普吉岛独特的地理位置，旅行社通常会将普吉岛作为一个单独的旅游产品。

笔者所带的"4 晚 6 天普吉豪华游"行程十分顺利，宾主尽欢，主要得益于普吉岛的当地导游。他是个很有意思的人，在没有碰及其底线的时候，十分好相处。导游的父亲是中国云南人，母亲是泰国人，他尽管中文的书写能力不佳，但是口语却十分流畅，解说也很清晰，对中国客人也怀有别样的亲近感。客人们有时也会认为他就是个中国人。

但是尽管他有中国血统，却出生在泰国，成长在泰国，是一个典型的泰国人，因此他有泰国人的普遍生活习性和特点。比方说，他性子很慢；又比方说，他不喜欢别人碰他的头,因为泰国人认为自己的头部是最高尚的;他也忌讳别人用脚对着自己或用脚指东西。关于碰头这一点,尽管笔者行前已和客人打过招呼,但在行程中还是出现了一个不太和谐的音符。

游客中有个小朋友,在和导游熟悉之后,总喜欢找他玩,而导游出于职业道德,在讲解之余,会和团里的几个小朋友嬉闹一番。但是有一次玩闹中,小朋友不知怎的忽然拍了下导游的脑袋,使得导游之后一天脸色都不太好,并向笔者投诉。

晚饭时,这个小朋友先吃好,跑出餐厅玩耍。笔者趁机将小朋友叫到身边,跟他再次强调泰国人的这个风俗。此时,导游正在不远处,听见笔者和小朋友的沟通,似乎脸色稍好。而当小朋友懂事地和他说了"对不起"后,他才彻底消除了这个芥蒂。

[评析]

出境旅游者所处的文化环境与旅游目的地国家或地区的文化环境是不同的,在意识形态、文化风俗、宗教信仰、民族心理特征等方面差异巨大。如在泰国抚摸小孩子的头是不尊重人的行为,而在中国则是疼爱关心孩子的表现;在欧洲未经孩子家长同意,不允许和孩子拍照;中东国家不允许表扬孩子漂亮、眼睛动人等,而中国家长若听到这些溢美之词会挺开心的;外国人对中国人询问年龄、收入、婚否颇为反感;请人吃饭时不停劝吃,本是国人的热情,却让外国人难以接受。以上种种都表明,因文化习俗的不同,双方缺乏对彼此文化的了解,交流时就会产生误解。

泰国被人们称作"微笑的国度",泰国人性格比较温和、热情、有礼貌,人与人见面打招呼时通常双手合十于胸前,互相问候。但作为一个传统的佛教国家,在泰国,有着许多人与人相处时的禁忌。

《中华人民共和国旅游法》第二章第十三条明确规定:旅游者在旅游活动中应当遵守社会公共秩序和社会公德,尊重当地的风俗习惯、文化传统和宗教信仰,爱护旅游资源,保护生态环境,遵守旅游文明行为规范。出境游客的素质不仅涉及个人修养,而且涉及法律层面,不仅是道德问题更是法律问题。

　　旅途中,成人是能记住当地的一些习俗,但小孩就不一定记得住了。所以,对于小孩子的掌控是比较难的。案例中,出境游领队对此类问题的处理非常有技巧,他抓住了合适的机会教育小孩,同时也让泰国导游听见、看见。这种能力是在教科书上学不到的,需要领队在工作中不断去总结和锻炼。

A Child Accidentally Touched the Head of a Thai Tour Guide

After arriving in Thailand, if not careful, tourists might encounter a great deal of embarrassment and trouble.

One summer, I visited Phuket as a tour leader. Phuket Island is a southern Thai island, located in Thailand's Andaman Sea. The capital Phuket Town is located in the southeast of the island, and is a large port and commercial center. Phuket is Thailand's largest island, and also Thailand's smallest state. It is called "A Pearl of the Andaman Sea". Due to its stunning scenery and abundant tourism resources, the island is rich in natural resources, and has the reputation of the "Treasure Island". The main mineral in the island is tin. It is also rich in rubber, seafood and a variety of fruits. Thanks to its unique geographical location, Phuket often has guests playing at the beach and relaxing themselves. Travel agencies usually sell Phuket as a separate product.

The 4-night-and-6-day luxury trip in Phuket turned out to be very smooth, thanks to the Phuket local guide. He got along very well with us. The tour guide's father is Chinese and his mother is Thai, so his spoken Chinese is very fluent though he can't write Chinese. To us Chinese, he had a special kind of intimacy. Some guests sometimes even thought he was a pure Chinese.

Despite his Chinese blood, he was actually born in Thailand and grew up there. So he is a typical Thai. He has Thai people's general habits and characteristics. For instance, he has very slow temper. He hates people touching his head, because Thai people believe that their heads are the noblest. He also regards it as a taboo if someone points their feet to him or touches goods with feet. Though I had told the tourists that they shouldn't touch Thai people's heads before the trip, something embarrassing still happened.

There was a child in the group. After getting familiar with the tour guide, he liked to play with the guide. With professional ethics, the tour guide also played with the kid during idle time. But once the kid touched the guide's head, making the tour guide unhappy all day. And he complained about this with me.

After dinner, the kid ran out of the dining room for fun. I took the opportunity to tell him again the customs of Thai people. At this point, the guide was not far away, and heard me communicating with the kid. The guide seemed to look a little better. As the kid said sorry to him, he was not upset any more.

Comments

Chinese tourists' culture and values are different from that of the destination countries or regions. And the differences are sharp due to different ideologies, cultural traditions, religious beliefs, national psychological characteristics and so on. In Thailand people can't touch a child's head, but this is accepted as a expression of loving in China. In European countries, without the consent of parents you are not allowed to take pictures with their children. In Middle East countries, it's improper to compliment on children's physical appearance or beautiful eyes, while Chinese parents who hear these words would be very happy. Foreigners in China are rather offended when asked about age, income and marital status. Chinese people's advising guests to eat makes foreign people uncomfortable. All these scenarios derive from different cultural practices.

Thailand is called the land of smiles. Thai people are mild, warm and polite. Usually people meet and greet with each other with their hands together at chest. But as a traditional Buddhist nation, in Thailand there are a lot of taboos for people to pay attention to.

The 13th article in chapter 2 of the Tourism Law of the People's Republic of China, stipulates that tourists in tourism activities should observe the social and public order and public morality, respect local customs, cultural traditions and religious beliefs, protect tourism resources, protect the ecological environment, and observe civilized code of conduct for tourism. In other words, the quality of outbound tourists is not only regarded as an individual quality, but also involves the legal level. It's not only a moral but also legal issue.

During a journey adults are able to remember the local customs, but the children may not. So it's difficult to let children follow the local customs. In the above case, the outbound tour leader handled this type of problem very skillfully. He was not in a didactic manner, but seized the right moment to educate the child at the right time when the Thai tour guide could hear. If this sort of thing happens, the answer could not be found in textbooks. All these skills needs to be discovered and summarized by tour leaders during their work.

一对上海夫妇被"请"下飞机

　　上海的张女士和丈夫携女儿报名参加旅行社的关岛"半自助游"。半自助游是一种介于参团游与自助游之间的旅游方式,其特点是旅行社只负责交通和住宿等环节,而游览行程、餐饮等环节全让游客自己安排。所以,张女士他们一家都没有领队带领游览。他们定于北京时间 2012 年 2 月 1 日 18:30 乘坐航班从关岛返回上海。通过异常严格的安检,好不容易登机了。也许从来没有经受过类似举手投降、脱鞋、解裤带等安检程序,不少中国游客都有些不爽,但是大多数人都明白入乡随俗的道理,特别是到过美国的游客,已经习以为常。

　　上了飞机,美国空乘小姐开始整理行李舱。一位空姐要变动一下张女士他们放置包的位置,这样也方便别的乘客放行李。张女士不同意,空乘说等她放下别人的行李后,她再安排。抱着女儿进来的张先生正好走过来,他就觉得很奇怪,用英语问道:"为什么不能把自己的行李放置在自己头顶的行李架上?"两人通过一些交涉后不能达成一致,后来张先生的情绪明显激动起来了,他用英语让空乘闭嘴(you shut up)。空姐就问他为什么要让她闭嘴,而张先生却只是一直重复"你闭嘴"这句话。

　　接下来的事情发生得有点突然,让人一下子回不过神来。美国空乘打开已经关闭的机舱门,此时一位懂中文的地勤人员登机与张先生夫妇沟通,请他们带着行李下飞机,并表示:"你们不下飞机,飞机就不能起飞。"原因就是,他们不礼貌的行为致使空乘感觉被侮辱,情绪受到影响,只要看到他们就无法为其他乘客正常服务,这可能会成为飞行中的不安全因素。

此时,张女士大叫起来:"这不可能!就是打死我也不下飞机!"这时,机舱走廊上已经站好了5位荷枪实弹的美国警察,警察告知他们已经违反了相关安全条例,必须下飞机接受进一步审查,如果不配合,将依法采取强制手段。警察还对他们说:"你们必须下飞机,不然所有人今天都要留在关岛。"这时,他们才意识到事态的严重性。

见此情景,张女士表示自己情绪有点激动,"我向她赔礼道歉好吧?"但已经来不及了。美国警察用英语向他们宣读他们违反的条例,但是他们根本没能听懂其中的内容,就已被赶下飞机,还未满12岁的女儿留在了飞机上。张女士夫妇在警察的押送下走出舱门。紧接着,机舱门关闭,飞机滑向跑道起飞了。而张女士未满12岁的女儿自己一个人坐飞机回来。第二天张女士和丈夫乘坐经停韩国的航班,机票价格一共为1100美元。

[评析]

根据国际民航法的相关规定,在一架飞机上,机长是拥有最高处置权的,只要机长觉得乘客的行为可能会对飞机安全造成影响,就有权请乘客下飞机。《中华人民共和国民航法》第五章第四十六条也有相关规定:"飞行中,对于……扰乱民用航空器内秩序……以及其他危及飞行安全的行为,在保证安全的前提下,机长有权采取必要的适当措施。"

另外,自由行或半自助游的客人赴国外,在没有旅行社领队带领的情况下,语言一定要过关。尤其在国外登机时,语言是很重要的沟通工具,如果表达不清楚,让对方误解的情况时常会发生,而且矛盾会随着语言不通不断激化。所以,上飞机一定要听从机组人员的安排。另外,"shut up"在英语国家是不礼貌的用语,切勿使用。

Forced to Get off the Plane—an Experience of a Shanghai Couple

Mrs. Zhang joined a half self-organized Guam tour. Half self-organized tour is a kind of travel mode different from package tour and self-organized tour. The distinctive characteristic of this type of tour is that the travel agency only takes charge of transfer and accommodation, while the travelers are responsible for their itinerary and meals. That means the family of Mrs. Zhang traveled without the guide of a tour leader. On the night of February 1st, they finished the travel and were going to take the flight to go back to Shanghai. They went through very strict security check and finally got on board. We know in the United States, the passengers' bodies have to be touched to be examined. They were asked to put their hands up and take off shoes. Some Chinese people would be a little bit annoyed by this procedure, but most of them could understand the procedure since when you are in Rome, do as the Romans do.

Boarding on the plane, stewardesses were putting the luggage in order. One of the stewardesses wanted to move Mrs. Zhang's bag to make room for the luggage of other passengers. However, Mrs. Zhang refused to have her luggage moved, the stewardess explained she would rearrange Mrs. Zhang's luggage. Just at that moment, Mr. Zhang came with his daughter in his arm.

He felt weird and asked in English, "Why can't we put our luggage just right above us?" There was a negotiation between them. Somehow, the stewardess and the couple could not compromise with each other. Maybe language was one of the causes. All of a sudden, Mr. Zhang became angry. He ordered the stewardess to shut up. The stewardess questioned why she must stop talking. But Mr. Zhang only kept repeating the phrase "you shut up".

All of it happened in a sudden. The flight attendants opened the door that had been closed. A security checker who could speak Chinese got on board to talk with Mr. and Mrs. Zhang. He told them to get off the plane. If they didn't do that, the plane would not take off. The reason was they had insulted the stewardess, and the stewardess was unable to continue her work if the couple stayed here. If the stewardess was in an unstable emotion, it would affect the safety of the flight.

Hearing this, Mrs. Zhang yelled, "It is impossible! I won't get off the plane!" Meanwhile, the American police with guns were standing along the plane aisle. They announced to Mr. and Mrs. Zhang, "You have gone against the law. You must get off the plane to be investigated. If you don't cooperate with us, we will do it by force." The couple didn't realize the seriousness of the situation until they heard if they didn't get off the plane, all the passengers would be left in Guam.

Realizing the seriousness of the situation, Mrs. Zhang explained that she just lost her temper. She hoped she could get a chance to apologize to the stewardess. But it was too late to regret. The police announced the law they went against which they could not understand at all. They were pushed to get off the plane and left their daughter who was less than 12 years old on the plane. The couple walked through the gate of the plane. The gate closed again and the plane took off in a few minutes. Their daughter was left to take the plane by herself. The second day, the couple took a flight which first stopped in Korea, and then flew to Shanghai. The cost of the air tickets was totally USD 1,100.

Comments

According to relevant laws, captain comes the first place with the biggest power. If the captain thinks the behavior of a passenger will affect the safety of the plane, he can order the passenger to get off the plane. Such stipulation also can be found in Civil Aviation Law of the People's Repubic of China.

What's more, the passengers who go abroad by themselves or party by themseleves without any tour leader should know some English. Language is a very important tool for communication. If one cannot express himself very well, it will cause misunderstandings, and conflicts will be triggered. Therefore, when we are on the plane, we should follow the requests of flight attendants. Besides, the author wants to make it clear that "shut up" is a discourteous phrase in English-speaking countries and should not be used.

象牙可以购买与送人吗？

在安哥拉罗安达的中国人都知道,沿着大西洋海边的沿海公路旁边有一象牙市场,距罗安达有几十公里,规模不算很大,主要是一些象牙饰品、黑木的木雕和一些不知名画家的代表着非洲风土人情的作品。

一般要回国的中国人都会到这里买一些当地特色的小饰品或木雕带给亲友。慢慢地,在这里做生意的安哥拉人都会说一些简单的中国话,比方说"过来这里""真的是象牙,不是象骨""不贵了""你说多少钱?"等。

现在,在安哥拉的中国人渐渐多了起来,生意也一度火爆起来,这可给这些商贩们带来了不少的收益。每当中国人来到这里,小商贩们都会主动招手拉拢客人,但他们从不会走出自己的摊位一定范围去拉客人,这也许是他们定下的规则吧。当你看上某件物品问价时商贩都会漫天要价,你还得要经过一番讨价还价,才能买到适中价钱的物品。这就要看你的还价本事了。

一位大约 50 岁的男子谭某,是某建筑公司职工。2008 年 7 月,他被派驻非洲安哥拉工程项目部工作。来非洲前,谭某得知象牙是安哥拉的特产,于是他在象牙市场花 1200 美元买了 20 多磅非洲象的象牙,同时还买了 6 片大穿山甲的鳞片,准备回国送给朋友。

2011 年 7 月 14 日晚,谭某携带大批礼物高高兴兴地准备从安哥拉回国。他由萧山机场入境,也许是由于对相关法律规定不了解,又或许是想铤而走险,他在通关时并没有向海关申报任何物品。天网恢恢,机场海关在检查他的行李箱时,在箱内查获了这批象牙和穿山甲鳞片。海关当即告知他涉嫌刑事犯罪,谭某一看,大事不妙,便扭头就跑。

10 多天后,谭某在家属陪同下向机场海关缉私分局投案。

在法庭上,谭某辩解,这些东西买来真是送朋友的,并不是为了走私赚钱。他也知道象牙不能带回国,但一直抱着侥幸心理,以为最多是罚款,哪里想到会触犯刑法,要坐牢。

检察官建议判处 5 年以上有期徒刑。最后,法官宣布择日宣判。

[评析]

1980 年,中国加入《濒危野生动植物种国际贸易公约》(以下简称《公约》)。野象象牙被《公约》列为绝对禁止贸易的物种。但非洲和东南亚部分国家没有加入《公约》,允许象牙制品合法买卖,比如安哥拉。

此外,根据我国的《海关法》和《野生动植物保护法》,没有相关允许进口的证明,禁止贸易、携带和邮寄非洲象物种和制品进出我国国境。实际上,携带超过一定价值、数量的濒危动植物入境,将构成走私,是触犯刑法的。不仅象牙不能带回国,鳄鱼及其制品,沉香木、犀牛角等都不能带,甚至象牙项链、象牙手镯这样的象牙制品都不行。即便是你带双象牙筷子回国,也不行,一旦被海关发现,肯定会被扣下。数量少的话,受行政处罚;数量多,达到刑法规定的数额,就涉嫌走私罪,要受刑事处罚。

如果要将象牙或象牙制品带入国内,必须要向海关申报,并同时提交国家濒危物种进出口管理办公室(以下简称濒管办)出具的《濒危野生动植物允许进出口证明书》。这个证明书,除非所涉动植物有非常特殊而必要的用途,申请人一般拿不到,尤其对个人而言,办下来很困难。

所以,个人如果没有濒管办证明的情况下,要带象牙及其制品回国是不可能的。在通关时,最好提前向海关咨询,得到海关否定答复后,就直接放弃。

如果没有申报,直接走了无申报通道,那么即使在海关关员开箱检查前说这里面有违禁物品,也已经没用了,算是故意隐瞒。象牙一定会被扣,情节严重的话,个人也会被追究刑事责任。不过,如果同时满足"珍贵动物制品购买地允许交易""入境人员为留作纪念或者作为礼品而携带进境,不具有牟利目的"两种情形的,可以降格量刑。

Can Ivory Be Bought and Sent to Someone as a Gift?

As Chinese people in Luanda, Angola know, along the Atlantic Sea coastal road, there is an ivory market about dozens of kilometers away from Luanda. The scale is not big. Some ivory jewelry, Kuroki wood and works of some unknown artists of Africa are sold there.

Generally, before returning home, Chinese would come here to buy small jewelries or wood for friends and relatives. Gradually, people do business here can speak a little Chinese like "come over here""it is really ivory, not elephant bone""it's not expensive""how much did you say?"

Now that there are more and more Chinese in Angola, the business here goes on quite well, which can bring the dealers a lot of profits. When Chinese people come here, vendors will take the initiative to wave to the guests. But they never go beyond their stalls. You need to bargain with the vendor, to buy affordable price of goods, this is depend on your bargaining skills.

An approximately-50-year-old man, Mr. Tan who worked in a construction company in Angola, was told that the ivory is a specialty of Angola. In July, 2008, Tan spent USD 1,200 buying more than 20 pounds of African elephant ivory on the ivory markets. At the same time, he also bought 6 large pangolin scales as gifts when going back to China.

On July 14th, 2011, Tan carried the gifts happily to return home from Angola. At Hangzhou Xiaoshan International Airport, probably due to lack of knowledge of the relevant legal provisions or perhaps Tan wanted to take a risk, he did not declare to the customs any items. Unfortunately, later the airport customs checked his suitcase, found ivory and pangolin scales inside. The customs immediately informed him of criminal suspects. Tan turned and ran. 10 days later, Tan was accompanied by family members to airport customs to report.

In court, Tan explained that these things were really for friends, not for smuggling. He knew the ivory would not be allowed to be brought to China. He thought he would be fined rather than go to jail.

Prosecutors suggested Tan be sentenced to an imprisonment of no less than 5 years. Finally, the judge declared that the verdict date would be announced later.

Comments

In 1980, China joined the Convention on International Trade in Endangered Species (CITES). Ivory of wild elephants is listed as the species that is absolutely prohibited from being traded. However, African countries like Angola and some Southeastern Asian counties did not join in the CITES. Therefore, ivory trade is legal in those countries.

In addition, according to the Customs Law of the People's Republic of China and Laws of the People's Republic of China on the Protection of Wildlife, the trade, carrying and mailing of African elephants species and products are prohibited in and out of China if no certificates are presented. In fact, carrying a certain amount of endangered wildlife with a certain value to enter China's customs is considered to be smuggling and a violation of the Criminal Law. Ivory and its products like ivory necklaces, ivory bracelets, ivory chopsticks, crocodiles and their products, agarwood, rhinoceros horns are not allowed to be brought to China. Once found by the customs, the relevant products are detained immediately. Administrative penalties or criminal punishment are implemented according to the amount of products.

But if you want to take ivory and its products back to China, you must declare it to the customs, and in the meantime, submit to the customs the Endangered Wildlife Import and Export Permit Certificate issued by the State Endangered Species Import and Export Management Office (hereinafter referred to as the office). As getting the certificate has to go through very complicated procedures, so it is very difficult for an individual applicant to get one without justified reasons.

So, without the certificate from the office, it is impossible to take ivory and its products back to China. Travelers are advised to consult the customs in advance. If travelers get the reply "NO" from the customs, they have to give up the idea of taking ivory and its products back to China.

If travelers do not declare to the customs and choose to go through the "No Declaration" pass, and then say there are prohibited articles in the luggage before the inspection from the customs officers, they are considered to deliberately concealing. Ivory will be confiscated, and if the amount and value is big, travelers will be investigated for criminal responsibility. However, if travelers can simultaneously prove that they have the "trading permits of precious animal products in purchasing areas" and they belong to the "entry personnel carrying certain prohibited articles as souvenirs or as gifts without the purpose of making profits", they can be given lesser sentence. That's why in the above case, the procurator sentenced Mr. Tan to the imprisonment of no less than 5 years.

在香港免税店购物

2014年2月2—6日正值新春佳节,也是年轻的出境游领队小汪带领"经典港澳5日游"的团队赴香港及澳门旅游的日子。

行程的第一天是游览迪士尼乐园。由于航班晚点,领队、香港导游、客人三方协商,香港导游同意让客人们在迪士尼乐园从下午4点一直玩到晚上闭园,将近5个小时的时间。但在客人进入迪士尼乐园之后,香港导游对小汪提出第二天带客人前往DFS免税店购物的要求。小汪表示,因为此团队是纯玩团,不设置购物项目,所以不能同意导游的这一要求。

行程的第二天是游览海洋公园。春节期间,海洋公园的客人非常多,公园内每一个游览项目的等候时间都在90分钟左右,但旅游行程中规定的时间只是不少于3个小时。对于年轻的旅游者来说只游览3个多小时根本不尽兴,香港导游也没有灵活地将游览的时间再延长一些。之后,香港导游按部就班地带客人游览了星光大道,游览结束后他在车上再三推荐客人赴DFS免税店进行购物。领队小汪告诉客人,该团是纯玩团,不设置购物项目。但车上个别游客认为"盛情难却"。其后,香港导游拿出了一份写明游客自愿前往免税店购物的协议书,要求游客在协议书上签名,协议书上根本也没有规定在免税店购物的时间。

客人签完名之后，香港导游就带领客人前往免税店购物。进入商店一个小时以后，有部分客人坐在了免税店的门口，提出不愿继续待在店里，要求进行下一个项目的游览。随着时间的推移，团内要求前往下一景点的客人越来越多，香港导游以还有部分客人没有完成购物为理由，坚持没让司机将大巴车门打开。此时，大部分客人已然非常不满意，提出要投诉导游。在客人购物两个半小时之后，香港导游终于让司机打开车门，带领客人离开免税店，前往维港夜游。

[评析]

团体旅游中的购物与自费环节一直争议不断，被视为阻碍旅游业健康发展的顽疾。《中华人民共和国旅游法》实施之后，行业逐步规范。国家旅游局会同国家工商行政管理局在 4 月 17 日联合发布了 2014 年版《团队境内旅游合同》（示范文本）《团队出境旅游合同（示范文本）》《大陆居民赴台湾地区旅游合同（示范文本）》和《境内旅游组团社与地接社合同（示范文本）》。这些合同示范文本中对旅行社安排购物活动、另行付费旅游项目在原则和方式上设定了约束性条约。

在《团队出境旅游合同（示范文本）》第六条关于出境社的义务中规定，旅行社不以不合理的低价组织旅游活动，诱骗旅游者，并通过安排购物或者另行付费旅游项目获取回扣等不正当利益；但是，经双方协商一致或者旅游者要求，且不影响其他旅游者行程安排的除外。在第七条"旅游者的权利"中增加了旅游者的拒绝权。旅游者有权自主选择旅游产品和服务，有权拒绝出境社未与旅游者协商一致或者未经旅游者要求而指定购物场所、安排旅游者参加另行付费旅游项目的行为，有权拒绝出境社的导游、领队强迫或者变相强迫旅游者购物、参加另行付费旅游项目的行为。

在《国际出境旅游合同（示范文本）》的最后部分，还有自愿购物活动和自愿参加另行付费旅游项目的补充条款协议，如果消费者和旅行社达成一致意见，需签署这份补充协议进行具体约定。

案例中,首先领队对自己的身份与权力的认知不够到位。领队应掌握团队动向,履行计划内的行程,行程中有损团队利益的活动应坚决阻止,坚决维护客人与旅行社的利益。其次,领队对当地导游的监督不够到位。在沟通无效的情况应该立即打电话给组团社,让计调人员来处理。不要害怕惹事,要坚决维护领队的主导与话语权。领队小汪没有细看香港导游提供的协议书,如果他能及时阻止,那就不会出现案例中的现象了。

Shopping in a Hong Kong's DFS

During the Spring Festival in 2014, the tour leader Wang led a group for the "classic Hong Kong and Macau tour".

On the first day, the group was scheduled to visit Disneyland. Because the flight was delayed, the tour leader negotiated with the tour guide and guests for more time in Disneyland. Finally, the Hong Kong guide agreed to let the guests enjoy themselves in the park from 4:00 p.m. to the closure of the park, for nearly 5 hours. When the guests entered into Disneyland, the Hong Kong guide said he wanted to bring the guests to a DFS. But Wang disagreed because this group was a pure travel group.

On the second day, the schedule was to visit the Ocean Park. There were many tourists in the park during the Spring Festival. The waiting time for every program in the park was about 90 minutes. According to the schedule, the group may stay in this park in no less than 3 hours. 3 hours were really not enough for young people. But the Hong Kong guide didn't prolong the time. Later, he brought the guests to the Avenue of Stars as planned. After the visits, the Hong Kong guide again persuaded the guests to go shopping in a DFS. Wang told the guests that they were not allowed to enter into the shops, because they belonged to a pure travel group. But there were several guests who felt it was hard to turn down the warm-hearted offer. Later, the local guide took out an agreement, requiring the guests to sign their names on the letter of agreement of going shopping in a DFS. But the agreement didn't mention the shopping time.

After the guests signed, the Hong Kong guide led the tourists for DFS shopping. An hour later, some guests went out of the DFS, saying that they were not willing to stay in the shop and required to go on to the next scenic spot. As time passed by, more and more guests required so. But the Hong Kong guide refused to let the driver open the bus door because he said there were still some guests who did not finish shopping. At that time, most guests said they would like to make complaint against the guide. After two and half hours' shopping, the Hong Kong guide opened the bus door and moved on to the next scenic spot—Night Cruise on Victoria Harbor.

Comments

The disputes spring up constantly whether tourists should take part or not in the shopping and self funding activities. This problem is considered the obstacle that stands in the way of tourism developing healthily. After the implementation of the Tourism Law of the People's Republic of China, the tourism industry becomes more standard. The National Tourism Bureau and the National Industry and Commerce

Administration issued on April 17th the 2014 edition of Domestic Group Travel Contract (Sample) and Outbound Group Travel Contract (Sample), Travel Contract for Mainland Citizens Coming to Taiwan (Sample) and Contract Between Tour Organizing Agency and Local Travel Agency for Inbound Travel (Sample). Those newly issued samples set limitations for shopping activities and self funding activities in principles and methods.

The 6th provision in Outbound Group Travel Contract (Sample) provides that the travel agency should not organize travel activity at an unreasonable low price, cheat and lure tourists and arrange shopping activities or self-funded activities to get improper profit such as commissions, except for the situation that tourists and agency agree with each other and the activity will not affect other tourists' itinerary. In the 7th provision, the contract first adds tourists' right to reject. Tourists have the right to choose travel products and services. They have the right to refuse shopping and self-funded activities which are not agreed upon. They have the right to refuse the guide's or the tour leader's service if they are forced to shop or take part in self-funded activities.

In the last part of the newly issued Outbound Group Travel Contract (Sample), there are complementary provisions to voluntarily shopping and self-financed activities. If consumers and the travel agency come to a consensus, they need to sign this complementary contract and make a detailed arrangement.

In the above case, the tour leader firstly didn't know his identity and right properly. A tour leader should be in charge of the group and carry out the schedule. If there are activities that will harm guests' rights, he should firmly protect the rights of guests and travel agency. Secondly, the tour leader didn't cooperate with and supervise the local guide well. When the negotiation failed, the tour leader should call the operator in the organizing travel agency immediately, and let them handle the problem. The tour leader should not be afraid of the local guide. He or she should stick to the rights and discourse power of a tour leader firmly. The tour leader Wang didn't go over the complementary contract in detail and failed to notice the shopping time. If the tour leader could control the shopping time (normally about 1 hour), made an agreement with the local guide before entering into the shop or signing the contract, then the situation in the above case might be avoided.

让邓丽君的歌声伴着你漫游清迈

当下的年轻人对泰国北部城市清迈的认识,可能要归功于喜剧片《泰囧》,片中出现的具有异域风情的美景深深地吸引着今天的"80后""90后"。而对于出生于20世纪五六十年代的人来说,对清迈的印象可能源自那位美丽的台湾歌手邓丽君留下的足迹。据说,邓丽君很喜欢清迈的气候,她一生最后的岁月就是在清迈度过的。

某年春节,出生于20世纪50年代的孙先生带领一个30余人的出境旅游团队,前往清迈观光游览。在清迈城里,大家饶有兴致地参观了双龙寺、大塔寺,还乘坐了"嘟嘟车"环绕清迈古城一周。但让孙领队感觉最有意义的是,当地旅行社安排大家在湄滨酒店参观了邓丽君当年曾经住过的套房。

那天下午,按照计划团队来到了位于市中心的湄滨酒店。在酒店的咖啡厅里,大家一边品尝着具有泰国风味的下午茶,包括泰国当地的水果、糕点、小吃、咖啡和茶水,一边听着邓丽君的歌声。团中的客人还情不自禁地唱了几首当年在大陆流行的邓丽君的歌曲,比如《小城故事》《何日君再来》等。此时此刻,团队中对邓丽君了解不多的年轻人似乎也从中领悟到了什么。用完下午茶以后,大家乘电梯上楼参观邓丽君曾经下榻过的湄滨酒店1502套房。在地陪的带领下,大家鱼贯而入,首先参观了她当年入住的卧室,卧室既温馨又浪漫。出了卧室是一个走廊,通向套房里布置典雅的客厅。走廊间有个小架子,上面放置着一盆鲜花,花盆下放置着当年邓丽君与友人的照片。大家先在邓丽君的卧室里驻足追思,然后仔细地端详了卧室和客厅的布置,似乎是在捕捉什么信息,或许是在想象当年她在这里的岁月,有些游客还拍照留念。

参观完毕,按计划大家乘车回到下榻的香格里拉酒店。进入饭店大厅后,地陪向大家重申了次日的安排。孙领队在酒店总服务台向服务生交代了次日的叫早时间后,准备去自己的房间休息。这时候团里一对"80后"的年轻夫妻礼貌地叫住孙领队,问孙领队能否给他们较为详细地介绍一下邓丽君的情况。

孙领队找了大厅一处安静的地方,与这对小夫妻一起坐了下来。他说,邓丽君是出生于台湾的第二代外省人。她是在全球华人中社会影响力最大的歌手之一,并赢得了"有中国人的地方,就有邓丽君的歌声"的美誉;她更是首位登上美国纽约林肯中心的华人女歌手,曾经在美国、加拿大等国家巡演。2008年,邓丽君小姐的金曲《但愿人长久》伴随"神舟七号"飞上太空。据统计,邓丽君的唱片销售量已超过4800万张。听了孙领队的介绍后,这对年轻人又问道,为什么团里的有些游客对邓丽君如此推崇。孙领队告诉他们,邓丽君的歌在改革开放以后在大陆风行。她的声音甜美圆润、婉转动人。聆听她天籁般的歌声在当时来说是种美妙的享受。可以说邓丽君的歌声影响了许多人,也影响了中国流行音乐的发展。她是许多中国的"50后""60后"青春时代最美好的记忆,某些团友今天在这里的表现正是情感的自然流露。听了孙领队的简单介绍,这对年轻人好像懂了点什么。

[评析]

伴随中国人出游人数的不断增加,中国游客在旅游过程中的礼仪修养缺失问题层出不穷,导致中国游客正作为一个符号化的群体被一些西方发达国家所"歧视"。马尔代夫酒店为防止中国游客在房间内吃泡面而不去餐厅消费,拒绝为中国游客提供热水;在马尔代夫,只有中国游客潜水前需要考试;美国海关歧视性排查中国游客;法国奢侈酒店拒绝接待中国游客……其实,国人自身也对一部分中国游客的一些低素质行为表示羞愧和失落。

此案例中,中国客人在参观清迈的邓丽君寓所时表现出来的安静与有序,在一定程度上靠的是孙领队在行前做的功课。在客人参观过程中,领队的不断补充介绍,使客人觉得参观的内容非常有意义。其实,孙领队并不是邓丽君的歌迷,对流行音乐也了解甚少,对邓丽君的了解基本上停留在会哼几首当年听熟的歌曲他只是因为担任领队,在出行前做了功课。作为领队要在旅游者中间树立威望,脑子里总要有各种知识的积累的。

笔者认为,旅游者自身的素质是一个方面,但是,出境游领队对客人的提醒和自身的修养也是非常重要的。一名优秀领队的言行,会让旅游者受到影响。

A Travel in Chiang Mai Accompanied By Teresa Teng's Songs

The comedy *Lost in Thailand* has pulled the younger generation closer to Chiang Mai, a northern city in Thailand. The outlandish beauty there has left a deep impression on the youngsters born in the 1980s or the 1990s, while those born in the 1950s or the 1960s may better know obout the city because of the Taiwanese singer Teresa Teng's life in Chiang Mai. It is said that the singer loved the climate in Chiang Mai and spent the last years of her life there.

In a Spring Festival, Mr. Sun, born in the 1950s, led a group of 30 members to Chiang Mai for sightseeing. The group visited a couple of Buddhist temples such as Wat Phra That Doi Suthep and Wat Chedi Luang, and also took tuk-tuks around the old town. The most significant tour for Mr. Sun was the visit to Teresa Teng's former hotel room.

In the afternoon, the group came to the Mae Ping Hotel. First, they tasted the afternoon tea of the local flavor in the cafeteria with local fruits, refreshments, accompanied by Teresa's songs such as "Story of Little Town", "When Will You Return". Some group members even began to sing some of Teresa's old songs. At this moment, some young members who knew little about the female star also felt something special. After the tea, the group took the elevator to visit Teresa's former room suite 1502. Led by the local guide, the entire group went inside and visited the romantic and lovely bedroom. There was a corridor outside the bedroom leading to the elaborately decorated living room. In the corridor, there was a shelf with some flowers on it, under which there were photos of the singer with her friends. Everybody was thinking about something in her bedroom before looking closely at the arrangement of the rooms, possibly for some more information, or to imagine her past. Some of them even took photos.

After the visit, the group went back to Shangri-La Hotel. The local guide stressed next day's itinerary before leaving. Mr. Sun arranged a morning call and was ready to go back to his room. Then a young couple politely asked the tour leader to stay and introduce more details of Teresa to them.

In a quiet place, the tour leader sat down with the young couple and he gave a very detailed introduction to Teng's life and achievement. He said that Teng was born in Taiwan as an outsider of the second generation of people from the mainland. Besides, she was a famous singer with great influence in overseas Chinese society where there are Chinese, there are her songs. What's more, she was the first female Chinese singer who performed in America Lincoln Center in New York and had tour concerts in America, Canada and so on. In 2008, her famous song, "May We All Be Blessed with Longevity", accompanied Shenzhou Ⅶ spaceship into space. According to statistics, her records sold over 48 million copies. After the tour leader's introduction, the young couple asked him why some tourists of the group were so obsessed with her. The tour leader told them, Teresa Teng's songs became popular in the mainland after China's reform and opening up. Her sweet, gentle and moving voice was a kind of wonderful enjoyment at that time. Her singing has influenced many people as well as the development of Chinese popular music. Many people born in the 1950s and the 1960s regard Teresa Teng's songs as a treasure in their green days. Therefore the expressions of some tourists today were their spontaneous overflow of emotions. The young couple seemed to understand something after the tour leader's introduction.

Comments

With the increase of outbound tourists, Chinese people's uncivilized behavior has been drawn attention to by western countries. In Maldives, many hotels refuse to supply hot water to Chinese guests in fear of their not dining in the restaurant but just having instant noodles in their rooms. And only Chinese tourists need to take a test before diving. American customs give Chinese tourists stricter security check. Luxurious hotels in France refuse to take Chinese guests. Actually, most Chinese themselves also feel it a big shame for some tourists to conduct uncivilized behaviors.

In the above case, the Chinese tourists displayed polite behaviors when visiting Teng's former hotel rooms in Chiang Mai, partly thanks to the tour leader's previous efforts. The trip was also enriched by the tour leader's additional introduction of Teresa Teng. As a matter of fact, the tour leader is not a fan of Teng and knows little about pop music. However, he made sufficient preparation before the tour, which is important for an excellent tour leader.

The author believes that Chinese tourists' bad behaviors derive from themselves on the one hand, and on the other hand, it may also be caused by the tour leader's failure to remind them for better discipline. An excellent tour leader's words and deeds will influence his group members positively.

攻击性行为所引发的后果

出境游领队小陈和他所带的旅游团此次的行程是从上海飞往美国芝加哥，而后转机前往迈阿密，最后在迈阿密罗德岱堡港口登上皇家加勒比游轮，开始为期 8 天的东加勒比海上游轮之旅。领队小陈顺利办完了登船手续，全团 23 名客人顺利登上了游轮。就在游轮出发离港前约 40 分钟，小陈房间的电话响起，电话是团里一个客人打来的，他十分焦急，请小陈赶快去他房间一趟，他爸出事了。

这里有必要向大家介绍一下这位王姓客人的情况，姓王的客人带着一对双胞胎女儿和老父亲，一家四口出来旅游。一路上，这位老父亲有点独来独往，每次都一个人走在最前面。所以王先生电话里说父亲出事了，领队小陈就特别担心。

赶到客人房间以后，小陈看见客舱内外站着好多船上的工作人员，进去一看，老人正躺在地上，旁边还站着两位医护人员，他的儿子在旁边急得满头大汗。领队当时的反应就是老人可能突发心脏病之类的疾病。但是仔细一看，发现老人神志还比较清醒，也能清楚地与人对话，当时就放心了不少。

小陈与王先生沟通以后，了解了事情的概况：当时王先生和老人一个房间，两个女儿一个房间，王先生打电话要客房服务人员拿一些火柴过来，之后就去女儿房间了。当服务人员送火柴过来的时候，房间里只有老人一个人在，由于语言不通，双方可能产生了误会，结果导致了肢体冲突。接着服务员就通知了船上保安人员，保安到了以后就要求老人下船。老人一急，可能就因身体不舒服，躺倒在地上了。由于王先生当时不在现场，不知道老人和服务员之间究竟发生了什么事。于是领队小陈就立刻向旁边的工作人员了解情况。工作人员说，由于老人和服务员发生了肢体冲突，服务员通知了船上的保安主管，主管又请示了船长，说老人有攻击性行为，所以船长以影响安全为由，要求老人即刻离船。当时领队小陈就找到保安主管，解释说这一定是个误会，老人年纪这么大，不可能有攻击性的举动，并且要求和船长亲自谈一谈，解释一下事情的原委。但是保安主管说，船长一旦发布离船命令，是任何人也无法改变的。现在请他们自行离船，不然的话就要呼叫岸上的警察来强制执行了。

老人与保安人员发生冲突时，正好旁边有两位中国籍服务员，他们也跟领队小陈表示说确实是老人太冲动了。当时保安主管来了解情况的时候，请老人去他办公室解释一下事情经过，两位中国籍服务员对老人说，一会儿什么都不用说，他们会帮他解释的。结果到了办公室以后，老人情绪还是很激动，而且全然不顾自己儿子的劝阻，所以导致最终的离船。

王先生不得不陪他父亲一同离船，两个小女儿也一边哭哭啼啼一边带着行李下船了。由于船上还有其他19位乘客，领队也不可能陪他们一起下船，所以领队小陈立刻联系了迈阿密地接社的相关人员，说明情况后，希望他们能提供帮助，马上来码头接这4位客人，帮他们安排住宿，并在游轮航行期间，帮助他们安排在迈阿密的游览行程。最后，地接社安排4位客人入住，并帮他们安排了前往奥特兰的迪士尼公园游玩。在游轮返回码头的那天，重新和团队会合。

[评析]

中国历史悠久的传统文化是国民宝贵的精神财富，然而正像任何文化都有其精华与糟粕一样，中国传统文化中同样存在一些文化陋习。譬如，中国传统文化中的"主奴意识""争抢意识"和"公共精神缺失"，在社会历史变迁中遗留下来。

这些文化糟粕不可避免地对国民心态产生了不良影响。

案例中,虽然大家都不知道老人到底和服务人员发生了什么冲突,但有一点是可以肯定的,就是老人讲话的嗓音一定是很响的,情绪一定也很激动。旅行社尤其是出境组团社的领队是最主要的管理主体。旅行社是旅游活动的组织者,出境游领队则是旅游计划的真正实施者,尤其是出境组团旅行社中的导游和领队,则更是旅游者的随行者。旅游作为一项文化活动,导游和领队除了带领旅游者完成旅游行程之外,还应该是文化的宣传者。由于不同文化之间存在差异,导游和领队人员在带领旅游者到一个陌生的环境中去旅游时,应该提前告知旅游者异地风俗文化、礼仪禁忌等知识,并承担起旅途中随时监督提醒的任务,以避免文化习俗差异所带来的文化冲突。尤其是在出境旅游中,不同文化之间的差异性更为明显,由于旅游者不符合当地习俗礼仪的行为而引发矛盾和冲突的可能性就越大。

基于以上的案例,笔者认为旅行社应该形成一个系统的教育管理机制,设计教育形式、确定教育内容,制订导游和领队全程教育责任制。

Consequences of Aggressive Behaviors

Chen, a tour leader, took his group all the way flying from Shanghai to Miami. They finally managed to board Royal Caribbean Cruises at Fort Lauderdale. The 8-day cruise trip on the eastern Caribbean began. Chen went through boarding procedure smoothly and soon all of his guests went on board. About 40 minutes before the ship departed from the port, the phone in Chen's room rang. It was from a gentleman in his group. The man said that something happened to his father and wanted Chen to go up to his room immediately.

Before we go further, let's first get to know a little bit more about the guest. The guest's last name is Wang. He joined the group with his twin daughters and his father. Along the way, his father kept his own company and always walked in front. So Chen was worried that something might have happened to the old man when hearing from Mr. Wang.

So Chen rushed to Wang's room right away, and spotted there were quite a few staff members standing outside the room. He went in and found Wang's father lying on the floor with medical personnel standing nearby and his son beside him, sweating all over. Chen's first thought was the old man was probably suffering a heart attack or something like that. However, when looking closely, he found the old man was conscious and able to talk to others, which made Chen feel quite relieved.

After talking with Wang, Chen learned that Wang first accompanied his father to his room while his girls went to theirs. Then he called the housekeeping for some matchsticks and then went to his daughters' room to have a check.

When the room attendant delivered the matches, his father was in the room alone. Due to the language barrier, they had some misunderstandings which led to an altercation. Later on the attendant informed the security guards about the whole thing, and they asked the old man to get off the ship. The old man might felt physically unwell when getting anxious and then fell on the ground. Since Mr. Wang hadn't been present when the incident occurred, he had no idea what exactly had happened between the attendant and his father.

Therefore, Chen had to ask other attendants for details. They told him that there was a physical conflict between them. Soon the security supervisor was informed about the incident, then he went to the captain for instruction. Besides, the old guest had aggressive behaviors. So now the captain demanded that the old man get off the ship at once. Chen tried to explain to the security supervisor that Mr. Wang's father was too old to have aggressive behaviors, and asked if it was possible for him to talk to the captain in person. However, the supervisor refused him, and said that the order issued by the captain was not negotiable and asked the old man to leave right away. Otherwise, they would call the police. When the conflict happened, there were two Chinese attendants nearby. They told Chen what the old man had done was severely out of line. When the security superior showed up and asked the old man to his office to explain what had happened, these two Chinese attendants told the old man that they would help explain it to the superior for him. However, when they got the office, the old man fell into a rage again. As a result, Wang's family had no other choice but to get off the ship.

Since the rest of the group was still on the cruise, Chen wouldn't be able to accompany the Wangs. He contacted the local travel agency immediately, and hoped they would provide accommodation and arrange some activities for the family. Eventually, the Wangs checked into a hotel and the local travel agency arranged them a visit to Disneyland and other places for entertainment. Later they joined the tour group on the day when the ship returned to the port.

Comments

Just like other civilizations, traditional Chinese culture as a spiritual treasure of Chinese is a combination of essence and dross. The consciousness of mastery and slavery, scrambling consciousness and the absence of public spirit are the outmoded conventions.

In this case，although we have no exact idea about what happened between the old man and the attendant，one thing was clear that the old man's voice must be loud and he was definitely raging.

It is well known that tour leaders in outbound travel agencies are the essential part of the system of travel management. Travel agencies are the organizers of tourist activities，while tour leaders are the conductors of travel plans. Besides，tour guides and leaders are also the retinue of tourists in outbound travel agencies. Nowadays travel even serves as a culture activity. In other word，tour leaders and guides should play the role of culture ambassadors during trips. Due to cultural differences，it's essential for tour leaders and guides to inform tourists about local folk cultures and etiquette taboos before taking them to a foreign land. In addition，they should constantly remind tourists of the chances of cultured conflicts.

Based on the above case，I think travel agencies should establish a systematic training mechanism and a responsibility system of full-course training for tour leaders and guides.

谁该付超时费？

本次英伦之旅 12 日的行程，从英格兰首都伦敦出发，采用不走回头路的方式一路北上来到苏格兰爱丁堡，行程的第 9 天来到北爱尔兰首府贝尔法斯特，之后即刻前往位于北爱尔兰北部的海岸绵延伸展长达约 8 公里的巨人堤道，客人们参观后皆为之震惊。此次行程除了常规的英国行程，还增加了北爱尔兰和爱尔兰的游览，让客人非常期待。

行程的第 10 天，原定早餐后从贝尔法斯特直接前往爱尔兰的首都都柏林参观基督大教堂，午餐后游览凤凰公园，接着参观由英国伊丽莎白女王于 1592 年创建的都柏林大学圣三一学院及老图书馆，之后游览梅林广场和菲兹威廉姆广场。负责北爱尔兰及爱尔兰两地接待的华人导游小王考虑，直接坐大巴从贝尔法斯特离开，抵达都柏林时刚好是中午 11 点整（基督大教堂正在修缮，无法进去参观），用中餐的时间尚早。小王决定在贝尔法斯特增加泰坦尼克博物馆的游览，博物馆建在贝尔法斯特哈兰德·沃尔夫造船厂的旧址上，泰坦尼克号当年就是在这里设计、建造并下水的。所以，客人都对增加的这个项目十分满意。

午餐后客人提出在都柏林购物的要求，导游同意给客人一个半小时的购物时间并要求在 4 点半集合，然后继续游览。结果，5 位客人 5 点才赶到集合点，全团出发时正好赶上都柏林的晚高峰,这使得大家只能在车上观赏了菲兹威廉姆广场和梅林广场。晚餐后抵达入住酒店时,司机已超时工作1小时。此时,导游说:"由于客人迟到半小时,我们才遇到了堵车,现在超出1小时的工作时间,需付100英镑的超时费。"作为领队,我对导游说:"你的好意(增加景点与购物)我们都领了。但是你的安排也是缺乏经验的,既然预测到客人可能会迟到,为何不将集合时间往前提半小时呢?这样也许可以避免堵车。"导游听了,只给出一句:"反正超时是需要付超时费给司机的。"

我跟客人及时做了沟通,随后对导游说:"让没有迟到的人付超时费,明显是不合理的。在你的行程中,应把堵车和迟到的情况预测进去,所以我们只需承担一半的责任和费用。迟到的5人每人付10英镑,剩下的50英镑只有你自己承担了。"最后,导游虽觉得有些不服气,但也只能认了这笔账。

[评析]

在欧洲旅行中,有时需要支付超时费给司机,是一个非常敏感的问题。有时超时是客人拖延时间所引起的。但有时是入住的酒店太远,或者用餐的餐厅不顺路所引起的。这就需要导游、客人、司机的三者配合才能让整个行程不拖延。领队也必须多次向客人强调准时这一理念。

案例中确定有客人迟到的情况存在。但是,导游对整个行程时间估算的不准确,也是一个问题,不然也不会超时一个小时。

Who Should Pay for Overtime Fee?

This 12-day trip started from London, the capital of England, and continued north to Edinburgh in Scotland. On the 9th day of this journey we arrived at Belfast, Northern Ireland. Then we went to the northern part of Northern Ireland immediately. Tourists were amazed at the causeway which was about 8 kilometers long there. This trip, besides the usual England itinerary, encloses Northern Ireland and Ireland, which makes tourists very exciting.

On the 10th day, according to the itinerary, we went to Dublin, Ireland's capital, to visit Christ Church Cathedral. After lunch, we would visit the Trinity College of Dublin University and its old library built by Britain's queen Elizabeth in 1592. Then we would visit Merrion Square and Fitzwilliam Square. The tour guide Wang who was responsible for the tour in Northern Ireland and Ireland thought, if we took the coach from Belfast to Dublin directly, we would arrive at 11:00, which was too early for lunch. So he decided to add Titanic Museum to visit. The museum was built in Belfast Harland Wolff shipyard site where the Titanic was designed and built. The tourists thought it was very remarkable to add this scenic spot.

After lunch the tourists requested shopping in Dublin. The tour guide agreed and gave them one and a half hours for shopping and asked them to meet at 16:30. In the end, 5 tourists reached the meeting place at 17:00. That was why later the group encountered the rush hour and had to see Merrion Square and Fitzwilliam Square only from inside the coach. After dinner we checked into hotel. At that time, the driver had already worked overtime for 1 hour. Therefore we had to pay the driver 100 pounds extra. As the tour leader, I talked to the tour guide, "We accepted adding a new scenic spot and shopping, but the arrangement was not perfect. You could have predicted that tourists may not reach the meeting place on time. Why didn't you set the meeting time half an hour earlier? If you had done so, we could have avoided the rush hour." However, the tour guide just said we had to pay for overtime work.

After communicating with the tourists, I told the tour guide that it was unreasonable to ask those who were not late to pay for the overtime work. The tour guide should take traffic jam and possible delay into consideration. Therefore we would take half of both the responsibility and the cost. 5 people who were late had to pay 10 pounds each. Although the tour guide was not very happy, he had to accept this.

Comments

When traveling in Europe, paying extra money for drivers' overtime work is a sensitive issue. Sometimes it is caused by tourists' delay. Sometimes it is because the hotel is too far or the restaurant is not on the same way. That is why we need the cooperation between the tour guide, the tourists and the driver to implement the whole itinerary properly. The tour leader should emphasize this concept to tourists.

In this case, if the tourists had not been late and if the tour guide had arranged the schedule of the whole itinerary more reasonably, the driver would not have to drive overtime.

在斯里兰卡俱乐部召开行前说明会

　　绿色城市康提是斯里兰卡最后一个独立王国的所在地,也是斯里兰卡的佛教圣地,拥有大量世界遗产,一直是旅游者的圣地。康堤因佛牙寺而闻名,佛牙寺则因供奉着佛祖释迦牟尼圆寂后的佛牙舍利而名扬世界。相传佛祖释迦牟尼的佛牙只有两颗留存于世,一颗珍藏在中国北京西山八大处的佛牙塔内,另一颗便在佛牙寺内。康提每年8月都要举行一次长达10天的盛大纪念活动。

　　王教授是在杭州某高校研究亚洲文化的专家,他造访并研究过东南亚及北亚的多个国家,诸如新加坡、泰国、印度尼西亚、韩国、日本等国家。对于南亚的印度等国他也有浓厚的兴趣。听说近年上海可以直飞斯里兰卡的首都科伦坡,王教授兴奋得不得了。因为,他准备参加一年一度的斯里兰卡佛牙节。

　　于是,王教授召集了一批佛教文化方面的专家,组成了一个佛教朝拜专业团队,线路套用的是旅行社常用的"6晚7天斯里兰卡深度游"的路线。一想到马上要游览斯里兰卡众多的世界文化遗产,马上可以欣赏到以大象的形象为载体的古典工艺品,王教授就激动不已。临出发前的一周,旅行社准备为全体团员召开一次行前说明会,开会的地点不是安排在旅行社的会议室,而是安排在杭州斯里兰卡俱乐部。

等到开会那天下午，王教授早早地来到了位于杭州西湖区黄姑山路的杭州斯里兰卡俱乐部，先参观了俱乐部的陈设，包括佛像观摩区、锡兰红茶品尝区、斯里兰卡宝石观赏区。"6晚7天斯里兰卡深度游"的说明会就在俱乐部的3楼会议室举行。

在3楼会议室，团员们一边品尝着享誉世界的锡兰红茶，一边聆听领队小陈的介绍。他先自我介绍，再从集合时间与地点、行程简述、着装与气温、饮食、入住酒店、交通方式、行李托运、货币与汇率、小费支付、个人物品、自由或夜间活动的注意事项、安全问题、签证及海关规定、购物及境外通讯方式、出境游的礼仪及中国与斯里兰卡的文化差异等方面向客人讲述了赴斯里兰卡旅游的注意事项。尤其是小陈讲到旅游者进入寺庙时一律脱鞋，服装必须整洁等细节时，团员们无不为陈领队的专业与细致所折服。

尽管这些专家、教授走过世界许多地方，但是类似于这样的行前说明会还是第一次参加，大家都觉得非常有新意，既听到了出境游时的注意事项，又提前感受到了斯里兰卡灿烂的文化，让所有团友对即将到来的斯里兰卡旅行充满了憧憬。

[评析]

斯里兰卡是一个热带岛国。它拥有一个美好而又梦幻的名字——"印度半岛的一滴泪"。中国古代称其为狮子国、僧伽罗。它曾经被马可·波罗认为是世界上最美的岛屿，因为它有美妙绝伦的海湾、神秘莫测的古城、丰富的自然遗产及独特迷人的历史和文化。

2012年9月成立的杭州斯里兰卡俱乐部是浙江第一个有关出境游目的地国家的俱乐部，是一个全面介绍和推广斯里兰卡文化的交流平台，也是集商务与休闲为一体的俱乐部。自2013年《中华人民共和国旅游法》开始实施以来，各家旅行社更加注重出境游行前说明会的召开，而该旅行社将说明会迁移到相关俱乐部召开也可以说是一个创新，是旅行社与俱乐部战略合作的一种新模式。

目前，在浙江的出境旅游市场，杭州招商旅游公司是办理斯里兰卡出境旅游的专业机构。自斯里兰卡航空开通上海至科伦坡的航线后,旅游公司得到了斯里兰卡航空公司和当地26家地接社、酒店的大力支持,推出微笑兰卡与斯航假期:一起发现斯里兰卡的奇迹专线。为方便游客出行,斯航每周都有多个航班往来与科伦坡与上海之间,两人便可出发成行。同时,针对不同的客户需求,杭州招商旅游公司还设计出新婚团、摄影团、佛教朝圣团、自行车团、潜水团、珠宝古董淘宝团等特殊旅游团体,以满足不同客户的需求。

　　旅游者的旅游经历过程可以分为旅游前、旅游中、旅游后3个环节。旅游者在出发之前参加的由旅行社组织召开的行前说明会,是一个非常重要的环节。除了让旅游者了解出境游的注意事项,还可以让客人预先了解到目的地国家(地区)的风俗与习惯。杭州斯里兰卡俱乐部的成立正好让旅游者在旅行之前提前了解斯里兰卡的历史与文化,让旅游者对即将要去的目的地国家充满期待。

中国公民出境旅游服务质量解析

Orientation at Sri Lanka Club

Kandy, an environment-friendly city, is the location of the last independent kingdom of Sri Lanka, and a land of Buddhism with abundant world heritage resource. Kandy is a tourist resort famous for the Temple of Tooth Relic in which one of Sakyamuni's teeth was enshrined after the Buddha passed into Parinirvana. According to the legend, there are only two teeth of the Buddha left in the world. One is in the Buddha Tooth Tower in Eight Great

500

Temples of the Western Hills in Beijing, China and the other is in the Temple of Tooth Relic. Every August there is a great memorial event lasting for 10 days.

Professor Wang is an expert in Asian culture. He has visited and researched many countries in Southeast Asia and north Asia, such as Singapore, Thailand, Indonesia, South Korea, Japan and so on. He is also interested in countries in South Asia, such as India and Sri Lanka. Prof. Wang was so excited when he heard that there's a direct flight from Shanghai to Colombo, the capital of Sri Lanka, since he planed to participate in the annual Buddha Tooth Festival.

Therefore, Prof. Wang organized a pilgrim group consisting of culture and Buddhism experts. They adopted the travel agency mode—a 6-night-and-8-day trip in Sri Lanka. Prof. Wang got excited as soon as he thought of the world culture heritages in Sri Lanka, and the classic art crafts in the form of elephant. One week before departure, the travel agency planned an orientation in Hangzhou Sri Lanka club instead of the office in travel agency, which brought Prof. Wang more expectations for the trip.

Prof. Wang came early that afternoon to Hangzhou Sri Lanka Club which was located at Huanggushan Road, West Lake District. He first visited the displays in the club, including the Buddharupa appreciation area, Ceylon black tea taste area, and Sri Lanka precious stone area. And the orientation of the trip in Sri Lanka was held in the meeting room on the third floor of this club.

The group members were enjoying the famous Ceylon black tea while listening to the introduction delivered by the tour leader Mr. Chen in the meeting room. Mr. Chen started with self-introduction and explained carefully about gathering time and place, route map, clothes and temperature, diet habit, hotel information, communications, luggage check-in, money and exchange rate, tip payment, personal belongings, free time or night activities, safety, visa and customs regulations, shopping and telephones outbound, politeness while traveling abroad, cultural differences between China and Sri Lanka. Mr. Chen gave more emphasis on the dress code when entering a temple. The group members appreciated Mr. Chen's professionalism and carefulness. Holding an orientation in such a place made people feel that they had already been in the destination.

Although many experts and professors in the group had already been to many countries, it was their first time to take part in such kind of orientation. They thought it was very creative to learn the rules and notices for the trip as well as Sri Lanka's culture in this way. The group members were looking forward to the trip.

Comments

Sri Lanka is an island country in the tropical zone south Asia. It is named as "a teardrop of India Peninsula". In ancient China, Sri Lanka was called lion country or Sinhala. It was considered the most beautiful island by Marco Polo for its wonderful bay, mysterious ancient cities, rich natural heritages, distinguished and charming history and culture.

Established in September 2012, Hangzhou Sri Lanka Club is the first destination club of its kind, a platform for introducing Sri Lanka, and a combination of business and leisure. Since the new tourism law was published in 2013 in China, the travel agencies have been paying more attention to orientation. And it is an innovation for travel agency to hold the orientation in the destination club.

So far, Hangzhou Merchant Travel Company is a professional organization dealing with Sri Lanka outbound trips. The company has been supported greatly by Sri Lanka Airline Company, 26 local travel agencies, and hotels since the flight from Shanghai to Colombo was initiated. It has promoted Smile Lanka and Sri Lanka

Airline Holiday as well as Miracle Airline of Discovering Sri Lanka. For tourists' convenience, Sri Lanka Airline runs flights every week. It sends off its guests to the tour even if there are only two people. Meanwhile, Hangzhou Merchant Travel Company has designed special tours to meet the different demands from guests, such as wedding tour, photographing tour, Buddha pilgrim tour, diving tour, jewelry and antique tour, etc.

The travel experience of tourists can be divided into three stages: before the travel, during the travel and after the travel. The orientation is an important activity before the travel. It provides an opportunity for tourists to know not only about the outbound travel rules and how to improve their qualities, but also about the customs and habits of the destination. The establishment of Hangzhou Sri Lanka Club also helps the tourists know about Sri Lanka in advance to build up their interest in the destination country.

译，或者不译，这是一个问题

许多伊朗人非常热情，而且自尊心很强。笔者所带的中国公民赴伊朗的旅游团队的导游就是一位典型的伊朗人，他以自己是米底（米底王国：公元前639年至公元前550年。米底人起先是中亚的雅利安人的一支，南迁至伊朗高原，并逐渐与土著居民融合、同化，形成了后来伊朗人的主体）后裔而感到无比自豪。

旅游途中，导游和领队都会尽量避免谈论一些敏感的政治经济、宗教信仰问题，这倒并不仅是为了减少麻烦，更多考虑的是因为毕竟文化差异不可能在几天内消除，客人们出门旅游，主要为了放松和开心，没有必要无事生非。但是笔者所带的这个团不同，游客具有较高文化层次、审美情趣和丰富的旅游经验。他们有时会主动要求导游多说一些当地的风土人情、政治情况，目的可能也只是与国内报道对比一下或者好奇使然。

行程中的某一天，一位客人再一次提出让导游谈谈伊朗人民目前的生活情况。其实，这位客人已经多次提出类似要求，但是前几次导游要么一带而过，要么不着痕迹地转而讲到一些他们国家的辉煌历史，以及即将要去参观的景点。作为领队，笔者已经意识到导游并不是很愿意多谈本国人民目前的生活状况。事实上，由于经济制裁，现今普通伊朗人民的生活水平并不高。导游不愿在其他国家的人民面前多讲本国人民的生活困难。但是那天要赴另外一个城市，车上的时间比较长，正好有机会谈谈那位客人要求讲的话题。

基于导游的敬业精神，他开始讲一些伊朗人民现今的生活状况，讲着讲着也谈到了经济制裁和中国的帮助。这时候，游客们表现出了对伊朗人民的同情，他们开始和导游互动。此时的笔者因为已经连续翻译了几个小时，有些疲惫，基本是在机械口译中，等意识到车内气氛不对，赶紧回忆下刚翻译的内容时，才发现是导游因为觉察到中国游客脸上的同情神色和他们的一些话语使他的自尊受到了伤害。

为了扳回一局，争个面子，导游说了一句："现在中国很多成功人士会养情人，而伊朗人民不会。"这一句本来没什么，团里其他客人也就当笑话听听。可是车上有一位60多岁的老人家，他表示非常不满，认为这样的人在中国不是很多，只是个别现象，一时气氛有些僵持。当笔者意识到这个情况时，话已翻译出口。笔者做的是将老人的不解和恼怒传达给导游，希望他能够态度有所调整或者能理解老人的观点——中国养情人的成功人士并不多，但是伊朗导游不愿改口。此时，笔者意识到，不能再直接将双方的话语翻译给对方了，否则可能引发口角。思索了一会儿，笔者先和老人解释了导游这样说的原因，并委婉地表示他起先也只是当笑话说说而已。同时，笔者也再次和导游强调，虽然中国是有他说的那种现象，但那并不是中国社会的主旋律。

就这样，因为一句速度太"快"的翻译，笔者花了一个多小时进行调解，车内气氛才恢复如常。

[评析]

在伊朗做领队，和在其他目的地国家（地区）稍有不同，不仅要完成常规的服务工作，还需要全程当翻译，因为目前大多数的伊朗导游还不会说中文，英语才是他们的工作语言。

伊朗历史悠久，文明灿烂，在受到经济制裁之前，这个国家对人民的教育投入也是巨大的。当今能在伊朗成为入境导游的，都是属于享有较高社会地位的人，他们充满了骄傲和民族自豪感。

要做好赴伊朗旅游团的称职领队，首先要做的是，在行前就客人需求进行了解和分析。因为此目的地国家是一个文明古国，可讲的历史文化典故很多。因此，领队应该在行前做好充分的目的地文化知识储备工作。

其次，在旅途中，针对双方提出的问题，应该稍加思考，再翻译，避免由于文化和政治等方面的差异产生不愉快。领队和导游在沟通时，也应注意换位思考，考虑导游的立场，再将客人的问题有选择地传达给导游。也就是说，译，或者不译，这是一个问题。

To Translate or Not, This Is a Question

Many Iranian people are very enthusiastic and dignified. The tour guide, an outbound tour leader whom I worked together with while we were visiting Iran, was a typical Iranian. He was proud of being an offspring of Media (Median Dynasty: between 639 BC—550 BC. Its people were primarily a branch of Aryans in the Middle Asia. Then they moved southward to Iranian plateau, fused with the local people and became a major group of Iranian.)

Normally, tour guide and outbound tour leader would not talk about sensitive political issues or religions during a trip, not only for the sake of avoiding trouble but also because of the truth that people's cultural differences couldn't disappear just in one trip. After all, tourists go out for leisure and happiness, not for conflicts. But in this trip, I went to Iran with a distinguished group. The tourists in this group were mostly well-educated people with much aesthetic consciousness and abundant travel experience. They would like to interact with the tour guide more often than normal tourist groups to get further information about the local customs and political situations, either for making comparison with the reports in China or just out of curiosity.

One day during the trip, a guest in the group requested again that the tour guide talk about the Iranian current living situation. In fact, this guest had asked for several times similar questions. But the tour guide had avoided the questions by beating around the bush or concentrating on the scenic spots. I had sensed that the guide was not willing to talk too much about such kind of topics. Because of the economic sanction, the living condition of ordinary Iranian was not quite good. The guide would not like to talk about the difficulties of his people, especially in the face of people from other countries. It was a way in which the guide showed his patriotism and protected his people. But that day, the group would have a long journey to get to the destination. Maybe it was a proper time to say something on the topic.

Out of duty, the guide started to talk about the current Iranian living situation. He also mentioned the sanction and China's assistance. Our guests started to interact with the guide and showed the sympathy for the Iranians. As the interpreter and tour leader, I had been working several hours and felt really tired. Therefore, when interpreting, I was just doing mechanical job. Suddenly, I felt there was something wrong in the bus. And I quickly reviewed what I'd just interpreted and found that the tour guide was hurt because of the sympathy and some words from the guests.

To fight back, the guide said, "Many Chinese businessmen have mistresses, but the Iranians don't. " It was a joke. The other guests in the group also thought so, but one guest in his sixties got angry. The guest stated that such men were few in China and the situation was not like what the guide had said. Before I realized all these, the words had been interpreted and the atmosphere became awkward. To try to ease the atmosphere, I tried hard to explain to the senior guest on the one hand and pass the guest's anger and confusion to the guide on the other hand, hoping that the guide would change his words or understand that men who had mistresses were few in China. Unfortunately, the guide refused to take his words back. At that moment, I realized I could not just directly interpret the words to each party any longer. Otherwise the situation would get worse. After a second thought, I explained first to the senior guest and then emphasized again to the guide that the situation he talked about was actually not common in China. It did exist, but it was not the main stream of our society.

Because of the "fast and direct" interpretation, I spent over one hour making explanation before the atmosphere in the bus gradually came back to normal.

Comments

It is quite different to be an outbound tour leader in Iran from in other destination countries/regions. The tour leader is not only responsible for normal work, but also for interpretation since most Iranian tour guides don't know any Chinese. English is their working language.

Iran has a long history and splendid culture. Before the economic sanction, the country invested a lot in its people's education. Iranian tour guides are people of high social status. And they are full of self-esteem and national pride.

First, A qualified tour leader should know and analyze the needs of the guests before the trip, for the destination is an ancient country with a long history and the guests are well educated. The tour leader should fully prepare the knowledge about the destination. Second, the tour leader should think twice before interpreting to avoid the dilemmas arising from cultural differences. When communicating with the local guide, the tour leader also should try to be in his shoes and then selectively deliver the information from the guests to the guide. In other words, to translate or not, this is a question.

参考文献

[1] 黄荣鹏.领队实务[M].台湾:扬智文化事业股份有限公司,2012.

[2] 徐辉.出境旅游领队实务[M].北京:中国旅游出版社,2014.

[3] 徐辉.国际旅游业对客服务艺术案例[M].杭州:浙江科学技术出版社,2008.

[4] 李天元.旅游学概论[M].天津:南开大学出版社,2003.

[5] 中国旅游研究院.中国出境旅游发展年度报告 2015[M].北京:旅游教育出版社,2015.

[6] 中国旅游研究院.中国出境旅游发展年度报告 2016[M].北京:旅游教育出版社,2016.

[7] 北京凤凰假期国际旅行社有限公司.出境旅游操作实务[M].北京:兵器工业出版社,2006.

[8] 徐辉.出境旅游领队实务(双语)[M].北京:中国财政经济出版社,2016.

[9] 陈亚轩.世界风云人物励志演说精粹(英汉对照)[M].杭州:浙江工商大学出版社,2015.

[10] 黄荣鹏.观光导游与领队[M].台北:松根出版社,2013.

[11] 饶华清.中国出境旅游目的地概况(双语)[M].北京:中国人民大学出版

社,2014.

[12] 石定乐,孙嫘.旅游跨文化交流[M].北京:旅游教育出版社,2014.

[13] 袁良平.外国人品味杭州(中英双语版)[M].北京:科学普及出版社,2010.

[14] 周彩屏.导游技能训练(第2版)[M].北京:高等教育出版社,2015.

[15] 杨天庆.沿途导游掌中宝[M].北京:旅游教育出版社,2007.

[16] 张瑞奇,刘原良.领队与导游实务[M].台北:扬智文化事业股份有限公司,2013.

[17] 潘海颖,王菘.酒水服务与酒吧经营[M].武汉:华中科技大学出版社,2015.

[18] 仉向明,黄恢月.出境旅游领队工作案例解析[M].北京:旅游教育出版社,2008.

[19] 国家旅游局.中国旅游年鉴[M].北京:中国旅游出版社,1997—2016.

[20] 吕尔欣.中西方饮食文化差异及翻译研究[M].杭州:浙江大学出版社,2013.

[19] 张晓青,周淑敏.市场营销实务[M].北京:中国财政经济出版社,2014.

[21] 韦福祥.华信经管创优系列:服务营销学[M].北京:电子工业出版社,2013.

[22] 刘会远,李蕾蕾.德国工业旅游与工业遗产保护[M].北京:商务印书馆,2007.

[23] 徐辉.墨尔本一日游开发与经营对杭州旅游业的启示[J].浙江外国语学院学报,2012(6):86—90.

[24] 徐辉,潘海颖.公民道德视域下的中国出境游客素质提升研究[J].杭州电子科技大学学报(社会科学版),2016,12(2):33—37.

[25] 关肇远.旅游英语口语[M].北京:高等教育出版社,2004.

[26] 姚宝荣,魏周.模拟导游教程[M].北京:中国旅游出版社,2007

[27] ZHANG Y, ZHANG X. Beyond competence:professional operations of international tour guiding[M].Beijing:China Science Technology &

Culture Press, 2003

[28] YUAN P. Hangzhou from foreigners' perspectives [M]. Beijing:
Popularization of Science Press, 2010

[29] LEW A A, YU L, ZHANG G, et al. Tourism in China[M]. New York:
The Haworth Hospitality Press, 2003.

[30] SONG H, CHON K. Experiencing China: travel stories by tourism experts
[M]. Hong Kong: The Hong Kong Polytechnic University School of Hotel &
Tourism Management, 2008.

中国公民出境旅游服务质量解析